A History of Spain and Portugal (2)

Stanley G. Payne

A HISTORY OF
Spain and Portugal

IN TWO VOLUMES (2)

The University of Wisconsin Press

Published 1973
The University of Wisconsin Press
Box 1379, Madison, Wisconsin 53701

The University of Wisconsin Press, Ltd.
70 Great Russell St., London

First printing

Printed in the United States of America
For LC CIP information see the colophon

ISBN 0-299-06280-5

Contents

Illustrations

at end of volume

Maps

A physiographic map of the Iberian Peninsula will be found on the last two facing pages of the book

Tables

Genealogical Chart and List of Presidents

A History of Spain and Portugal (2)

16

The Eighteenth-Century Bourbon Regime in Spain

The eighteenth century began in Spain with a change in dynasty as, in accordance with the will of Carlos II, a grandson of Louis XIV of France ascended the Spanish throne as Felipe V. The advent of a Spanish Bourbon monarchy was eventually decisive in establishing a new and much more effective pattern of government, but in the short run it involved the peninsula in a disastrous thirteen-year succession war that engaged all the great powers. The remaining imperial possessions on the continent were swept away, and the English seized Gibraltar and took over the island of Menorca as well. Thus, paradoxically, a decade of Bourbon regenerationism proved more fatal to the old European inheritance than had a century of Habsburg decadence. The final and irrevocable loss of Spanish Italy and the Spanish Netherlands was, however, an almost inevitable process for which the dynasty could not realistically be blamed. Though the cost of the war did in some ways retard Spanish resurgence for one more generation, the new regime provided leadership and administration so much superior to that of its predecessor that it contributed greatly to the eventual renovation. Spanish America held fast from foreign assault, and its further development after mid-century was a major factor in the later advance of the Spanish economy.

The War of the Spanish Succession, from 1702 to 1714, was made almost inescapable by the mere fact of inheritance of the Spanish crown by a French Bourbon prince. Though the new Spanish dynasty was to be completely separate and independent from that of France, political and family ties were nevertheless close. If Louis XIV's jubilant exclamation "Now there are no more Pyrenees!" proved a considerable exaggeration, other European powers read the darkest omens in the dynastic succession, and were determined not to permit a great new Bourbon power bloc in southwestern Europe. Hence the coalition organized in 1702 ranged nearly all the other states of western and central Europe in a grand alliance against France and Spain, with the aim of annulling the succession and reducing the extent and power of the Bourbon domains.

The young Felipe V, born Philippe d'Anjou, was fully accepted by most opinion in Castile, for his succession promised continuation of an imperial Spain based on traditional unitary Castilian values. By contrast, the rival candidacy of the Austrian Archduke Karl, backed by the anti-Bourbon alliance, stressed Habsburg pluralism and relied to a considerable extent on the main Protestant powers of Europe.

The response of the Aragonese principalities was somewhat less certain. At the beginning of his reign in 1701, Felipe V specifically reconfirmed the traditional privileges and exemptions of the Catalan constitution; in the following year his new queen, María Luisa of Savoy, did the same during his absence with respect to the laws and fueros of Aragón. However, when the war started in 1702, Felipe V hurried to his new Italian possessions to assure their loyalty without having given detailed attention to the Aragonese principalities. Nevertheless, their ruling strata showed little opposition to the Bourbon succession and were swept into the Habsburg cause only after allied forces had landed in eastern Spain. Archduke Karl stressed the traditional Habsburg respect for Aragonese federalism and played upon the fear and hatred of French imperialism and centralization. In Aragón and especially in Valencia, the Habsburg candidacy took full advantage of social tensions and encouraged a peasant revolt against the seigneurial control of the aristocracy. Amid rural social conflict, local districts and towns in Valencia were reincorporated into the royal domain by Archduke Karl, freeing them of many seigneurial exactions. On the other hand, most of the aristocracy, ecclesiastical hierarchy, and state officials in Aragón and Valencia remained loyal to the Bourbon succession; the cause of the Habsburg pretender was embraced particularly by peasants and village clergy. Only in Catalonia did opposition to the Bourbon crown include all social classes, and there, too, it was more intense among the lower classes.

The Spanish phase of the Succession War began in 1705, with the landing of Archduke Karl and strong allied forces in both Valencia and Barcelona. The Habsburg effort was backed by the powerful

The Spanish House of Bourbon, 1700-1931

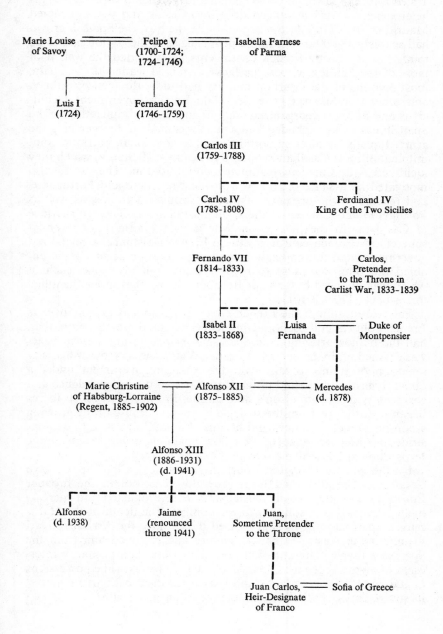

English fleet, sizable contingents of German professional troops, the armed forces of Portugal, and Catalan and Valencian volunteers. This heterogeneous army advanced deep into Castile and twice occupied Madrid (1706, 1710). At the beginning of the war, the Spanish crown had scarcely 18,000 troops in the peninsula, and these soon had to be reinforced by strong French contingents, who carried the weight of most of the fighting. Given the lack of trained leadership in Spain, most sections of the Bourbon military had to be directed by French and other non-Spanish generals, while French government technicians and advisors reorganized state finance and administration. The Spanish navy was expanded and a start was made in reorganizing the army. Equally or more important was the emotional, patriotic commitment of most Castilian people to the cause of Felipe V, which they identified with Castilian legitimacy and tradition. They were also motivated by a sense of rivalry with the Aragonese and Portuguese, and reacted to the presence of foreign Protestant troops, as well as Portuguese and Catalan soldiers, on Castilian soil. The self-sacrifice of Castilians in the Succession War drew the admiration even of supercilious French courtiers. Strong French assistance, a revitalized government and administration, and popular support in Castile enabled the Bourbon cause to recover from both invasions, each of which was followed by a major Bourbon victory that threw the allied forces back (1707, 1710).

The relationship of the French crown to Spain was exploitative, as French political and economic influence increased greatly; more than half the bullion arriving from Spanish America during the war years was drained off by payments to France. Yet Louis XIV never had any intention of trying to take over the Spanish government under a direct dynastic union, and ultimately respected the independence and sovereignty of his grandson's new throne. From 1709, French forces began to withdraw from the struggle in Spain, because of the growing strain on French resources and because Louis XIV wished to demonstrate the independence of Bourbon Spain in order to encourage recognition and a settlement from the other powers.

By the end of 1710, the Bourbon forces held all of Spain, save Catalonia. The allies had been generally victorious in the broader European struggle, but all participants were exhausted and increasingly interested in a solution to the conflict. The death of the Habsburg Emperor Josef I in 1711 cleared the path for the Archduke Karl to inherit the Austro-Habsburg empire and removed him from the Spanish struggle. The anti-Bourbon allies were then primarily interested in divesting the new Spanish dynasty of its erstwhile possessions in Italy and the Netherlands and ceased for the most part to contest its sovereignty over the principalities of peninsular Spain.

The chief remaining obstacle facing the regime of Felipe V was Catalonia, which still held firm against it. At a meeting of the Catalan Corts in 1713, the military and ecclesiastic branches at first voted to come to terms. Only the *Braç popular,* representing the third estate, resisted, and this only by seventy-eight to forty-five votes, but it was enough to turn the tide, bringing the nobility back to a position of all-out resistance.

The crown would have been willing to compromise, and in the face of Catalan intransigence was able to subdue the principality only with the renewed assistance of French arms. The ensuing siege of Barcelona (1713-1714) evoked the wonder and admiration of Europe. It was the last stand of traditional Catalonia, glorious, but doomed to failure under the overwhelming weight of royal arms. The slogan of *Privilegis o mort,* as some of the Catalan banners read, sustained patriotic fervor but helped make it impossible to come to terms with the new regime. When Barcelona surrendered, the city was a wreck, the region's economy ruined, and the historic Catalonia a thing of the past. The region did not recover for an entire generation or more, but when it did there emerged the beginning of modern Catalonia, for nearly two hundred years the most dynamic region of modern Spain.

Unification of Government and Administration

The most enduring achievement of the reign of Felipe V was to establish, for the first time since the Romans, a unified, centralized administration over nearly all of Spain. Spain as a single united polity dates from approximately 1715, and the model for its eighteenth-century royalist regime was the governing system of the Bourbon dynasty of France. The separate fueros of Aragón and Valencia were abolished in 1707 and the administrative system of Castile extended over those territories. This brought abolition of the socially progressive changes in legal jurisdiction over peasant lands that had been decreed by the Habsburg pretender. Catalonia was also incorporated into the central system under terms of the Nueva Planta decree of 1716. The only concession to the particularism of the former Aragonese principalities was retention of their law codes, but these were henceforth applied by the centralized royal administration. The only regions to retain historic fueros more or less intact were Navarre and the Basque country, which had accepted the new dynasty without resistance, but even there royal delegates assumed greater authority than before. All the eastern parliaments were abolished save that of Navarre, which was essentially a council of local aristocrats. Aragonese and Valencian deputies were first summoned to a common all-

Spanish Cortes in 1709, and Catalan representatives were incorporated in 1724. A total of eight ceremonial Cortes were called between 1700 and 1789, but they were not permitted, nor did they show any interest in, the slightest political or legislative initiative.

The Bourbon government swept away the old Habsburg council system of executive administration, replacing it in 1714 with four *secretarías,* the predecessors of a modern ministerial system. The secretaries or ministers together formed a "cabinet council." For the first time in Spanish history the main areas of state administration were directed by specialized authorities personally and directly responsible to the crown. The original ministries were State and Foreign Affairs, Charity and Justice, Army and Navy, and the Indies. A ministry of finance was added in 1754, and under Carlos III, the ministries were increased to seven, splitting Army and Navy into separate departments and dividing that of Indies as well. The traditional Council of Castile, however, was modernized somewhat and retained for general domestic administration.

One of the chief consequences of Bourbon government was to exclude the *grandes* from major government positions and end their era of political dominance. There was no attack on the social and economic position of the high aristocracy, although a few who rebelled had their properties confiscated. Felipe V was not opposed to nobility, but he demanded an aristocratic elite obedient to royal authority. During his reign approximately two hundred new titles were created as a reward for service and loyalty, not as recognition of wealth and status alone.

The kingdom was divided into eight sections, or *reinos,* for local administration. Each district was headed executively by a military captain general, with a regional audiencia (court) as advisory and judicial organ. In addition, a separate audiencia was created for Mallorca in 1715. The Castilian institution of appointing corregidores with broad administrative powers in local areas was extended throughout Spain. Urban government was reorganized under the general principle of hierarchy, and urban guilds were also brought under stricter supervision.

The royal fiscal system was reorganized by French officials and centralized much more than it had been under the Habsburgs. Some state bonds were repudiated and others converted to a lower rate of interest. In general, state income approximately doubled during the period of the Succession War, due primarily to greater efficiency of collection and administration. The tax burden of the former Aragonese regions, which had previously not been subject to general royal taxes, was greatly increased, and it has been calculated that the actual levy in Catalonia grew nearly six times heavier under the eighteenth-century regime. A general land cadastre was carried out there in 1717 to serve as a basis for assessment. A unified Junta del Catastro was eventually established for all Spain under Carlos III to work toward a unified tax system.

A corps of intendants (district administrators) was created on the French pattern to oversee taxation and local security, but it never became a general administrative system for the entire kingdom. Under Felipe V, intendants were named primarily for regions where large military detachments were stationed and where security was a problem, that is, mainly in the former Aragonese principalities. After 1720 their use declined, though there was a partial revival of the intendant system at mid-century to try to stimulate economic development.

Another key institution to be restructured was the armed forces, which had nearly withered away under Carlos II. The Spanish army was slowly reorganized on the modern French pattern and the historic *tercios* replaced by regiments. This transformation was not completed until the reign of Carlos III, when Prussian influence also became noticeable. Many foreign commanders were appointed, preempting the places formerly held by native grandes, and the military hierarchy was given a major role in regional administration through the naming of district captains general. These served as the chief state executives in every part of the country, and replaced the viceroys formerly appointed for the eastern regions. In Catalonia, local guerrilla bands were still active in 1718-1720 and 1725-1726, and a local Catalan rural militia, the "Mossos d'esquadra," was formed to keep peace in the countryside. Its success encouraged establishment of a local militia system in most other parts of the kingdom by the time of Carlos III.

The Reign of Felipe V (1700-1746)

During the first fifteen years of the rule of the first Bourbon king, Spanish government was directed largely by French officials brought in to reform and improve administration. This "French phase" came to an end after the marriage of D. Felipe to his second queen, Isabella Farnese (Maria Luisa having died prematurely). She was the niece and stepdaughter of the Duke of Parma, and brought with her a new cadre of Italian advisors and officials, who replaced most of the French appointees, and inaugurated a brief "Italian phase" of Spanish government. A Parmesan church official, Cardinal Alberoni, became the new *primer ministro* of the Spanish state.

The crown, like many patriotic Spaniards, much resented the fact that France had made peace with the other powers in 1713-1714 at the expense of Spain and the integrity of its European dominions. At first, the Spanish crown refused to recognize the loss of all the territories that had been seized, particularly those in Italy, and the new Italian queen stimulated plans for restoration of Spanish influence there. Alberoni hastened re-expansion of the armed forces, especially the navy, and adopted a new mercantilist policy to stimulate commerce. In 1717, a surprisingly strong expedition of more than 10,000 men was sent to reoccupy Sicily, and in the following year a great force of 36,000 troops and 8,000 horses was moved in 439 ships for the reconquest of Sardinia. The size of this expedition made it the largest single effort that had yet been made in the military history of the Spanish crown.

Though the returning Spaniards were welcomed in Sicily, it was all for naught. Military and naval competition had grown incomparably stronger in the eighteenth century. Much of the new Spanish fleet was destroyed off Sicily, a large Austrian force successfully launched a counteroffensive in the island in 1719, and a British force actually landed in the Galician port of Vigo. The partition of the Spanish empire at Utrecht had finally to be conceded, together with token British participation in the American trade.

Felipe V was a neurotic, vacillating ruler, concerned with outward decorum and brave only in battle. He had little sense of Spanish interests and needs. After the realities of his shrunken and impoverished realm had become clearer to him, he sank further into melancholy and mental withdrawal. Between 1721 and 1724 he abjured the throne in favor of his eldest son, Luis I, but the latter's death from smallpox required the return of Felipe V in 1724. From that time on the influence of the queen became even stronger, and Spain's first Bourbon ruler passed the last two decades of his reign in a state of intermittent madness.

The phase of recovery from the Succession War was not completed before 1726. In that year the first native Spanish chief minister of Felipe V's reign, Baltasar Patiño, was appointed. The next twenty years, until the death of Felipe V in 1746, were years of modest reform and expansion. The main concern of government lay in improving the state administration itself, but under Patiño the era of foreign advisors and administrators largely came to an end, and the Spanish Bourbon administration was increasingly nationalized. Spanish forces made an unsuccessful attempt on British-held Gibraltar in 1727-1728. Patiño, as minister of the navy, Indies, and finance, concentrated on a policy of state mercantilism, encouraging the colonial trade, new commercial companies, and the expansion of the fleet.

After the death of the duke of Parma in 1731, Spanish forces were authorized to occupy the Italian duchies of Parma, Piacenza, and Tuscany to hold for the heirs of Felipe V and Isabella Farnese. During the next major European conflict, the War of the Polish Succession, the Spanish crown joined France against Austria to further its anti-Habsburg interests in Italy. The first Family Compact, or mutual assistance pact, was signed between the French and Spanish Bourbons in 1733. In the ensuing war, the dynasty regained Naples and Sicily as a separate patrimony for Felipe V's second son, D. Carlos, though the north Italian duchies had to be relinquished.

It had long been clear that Spain's main concern was not the Mediterranean but the Atlantic, lifeline to the empire, then as before the kingdom's main source of wealth. Spain could not possibly compete with the British fleet, so Patiño, who dominated foreign policy between 1728 and 1740, followed a policy of peace with Britain, while doing everything possible to exclude interloping British traders. Spanish *guardacostas* were active in American waters in a vain effort to enforce the trade restrictions. In one of many incidents, a British sea captain, one Jenkins, was said to have had an ear cut off by a Spanish naval commander. This was used by the British parliament as the excuse for an Atlantic naval and commercial war against Spain. The so-called War of Jenkins' Ear was popular in Spain as a struggle against a proud and aggressive naval rival currently occupying Spanish territory, though it proved very costly to Spanish shipping.

It was soon followed by participation in the next general European struggle, the War of the Austrian Succession, once more against Austria in the hope of regaining control of the Milanese. A second Family Compact was signed with France in 1743. Felipe V finally entered Milan as an elderly conqueror in 1744, though his forces were driven out the following year. When peace was eventually made in 1748, D. Carlos was fully recognized as king of the Two Sicilies and his younger brother (Isabella Farnese's second son by Felipe V) was awarded the duchies of Parma and Piacenza. This finally satisfied the dynastic ambition of Isabella Farnese, ending Spain's involvement in Italian conflicts.

Fernando VI (1746-1759)

Felipe V was succeeded by the last surviving son of his first marriage, Fernando VI , who was married to a Portuguese princess, Barbara de Bragança. Though childless, theirs was a pleasant and harmonious royal household, devoted to music and quiet pleasures. The great virtue of Fernando VI as ruler was that he kept Spain at peace and avoided further entanglement in European struggles. His outstanding ministerial appointee, the Marqués de la Ensenada, was the first high aristocrat to be given a central position in government under the Spanish Bourbons. Ensenada, however, was a reformer who continued the efforts of Patiño and others before him to reform taxes, advance commerce and the navy, and promote the professional interests of the middle classes. Traditionalist foes managed to force Ensenada from government in 1754 after the colony of Sacramento in South America was returned to Portugal. The last five years of the reign of Fernando VI, who ultimately lapsed into madness like his father, were a time of vacuity and inaction.

Carlos III (1759-1788)

Fernando VI was succeeded by his half-brother Carlos III, eldest son of Isabella Farnese and until 1759 king of the Two Sicilies. Judged by comparative standards, his was the most enlightened and most prosperous reign in modern Spanish history. This was in part because it spanned the last generation of Spanish history under the Old Regime, while Spanish society was still at peace with itself, but also because of the many enlightened initiatives taken, if not by Carlos III himself, by his chief ministers. Carlos III was an ambitious prince but a very well disciplined one, level-headed, and much given to the out-of-doors and the chase, even to the extent of having a rather rustic air. His record as ruler of the Two Sicilies was good. There he had learned most of the principles of eighteenth-century enlightened despotism, and he brought a number of Italian administrators and reformers to help staff his government in Spain.

Yet the government of Carlos III did not maintain the European neutrality that its predecessor had. Spanish commerce had taken a severe mauling from the British fleet during the wars of the 1740s and 1750s. When the British government refused to come to an agreement, Carlos could not resist signing the third Family Compact with the French crown in 1761. Thus Spain became involved in the two concluding years of the Seven Years' War, and suffered on the seas as a result. In the peace treaty of 1763, the Spanish crown had to give up the American territories of Florida (to Britain) and Uruguay (to Britain's ally, Portugal), but received the vast, almost uninhabited territory of Louisiana in return. Uruguay was regained after a brief war against Portugal in 1776-1777; then, after Spain joined the anti-British coalition during the War of American Independence, Menorca and Florida were rewon in 1783. This was the most favorable peace settlement made by the Spanish crown since 1598. During the felicitous reign of Carlos III, the Spanish empire overseas reached its greatest extent.

The crown also enjoyed success in its relations with Muslim northwest Africa. Several assaults on the Spanish presidios earlier in the century had been beaten off, and the reduction of piracy made it possible to complete the resettling of the coastline of Catalonia and the Levant. After the Spanish Moroccan stronghold of Melilla withstood a joint assault from Morocco and Algiers, the crown retaliated with a major expedition of 18,000 troops against Algiers in 1775 which in turn was beaten back. However, Morocco came to terms in 1780, and Algiers, after being bombarded by the Spanish fleet in 1783 and 1784, signed a general treaty in 1785. Satisfactory agreements were also made with Tunis and Tripoli.

Expulsion of the Jesuits

Despite its religious orthodoxy and the relative piety of its rulers, the eighteenth-century monarchy, ever jealous of its preeminent authority, was not infrequently involved in conflict with the church or elements thereof. During the feeble reign of Carlos II, the papacy had succeeded in reasserting control over a broad spectrum of Spanish church affairs and appointments. In the eighteenth century, there remained long-standing uncertainties about various areas of jurisdiction, and about such key issues as the extent of the church's liability to taxation and the *pase regio,* or royal right to regulate or veto publication of nondogmatic papal pronouncements. Those both inside and outside the church who supported an increase in royal power for purposes of reform were known as *regalistas.* Local jurisdictional conflicts became so severe that the regalists were wont to say that any corregidor who had not been placed under excommunication for at least half of each year could hardly be discharging his administrative responsibilities zealously. The Concordat of 1753 resolved some of the main points at issue, restoring to the crown control over most major appointments, but other difficulties remained.

The major church controversy during the first years of Carlos III's reign concerned the power and loyalty of the Jesuit order. For two hundred years, the Jesuits had been the chief institutional representative of papal influence in western and central Europe. Their talent, their control of quality education, and their influence as confessors of aristocrats and royalty had made them a force to be reckoned with and had drawn the suspicion and envy of Catholic rulers in various countries. Some of the strongest opposition to the Jesuits in the 1760s came from within the church itself, for their wealth and influence had also elicited keen rivalry from other orders. In turn, Jesuits called regalists among both government officials and church reformers "Jansenists," illogically applying to them the name of the Jesuits' earlier chief religious foe within French Catholicism. Yet the name stuck, and Spanish regalists have frequently been termed *jansenistas*.

The beginnings of secularization in Spanish culture and education were just making their appearance, as was Spanish Masonry. The first English-rite lodge had been established in Spain in 1727, followed by influential currents from French Masonry. After papal condemnation, Fernando VI banned Masonry from Spain in 1751, but it returned to the 1760s in a number of small lodges. One of the king's chief advisers, the deist grande Conde de Aranda, was the grand orient of the principal Masonic rite. Moreover, steps were being taken to further curb the powers of the Inquisition, which had become relatively inactive. To all this the Jesuits were strongly opposed.

The crown was determined to extend royal power and press positive reforms. In addition to all the common charges, D. Carlos was especially apprehensive of the Jesuits because of two recent developments. First, the Jesuits had attempted to use the crisis provoked by the Lisbon earthquake to gain further leverage on the neighboring Portuguese monarchy. Second, they had strongly protested the 1763 treaty with England and Portugal (which had given Uruguay to Portugal and so provided further opportunity for Brazilian attacks against the Jesuit settlements in Paraguay).

The latent struggle came to a head after the "Motín de Esquilache" in 1766. The king's Italian finance minister, Squillaci ("Esquilache"), was extremely unpopular because of his enforcement of tax reforms and sumptuary edicts. There had been a long list of such endeavors in the past, but Squillaci was particularly resented as a foreigner and because harvests had been poor for six years in a row, raising the price of bread. A new decree of 1766 forbidding the citizens of Madrid to wear the traditional long cape and broad-brimmed round hat (in order to expose criminals more easily) provoked a popular riot in which Squillaci's house was sacked. The outburst was apparently encouraged by obscure elements drawn from the aristocracy, clergy, and middle classes of Madrid. This was, however, a bread riot as much or more than anything else, and was accompanied by similar disturbances in a number of provincial towns. The king was forced to dismiss his minister, but frightened by the riot and more jealous than ever of royal power, he determined to prevent such a thing from ever happening again.

The deist anti-Jesuit Conde de Aranda was appointed chief minister, and in the months that followed the Jesuits were made scapegoats for the whole affair. The contemporary movement to expel the Jesuits from Portugal was strongly felt in Spain, and the enemies of the Jesuits in the church were eager to be rid of rivals. On the grounds of subversive agitation and plotting for a "universal government," the Jesuits were expelled from Spain in 1767, and after pressure from the crowns of France, Spain, and Portugal, the order was dissolved six years later by the papacy.

The Domestic Reforms of Carlos III

Though its achievements on the international plane were notable, the reign of Carlos III owes its fame chiefly to its many domestic reforms. These were predicated on the overriding authority of the crown, which was much more nearly absolute under the eighteenth-century Bourbons than under the Habsburgs. The glory of the monarchy and its concern for a strong, enlightened kingdom were held to require a program of basic reform that would make Spain more orderly, rational, educated, and productive. Monarchist reformism had little to do with representative government or the subsequent era of liberalism, for it functioned almost exlusively from the top downward. Carlos III always remained jealous in the extreme of the prerogatives and majesty of the Spanish monarchy.

The initial phase commenced in the early years of the reign with the revival of the financial and economic reforms of Ensenada, favoring the activity of the middle classes. New efforts were made to improve urban government and administration, encourage better dress and behavior, make taxation more equitable and efficient, and raise the level of church appointments.

For two decades reform policy was led by the Conde de Campomanes, whose post as president (fiscal) of the Council of Castile gave him supervision of much of domestic administration. In general, it was the policy of the crown and some of its ministers to introduce more of the educated hidalgo class into the Council of Castile to get fresher and more objective administration. As the regime wore on, there was increasing rivalry between the educated *manteístas* or *golillas* from the middle and hidalgo classes (the names refer to common students and the jurist's collar of law graduates) and the *colegiales,* aristocrats who came from the exclusive *colegio mayor* residences of the universities. This rivalry within and behind the government was never resolved, though most of the aristocracy became increasingly hostile to change. The major exception was the small *partido aragonés* of liberal reformist aristocrats grouped around Aranda.

Between the 1760s and the 1780s, the government sketched out an incomplete but basic and far-reaching reform program that anticipated most of the reform goals of Spanish government for the next one hundred and fifty years. The agrarian difficulties of 1760-1766 encouraged the first effort at agrarian reform in modern Spanish history. A law of 1765 established free internal commerce in grain. Between 1766 and 1770, a series of decrees were promulgated to divide up portions of town council and waste land in order to increase direct cultivation. It was also hoped to encourage peasant smallholders, though most of the land divided up in New Castile, Andalusia, and Extremadura seems to have fallen under the control of the aristocracy. Other efforts, somewhat more successful, were made to control peasant land rents, which had been rising rapidly. Later, several small colonies of immigrant German peasants were established in the Andalusian hills to bring barren land under cultivation and encourage a more productive attitude. The imperial canal of Aragón, begun generations earlier, was completed during this reign, and new irrigation projects were started in Aragón and in Murcia.

In church affairs, government administration intervened directly to strengthen discipline among the orders, reduce the number of monks (one order of which was abolished entirely), reconfirm the pase regio that restricted publication of papal pronouncements, and limit the legal power of the church, including the right of asylum. There was also a great deal of intervention in details of payment of priests and the administration of charity. Like that of the Catholic Kings, the government of Carlos III endeavored to raise the level of appointments, improve the qualifications of priests, and discourage the grosser forms of popular superstition. A good deal had been accomplished, at least among the higher clergy, by the close of the reign. Yet there was little effort to curb the Inquisition, which remained popular, respected, and potentially powerful. During the eighteenth century, the Holy Office was exercised with comparative restraint, but in 1778 it still retained the power to try, disgrace, and force from Spain Pablo de Olavide, Campomanes's chief collaborator in agrarian and educational reform. That Spanish regalism provoked no more reaction from the church than it did was due to the undeniable orthodoxy and reputation of the Spanish crown and to the tact shown by some government officials, especially the king, whose personal piety was irreproachable.

Spanish enlightened despotism had no more of a theory of politics or representative constitutionalism than did any other contemporary continental monarchy, but the crown's ministers saw the wisdom of involving the more capable middle class subjects in decisions on the lower levels of administration. A decree of 1766 provided for *vecinos* (heads of houses or householders) and *pecheros* (taxpayers) to choose local electors who would elect *diputados de común* in every town to consult with municipal *regidores* about local problems. It also arranged for election of district *alcaldes de barrio* (aldermen) in the larger towns. Two *diputados de común* were to be chosen in towns with less than one thousand *vecinos*, and four in the larger towns. Yet there was almost no interest in representative government in eighteenth-century Spain, and little enthusiasm or concern demonstrated in the selecting of these municipal *diputados*.

The royal government took direct measures to improve education. Official recognition had earlier been given to learning and the arts by the establishment of the royal academies (Real Academia de la Lengua, 1713; Real Academia de la Historia, 1736; Real Academia de Bellas Artes, 1744), and in 1759 the Barcelona Academia de Buenas Letras was raised to royal status. During the reign of Carlos III, the government intervened directly in the university system for the first time in Spanish history. An effort was made to modernize administration, appointments, and curriculum, and later some of the endowments were taken over for reorganization. There were positive accomplishments, but in general, the university reform was undertaken only in bits and pieces. Higher education remained retrograde in Spain, though it was closer to modern knowledge by the 1780s than it had been earlier. In addition, ministers encouraged development of new secondary schools and institutes, with several new schools of mining, engineering and surgery. Further general plans were made by Godoy in the following reign but came to naught.

The government also prepared the first really reliable Spanish censuses, carried out basic work in peninsular cartography, and organized the historical archives of the Indies and the crown of Aragón. It subsidized foreign travel and study and paid for new pilot projects in the improvement of agriculture and artisanship. A national road network was planned, and an unsuccessful attempt was made to set up a corps of engineers. The idea of trade schools was encouraged, but there were severe limits to state resources. The two most important new scientific and economic institutes, the Basque Seminario de Vergara and the Instituto Jovellanos, were both the result of private initiative.

The financial reform instituted earlier in the century was carried still further. No new taxes were imposed, but assessment and collection were somewhat improved, even though local resistance prevented the planned national land register, or cadastre, from ever being completed. Paper money was first introduced in 1780 for war expenditures, and the first attempt at a national bank, the Banco de San Isidro, was formed to support state finance in 1782. During the course of the century, currency was slowly becoming standardized in the peseta (a unit of coinage taken from the Catalan silver *pecete*).

Campomanes eagerly encouraged local commercial and economic improvement societies. The first had been founded by a small group of hidalgos and priests who met in the town of Azcoitia (Guipuzcoa) in 1748 to discuss social and economic problems. This body was officially organized in 1765 as the Sociedad Vascongada de Amigos del País, setting itself the goals of studying the principles and bases of economics, gathering more precise information about local conditions and problems, fostering technological improvement and better use of labor, and promoting government assistance and tariff protection. During the reign, approximately seventy local Sociedades de Amigos del País were formed, engaging in technical education, charity, and sometimes in agricultural improvement.

The reforms of the reign of Carlos III were as important for Spanish America as for the home kingdom. Beginning in the 1720s, the Bourbon regime had encouraged intra-Hispanic trade through the formation of new trading companies. Some efforts were made to improve administration of the colonies during the reign of Felipe V, but reform and regeneration blossomed in the 1760s and 1770s. The intendant system was extended to America in 1768, and adminstrative units were reorganized. The level of appointments, efficiency, and supervision was raised. Most important, the volume of trade increased greatly and facilities were broadly liberalized, as new regulations of 1765 and 1778 finally broke the Board of Trade monopoly through Cádiz and opened direct American commerce to thirteen major ports along the Spanish coastline. The opportunity for direct American trade was one of the major single factors in the resurgence of the eighteenth-century Catalan economy.

The effect of the Caroline reforms in Spanish America was not merely to stimulate the American economy but also to awaken new feelings of resentment and patriotic identity among Spanish Americans. The reasons for this were several. The administration of Carlos III was much more overtly interventionist in the affairs of colonial Spanish America than its predecessors had been, and pursued an avowed policy of colonial development that made the object status of the colonies explicit. Under the Habsburgs, Spanish America had increasingly been allowed to deal with its own affairs as part of the pluralistic patrimony of the crown. By the time of Carlos III, the imperial patrimony in Europe had been lost, and the idea of autonomous pluralism had been replaced by that of centralized authority. Spanish imperial economic policy stimulated parts of the Spanish American economy, but the controls and limitations that it imposed restricted other parts and required costly adjustments. Moreover, the Caroline reform period coincided with the first reception of critical Anglo-French ideas of enlightenment in Spanish America. Perhaps most important of all was that the prosperity of the late eighteenth century served to develop a Spanish creole elite in America with the income and culture to exist as a separate society, no longer merely an appendage of peninsular Spain. The era of Carlos III brought the Spanish empire to its climax and sowed the seeds of Spanish American independence.

Within the peninsula, this was one of the two greatest reform periods in Spanish history, surpassed only by that of the Catholic Kings. It was not a time of political change but of institutional, legislative, and educational improvement, designed to permit the existing Spanish society to increase its talents and opportunities and raise its level of achievement. The enlightened ministers of Carlos III were indeed social reformers, but they never envisaged any drastic reordering of society as a whole. Just as government was based on the firmest of autocratic monarchist principles, so enlightened despotism was conceived as operating within the framework of the traditional three-class society. Though, as will be discussed in the next chapter, fiscal and economic reforms had the effect of shrinking the numbers of those who claimed aristocratic status, there was no direct assault on the prerogatives of nobility itself. A decree of 1716 had declared that all criminal jurisdiction in Spain, without exception, pertained to the crown, but in practice there was never a concerted effort to limit the extent or prerogatives of seigneurial domain. The hierarchic order remained unaltered. Carlos III was himself quite rigid regarding the principles of authority and obedience, and became considerably more cautious with respect to reform during the last years of his reign. Very few government appointments of any importance were made from among the middle classes. The state was administered mainly by nobles and hidalgos, especially the latter, for appointments were drawn increasingly from among the hidalgos of the northern regions. Their attitudes may have become increasingly like those of the middle classes, but the state appointees were not themselves genuinely middle class or bourgeois.

The Eighteenth-Century Enlightenment in Spain

The century from 1650 to 1750 may be seen as the last phase of classical Spanish culture. Though relatively sterile and uncreative, with the possible exception of a few late achievements of the Golden Age, Spanish culture retained its traditional structure during those years. When finally that form began to change during the second half of the eighteenth century, it was not from the sudden victory of an aggressive new rationalist culture, but was rather a natural death from general exhaustion of a traditionalist Catholic culture unable to sustain itself.

The reformist, quasi-rationalist culture of the enlightenment began to make significant progress in Spain only with the reign of Carlos III. Those new ideas that penetrated Spain from abroad had to do almost exclusively with natural science, especially physics and medicine, and with abstract philosophy. The religious criticism applied by French philosophers was almost completely rejected, even by rationalistic Spanish reformers themselves. The enlightenment in Spain was a Catholic enlightenment, in some respects reminiscent of Erasmianism but altogether different in character from the deistic, anti-Catholic, increasingly radical enlightenment of the French philosophers.

The precursor of the Spanish enlightenment was a Benedictine monk and professor at the University of Oviedo, Benito Gerónimo Feyjóo, whose multivolume *Teatro crítico universal* and *Cartas eruditas* first set the tone for a more critical and empirical attitude in eighteenth-century Spanish thought. Feyjóo was in no way an original thinker. In the sciences he was a dilettante, and his opposition to traditional scholasticism was that of a moderate reformer, but he proved an extraordinarily able publicist who touched on a great variety of topics and was rarely afraid to speak out. He encouraged a more critical and empirical attitude toward knowledge and laid particular stress on the improvement of medicine. He was especially concerned to get rid of the innumerable superstitions and false religious beliefs plaguing Spanish Catholic thought and practice. Feyjóo was more destructive of the old than constructive of the new, but served the important function of preparing the way in intellectual circles for rationalist and reformist ideas. A royal decree of Fernando VI in 1750 forbidding restrictions upon or denunciation of Feyjóo's writings may be taken as the turning point that marked the official beginning of the Spanish enlightenment.

The main cultural influence on Spanish reformism came from France, with considerable influence also from Italy, especially through the Parmesan and Neapolitan connections of Carlos III. Italian officials, as well as Italian musicians and artists, were prominent in Madrid. The principal inspiration for juridical reform came from Beccaria and Filangieri. English theorists and reformers, too, were by no means ignored.

After Feyjóo, the three leading figures of the Spanish enlightenment were Andrés Piquer, Gregori Mayans, and Gaspar Melchor de Jovellanos. Piquer, who taught medicine and philosophy at the University of Valencia, was a Catholic traditionalist who introduced modern physics to Spain and did much for the reform of medicine. The Valencian Mayans was the first great modern polymath in Spanish culture and has sometimes been called the Menéndez y Pelayo of the eighteenth century. Jovellanos was Spain's greatest didactic prose writer of the century and the leading philosopher of economic liberalism and economic reform. His *Informe sobre la ley agraria* became a prose classic.

It is well to remember, however, that at no time had the most resourceful elements among the Spanish intellectuals completely lost touch with the advances of modern European culture. In 1697 a new philosophical society in Seville, striving to study recent European achievements in science and philosophy, was granted the protection of the crown. The University of Valencia, possibly because of the more cosmopolitan atmosphere of a port that never fully lost its trade connections, maintained better contact with the main currents of modern science than did most Spanish schools. Though the traditional Catalan universities were closed by the repression of Felipe V, the one new Catalan university that was authorized (at Cervera, outside Barcelona) had the advantage of developing when it could be open to contemporary ideas. Moreover, the Jesuits, who were somewhat more sophisticated than other teaching orders, played a major role there.

The formation of the seventy-odd Sociedades de Amigos del País and of a considerable number of schools and training institutes was of course an expression of "enlightened," critical, and reformist attitudes. There was considerable interest also in certain practical fields of knowledge such as chemistry, which was especially useful for mining and the nascent metallurgical industry. In general, however, the enlightenment touched only a few hundred thousand people of the upper and upper-middle classes, probably little more than 5 percent of the population.

The fine arts followed the vogues of neoclassicism and then of romanticism, restrained to an almost purely esthetic level, with the sole transcendant exception of Goya, who sounded the only really jarring notes in the Spanish culture of the late-eighteenth century with his *Caprichos, Disparates,* and *Pinturas negras.* Goya has often been called the first modern painter for his creation of new forms employing both realism and subjective expression rather than the stilted motifs of formal style. He was an artist of more profound insight than the European painters of his time, drawing attention to the irrational and demonic beneath the surface of the enlightened century.

Modern Spanish journalism had its roots in the second half of the eighteenth century. Periodic newspapers were already being published by 1700, but systematic Spanish journalism began with Francisco Mariano Nipho in the years 1750–1770. Nipho strove for originality and explicit didacticism in laying the groundwork for a regular press in Madrid.

Spanish conservatives and antireformist traditionalists by no means simply accepted the critical attitudes of the enlightenment, even in its moderate Catholic Spanish form. By the 1770s, they launched all-out assaults on heterodoxy and reformism, assisted socially and politically by some aristocrats who feared economic and administrative change. State censorship of all printed material was maintained, and the Inquisition showed its power by the trial and disgrace of the prominent intendant Olavide in 1778.

Though the absolute orthodoxy of Spanish culture and religion was maintained, by the midpoint of the reign the Spanish elite was nonetheless beginning to split between modernist and traditionalist attitudes. As Andrés Piquer wrote in 1771,

> There reign among us two equally concerned factions. One cries against our nation in favor of foreign lands, praising highly the flourishing of the arts and sciences, politics and the enlightenment of the understanding in them. Others abhor whatever comes from without and reject it merely for being foreign. The concern of both factions is equal, but in number, activity, and power the first prevails [among the elite].*

Piquer exaggerated the influence of the modernists. Fifteen years later the conflict was commented upon by the chief literary historian of the time, Sempere y Guarinos:

> Many will not let themselves be persuaded that it is possible to know more about anything than did the Spanish of the sixteenth century ... But there are those who, thinking that to criticize their nation and go against the current is manifest proof of genius and erudition, censure our customs, ridicule efforts for the restoration of literature, and find nothing good unless it comes from foreigners.†

Conflict between intransigent traditionalists and uncritical imitators of foreign ideas was already beginning during the reign of Carlos III, though it would not become violent until after the turn of the century.

The article "Espagne" in the first geographical volume of the Parisian *Encyclopédie méthodique,* appearing in 1783, had an almost traumatic effect on both traditionalists and reformers, for it was devoted to a hyperbolic, one-sided denunciation of Spanish ignorance, sloth, cruelty, bigotry, and tyranny. This led to a series of replies by Spanish writers and induced a more critical approach to

---

* Andrés Piquer, *Lógica moderna* (Madrid, 1771), pp. 184-85.

† Juan Sempere y Guarinos, *Ensayo de una biblioteca de los mejores escritores del reinado de Carlos III* (Madrid, 1786), 4:5-6.

French ideas and fashions among the Catholic reformers of Spain, incensed at the injustice done their country.

Though Spain in the 1780s was still quite backward compared with northwestern Europe, a great deal of progress had been made in the preceding thirty years. Among the most striking characteristics of the country during the last years of Carlos III were the unity of the people and the solidity of the regime, especially when contrasted with France of the 1780s. Carlos III was probably the most successful European ruler of his generation. He had provided firm, consistent, intelligent leadership. He had chosen capable ministers and then supported their authority effectively, thus preventing the development of political factions at court. Almost as much a non-Spanish ruler in 1759 as Felipe V in 1700 or Carlos I (V) in 1517, he learned to Hispanize himself, and his sober, pious, firm rule and simple, chaste personal life had won the respect of his people. In Spain both traditionalists and reformers were agreed upon devotion to orthodox Catholic religion and the authority of the throne. There was no division of major importance between court and country, and less tension between the intellectual elite and established values than in France. The prosperity of the 1770s and 1780s accommodated the interests of landholding aristocracy and mercantile middle classes alike, discouraging the sense of conflict that was developing north of the Pyrenees. The government of Carlos III had shown that in Spain being non-noble was not necessarily a barrier to advancement. There was much less selling of places in court, church, and army and there were more merit appointments than in prerevolutionary France. The great gap between the high and low French clergy scarcely existed in Spain, and recent fiscal reform had probably made the Spanish tax system generally more equitable than that of France. Though its society and economic structure were much less developed than those of its northern neighbor, Spain by 1788 had achieved unity, order, and progress under the most enlightened of contemporary European "despotisms."

17

Society and Economics in Eighteenth-Century Spain

The resurgence of Spain in the eighteenth century is shown most clearly by the demographic statistics. During the first half of the century the population grew only slightly. The Succession War did not cause great loss of life, largely because both sides were eager for popular support and comparatively respectful of civilians. There were, however, bad weather conditions between 1708 and 1711, and economic revival remained comparatively slow throughout the generation that followed the war. All this discouraged any rapid advance in population, but growth subsequently accelerated, and the population increased by about one-third during the second half of the century. The most rapid rise occurred during the two peaceful, fairly prosperous decades of 1748 to 1768. That was also a time of sustained emigration to Spanish America, averaging for several decades as many as 15,000 a year of the most vigorous inhabitants of the peninsula. Approximate figures* for the years 1717-1797 show the following growth in population:

1717	7,500,000
1768-1769	9,308,000

* Based on recent adjustments of incomplete censuses taken in those years. The figure for 1797 is low, and should probably be adjusted upward.

| 1787 | 10,409,000 |
| 1797 | 10,541,000 |

The increase in urban population was only slightly more rapid than that of the country as a whole, the bulk of the expansion coming among the peasantry in the countryside and villages. Swollen Madrid may actually have declined, totalling little more than 200,000 in 1800. Barcelona tripled its size between 1714 and 1800, reaching 115,000, followed by Seville (95,000), Valencia and Granada (80,000), Cádiz (70,000) and Málaga (50,000). This distribution underscores another feature of the period—the demographic and economic rise of the coastal peripheries. Not only were nearly all the large cities on the coast, but the densest rural populations were also found in the outer regions (Galicia, Valencia, the Basque region). During the second half of the century, after the threat of Muslim pirate attacks had finally been overcome, depopulated regions of the eastern and southern coasts were reinhabited. The Castilian heartland did not itself make a real demographic or economic comeback, and the weight of demographic and economic power shifted outward.

The balance between social classes finally began to change during the reign of Carlos III, as a much more stringent effort was made to define *hidalguía* and to remove the tax barriers and exemptions which had stimulated the desperate striving after aristocratic status. Growth of economic opportunity and administrative reform removed injustices, made taxation somewhat more equitable, spurred precise economic records, and made it less useful to seek special exemption. This helped reduce the proportion of the population identified as *nobleza* from at least 7.5 percent in 1768 to only 3.8 percent or less by 1797.

It should be understood that the decline of the Spanish aristocracy in the eighteenth century involved only shrinkage in the numbers of lower-rank hidalgos, and that the power and influence of the high aristocracy was curtailed in the political sphere alone. The upper nobility retained most of its social prestige and economic power. It still held seigneurial jurisdiction over slightly more than half the land in Spain. Indeed, aristocratic seigneuries probably contained about 65 percent of the cultivated land in Spain, since mountainous and waste land was disproportionately concentrated on royal domain. In most cases, the upper aristocracy's income increased during the second half of the century with the rise in food and cattle production and in agricultural prices.

According to a land survey of 1811, legal jurisdiction over the lands of Spain near the end of the old regime was divided as follows:

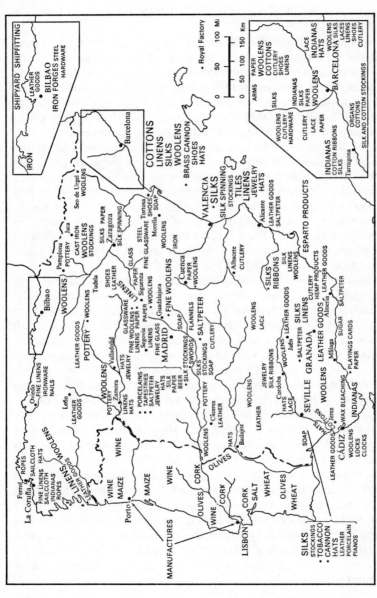

Manufacturing in Late-Eighteenth-Century Spain and Portugal. Abridged from a map by Richard Herr, with his kind permission

Señorío laico	28,306,700 aranzadas
Realengo (royal domain)	17,599,900
Abadengo (church domain)	9,093,400
	(an aranzada equals about one acre)

Thus local land jurisdiction was divided in rough proportions of 3:2:1 between the aristocracy, crown, and church. The church held particularly large proportionate jurisdictions in certain regions such as Galicia and Extremadura. The best-balanced region jurisdictionally was Catalonia, where as a result of eighteenth-century changes, aristocratic jurisdiction was less than half the total.* The region freest of private seigneuries was the Balearics, where most land was under the royal domain. But in areas such as La Mancha, Guadalajara, and Valencia aristocratic jurisdiction was overwhelming. At least three different kinds of seigneurial jurisdiction might be defined: full administrative and juridical control with the right to name local judges, priests, and town officials; limited administrative and juridical power, such as the right to confirm elections or other acts of local concejos (deriving from old behetría jurisdiction); and mere economic lordship to collect rents or other fees, leaving local townships or concejos autonomous. More than 25 percent of the villages and towns of Spain were administratively controlled by and had their own officials appointed by seigneurs. The only practical restriction upon their jurisdiction in these areas was a decree of Carlos III reserving for the crown the appointment of a public attorney in each town under señorío.

In general, the Spanish aristocracy showed itself somewhat disaffected from the cause of Felipe V in the Succession War, evidently fearing the imposition of a strong and centralized Bourbon monarchy. But after 1714, there was no general purge of the nobility save in Catalonia. The special rights of grandes to be tried only by the royal council and to keep their heads covered in the presence of the king were maintained. The upper aristocracy remained especially powerful and numerous in the central and southern regions and in Valencia. Felipe V also created many new titles. A total of 200 were established in his reign, compared with the 215 created in the equally long reign of Felipe IV.

At the beginning of the century, the hidalgo class of petty nobles

---

* According to Salvador de Moxó, La disolución del régimen señorial en España (Madrid, 1965), division of jurisdiction in 1811 was as follows, in terms of aranzadas:

	senorío laico	abadengo	realengo
Galicia	2,677,734	1,519,988	264,460
Extremadura	2,149,898	1,506,306	741,510
Catalonia	1,671,744	1,020,688	1,068,390

and pseudo-nobles remained concentrated in the north. The entire population of Guipuzcoa claimed the status of hidalguía in 1700, and the pretension was almost equally extensive in Asturias. One-half the population of Vizcaya, one-eighth of Alava, and one-twelfth of Navarre laid claim to hidalguía. In Old Castile and León there were common sheepherders who insisted on their hidalguía. It was these marginal elements that were peeled off the aristocratic rosters by economic change and fiscal reform.

The most serious thing that happened to the upper aristocracy between the sixteenth and eighteenth centuries was that although it had retained wealth and status it had slowly been losing its utility. The nobility was no longer needed for military protection, since the army had become fully institutionalized and professionalized. It was not as necessary to government, because of the extension of organized administration. The change was gradual, but was speeded up during the second half of the eighteenth century. A not insignificant proportion of nobles still served in government, but even by the beginning of the century so many had abandoned military activities and horsemanship that in 1725 the government had created a Junta de Caballería del Reino to encourage cavalry activity. The nobles retained great social prestige and wealth, but they were losing the practical role in society that they had to some extent played even under the Habsburgs in the sixteenth and seventeenth centuries.

No serious conflict developed between court and aristocracy or between the aristocracy and the third estate. Many of the rural landholding nobility reacted with varying degrees of hostility to the reforms of Carlos III, but such feeling was diffuse and did not usually take the form of organized factionalism. Educated aristocrats in fact constituted the principal support of the enlightenment in Spain. Such liberal noblemen were more prone to form voluntary associations than was any other social stratum, and at first they formed the backbone of the secret Masonic societies. If the bulk of the aristocracy was sunk in indulgence, conformity, and routine, a minority actively promoted the changes that proved a precursor to the alteration of the structure of society itself. Moreover, the nobility narrowed the social and cultural gap somewhat, as the century wore on, by tending to adopt plebeian styles in speech and aspects of dress and amusement, a form of sentimentalism and bored "campish" styles.

The Clergy

At the beginning of the eighteenth century, the Spanish church was still at the height of its wealth and influence, and the proportion of clergy was as high as in the seventeenth century. Yet though the authority of the Catholic religion was never challenged during the course of the century, subtle changes began to take place in the structure and property of the clergy that foreshadowed the momentous alterations of the nineteenth century.

It would appear that at mid-century between 15 and 20 percent of the gross national income of Spain went to the church. Over half of this came from church properties, and the remainder from tithes and *primicias* (a portion of which had to be accorded to the crown and to local seigneurs). Three-quarters of all *censos* (agrarian loans) in Castile were made by the church, and Toledo continued to be the second richest diocese in the Roman Catholic world. Church wealth remained a major source of royal taxes. The church was also the principal, almost the sole, dispenser of charity in the country and the chief educator; most of those who held positions in higher education were clerics.

A significant shrinkage in the number of the clergy began by mid-century, increasing during the reign of Carlos III and accelerating slightly more in the 1790s:

Year	Number of Clergy	Percent of Population
1768	226,187	2.5
1787	191,101	1.9
1797	172,231	1.6

This relative decline was a result of a change in the temper of society. Economic and social opportunities were much greater in the late eighteenth century than a hundred years earlier, and a more critical spirit was stirring among those in school. While strongly Catholic, their personal emphases were beginning to shift.

Despite such numerical decline, the proportion of clergy to population was still higher than in any other European country save Portugal. During the last years of the century there were about 60,000 monks and friars and 25,000 nuns. By that time the meditative orders were in a state of general decadence, but those engaged in teaching and charity remained fairly popular.

During the course of the century the structure of the Spanish clergy grew somewhat less democratic as the proportion of prelates of plebeian background declined, but there was no particular increase in aristocratic influence. High prelates tended to be *segundones* from the hidalgo class, perhaps reflecting the vigor and ambition of the new hidalgo and middle class elite forming in some regions.

Some of the clergy became notably more liberal in outlook. Feyjóo, father of the Spanish enlightenment, was a monk. While the great majority remained traditionalist and culturally xenophobic, a significant new progressive strain was developing that played a brief but prominent role in the early nineteenth century.

The regions of the peninsula were still served quite unevenly in the proportion of churches and priests available for religious work, reflecting inequities of endowment established in the Middle Ages. The ratio of priests to population was highest in the areas of Burgos, Avila, and surprisingly, Almería. It was lowest in mercantile, materialist Cádiz, which had only one parish priest for each 5,000 people. The region in which resources were distributed most equitably within the church was Catalonia. One-fourth of that region's land was held by the church, but a greater part of it was devoted to the lower clergy and prelates there were proportionately less wealthy.

In general, clerical mores and training improved, but there was still a certain amount of concubinage and the educational qualifications of Spanish priests continued to be low.

Agriculture, Land Tenure, and the Peasantry

There was a significant increase in agricultural production during the eighteenth century. This was stimulated by the growth of population, loosening of regulations, and a rise in food prices, resulting in an expanded market. It encouraged increased output of the three chief grains—wheat, barley, and rye—and by the early nineteenth century, grain occupied three-quarters of the land under cultivation. There was also expansion of maize and potato production. Severe crop failures occurred in 1709 and 1750, but there were none of such severe intensity during the second half of the century.

Cattle, on the other hand, became less important, and the Mesta continued to decline. Some slight restrictions were put upon it by a decree of 1758 and more severe ones by a decree of 1786, but its deterioration came more from the natural processes of economic change than from government restriction.

There was little improvement in technique or intensification of agriculture during the eighteenth century. Productivity remained low, and grain sown rarely brought a ratio of return higher than three to one. As in the sixteenth century, increased production was brought about mainly through extension of the amount of land under cultivation. This, along with a string of fairly good harvests, raised food production at a rate equal to or slightly exceeding the growth of population, but there was nothing approaching the technological transformation of modern agriculture occurring at that time in England and Holland. Improvements in technique and productivity were always difficult in Spain because of deficiencies in soil and climate, and because of a variety of social and legal obstacles as well. Among these were disputes over tenure rights and joint exploitation of municipal and council lands, the start of modern development of latifundia in the south, and the tendency of the peasants there to live crowded into large villages and towns. Transport facilities improved slightly but were nevertheless still insufficient and extremely expensive, especially in central Spain. Failure to achieve technological development meant that Spanish agriculture was not building the productive base for broader economic modernization. Elsewhere, in much of western Europe, a technical transformation in eighteenth- or nineteenth-century agriculture preceded the urban industrial revolution.

What was occurring, however, during the second half of the eighteenth century, was a social and commercial transformation from traditional usufructual, semisubsistence agriculture to greater production for the market. This movement toward market agriculture in turn brought important changes in land cultivation and tenure. In most regions, there was a general effort to revise terms of rent for peasant properties, taking advantage of the price rise and increase in land values. The big decade of the rent squeeze in Andalusia was the 1760s. This had especially severe effects in the most overpopulated peasant region, Galicia, where rents were raised and cultivation units persistently subdivided until thousands of relatively high-priced but uneconomic minifundia had been created. Holders of censo mortgages and *foro* landleases among the middle classes and more prosperous peasants tended to buy up rental properties held by the aristocracy as the movement toward a more capitalist agriculture developed. Others speculated on long-term leases that were divided up, sometimes microscopically, into numerous *subforos* for a perpetually land-hungry peasantry that was now beginning to emigrate in increasing numbers. A government decree of 1763 endeavored to hold the line of *forero* rents but was not fully successful.

In the southern and south-central regions, where aristocratic domains were large, there began a trend to evict peasant renters in order to form single bloc *cortijos* and carry on large-scale cultivation. Property was also rented in larger blocs in *subarriendo* to astute peasants who sublet it on their own terms to poorer peasants or hired laborers to cultivate large tracts for them. This encouraged further concentration of the rural population of Andalusia, Extremadura, and New Castile. The formation of a capitalist, not merely rentier, agricultural class laid the basis for the rural elite or oligarchy of the large-estate districts of southern and south-central Spain—also of certain northwestern regions such as Galicia and to some extent Salamanca. District leaders and economic overlords formed the background for the nineteenth-century system of rural bosses, known as *caciques* (from a Mexican word for tribal chiefs), a term that first began to gain usage in the 1770s. The new elite was composed of aristocratic landholders, middle class investors able to buy land, and the more prosperous *labradores* (landowning farmers), who could take advantage of the new system.

Land remained by far the chief source of wealth, and enterprising aristocrats, as well as some monied middle class elements, took advantage of reform attempts of Carlos III's ministers to snatch off a further portion of common and municipal or council lands from the towns or concejos. *Mayorazgos* continued to spread during the eighteenth century, especially in Castile and Navarre. The entailed estate remained the dominant socioeconomic ideal, not merely of the aristocracy but of the successful new upper middle class as well. A great deal of money made in commerce was invested in land, and some wealthy middle class people even established legal entailment of family heirlooms such as jewels. Thus the agricultural expansion of the eighteenth century was fit into the traditional status-oriented value system of upper class society. There was no serious attack on secular entailment by any eighteenth-century government.

Social and economic categories in eighteenth-century censuses were notoriously inexact, but even at the end of the century more than 75 percent, and probably more than 80 percent, of the Spanish population were peasants. The census of 1797 listed 1,677,172 peasant households (probably an undercalculation). Of these, nearly half— 805,235—were without land of their own and classified as *jornaleros* (laborers). Only a little more than 20 percent were listed as property-owning peasant farmers (*labradores propietarios*) but nearly one-third—507,423—were categorized as renters (*arrendatarios*). Since there were no usable agrarian censuses before the late eighteenth century it is impossible to compare these categories with earlier periods, but it may be inferred that they reflected considerable change during the second half of the century.

The property structure of peasant society fell generally into three categories: a) areas in which less than 25 percent of the peasants were landless; b)areas in which between 25 and 50 percent fell into that category; and c) areas in which more than 50 percent were without land. Category *a* embraced the Basque region and the districts of Santander, Soria, Asturias, and Galicia. Category *b* included most of the rest of Old Castile, León, Aragón, Navarre, Guadalajara, Cuenca, and Valencia. Category *c* was made up of the entire southern half of Spain, as well as Palencia, Catalonia, and the Balearics. The largest proportion of absolutely landless peasants were in the districts of Seville, Córdoba, and Jaén.

Yet that sort of categorization can be misleading, for distinctions should be made between the stable, long-term renters and the precariously situated short-term renters. In Catalonia, the great majority of peasants were technically propertyless, but a majority also held fairly secure, long-term emphyteutical tenure. Such leases were also common in Valencia, and long-term rents were the norm in Vizcaya, Navarre, and parts of Aragón. Rental conditions were somewhat more precarious in Old Castile and Asturias. The most inequitable property distribution was found in the region of La Mancha, where only one of every fifty-four peasant families was an owner. On the other hand, the situation was worse than it appeared in Galicia. That region had the highest proportion of peasant owners—91,759 peasant smallholders, 57,571 renters, and only 31,500 laborers, according to the 1797 census—but the peasant owners were mostly dwarfholders who also rented other strips or worked as laborers. During this period the number of peasant renters may have declined in the south, while increasing in the north.

Overall, peasant living standards seem to have improved somewhat. This was reflected in new (though frequently unsuccessful) efforts by rural townships under señorío to buy up their obligations to their lords. Even for those with little or no land, the rural system provided some benefits. Though common lands had been reduced during the seventeenth century, and again by the decrees of 1767 and 1770, they remained extensive in most of the center and north. Almost no district was without some collective property, much of it used to relieve the wants of poorer peasants. Most rural laborers lived at least above the subsistence level, and their real wages may have been a trifle higher in the late eighteenth century than in 1900. Moreover, a well-endowed church made not insignificant provisions for charity in many areas, and peasants frequently supplemented their income by their artisanry.

Many rural municipalities were better off financially in the eighteenth than in the nineteenth century, because income from their lands provided funds for charity, village schools, and a degree of medical assistance. These provisions contributed to the stability of the Spanish countryside in the eighteenth century. Yet though there were more rural or small-town schools supported by the church or local endowments in the eighteenth than in the nineteenth century (after the seizure of church and common lands), rural educational opportunities may already have begun to decline in the late seventeenth century, when the first major reduction in charity funds took place.

At any rate, it has been argued that there was more general illiteracy in 1760 than in 1660.

In general, the Spanish peasantry suffered less than that of France from efforts by the aristocracy to squeeze as much as possible out of new seigneurial exactions in the eighteenth century. Relations between overlords and peasants on many domains were fixed by custom and could not easily be changed. The domains of grandes and large church holdings were still, in many cases, administered on easy terms, and the overseers of the huge properties of the crown-dominated crusading orders were reputed to permit the easiest terms of all. But the movement toward creation of latifundia and the raising of rents was particularly strong among lesser aristocrats, middle-class owners, and some of the more compulsive monastery administrators. Conditions on land under aristocratic and church domain had changed considerably by the last decades of the century, and it was no longer generally true that peasants could expect easier terms and lighter taxes under señorío, than under royal domain. Tension over the raising of rents seems to have been particularly strong in the districts of Avila and Valencia. These changes in land relations were not the result of an increase in "feudal" dues, but of pressures being created by a capitalist market agriculture geared to more extensive production. Despite resentment over higher rents, however, the Spanish countryside stayed relatively calm and peaceful. It presented a picture of social unity and cohesion; no serious social splits occurred during the course of the century.

The Middle Classes

The second half of the eighteenth century was a time of expanded economic activity for the middle classes. Their proportion in the population increased somewhat, but it would be altogether mistaken to see this as a time of general embourgeoisement or the beginning of a social and economic "bourgeois revolution" in Spanish affairs. The growth of manufactures, save in Catalonia and in a few particular towns, was slight, and the mercantile middle classes were concentrated in the capital and a number of thriving ports. There existed a second stratum, the provincial middle classes in the smaller inland towns, whose economic existence was much more precarious and who had less thrust and vigor. If skilled artisans as a lower middle class are excluded, the socially and economically intermediate Spanish middle classes were only a slightly larger group proportionately than the aristocracy—a middle stratum of 5 to 6 percent compared with a remaining aristocracy of 3.8 percent.

There was no bourgeois ideology in eighteenth-century Spain as there was in England and France during the same period. Political ambition in the Spanish middle classes before 1800 hardly existed, and monarchist paternalism was fully accepted. Aside from those in Catalonia and a few towns, the middle classes tended to wait for economic ideas and incentives from government reformers rather than developing their own goals. While not ignorant, they were almost untouched by the enlightenment. They had no sense of being the social equals of the aristocracy and they continued to feel their inferiority acutely. Throughout the eighteenth century, the great goal of nearly all wealthy middle class Spaniards was to rise to the nobility.

The psychology of the status society—status based on position, not on achievement—was only slightly altered during the eighteenth century. Society remained highly dependent on external opinion. The dependence for security on appearance and social artifice, the lack of a personal sense of worth coming from a feeling of uniqueness or accomplishment, continued almost unchallenged. Honor, status, and group remained the primary categories of social value, and the eighteenth century was full of lawsuits and quarrels of all manner over social status, by the middle classes as well as by the aristocracy.

Economically expanding Barcelona, for example, still retained its society of four *estamentos* (estates): nobles, clergy, *ciutadans honrats* or nonmilitary oligarchs, and a fourth estate of merchants (*mercaders*), professional men (*artistes*), and artisans (*menestrals*). All of society accepted this, and upward-striving was defined exclusively in terms of these categories. Petty shopkeepers or artisans wanted to be *artistes*, and prosperous merchants hoped to establish themselves as rentier, oligarchic ciutadans honrats. In 1770, the most potent private association of merchant entrepreneurs in Spain, the Junta de Comercio of Barcelona, refused trading privileges to a merchant whose brother had been condemned by the Inquisition.

In Cádiz, the attitude and psychology of the prosperous merchants battening off the Spanish American trade could scarcely have been called bourgeois. The most visible goal was to buy land and obtain aristocratic status. Much money was wasted on conspicuous consumption; little was saved for productive reinvestment. There was a spirit of profit abroad in late-eighteenth-century Spain, but less interest in creative economic enterprise.

The comparatively small population of urban artisans and laborers was by and large a stable and orderly group at a time when the people of London and other western cities were showing a propensity to riot. The major disturbance of this quiet was the "motín de Esquilache" of 1766 in Madrid, which came as a great surprise but was in fact in part a political ploy by certain upper-class elements. There were accompanying bread riots in a number of other towns, riots that would never be repeated on such a scale. The only disturbance of the time worth noting was the greatest bread riot of the century, the *rebimboris de pa* in Barcelona in 1788, which kept the whole city in turmoil for three days. In general, the urban economy was less given to fluctuation than that of the countryside, and life in the Spanish towns of the eighteenth century was quite peaceful compared with either the seventeenth or nineteenth century. In a few regions there were, however, distinct social tensions between town and countryside, and at least two town-and-country riots occurred in the Bilbao district during the latter part of the century.

The traditional Spanish or Castilian prejudice against physical or "mechanical" labor persisted, and there was great concern among artisans to show that their work was not *vil* or *mecánico,* but intellectual or artistic. Nevertheless, there was little sense of servility in the Spanish lower classes, rural or urban, and common people continued to hold a fairly high opinion of themselves. Formal respect for women was normal, but even among the middle and upper classes there was not at all the concern for the education of women that could be seen in France.

In the larger cities the *gremio* or guild system of skilled labor (and of part of commerce) remained little altered. Great concern was shown by merchants and artisans for guild rights. Gremios continued to expand but their rigidity was more of a restraint on production than ever, and edicts of the 1770s and 1780s reduced their authority. In the smaller towns, however, there were frequently no guilds at all. Moreover, the major new manufacturing undertakings of the period—the royal textile factories that were begun at Guadalajara, Avila, Barcelona, and Valencia—were established completely outside the guild network. The first modern strikes or labor stoppages in Spain occurred at several of these factories, beginning at Guadalajara in 1729, when wages were cut.

Eighteenth-century Bourbon reformism was especially concerned to improve or eliminate the dregs of society. The proportion of *vagabundos* (bums and vagrants) had notably increased during the seventeenth century, and the Succession War had added to the ranks of the disorderly and criminal. Felipe V had at one point decreed the death penalty to try to control thieves. The government of Fernando VI attempted draconian measures against gypsies, without success, and a law of 1775 declared that all *vagos* between the ages of seventeen and thirty would be drafted into the army. This proved impossible to enforce, and by 1793 there were said to be 6,000 vagabundos in the Granada district alone. There was considerably less semi-organized banditry or delinquency during the greater part of the eighteenth century than in the preceding or following periods, however.

Commerce and Manufactures

Numerous eighteenth-century reforms contributed to the growth of Spanish manufactures. Among them were reform of taxes, suppression of most internal customs between 1714 and 1717, establishment of pilot factories for textiles and arms, attraction of foreign craftsmen to Spain, and a more extended program of protection and prohibition of raw material exports. Domestic manufactures increased considerably in volume, but this increase was accompanied by comparatively little technological development, except in the case of Catalan textiles toward the very end of the century.

In general, Spanish commerce abroad rose greatly from 1745 to 1755, fell off a bit for the next two decades, then increased very rapidly after 1778. France was the principal European customer, but the main axis of trade was between Spain and Spanish America. After the second and broader decree of 1778 liberalizing terms of commerce, the colonial trade increased approximately four times within a decade and remained very high throughout the 1790s. This encouraged further expansion of domestic manufactures, which reached a high in 1804 before the export market was ruined by the full impact of the Napoleonic wars. America was crucial not merely as a commercial outlet but also because its silver production increased during the second half of the century. This helped to balance what would otherwise have been large trade deficits between Spain and western Europe, although the influx of silver also contributed to the inflation of the period.

Beginning with the steady expansion of the 1760s, the price of industrial products rose more rapidly than did that of agricultural products, as shown in table 1. Moreover, in key regions urban wages

Table 1.   *Index of Industrial and Agricultural Prices, 1700–1800*

Year	Industrial price index	Agricultural index	Difference in indices
1700	103.1	107.4	−4.3
1720	83.2	96.9	−13.7
1740	114.4	104.8	9.6
1760	110.0	111.8	−1.8
1765	149.9	125.7	24.2
1780	144.4	135.5	8.9
1790	181.2	157.1	24.1
1800	200.0	187.6	12.4

Source: J. Vicens Vives, ed., *Historia social y económica de España y* América (Barcelona, 1958), 4:162.

lagged considerably behind the price rise. Between 1751 and 1790 urban prices increased nearly 22 per cent in New Castile and almost 32 per cent in Valencia, while nominal wages declined by approximately 18 per cent, indicating a great loss in purchasing power. Population increase may have been a factor in permitting the depression of urban wages. Prices shot up even more rapidly after 1780, while wages lagged far behind. Real wages probably hit their peak under Fernando VI, declined slightly under Carlos III, then fell drastically during the 1790s. Statistically, the real wages of a Madrid worker in 1800 were only 60 percent of those in 1726, though that was due in part to abnormal wartime conditions.

Regional Development

The region that benefited most from eighteenth-century reformism and expansion was Catalonia, even though it lost more politically to the Bourbon regime than any other part of Spain. Though taxes increased considerably, they were levied on a more proportional basis. Increased tariff protection after 1717, the reduction of internal restrictions, and the beginning of a broadly national market for the first time in Spanish history were all major stimuli. Nearly thirty years were required to overcome the losses of the Succession War, but the level of 1700 was far surpassed during a major growth phase from 1745 to 1760.

Catalan commerce and industry could not have developed as vigorously as they did had not the region's economy been based on a strong agricultural system. Though it may be something of an exaggeration to call eighteenth-century Catalan agriculture prosperous, there was a significant extension of cultivated land as well as some improvement in technique, and the rise in production was an important stimulus to the region's economy.

The two main exports of Catalonia were textiles (increasingly cotton textiles) and one popular rural product, *aguardiente* (brandy). The first modern "factory" in Spain, aside from the several new royal textile mills, was Esteban Canals' cotton textile factory established in Barcelona sometime before 1738. The partial prohibition of foreign textiles enacted in 1717 was reversed in 1760, but protectionists won out in a new decree of 1771 banning all cotton textile imports. By 1772 there were about twenty-five cotton cloth factories in Catalonia, and Catalan producers were making significant advances in new textile dyes. Modernization of the textile industry got under way about 1780 when new machines were imported from England, and later from France. A major wave of importation of textile machinery in 1803-1804 helped raise productive capacity, but the ensuing ravages of the Napoleonic wars halted any further gains for Catalan industry until the 1840s.

The expansion of Catalan commerce became so aggressive that in 1742 tariff barriers between Catalonia and the rest of the peninsula had to be raised again to protect merchants elsewhere. After 1778 more than half of all Spanish trade with America originated in Catalonia, and a sizable Mediterranean commerce had also been developed. The Catalan fishing industry expanded even though Spanish fishing in general languished during the eighteenth century. Moreover, the Catalan towns were perhaps the only ones in Spain where wages kept pace with prices. The disparity between the real wages of Barcelona and Madrid workers was very noticeable by the close of the century.

The other regions making significant economic progress were the northern coastal districts from the Basque country to Asturias, and to some extent, the Levant. The Basque region and Navarre retained their special fiscal systems, which were a definite advantage, and the Basque region and Santander also retained a differential tariff, which stimulated their commerce. The advance of the Basque region in the late eighteenth century was second only to that of Catalonia. Its economic leadership proved vigorous and resourceful; the first of the creative Sociedades de Amigos del País was formed in the Basque country in 1765. Basque agriculture was more productive than the Spanish norm, and the Basque custom of transmitting a family farm intact to a single heir perpetuated efficient productive units. The Basque shipbuilding industry continued to be the first in Spain and it expanded considerably. Yet during the course of the century Basque metallurgy made few advances and in fact barely held its own. It might have failed altogether had it not been for sweeping government action in 1775 to protect the entire iron industry. The rural economy also expanded in Santander, where the peasants were able to rely upon the broadest system of common lands that had been preserved anywhere in Spain. In Asturias, the local hidalgos and urban middle classes also showed initiative, in government as in the local economy. Though there were fewer peasant owners there, rental conditions were perhaps the best in Spain. Improved transportation assisted the beginning of the modern Asturian coal export industry.

The only area besides Catalonia where textiles expanded was Valencia, which greatly developed its silk industry as well as increasing its commerce. The Madrid region, by contrast, remained essentially nonproductive, an administrative, social, and cultural center. Its commercial elite were the members of the Cinco Gremios Mayores, the five big merchant guilds that controlled the wholesale trade of the capital.

Before the end of the eighteenth century, the two contrasting social and economic Spains of modern times had begun to take clear shape: on the one hand a fairly prosperous, commercially expanding proto-industrial north center and northeast, with a stable peasantry; on the other, an almost exclusively rural center and south, lacking industry, its commerce limited almost exclusively to an archaic colonial trade, its peasantry poor, backward, in large proportion landless, and socially unincorporated.

Periodization of the Eighteenth-Century Spanish Economy

Gonzalo Anes has suggested that the Spanish economy between 1700 and 1789 might be divided into five periods having the following general characteristics:

1. 1700–1715. The War of Succession and its aftermath. The war provoked a crisis in food production and consumer goods, which reached its height in a great agrarian crisis in 1709. The resulting mortality checked population growth, though some merchants prospered from the war and expanded their capital.

2. 1716–1735. Agrarian expansion and low prices. After the war the area under cultivation increased considerably. This came partly from population growth and increased demand. Though that pushed up land rents and dues, the increase in area of tillage held prices down. The major exception was the higher price of wine, which encouraged extension of vineyards. The greatest increase in agricultural production came in Catalonia, where the level of investment was highest.

3. 1735–1753. General price increases and lowered consumption, retarding population growth. Redistribution of income benefiting landowners, merchants, and manufacturers. Land rents increased while wages tended to drop.

4. 1754–1774. Proportionaly lowered food production resulting from bad weather, backward technique, and greater use of marginal land. Sharp price increases accompanying rapid population growth, leading to higher land rents and vocal peasant discontent. Increase in commerical activity and manufacturing along the periphery.

5. 1775–1789. Rapid population growth accompanied by higher prices and further increase in land rents. Great increase in commerce along the periphery and in Catalan manufacturing.

Conclusion

Traditional Spanish society and its economic system reached their apex during the reign of Carlos III. Population and the volume of economic activity expanded greatly. The improvement in the standard of living was much slighter, however. Though the bulk of the population was lifted out of such depths of misery as they had suffered in 1680-1682 and 1709 and mortality was reduced, the actual income of the poorer peasants increased little during the century.

The traditional structure of society underwent only limited change. The sole indication of the emergence of a modern capitalist entrepreneurial society was in Barcelona. On the other hand, the ranks of the lesser nobility were greatly reduced and the transition to a modern capitalist market agriculture was begun, even though accompanied by very little improvement of technique. While Spain had not achieved the basis for social and economic modernization on the northwest European model, some progess had been made. Continued state unity and enlightened administration were preconditions for sustaining and accelerating this process. During the following generation, a combination of royal ineptitude, internal division, and overwhelming foreign pressures destroyed the Spanish state and completely disrupted the economy. Such progress as had been made proved insufficient to meet the catastrophic challenges brought by the Revolutionary and Napoleonic era.

18

Portugal in the Seventeenth and Eighteenth Centuries

The early seventeenth century was a time of recuperation for Portugal. Union of the Hispanic crowns provided greater security and eased the financial strain, while offering Portuguese merchants major commercial opportunities in Spanish America that they were not slow to take advantage of. The Moroccan crusade was definitively abandoned, and Atlantic commerce increased considerably, particularly with Brazil, which emerged as the most important and lucrative of Portugal's overseas possessions. The hypertrophy of Lisbon was reversed, at least during the years 1580–1620, when lower taxes encouraged expanded use of the smaller ports, particularly Porto and Viana. The narrow oligarchy of the sixteenth century no longer dominated trade to the extent it had, and the restrictive effects of commercial monopoly were lessened, enabling the mercantile middle class to increase slightly over a period of several generations. Terms of peasant agriculture did not change, but rural depopulation was halted and domestic production began to expand once more.

The first half of the seventeenth century was, however, a time of severe stress and decline for Portugal's eastern thalassocracy. Clearminded advisers had long recommended against trying to maintain so far-flung a network. As early as 1520, an elderly Vasco da Gama had urged contraction and reconcentration of the Portuguese position in the East. The Portuguese had never had a strong base in the Moluccas, the most important source of spices, and the loss of Ternate in 1576 further weakened their position. Henceforth, operations in the Moluccas were carried out on a strictly commercial basis, on the sufferance of or in alliance with native rulers, of whom Portuguese traders were respectful. Though the spice trade continued a slow increase, the margin of profit steadily decreased. The balance was restored in part by the expansion of far eastern (Chinese and Japanese) trade, but profit from the thalassocracy tended more and more to remain among the Portuguese in Asia as a result of their intra-Asian activities. Even during the late sixteenth century, however, Portuguese expansion did not completely cease. Control of Ceylon was won mostly after 1597, though it would last less than half a century.

Throughout the sixteenth century, the eastern empire had managed to weather heavy assaults from Asian powers, particularly in India and the Persian Gulf, and to survive largely intact. The great losses of the seventeenth century were suffered not at the hands of Asians but at those of Portugal's aggressive and dynamic western rival Holland. The initial hostilities with Holland were brought on by the policies of the Spanish Habsburg crown, starting with the decision of Felipe II in 1594 to crack down on Dutch commerce, leading to the seizure of some fifty Dutch ships in Lisbon harbor. It is unlikely that armed conflict with Holland could have been avoided for long, however, for the Portuguese thalassocracy lay directly in the path of Dutch overseas expansion. Holland's superiority came from the great increase in her naval strength. The Portuguese fleet did not decline greatly—it was only slightly smaller and weaker in 1600 than in 1500—but it fell behind technologically and could in no way equal the pace of Dutch expansion. The Dutch were able to draw on naval resources and seamen from northern Germany and Scandinavia, while the Portuguese position was further weakened by attempts of English expeditions to build positions of their own in the Persian Gulf and the Indian Ocean.

Portuguese naval construction at home concentrated on unwieldy carracks and galleons, and was slow to adapt to the new heavily armed yet swift and maneuverable frigate of the Dutch or English type. In Asia, on the other hand, the Portuguese made the mistake of overadapting to local conditions of sailing and fighting. They relied to a great extent on small, maneuverable, lightly gunned, oar-driven *fustas* and *fragatas,* effective enough against Asian foes but hopelessly outclassed by the more powerful Dutch and English vessels. Thus to a certain degree, their two rivals enjoyed some of the same maritime and military advantages against the Portuguese that the Portuguese had held a century earlier against the Asians.

According to a tabulation of 1627, there were about 5,000 Portuguese fighting men in Asia, some 3,500 of whom were stationed in the fleets of the west Indian coast. Only 300 manned the Persian Gulf fleet and only 200 the Malaccan. Most local stations had to depend on their own militia of settlers, half-castes, and armed slaves. There were permanent garrisons of troops only in Ceylon (800 men), Malacca (100) and Moçambique (100) on the east African coast, with presumably some sort of unspecified force at Macau. At the same time there were large numbers of Portuguese deserters acting independently for their own profit. According to one estimate, these freebooters numbered 3,000 in Bengal (western India), 1,500 in Siam, and 500 at Macassar in the Celebes. Portuguese mercenaries also turned up in China and were employed by the emperor to help resist the Manchus. The numerical weakness of Portuguese military units was compounded by their general disorganization and indiscipline. The Portuguese had never developed the systematic professional organization achieved by the Spanish tercios.

Though the ten-year truce between the Dutch and the Habsburg crown never applied to Asian waters, the principal phase of struggle with the Dutch did not begin until the truce ended in 1619. Development of the main Dutch base at Djakarta on Java threatened the key Portuguese position of Malacca (near Singapore), and Portuguese operations in the Moluccas were eliminated almost altogether. Simultaneously, Dutch incursions greatly reduced the trade with China and Japan, though a Dutch attempt to seize Macau in 1622 was dealt a crushing defeat. That same year, however, an Anglo-Persian alliance resulted in the capture of Ormuz, the Portuguese base in the Persian Gulf. Between 1629 and 1636, nearly one hundred and fifty ships were lost to the Dutch in Asian waters alone, and this was far more than the Portuguese capacity to replace. The trough of Portugal's eastern trade occurred between 1625 and 1640; in only one of those years were more than three ships dispatched to India. Goa was under Dutch blockade from 1637 to 1644, and the Dutch conquest of Ceylon began in 1638. All Portuguese traders and missionaries were expelled from Japan in 1639, bringing the once highly profitable Japanese trade to a complete end, and Malacca was finally lost to the Dutch in 1641.

It was already abundantly clear that the future of overseas commerce and expansion for Portugal lay in Brazil, not in Asia, but the struggle to maintain the eastern empire diverted vital supplies and manpower from Portuguese America. A crucial thirty-year struggle for control of Brazil and Angola was waged with Holland from 1624 to 1654. The ultimate defeat of the Dutch in those two regions was due more to the determination and resilience of Portuguese colonial society than to assistance from the homeland. The Spanish government of Felipe IV took the initiative in organizing several relief expeditions to Brazil, yet did not succeed in getting wealthy and influential Portuguese to cooperate fully in the expedition of 1630 to rescue Pernambuco. By the 1630s, the Portuguese elite was disillusioned by association with the Spanish Habsburg crown and resisted participation in Spanish-led projects.

Portuguese Independence Restored

The Spanish crown did not completely fulfill its pledge of 1581 to respect the integrity of Portuguese institutions, but the essentials of the agreement were honored. Though a few small Spanish garrisons were established in Portugal, there was never any general military occupation. After leaving Lisbon in 1583, Felipe II never returned to Portugal, and Felipe III visited the kingdom only on one brief occasion during a reign of twenty-three years. Portuguese interests were less respected during the latter reign, especially during the domination of the Duke of Lerma, and there was a tendency to name more and more Spanish officials to offices in Portugal.

In general, however, the benefits of the union of crowns at first considerably outweighed the disadvantages. The Portuguese were never required to contribute to the Spanish treasury, while the Spanish crown helped to bolster Portugal's Atlantic defenses. Little could be done to halt the decline of Portuguese Asia, but the Portuguese themselves recognized that that was neither the responsibility of the Spanish crown nor within the scope of its resources, while the Atlantic route to Brazil had become much more valuable. Access to the Spanish American economy alone was worth a great deal to enterprising Portuguese. Wealthy cristão novo financiers found a major new field for activity in the Spanish money market, and many of them gravitated to Madrid.* Positive aspects of Habsburg rule included a new compilation of Portuguese law, the *Ordenações Filipinas,* completed in 1602, and a number of efforts to stimulate agriculture. Several decrees were issued to limit hunting and certain abuses of *senhorio,* to encourage local officials to distribute idle land for cultivation, to protect peasants in debt, and to give greater legal power to village councils.

Discontent with Habsburg government became severe only after the reign of Felipe IV was well under way, and stemmed from three

---

* Within Portugal, however, certain legal concessions purchased by cristãos novos were cancelled in 1610, and the activities of the Inquisition were revived.

sources: losses from the Dutch invasion of Brazil, efforts to exclude Portuguese from the Spanish-American economy, and attempts by the crown to levy new taxes for imperial defense. The Spanish crown tried to give the defense of Brazil priority equal to that of its own territories, but after the main Dutch invasion of Pernambuco began in 1630, lacked the resources to drive them out. A large joint Spanish-Portuguese expedition under a Portuguese commander was defeated by a much smaller Dutch force off the Brazilian coast in January 1640. Retention and development of Brazil was now much more important than what remained of Portuguese Asia, and it became increasingly clear that the Spanish crown would be hard put to defend Portuguese America.

The Spanish imperial economy, which had absorbed many Portuguese immigrants, went into a phase of seemingly irreversible decline after the 1620s, and by the end of that decade the Spanish government had begun to take measures to exclude Portuguese from Spanish America. Thus a major source of opportunity was closing. The Portuguese peasantry and lower classes had never felt enthusiasm for the Habsburg dynasty. A new pro-Habsburg upper aristocracy had been created by the awarding of a whole group of new titles since 1580, but the lesser nobility became increasingly disillusioned. Under the Habsburgs, they were becoming a parochial rural class, living beside the peasants on small estates, lacking major imperial posts, yet still fed on a culture of chivalry and adventure in which they could no longer participate.

During the 1620s, the crown raised a number of forced loans in Lisbon, provoking discontent among the economic elite. Olivares subsequently endeavored to make the Portuguese pay increased taxes for their own defense. In 1637 agricultural prices took a downturn throughout Portugal and the peasantry faced a new crisis. When further excises were levied, a popular revolt broke out at Evora that spread through most of the Alemtejo and the Algarve, with repercussions in the northwest. The tax revolt did not lead to widespread violence and was soon put down by Castilian troops, but it was an indication of popular feeling. At that time the leading descendant of the Portuguese royal family, D. João, eighth duke of Bragança, was acclaimed as a national leader, raising the possibility of a revolt for independence. This was encouraged by messages from the French crown in 1638 promising strong French military assistance.

The moment of decision came two years later, in 1640, when Olivares applied heavy pressure for Portuguese assistance in putting down the revolt that had broken out at the opposite corner of the peninsula, in Catalonia. Some 6,000 troops had already been impressed from Portugal, and D. João of Bragança, as leading aristocrat of the kingdom and nominal commander of Portuguese military forces, was ordered to Spain with a new levy of Portuguese troops. A conspiracy to revolt was already under way among a group of lesser nobles and some state officials, encouraged in part by fear that if the upper classes did not act, popular discontent would get out of hand. Grandson of a daughter of João III, and the greatest landholder in Portugal, with 80,000 peasants on his Alemtejo estates, João of Bragança was the natural leader of Portuguese society. Fearing that Olivares's summons was merely a means to gain control of him, the conspirators acclaimed D. João king of Portugal on December 1, 1640. The revolt was justified as a return to established law, contravened by the centralizing measures of the reign of Felipe IV. The moment was propitious: not only were Spanish land forces tied down in Catalonia, but Spanish naval strength had been disastrously weakened by defeats at the hands of the Dutch in 1639–1640.

Dom João had shown considerable caution, and even reluctance, in the development of the conspiracy, but his prudence and calculation served him well in the difficult years ahead. The restored monarchy made no effort to change anything in the structure of Portuguese government and society, ratifying the position of all officials willing to serve the independent Portuguese crown. The traditional Cortes was summoned in 1641 to recognize the king as João IV and provide financial support for the struggle. The restoration was popular with all social classes and was strongly supported by the most influential of the clergy, the Jesuits, who were of prime importance in winning support for the independence movement in Portuguese Brazil. There was, however, a significant pro-Spanish faction among the upper aristocracy, church hierarchy, and coastal bourgeoisie.

One hope in the minds of the Portuguese rebels was that a break with the Spanish crown would make it possible to achieve peace with Holland, and even to restore many of the losses overseas. The Dutch refused to return any conquests in the East, but a ten-year truce was concluded in 1641, restoring Dutch trading privileges in Portugal and taking effect in Asian territory one year later. The Dutch also obtained a virtual monopoly of foreign shipping to Portugal and Brazil.

After independence, the French provided very little of the help they had led the Portuguese conspirators to expect. Moreover, it proved impossible to establish friendly relations with the papacy, which was strongly under Spanish influence. Though most sees in Portugal were or became vacant during the next quarter-century, the papacy did not officially receive a Portuguese ambassador until 1669.

During the first years, independence was maintained more through Spanish weakness than Portuguese strength. Until 1652 the Habsburg crown had to concentrate on the Catalan revolt and engaged in no more than border harassment on the Portuguese frontier. It relied primarily on internal subversion in Portugal, which first took form in a pro-Habsburg conspiracy of 1641 among aristocrats and upper clergy (as well as some merchants and financiers whose main business lay with the Spanish empire). This was crushed, but several years later there was a revival of activity by the Portuguese Inquisition, very possibly due to Spanish encouragement, against the wealthy cristão-novo merchants and financiers whose economic assistance was vital to the Portuguese resistance. The only direct attempt at invasion, however, a comparatively small Spanish expedition of 1644, was beaten back.

João IV proved a capable and prudent king. He maintained an active diplomacy, making the most of Spain's hostile relations with the other powers of western Europe. His government husbanded Portugal's limited resources and built a modest military strength, while it conciliated all sectors of Portuguese society through a balanced domestic policy. João IV called five Cortes assemblies during his sixteen-year reign (1640-1656), and never tried to raise new moneys without the approval of the third estate. He was not a bold and inspiring king, but as one English visitor put it, "an honest plain man ... faring as homely as any Farmer."* Though at one point he considered abdication in favor of his son, his shrewdness and persistence were essential to the new Portuguese state. His personal qualities were not unlike those of the founder of the second (Aviz) dynasty, João I.

The success of the Portuguese restoration may be contrasted with the failure of the Catalan revolt of 1640-1652. The Catalans had about as much sense of uniqueness and "nationality" as the Portuguese, and differed even more from Castile in their values, social structure, and psychology. A crucial difference lay in economic base—Portugal could rely to some extent on Brazilian resources, but Catalonia had no empire or overseas resources and was not economically self-sufficient. Another advantage for Portugal was that it had a traditional independent political structure and an acknowledged leadership, for only sixty years had passed since the loss of independence. Moreover, the Catalans were handicapped by the fact that their society was more European, political, and constitutionally minded than that of either Castile or Portugal. Under their restored system of semi-absolute monarchy, the Portuguese had no equivalent of the elaborate constitutional system of Catalonia, making it easier to channel civic concerns and direct government. Geography also aided Portugal. The Castilian crown could not afford an independent Catalonia under French protection and concentrated on the conquest of

---

* Quoted in an unpublished study of seventeenth-century Anglo-Portuguese relations by Bentley Duncan.

that principality. Nor did the French in the long run stiffen Catalan resistance, for their intervention ultimately had a divisive and weakening effect on Catalan society. Portugal was better situated to go its own way, bolstered by its tradition of independent monarchy and isolated by Castile from direct French assistance but also from the negative effects of French intervention. The Catalan resistance became revolutionary and could not hope for a general rising of all the lands of the traditional crown of Aragón, while the Portuguese restoration rested upon a completely traditional system. Finally, the very cost of the long struggle to subdue Catalonia nearly exhausted the already deteriorating resources of the Spanish crown, leaving little with which to conquer Portugal.

During the second half of the reign of João IV, the Portuguese seized the initiative against the Dutch who still held territory in Brazil and Angola. The struggle was begun by Portuguese Brazilians who rebelled against Dutch control of Pernambuco in 1645, when Holland and Portugal were nominally at peace. Three years later, the Portuguese managed to regain Luanda, the focus of the Angolan slave trade, which had been seized by the Dutch in 1641. Resources were then concentrated on the struggle in Brazil, whence the Dutch were finally expelled in 1654.

Thus despite renewed Dutch naval assaults, the Portuguese position in the Atlantic held fast, but further severe losses were suffered in the Indian Ocean. Throughout this period, Portuguese bases in the East were intermittently attacked or harassed by a wide variety of native Asian and east African foes, and the Dutch proved relentless. They gained full control of Ceylon in 1655 and during the next eight years took over most Portuguese positions on the Malabar coast of India. The new Arab state of Oman seized Muscat, the last important Portuguese possession in the Persian Gulf, in 1650, and raided other Portuguese strongholds in the west Indian Ocean. The main pressure was ended when peace was finally made with Holland in 1663. Dutch recognition of Portugal's full possession of Brazil was gained after paying an indemnity, but at the same time the Portuguese crown had to acknowledge loss of nearly all its Asian possessions. There remained only Macau and Goa—the latter but a shadow of its former self—together with Timor and a few smaller stations. Even so, Portuguese traders in Asia had in the few decades before managed to expand their commercial position in Siam, Indo-China, and the Celebes.

The bases of what was to become the historic Anglo-Portuguese alliance were laid by the commercial treaty of 1654 and the dynastic alliance between Portugal and England negotiated in 1661. The latter provided for the marriage of D. Catarina, daughter of the late João IV, to the newly crowned Charles II of England, together with the payment of a sizable dowry and the cession to England of the Portuguese coastal enclaves of Tangier and Bombay. In return, the Bragança dynasty gained the prestige of arranging an interdynastic match of the first order, and more important, the two crowns signed a mutual defense pact providing Portugal with a formal ally in the still undecided struggle with Spain. The Anglo-Portuguese association remained a perpetual alliance ever after that date, giving Britain useful commercial opportunities and strategic bases, while providing Portugal and its empire with the shelter of what was soon to become the strongest fleet in the world. This became a significant factor in sustaining Portuguese independence.

Pressure from the Habsburg crown had increased after the end of the campaign in Catalonia (1652) and the signing of the peace with France (1659). A minor invasion attempt was thrown back in 1653, as was a slightly stronger one five years later. The most serious effort was made by a Spanish invading force of more than 10,000 men, under D. Juan José, that captured Evora in 1663. Assisted by foreign experts, the Portuguese crown had built a home army of 15,000, including 1,500 elite English regulars and 5,000 cavalry, 20 percent of which were British or other foreign forces. These troops defeated the Spanish in several pitched battles between 1663 and 1665, with the English brigade winning special distinction. By this time, the Spanish forces were made up of German and Italian mercenaries or local militia and were nothing like the conquering elite of a century earlier. After the defeat of a final Spanish invasion attempt in 1665 and the death of Felipe IV that same year, peace was eventually signed in 1668. The Habsburg crown recognized the full independence of Portugal and in the following year the papacy also resumed official relations. Carlos II continued to call himself king of Spain even after Portuguese independence, so the Portuguese in turn began to drop the traditional custom of calling themselves, along with the other inhabitants of the peninsula, Spanish. As late as 1712, however, in negotiations for the Treaty of Utrecht, Portuguese representatives insisted that the monarchy in Madrid be referred to simply as Castile and not as Spain.

The Reigns of Afonso VI (1656-1667) and Pedro II (1667-1706)

The eldest surviving son of the first Bragança was a mentally deficient youth named Afonso, the nature of whose malady was uncertain. For six years after the death of João IV the kingdom was governed by a regency under Afonso's mother, the queen-widow Luisa de Guzmán, daughter of the powerful Spanish noble the duke of Medina-Sidonia. Afonso's only interests were in the brawls provoked by his personal gang of ruffians in the streets of Lisbon. When his favorite was arrested by the regency in 1662, however, one of his courtiers, the young Conde de Castelo Melhor, encouraged D. Afonso to seize the powers of government directly. Since Afonso VI could not rule, the Portuguese state was dominated for the next five years by Castelo Melhor. Ironically, it was during these years that the crown's military leaders won the decisive battles in the long struggle with Castile, bringing the mentally incompetent king the nickname Afonso the Victorious. The downfall of Castelo Melhor and his sovereign occurred in 1667, when the favorite negotiated a marriage for Afonso with a French princess, Marie Françoise of Savoy. D. Afonso was sexually impotent, and the ambitious Marie Françoise, once installed as queen, soon took direction of government. Together with Afonso's younger brother Pedro she forced the dismissal of Castelo Melhor and the personal retirement of Afonso. Pedro took power as regent and heir to the throne; in the following year the marriage to Afonso was annulled and Pedro and Marie Françoise were wed. Afonso lived the remaining fifteen years of his life in confinement.

In 1668, a convocation of Cortes recognized D. Pedro as regent and heir to the throne. Pedro II signed the final peace with Spain, governed for fifteen years as regent, and after the death of Afonso for twenty-three years in his own right. His long reign was a time of modest economic expansion and of recuperation from the restoration struggle. It also saw the rise of the Brazilian economy to a place of overwhelming importance in Portuguese commerce and taxation. The crown was still quite poor when Pedro inherited it, but receipts increased by the middle of his reign. After 1680, he ceased altogether to summon the Portuguese Cortes, save for a perfunctory assembly in 1697 to recognize the next heir to the throne. That meeting agreed that the crown could make whatever laws it desired to legitimize the succession, and the traditional Portuguese Cortes was never called again. The eighteenth-century system of authoritarian monarchy had taken form. Henceforth the only contact that the Portuguese state of the Old Regime had with representative assemblies were its relations with the guild representatives in the municipal councils of the larger towns, themselves in large measure controlled or manipulated by royal administrators.

The Portuguese Economy in the Seventeenth Century

The recuperation of Portuguese society and economy in the early seventeenth century was attested by steady growth of the population, which reached 1,800,000 by the time of the restoration in 1640, and grew to more than 2,100,000 by 1730 and nearly 3,000,000 by 1800. All the while there was a small but steady emigration to Brazil, which had a European population of approximately 30,000 in 1600, and contingents were still sent to man the *praças* (strongholds) remaining on the Asian coast.

In economic perspective, it was the upswing of Portugal's Atlantic commerce during the 1620's and 1630s, at the very time that the major Spanish decline had set in, that helped to pull Portuguese interests apart from those of Spain and provide an economic base for the restoration. The cyclical phases of overseas commerce moved approximately as follows:

1570–1600	expansion
1600–1620	depression
1620–1640	expansion
1640–1670	depression
1690–1760	expansion
1760–1780	depression
1780–1805	expansion

All in all, the century from 1570 to 1670 was a time of relative commerical strength for Portugal, more stable than most of the sixteenth century had been. Domestic exports were still primarily the traditional items: salt from Setúbal, wine, oil, and fruit. Lisbon remained the chief port, and after 1620 once more began to grow at the expense of some of the smaller port cities. Its major trade, however, was in sugar and tobacco (and to a much lesser degree wood), reexported from Brazil and Madeira. The production of sugar and tobacco in Spanish, French, and English America cut heavily into the Luso-Brazilian market from about 1670 and forced prices downward.

The commercial depression of the 1670s led to the first serious government attempt in Portuguese history to develop domestic manufactures. Heretofore the state and the upper level of the economy had lived largely off overseas trade. There had been scarcely any per capita growth in domestic artisan manufactures for two hundred years. The modest expansion of the country's agriculture in the seventeenth century scarcely kept up with the population growth, and Portugal normally had to import 15 percent or more of its grain. In general, the domestic economy was nearly static, a part of the backward agrarian belt of southern and eastern Europe.

Since the early part of the century, there had been growing discussion among critics and economic writers—the Portuguese equivalent of the Spanish *arbitristas*, or reform writers—about the need to concentrate on the development of the domestic economy. They advocated a policy of *fixação* (concentrating at home) rather than *transporte* (overseas commerce). Various plans were formulated for supporting agriculture, setting up peasant colonies, and stimulating manufactures. The Conde de Ericeira was made supervisor of finance in 1675 and dominated economic policy for the next fifteen years. It was clear that the kingdom could no longer pay for the volume of imports to which it had grown accustomed in recent decades. Under the stimulus of Ericeira—"the Portuguese Colbert"—a series of decrees tried to control imports and nonproductive spending. Measures were taken to stimulate silk, woolen, and other cloth manufacture, and there was some effort at tariff protection. The achievements were limited, and after 1690, when profits from overseas commerce began to rise once more, the attempt to stimulate domestic manufactures for the most part lapsed.

The main factor in the transformation of the commercial economy at the end of the seventeenth century was the development of Brazilian gold production. The arrival of gold in Lisbon reached the following annual levels:

1699	725kgs.
1701	1,785
1714	9,000
1720	25,000
1725	20,000

The early eighteenth century Portuguese economy was thus keyed to the balance of trade provided by Brazilian gold. It was this reliance on *transporte,* rather than the supposed domination of Portuguese commerce by Britain, that guaranteed the protracted anemia of domestic production. With the peasant economy completely undeveloped and the upper classes relying upon imports paid for by the profits of the colonial economy, manufactures were persistently ignored.

Commercial ties with England became particularly close after the treaty of 1654 that placed a tariff maximum of 23 percent on all English exports to Portugal and gave the English merchant colony in Portugal extraterritorial religious rights, though neither provision was fully honored by the Portuguese. After 1670, England increasingly dominated the Portuguese market, and in turn, the export of Douro wines, which had increased since the early seventeenth century, rose erratically but significantly. The nominal landmark of Anglo-Portuguese commercial relations, the famous Methuen treaty of 1703, provided for a preferential duty protecting Portuguese wine from foreign competition in the English market, in return for a Portuguese guarantee of removal of all restrictions on the importation of English textiles. Eleven percent of England's exports already went to Portugal, and the Methuen treaty had no revolutionary consequences, merely ratifying officially a well-established trend. French and Dutch textiles were normally admitted to Portugal on terms equal to those of Britain, and British dominance was due mainly to superior quality, volume, and financing.

State income in Portugal came primarily from the levies on colonial trade, and agrarian exports continued to be quite low during the seventeenth century. During the commercial depression of the 1670s and 1680s, the crown's receipts were sometimes 50 percent lower than those of the early years of the century. Brazilian gold created a marked upswing after 1700; by 1715, state income was nearly twice the level of 1680. This revolutionized the finances of the crown. The restored monarchy had been a poor regime, barely able to keep its head above water; for a few short years in the early eighteenth century the crown enjoyed a comfortable surplus, leading to great sumptuary spending but also to the rehabilitation of public institutions.

As in the sixteenth century, the expanded overseas activity and increased income of the state and upper classes in the early eighteenth century had little effect on the condition of the lower classes. The rural standard of living was scarcely above subsistence level, little changed from the late Middle Ages. Though seigneurial domain was extended in Portugal as in Spain during the early modern period, this had less effect on the terms of agriculture in Portugal. The long-term family rental and share-crop farm were still characteristic of most of the country and provided rural stability, even though it was one of stagnation and grinding poverty. Portuguese society remained surprisingly cohesive during the seventeenth century; indeed, Portugal was perhaps the only country in Europe not to undergo at least a few notable social revolts or internal upheavals. The traditional, paternalistic society showed little uneasiness, only quiescent and accepted misery. Even in Castile there were occasional bread riots, while in Catalonia for some time there was widespread banditry. The only Portuguese equivalent was an increase in the number of town beggars.

Remnants of the Thalassocracy

Portuguese power in southern Asia and southeast Africa continued to decline in the late seventeenth and early eighteenth centuries. The chief pressure came, not from European competitors, but from the resurgence of native Muslim states. The foothold in the Celebes was lost in 1667. The island fortress of Moçambique, with its profitable trade in slaves and ivory, was retained, but the other east African stronghold of Mombaça was finally lost to the Arabs in 1698 and was regained only briefly in 1728-1729. Portuguese commercial influence on the west coast of India, vastly diminished in the seventeenth century, declined further. Some territory surrounding Goa was acquired between 1763 and 1783, but nearly all the remaining outlying ports were lost. Commercial competition from the French and English grew more severe as the latter commenced their domination of the subcontinent. The trading stations and fortresses on the Angolan coast of west Africa became increasingly valuable, however, as the volume of the slave trade to Brazil mounted.

The Reign of João V (1706-1750)

The reign of João V bears modest comparison with that of Manuel I at the beginning of the sixteenth century. Whereas Manuel the Fortunate reaped all the advantages of the establishment of the eastern thalassocracy, João V ruled during the heyday of the Atlantic Brazilian economy and its gold production. Unlike his father, Pedro II, and his grandfather, João IV, João V was not severely limited by fiscal restraints. He was one of the best-educated princes of his time, devoted to pomp and luxury but also generous in charities.

When his reign began, Portugal was already deeply involved in the Spanish Succession War. This was the only major entanglement of the kingdom between the restoration and the Napoleonic struggles, and was the result of British influence and the offer of two small slices of Spanish territory in return for support of the pro-Habsburg, anti-Bourbon forces (see chapter sixteen above). With British assistance, Portugal withstood a limited Bourbon offensive in 1704, then participated modestly in successful campaigns by the allies in Spain between 1705 and 1707. After that the Portuguese front in western Spain lapsed into stalemate. Portugal's anti-Bourbon allies failed to provide all the assistance promised, and peace was made on the basis of the status quo ante in 1713. During this conflict the Portuguese army of some 20,000 was transformed from the old proto-Spanish tercio organization of the seventeenth century into the more modern French regimental system, but altogether it was a very costly war from which Portugal derived little or no benefit.

For the remainder of the century the Portuguese crown carefully stayed out of continental conflicts. During 1716-1717 the revitalized Portuguese navy answered a call from the papacy to defend the Adriatic, and defeated a Turkish fleet. The only other military engagement of João V's reign was the colonial struggle with Spain over Uruguay in 1735-1737. Portugal's distant but axial geographic position, together with its alliance with Europe's premier maritime power, enabled it to avoid major involvement.

João V spent enormous sums on construction, the chief example of which was the luxurious palace, monastery, and library of Mafra, north of Lisbon. This pinnacle of Portuguese baroque architecture was constructed at great cost between 1715 and 1735. The crown also spent sums to beautify Lisbon, built a new library for Coimbra, founded a Royal Academy of History and an Academy of Portugal for artists. Hospitals and medical studies were supported and encouraged, and Lisbon enjoyed the finest opera in Europe outside Italy. The reign brought the flowering of the Portuguese baroque, but the emphasis of the time was on foreign, especially Italian, art and led to few striking achievements in Portuguese arts and letters. Its style of splendor was in imitation of the forms of the French monarchy, common to many European dynasties of that period.

This reign coincided with half a century of relative prosperity for the economy as a whole. Some decline in Brazilian gold production was balanced by the export of diamonds after 1728. The rate of emigration to Portuguese America increased. Between 1720 and 1740 there was a rise in domestic manufactures, stimulated by royal support for textiles, paper, and weapons and by the military and commercial uncertainties of the period.

In administration and government, the crown continued the centralizing policy of the Portuguese state. In Portugal, as in Spain, the district military commands set up during the Succession War were made the framework of regional administration. During the middle years of the reign an effort was made to reform and improve some of the central organs of government. In the 1740s, however, the declining vigor of João V led to a relaxation of governmental activity and the Portuguese state system began to atrophy. The corporative, aristocratic institutions of local government, little altered for two or three centuries, were unequal to the tasks of a larger, more complex society. At the top, the centralized monarchist administration was overloaded with tasks and lacked the imagination, flexibility, and leadership to face new problems.

Pombal

João V was succeeded in 1750 by his son José I (1750-1777), an indolent prince already of middle age who had had no experience in government and lacked talent or energy for it. The Portuguese state was facing crisis arising from the paralysis of government in the last decade of D. João's reign, coupled with a decline in trade revenues. As a consequence the new king appointed several new ministers whose only common denominator was their dissatisfaction with the breakdown of the state machinery and their determination to institute administrative and economic reforms. Chief of these was a fifty-one-year-old sometime diplomat of petty fidalgo background, Sebastião José de Carvalho e Melo, later created Marques de Pombal in 1770. He soon became the strong man of D. José's reign, relieving a disconcerted king of the main responsibilites of government. Becoming the secretary of state, he firmly took control of affairs at the time of the catastrophic Lisbon earthquake of 1755 and with royal assent served as minister-dictator for the balance of the reign. He became far and away the dominant figure in eighteenth-century Portuguese history.

Pombal's ideas and goals were formed largely from observation of contemporary west and central European policies of enlightened despotism and mercantilism, and from some of the values and laic, anticlerical attitudes of the west European enlightenment. There has been much debate over the relative "enlightenment" of Pombal's government, but of its despotism there was never any doubt. It was more authoritarian than any of its contemporaries in western and central Europe, not excluding the Prussia of Frederick the Great. The Cortes had made no decisions of consequence since 1668 and was never summoned during the eighteenth century. Juridically, there were few checks to royal authority as exercised by Pombal.

Pombal's regime may be divided into four phases: 1) 1750-1760, devoted to government and mercantile reforms; 2) 1760-1763, dealing primarily with the military challenge of the last phase of the Seven Years' War and the colonial struggle with Spain; 3) 1764-1770, facing a commercial and fiscal crisis, devoted to mercantile and tax reforms; and 4) 1770-1777, concerned mainly with educational reform and the stimulation of domestic manufactures.

Under Pombal the government moved to reform administration, tighten the legal system, and make tax collection more efficient. Strong measures were taken to cut down on contraband, particularly in gold, which had swollen to great proportions in the 1740s. The production of Brazilian gold was declining, and it was all the more important to see that the full royal share was received. Private export of gold was forbidden. Direct steps were taken to reduce the powers of influential church institutions and the most privileged groups of nobility. In 1751, the scope of the Inquisition was drastically curbed, and six years later the jurisdiction of the Jesuits in Brazil and their influence at court were both eliminated. The prerogatives of influential aristocratic families, such as the Aveiro and Tavora, who were realizing great profits from their connections with foreign trade, were sharply reduced.

Pombal took charge of the reconstruction of Lisbon after the great earthquake of 1755, which claimed more than 5,000 lives and shook the optimism of rationalist thought in France and England. From his efforts emerged a spacious, elegant, modern district in the center of the Portuguese capital.

Pombal installed a concentrated state mercantile policy designed to squeeze out or control less effective small merchants. It established a series of monopolistic trading associations for both colonial and domestic exports. Between 1753 and 1759, three new trading associations were formed for sections of the Brazilian trade, one for Asia, one for whaling, and another to monopolize the export of Douro wines. Wine prices had been falling as a result of overproduction in Portugal and superior organization among British traders. The aim of the new mercantile companies was to regulate and make more profitable the sale of wine, tobacco, and diamonds. In 1756, the government established an official Junta do Comércio.

Pombal fully recognized the importance of Brazil, which benefited from his rule. Trade restrictions were relaxed somewhat and colonial production, notably shipbuilding, was encouraged. Emigration to Brazil, on the increase since the turn of the century, rose more rapidly and averaged neárly 1,000 per year, mostly from the poor, already overpopulated Azores.

Pombal's policies eventually elicited a strong reaction. In 1757, there was a five-day riot in Porto against the new wine company monopoly. Important local merchants and officials were involved in exciting the disorders, which were firmly suppressed with nine executions and seventy-eight penal deportations. The following year, 1758, resentment among elements of the nobility connected with the colonial trade, whose privileges had been sharply reduced, led to a confusing attempt on the life of the king, which in turn brought the prosecution of several of their number and execution of a leading aristocrat. The crackdown on opposition was climaxed by the decree of 1759 dissolving the Jesuit order in Portugal and expelling its members.

Pombal pursued a foreign policy of general neutrality, but identified Portugal closely with British commercial interests. After the signing of the third Family Compact bringing the Spanish Bourbon crown in on the French side of the Seven Years' War in 1762, Portugal found itself involved on the side of the British, anti-Bourbon alliance in defense of its territorial aims on the Brazilian frontier. Pombal detested war, considered the military wasteful, and had neglected the armed forces during the previous decade. Weakened military resources led to several anxious moments before the crown was extricated by the general peace of 1763.

After the close of the war, Portugal was faced with the most severe colonial commercial slump of the century. Brazilian exports declined 40 percent during the decade 1760–1770. Suffering from foreign competition, sugar sales dropped by the same percentage between 1760 and 1776. Brazilian gold production decreased steadily during the second half of the century. Royal gold revenues declined from an annual average of 125.4 arrobas (an arroba equals 33 lbs.) in 1736–1751, to an average of 86.1 in 1752–1787, and then to 44.3 in 1788–1801. (The actual ratio of decline was proportionately greater, since Pombal made collection of the royal shares more efficient.) During the decade of the 1760s, imports from Britain, Portugal's main trading partner, dropped 50 percent. By 1770, ship movements in Lisbon had diminished by one-third from the level of 1750. In the general depression, the Portuguese African slave trade also dwindled. The trough in the decline of state revenues occurred between 1768 and 1771, and the government's response was a series of moves to improve tax collection and reorganize and stimulate the most lucrative exports. Parallel to this, a central tax and treasury system had finally been established in 1766.

By 1769, the commercial depression was so severe that it led to the only major attempt by the Portuguese government during the eighteenth century to develop domestic manufactures. What no longer could be imported would have to be produced at home. Between 1769 and 1778, the Junta do Comércio set up seventy-one manufacturing establishments (60 percent of them in Lisbon and Porto) to make such products as textiles, ceramics, clothing, paper, and glass, and to refine sugar.

The economic policies of the Pombal regime achieved no more than a temporary and limited success. They were often poorly conceived and uncoordinated, and tended toward overregulation. Most of the commercial companies fared badly, but some increase was made in domestic production. The greatest increase came in textiles such as cottons and silks, enabling Portugal very briefly to become self-sufficient in clothing and a few other goods that had been imported.

With this came such positive accomplishments as the weakening of the color bar in the colonies during these years. Pombal abolished slavery in metropolitan Portugal in 1773, ending the import of slaves for household service and the cultivation of estates. Equally notable were the educational reforms of the 1770s. In 1772, the curriculum and organization of the University of Coimbra was modernized for the first time in two and a half centuries, introducing more study of the natural and physical sciences. A series of new schools for the upper and middle classes were established, with greater emphasis on education in the vernacular. During the second half of the century there was an increase in middle-class literacy and in the production of trained clerical and administrative personnel, but the peasantry and urban lower classes remained almost completely untouched, and had if anything an even lower literacy level than in Spain. Moreover, Pombal suppressed discussion of the liberal political ideas of the English and French enlightenment and established a government censorship board in 1768.

In 1774 Pombal reached the age of seventy-five, but had no thought of relinquishing power and even planned to remain in control after the death of José I, whose health was much more delicate than his. He had grown increasingly arbitrary and did not blanch at the arrest and torture of innocent suspects. He had become the most hated figure in Portuguese government since Leonor Teles four centuries earlier—indeed, perhaps the most hated in Portuguese history. Despite widespread opposition among all social classes, he remained omnipotent under the Portuguese system of authoritarian monarchy so long as he enjoyed royal favor. When José I died in 1777 and was succeeded by his daughter Maria I, there occurred the *viradeira* (upset). The new queen accepted Pombal's resignation and released 800 political prisoners from jail. The seventy-eight-year old despot was then arrested, brought to public trial, and finally allowed to live out his few remaining years in disgrace on a rural estate.

The government of Pombal has provoked much controversy in both historiography and political polemics. His rule cannot, on balance, be termed a success even with respect to his own chosen goals. He did shake up and reform the government and made it more efficient, as well as reforming elite education and to some extent stimulating economic activity. Yet it is doubtful that the slender margin of accomplishment was sufficient to justify the harshness of his rule. Portuguese society was affected little by it all; only administrative efficiency showed a significant improvement. But by 1777, the state treasury was disastrously in debt and the navy in decay.

Religion

The religious orthodoxy of Portuguese Catholic society and its general influence over Portuguese culture were scarcely changed from the fifteenth and sixteenth centuries. Church-state relations, however, had become much more strained. After the restoration in 1640, much of the Portuguese Catholic hierarchy remained pro-Habsburg. The papacy did not officially recognize the new dynasty until 1669 and did not grant its blessing to the filling of many new vacancies in the Portuguese episcopate until then. Aside from several prelates who participated in anti-Bragança conspiracies, the sharpest antagonism within the Portuguese church came from the administrators of the Inquisition, who renewed an all-out campaign against wealthy cristão-novo merchants. Since the latter's mercantile and financial resources were indispensable for Portuguese commerce and military strength, the crown exempted the wealth of cristãos-novos from confiscation. Hostility remained intense between João IV and the inquisitors, who posthumously excommunicated him after his death in 1656. Persecution of the cristãos-novos was then resumed, and continued intermittently for more than a century.

By the eighteenth century the landed wealth of the Portuguese church was apparently proportionately greater than that of the Spanish church, amounting to nearly one-third of the cultivated soil in the kingdom. There was one cleric for every thirty-six inhabitants—the highest ratio in Europe. The number of monastic establishments continued to increase, mounting from 396 in 1600 to approximately 450 in 1650 to 477 by 1739. In general, this reflected the same swelling of clerical ranks and increase in endowments that Spain had seen during the seventeenth-century, but in Portugal the process began earlier and did not start to reverse as early during the eighteenth century. Moreover, though the church was responsible for nearly all the charity in the kingdom, it did not use its resources for educational and cultural work to the same extent as in Spain.

The splendid and wasteful João V was very generous with church endowments, but eager to increase royal control over the church and hopeful of establishing a sort of Portuguese Gallicanism modelled on the royal domination of the church in France. This led to a major quarrel with the papacy in 1728–1730 that was finally settled by a new concordat in 1737. Thanks in part to the crown's generous contributions, the papacy recognized the right of royal *padroado,* or investiture, to all Portuguese sees; the nuncio to the crown as well as the patriarch of Lisbon were both raised to the rank of cardinal. During the late 1740's, as his health declined, João V became increasingly pious, and in the last years of the reign virtually turned the government over to clerics. His efforts toward caesaropapism thus ended in virtual, if temporary, theocracy.

The work of Portuguese missions in colonial areas continued fairly steadily, though no spectacular new triumphs were achieved. The crown, however, preserved the right of padroado only in Brazil, losing it to the papacy in the Portuguese dioceses of Asia and Africa. The Jesuits remained the most active Portuguese missionaries, and suppression of the order by Pombal in 1759 was a serious blow to evangelism overseas. During the reign of Maria I in the last quarter of the eighteenth century, a sustained effort was made by the crown and church to expand once more the work of colonial missions.

If there was never any religious competition for Portuguese Catholicism, and the great mass of the population remained totally orthodox and devout (and highly superstitious), the eighteenth century was a time of growing latitude in practice for the upper classes. Indifference to religious norms was increasingly common among aristocracy and intellectuals. During his pleasure-centered earlier years, João V took at least one nun for a mistress. Since the seventeenth century the notion of seducing a nun had particularly inflamed the erotic imagination of the Portuguese (and to some extent, the Spanish) aristocracy. During the 1730s there were flagrant violations of discipline in some convents and monasteries, though conduct was tightened up somewhat after signing of the concordat of 1737.

By the middle of the eighteenth century, a mood of anticlericalism (though never of anti-Catholicism) had become widespread among politically reformist elements, and anticlericalism became official policy throughout the long dictatorship of Pombal, climaxed by the suppression of the Jesuit order in 1759. The Jesuits were particularly hated by anticlerical reformers for their widespread influence in education, missions, and among the upper classes and the Catholic courts of Europe. Pombal's act was subsequently emulated by the crowns of Spain and France, and during the commercial and fiscal crisis of the 1760s the Jesuits were made scapegoats for the problems of the kingdom. Their properties were confiscated and their remaining members in Portugal severely persecuted. In 1760, the papal nuncio was expelled from Lisbon, and relations were not satisfactorily reestablished for ten years. Pombal also restored the right of beneplácito regio by which the crown could censor church decisions and proclamations. Pombal had his own brother made a cardinal and turned the Inquisition into a mere royal tribunal. One of his great achievements was to put a final end to the persecution of cristãos-novos. He ordered all lists of cristãos-novos destroyed and, in 1773, abolished the statutes of limpeza de sangue, "purity of blood." This also reflected and encouraged a social change that was occurring in the eighteenth century: the influence of the nobility was declining while the independent strength of the upper middle class was slowly increasing.

The Enlightenment in Portugal

The culture and ideas of the west European enlightenment first began to enter Portugal during the reign of Pedro II, and slowly gained influence until a measurable impact was achieved under Pombal. The third Conde de Ericeira, "the Portuguese Colbert," introduced an active mercantile policy, though subsequently largely ignored until Pombal, and his son led in introducing the norms of French artistic neoclassicism at the very end of the seventeenth century. During the eighteenth century, the trend in Portuguese art and literature was away from the baroque and toward French neoclassic standards. The reign of João V brought the founding of the academies of history and art and greater attention to the sciences. The strongly Castilian orientation of a century earlier was replaced by a mood of ever more intense cultural hostility toward Spain. Castilian-language culture came to be associated with all the retrograde aspects of Portuguese life and was considered an obstacle to modernization.

Concentration on foreign culture and ideas led toward *estrangeiramento* (foreignization), combatted, as in Spain, by the *castiço* supporters of native traditionalism. The greatest of estrangeirados was, of course, Pombal. Married to an Austrian wife, he derived many of his ideas from observations as ambassador in London and Vienna. Anticlericalism, along with the criticism of tradition, Aristotelianism, and superstitious practices gained the day among the cultural and political elite. The educational reforms of the 1770's and the founding of the Academy of Sciences in 1779 formed the apex of the Portuguese enlightenment. The vogue of French literature reached its height in the last decades of the century. Yet the influence of the west European enlightenment reached only a tiny few of the aristocracy and middle classes and was not diffused through society.

Agriculture

There were no major changes in the social and economic structure of Portuguese peasant agriculture during the eighteenth century, but it was a time of modest expansion and fairly steady price increases and also, to some extent, of improved conditions for the peasants. Terms of land tenure had changed comparatively little over three centuries. In the heavily populated northwest, most land was held under seigneuries by the nobility and the church. Despite the prevalence of seigneurial domain, peasant society remained quite stable because most land was worked under long-term emphyteutic arrangements. The Pombaline reforms were directed almost exclusively toward commerce and manufacture, largely ignoring agriculture. Nonetheless, several measures were taken by the crown in the second half of the century to encourage emphyteusis and protect renters.

The difference between the south and north—between the Minho at one extreme and the Alemtejo at the other—was altered little. In the south most of the land was held in large domains, especially by the church and the orders, but there were also significant tracts of town lands dating from the medieval concelhos. Large-scale cultivation was uncommon. Most of the large domains were rented to *lavradores rendeiros,* renter proprietors, who worked the smaller estates themselves or let plots to sharecroppers (*seareiros*). Approximately 75 percent of the peasants in the Alemtejo were day laborers, but emigration and the end of slavery in 1773 left a constant shortage of farm labor. Consequently agrarian laborers' wages were sometimes twice as high in the south as in the north, and despite their low status the rural proletariat of southern Portugal were not a rebellious class. They may have been relatively more prosperous in the late eighteenth century than a hundred years later.

In general, the process under way in the countryside of southern Portugal was the same as that of southern Spain during the second half of the eighteenth century. Common lands were being divided up into private holdings by the more prosperous lavradores who dominated municipal government and subrented smaller estates (equivalent to the Andalusian cortijos) from large church or aristocratic domains. As in Spain, there occurred the modest beginning of an agrarian prereform in which small amounts of land were withdrawn from church jurisdiction, returned to royal domain, and sold or rented out to *lavradores* or peasants. The size of cultivation units was growing somewhat larger, and as had been true frequently since the thirteenth century, there was a tendency to revert from agriculture to cattle-raising. In a few parts of the south, such as the Beja district, there was a considerable degree of emphyteusis, however. In general, it was a time of relative prosperity, and food prices rose particularly after 1785.

Last Phase of the Old Regime in Portugal:
The Reign of Maria I (1777-1799/1816)

The heiress and successor of José I had even less experience than her father when she ascended the throne, but for the next two decades presided over the happiest and most prosperous period the Bragança dynasty had seen since the palmy early years of João V. Donha Maria was of a kindly, melancholy nature, and extremely devout.

Though not graced with special administrative talent or acute insight, she had several basic goals: to make amends for Pombal's offenses to the church, right the wrongs of the Pombaline dictatorship, make government more honest, and encourage the development of the kingdom. Many of Pombal's foes were judicially rehabilitated, and though the Jesuit order was not reestablished, all extremes of regalism were dropped and clerical influence became much stronger. Yet Maria's religious and cultural policy was not reactionary, for educational reforms were continued and during her reign the modest Portuguese enlightenment reached its height. The movement toward juridical centralization and regularization was carried further. A decree of 1790 theoretically abolished separate seigneurial justice throughout Portugal, incorporating all such functions under standard royal jurisdiction, though it was not enforced in many parts of the countryside.

In foreign affairs, Portugal was the only state that ranged itself on the British side in the North American war of independence, though the crown soon established a position of technical neutrality. Renewed conflict with Spain over the borders of Brazil was finally settled by negotiation in 1778.

Maria's government was generally benevolent and did not expel all of Pombal's administrative and juridical appointees, but most of the special economic projects of the reign of José I were either cut back or abolished. There was somewhat less concern to foster manufactures, because the 1780s and 1790s were a time of greatly increased commercial prosperity. Cotton had become a major new export from Brazil, while wine exports to Britain almost doubled. For the first time since 1740, the balance of trade with Britain began to run in Portugal's favor, with credits in 1790-1792 and 1794-1795. The period 1775-1805 was also the last era of prosperity in the Portuguese eastern trade. Between 1600 and 1775, there had been an annual average of scarcely more than two ships trading between Lisbon and Asia. From 1775 to 1805, the average ranged between ten and twenty, particularly after the French revolutionary wars of the 1790s restricted Dutch-Asian commerce. During this time, there was no similar increase in Portuguese manufactures. The first mechanical equipment for Portuguese textile production was imported from Britain in the 1780s, but on a very small scale. Portuguese capital remained geared almost exclusively to commerce, and British industrial exports nearly ruined the tiny Portuguese iron industry as well as several branches of the textile industry.

The main significance of the second half of the eighteenth century for Portuguese social structure was the development for the first time of a relatively strong, wealthy, and independent mercantile upper middle class not tied to the aristocracy. By 1800, the merchant class numbered only 80,000 in a kingdom of 3,000,000 (together with 130,000 from the professional classes), but certain individual merchants had achieved great wealth and a degree of social prestige that they had never known before. Most Portuguese merchants were, of course, small traders and shopkeepers of very modest resources, but they benefited from the opening up of commercial opportunities and the end of the Pombaline monopolist companies. The cultural level of the Portuguese middle classes was quite low compared with their proportionately more numerous counterparts in France and England. Their level of religiosity was higher than that of the French bourgeoisie. Though the truly wealthy among them were few in number, they were beginning to establish a place of influence and independence in Portuguese society.

By contrast, the eighteenth century was a time of relative decline for the aristocracy. The wealth of João V had made possible the granting of special honors and emoluments to the nobility, as well as the expansion in the number of offices held by the aristocracy, until about 1740. Pombal, however, had eliminated much of the influence of the powerful "ultramarine" aristrocracy (holding offices overseas) and had reduced the juridical powers of the provincial landholding nobility. The economic changes of the second half of the century were inimical to aristocratic wealth and influence. Nobles were less involved in overseas commerce than in earlier centuries and had difficulty adapting to the changes. The number of aristocratic titles nearly doubled in the early nineteenth century, but this was because they had depreciated in value and were awarded for all manner of services or gifts, often to commoners. The aristocracy was declining in number in proportion to the population as a whole.

In later years Maria I began to suffer from mental abberations, and her son D. João took over affairs of state in 1792. He was officially proclaimed regent seven years later in 1799. During the decade of the French Revolution, no country in western Europe felt as little pressure against its old regime as Portugal. Several factors stood out: the stability of peasant society, the relative prosperity of middle class commerce, the lack of a direct challenge to the aristocracy, the nominal strength of Catholicism, the weak development of a critical intelligentsia, and the comparatively benevolent government of the crown. Though a new mercantile middle class was evolving and would begin to come into its own in 1820, it did not yet have either the strength or inclination to seek fundamental change. In Portugal, as in Spain, the old regime still revealed a high degree of cohesiveness and general acceptance by the population at the end of the eighteenth century. It would be overthrown not from within but from without.

19

The War of Independence and Liberalism

The Reign of Carlos IV (1788-1808)

The Old Regime in Spain ended with the reign of Carlos IV, which collapsed beneath the weight of French Napoleonic imperialism. Spain seemed a comparatively peaceful and progressive land when Carlos IV came to the throne in 1788. The order and decorum shown by the many thousands of Spaniards who crowded into Madrid for the official coronation the following year contrasted sharply with the revolution that was developing in France. The new king was about forty years old, good-hearted but weak and simple-minded. He hoped to continue the general policies of his father's reign and retained as chief minister the Murcian lawyer José Moñino, Conde de Floridablanca, a strong-minded regalist who had long served Carlos III capably.

The beginning of the French Revolution in 1789 drastically altered the policy of the Spanish crown. Floridablanca adopted a sharply hostile course and imposed censorship on all news from France. The atmosphere was even more tense after the attempted assassination of Floridablanca by a demented Frenchman in 1790 and a tax revolt by the overburdened Galician peasantry in 1790-1791. The nascent Spanish press was also subjected to severe censorship, and the progress of the Spanish enlightenment was brought to a near halt. Early in 1792, Floridablanca's enemies, both personal and political, combined to force him from power. Carlos IV replaced him with the now elderly Conde de Aranda, who while no supporter of the French Revolution, was a liberal and a Francophile, convinced of the importance of the French alliance. He relaxed the censorship, allowing Spanish publicists and reformers to continue their proselytizing activities. Before the end of the year, however, Aranda was shoved out by palace intrigues, replaced as first secretary by a handsome, sturdy young guards' officer from Extremadura, Manuel Godoy, friend of the royal family and sometime social escort (*cortejo*) of the Italian queen, Maria Luisa di Parma. Carlos IV considered him a true friend, one of the few reliable counselors among a bevy of fops and intriguers, and made him Duque de Alcudia.

For most of fifteen years 1792–1808 Godoy was the real ruler of Spain. He was not a politician or administrator of great education or mental power, but considered himself a man of the new generation, a reformer and continuer of the policies of Carlos III. Throughout these years, the overriding concern of the Spanish crown was the challenge presented by revolutionary France and its successor, Napoleonic imperialism. Spain joined the alliance of legitimacy against the French revolutionary regime in 1793–1795 and scored some initial successes, occupying Hendaye and Perpignan. Despite a major effort by the French to inundate northeastern Spain with revolutionary propaganda, the anti-French struggle was quite popular among the Spanish people, whose religious and patriotic sentiments were fully aroused. This was most of all the case in Catalonia; there anti-French feeling was intense, popular volunteers were numerous, and the conflict was called *la guerra gran*. But the Anglo-Spanish fleets failed before Toulon, and the Spanish army lacked the cadres, equipment, training, or leadership to resist the new French military masses. The French briefly occupied San Sebastián and northern Catalonia. Peace was made in 1795 on the basis of the status quo ante, the French regime not pressing its terms, because of its interest in detaching Spain from the British antirevolutionary alliance.

The war against revolutionary France helped to open the first serious political fissures in the eighteenth-century Bourbon regime in Spain. Almost from the start, Godoy was resented as no minister of Carlos III had been because he was obviously a youthful favorite and his appointment was a throwback to the old system of *validos* which had always been unpopular. At a time of great stress, the vacillating and confused Carlos IV proved incapable of emulating his father, who had known how to choose professionally competent ministers and arbitrate among them himself. Libellous stories about Godoy and the queen brought the royal family under fire for the first time in a

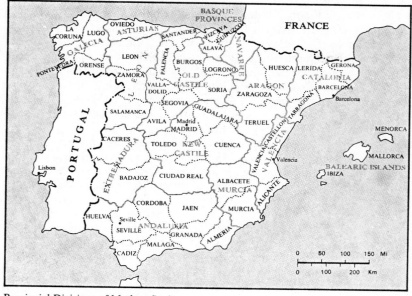

Provincial Divisions of Modern Spain

century, and lowered respect for the crown. Resentment became more intense after the crown awarded its first secretary the unusually prestigious title of prince after he concluded peace in 1795. Nor did Godoy's undeniably reformist measures win him support among the progressivist and critical-minded. He was still accused of being underhanded and too authoritarian in government. The reformist and progressivist currents of preceding decades all the while gathered force rapidly under the stimulus of the French example. While only a few small revolutionary cliques were formed in Spain, the scope of critical opinion among the upper and middle classes increased considerably.

Discontent first found public expression in mid-1794, after an increase in taxes and the apparent ineptitude of the Spanish army. In Madrid there were public demonstrations of sympathy for the French cause for the first time, and by the following year several small secret prorevolutionary juntas had been formed in Madrid and in the provinces. After peace was made, these were dissolved and some of the ringleaders arrested. In the meantime, the Inquisition had attempted a wartime crackdown on the dissemination of subversive ideas, decreeing in 1794 the abolition of all Spanish university chairs in public and natural law. Such measures had little effect, however, for after 1795 restrictions on publications were relaxed once more, and after French pressure a Spanish edition of the *Encyclopedia* was allowed to be published. The crown resumed its encouragement of education, and in the last years of the eighteenth century reformist and progressivist ideas were circulating more widely than ever before. The beginning of a nucleus of political liberalism, questioning complete royal sovereignty—however enlightened—was starting to form. This trend toward the expression of critical political ideas brought a reimposition of censorship on books at the beginning of 1798.

Aside from its semiliberal policy on education and printing, the crown's principal attempt to continue and expand reform policies came in the fields of taxation and commerce. Royal finances were sufficiently strong to permit Spain to enter the war of 1793-1795 on a fairly sound footing—sounder than that of Prussia, for example—but after a year of full-scale war fiscal pressures mounted. Taxes on salaried officials and on the church were raised, and new issues of paper money were backed by special levies on landowners and on the church. For the first time, the aristocracy was brought directly under taxation, and this explains part of the opposition to the government in central Spain. In 1795, Godoy's government took the step of abolishing the special *servicio* tax on peasants that had first been levied in sixteenth-century Castile, making the burden somewhat less inequitable.

The economy took a turn for the worse after 1796, when the government allowed itself to be maneuvered by French pressure and its longstanding trans-Atlantic rivalry with the British into declaring war against the latter in October 1796, after signing an alliance with France. During the next few years, Spanish commerce suffered grievously as the fleet underwent major reverses. This necessitated drastic changes that portended far-reaching consequences, as in the case of two significant new decrees issued in 1797. One permitted foreign craftsmen of Christian religions other than Roman Catholic to enter Spain and open shops or factories with a guarantee of freedom of religion. The second recognized the effectiveness of the virtual British naval blockade by suspending commercial restrictions within the Spanish American empire, permitting all neutral nations to trade freely. This was a fateful step toward the ultimate independence of the colonies, for it admitted that at least for the time being Spain could not maintain its pretended monopoly.

Another important precedent was set in 1798, when the government decided to raise money by auctioning off surplus buildings owned by municipalities. This was the first time that entailed property was seized and auctioned by the state to pay for war expenses. In

1798, the government also decreed the sale of the property of most church charitable foundations, as well as of all remaining unsold Jesuit property, and during the subsequent years further levies were agreed to by the church to meet military expenses. In 1799, a new property tax was levied on the wealthy. These measures roused the ire of aristocrats and the clergy, while discontent increased among the lower classes. As prices increased, real wages fell, and there were several minor riots in 1797-1798.

Godoy himself brought in a new group of liberal appointees at the end of 1797 but, because of French pressure, was forced to retire as first secretary in March 1798. He was replaced by the secretary of finance, Francisco de Saavedra, in turn succeeded a few months later by the anticlerical and regalist foreign minister, Mariano Luis de Urquijo. The financial situation continued to deteriorate, and the crown became increasingly confused by the pulling and hauling of factions. Conservatives among churchmen and aristocrats launched a counteroffensive against the new reform government of 1798-1800, bringing first the dismissal and imprisonment of Urquijo at the end of 1800, then that of the eminent progressivist and reformist minister of justice, Jovellanos, early in 1801. Thus within less than a decade the pressures of the French revolutionary wars had completely broken the unity of the Spanish polity.

After two years absence, Godoy returned to de facto control of Spanish government at the end of 1800 and held that influence until the whole Spanish regime was overthrown in the spring of 1808. During his second period in power he followed a more moderate line than before, since the *luces*—the critics and progressivists—remained his committed enemies. Yet Godoy successfully maintained a reform program in some areas and rejected a genuinely reactionary policy. One major reform was the partial abolition of the *señorío eclesiástico* in 1806. Papal permission was obtained to sell one-seventh of church properties in return for state bonds. This was the last great step of eighteenth-century regalist policy and opened the way to all-out disamortization of church lands by the succeeding liberal regime thirty years later.

Yet all domestic problems had become secondary to the irresistable pressure of French imperialism, whose military dominance of the western half of the continent had held Spain in satellite status since 1796. In 1799, Napoleon forced the cession of the vast Louisiana territory in North America that the Spanish crown had gained from Britain only sixteen years earlier. By 1801, Godoy had been maneuvered by France into the petty border "War of the Oranges" against pro-British Portugal. When peace was temporarily signed with Britain, Spain was able to keep the Extremaduran border district of

Olivença it had seized but lost the island of Trinidad to Britain. The peaceful years of 1802-1804 helped to revive the faltering economy briefly. A high volume of trade was momentarily regained with Spanish America, and the country's domestic production reached a new peak in 1805-1806. However, the resumption of war with Britain upon Napoleonic dictates marked the beginning of the end. The naval disaster of Trafalgar (1805) completed the virtual destruction of the Spanish navy, and the subsequent British domination of the Atlantic, coupled with the imposition of Napoleon's French-controlled economic "Continental System" the following year, threw the Spanish economy into profound depression. Commerce declined catastrophically, unemployment grew in the towns, inflation mounted, the government's financial situation became almost hopeless, and real wages for workers continued to decline.

This completed the discrediting of the government, and the unpopularity of Godoy increased year by year until he became the target of almost universal execration. Rumors about Godoy and the queen, coupled with the ineptitude of Carlos IV, dragged the prestige of the royal family in the mud. The regime drew the opposition alike of progressivists and of ultra-conservatives within the aristocracy and church. The latter found a rallying point in the heir to the throne, the prince D. Fernando, deeply jealous of Godoy and eager to succeed his father as soon as possible. Both the elite elements and the royal family itself had thus been divided by political rivalries. The conservative *fernandista* opposition began to intrigue with Napoleon to encourage removal of Godoy and of the king himself, who was hated for his weakness and for the reformist fiscal policies of his government. The Napoleonic vise grew all the tighter with the signing of the Treaty of Fontainebleau in October 1807 providing for the partition of Portugal and the entry of a sizable French army into the peninsula. A fernandista plot of vague dimensions was precipitated and aborted late in 1807, but French pressure forced Carlos IV to pardon his son almost immediately. Napoleon meanwhile had himself become eager to eliminate Godoy, who was trying to follow a double game in a futile attempt to free Spain of French domination.

Godoy's final effort was a desperate plan to remove the royal family to America, whence an independence struggle against French domination might be led just as the Portuguese crown was attempting to do from Rio de Janeiro. Before this scheme could be put into effect, Godoy was imprisoned by a riot at the winter palace of Aranjuez in March 1808 that had been encouraged by dissident fernandista aristocrats. Carlos IV was forced to abdicate. The resultant breakdown of Spanish government, precipitated as it was by a suicidal feud in the royal family, provided Napoleon with the excuse to intervene directly, deport both Carlos IV and D. Fernando to France, and install his brother Joseph (José I) as king of Spain.

The Bonapartist Regime of 1808-1812

The transitory monarchy of Joseph Bonaparte achieved the climax of enlightened despotism in Spain, just as, according to a common argument, the Napoleonic empire in western Europe as a whole climaxed the entire era of eighteenth-century autocratic reformism. The regime of "Don José" was, however, an arbitrary imposition of French arms and broke inevitably with the Catholic legitimist spirit of the Bourbon monarchy. It was based on Napoleon's Bayonne Constitution of 1808, which stipulated for Spain a legislature composed of a lifetime appointive senate and a three-estate assembly—clergy, nobility, and commons—in part elected, in part chosen by town councils, in part appointed by the king. Once in power, the Bonapartist administration tried to enact the same reforms brought by French rule to other lands. The legal and administrative systems were reorganized, establishing greater uniformity and opportunity for the middle classes, the Inquisition was abolished, the church was brought under closer state regulation, and in 1809, most monasteries were abolished and their properties seized. Yet for much of the country these were mere paper reforms that could not be put into effect because of the warfare that raged throughout the brief years of French dominion.

Despite a conscientious effort by the new Corsican monarch, he was rejected by the great majority of Spaniards, who referred to him sneeringly as Pepe Botellas (Joe Bottles) because of his supposed fondness for drink. The only real support for the regime came from a small minority of the *afrancesado* intelligentsia, supporters of Napoleonic-style enlightened despotism, who were no more than twelve thousand or so in a population of more than ten million. Some of the afrancesados were mere opportunists interested in positions. Others, however, were concerned patriots who chose to serve the new regime out of a desire to Hispanize it, reform the country along more modern lines, and above all save their homeland from the anarchy and destruction that threatened it in 1808. Yet the Bonapartist regime, imposed by force, remained always at the mercy of military events and never effectively controlled as much as half the country.

The War of Independence

The reaction of the Spanish people to French domination was the great revolt of May 1808—the broadest popular uprising anywhere in Europe during that era. The rebellion started on May 2 in Madrid as the last member of the royal family was being hustled into French exile, and spread throughout the country within a few weeks, even before Napoleon had officially imposed a Bonaparte king. It was supported by all classes of the population (though the nobility were the most tepid), to save national independence and also to save the primacy of traditional religion. The whole experience was incomprehensible to Napoleon, for nothing of the sort had happened in any other area occupied by French troops. In Spain, however, even the upward-striving middle classes—among the elements that elsewhere seemed to have most to gain from Napoleonic reform—were part of the backbone of resistance.

By June 1808, the Spanish resistance fielded an army with a nominal strength of 130,000 men. The southern contingent under General Castaños scored the first clear-cut field victory over a Napoleonic army in Europe by defeating and capturing Dupont's corps of nearly 20,000 French troops at Bailén (north of Córdoba) in July 1808. That summer, the French army of occupation was nearly swept from the peninsula, and the Spanish forces were increased to more than 200,000. During the final two months of the year, however, Napoleon concentrated his attention on Spain, personally leading an invading force of 300,000 men from his best units. Madrid was seized, and during 1809 the French occupied most of the key points in the north, center, and northeast, moving into the south and east in 1810. The organized Spanish field forces dwindled to no more than 100,000 by the close of 1809 and were hard put to maintain that strength for the remainder of the war.

Britain immediately joined hands with the Spanish governing junta, and dispatched an expeditionary corps under Sir Arthur Wellesley (later the Duke of Wellington) to establish a firm redoubt in Portugal. Wellesley proved a master of defensive tactics in holding his position against heavy odds for three years. On the other hand, Britain never committed more than 50,000 troops to the "peninsular war," as British commentators have termed it, and Wellesley's strategy proved cautious in the extreme, refusing opportunities to seize the strategic initiative after French forces had grown weaker. Britain's other main contribution was economic, providing money and many of the military supplies used by the Spanish and Portuguese forces.

The heart of the Spanish War of Independence of 1808–1813 lay not in the maneuverings of the field armies but in the massive popular resistance of all classes. It became the first great people's war of modern history. Though the Spanish field forces were no match for the Napoleonic armies, the main burden of the war was carried by irregular forces waging a *guerrilla* (little war). This *guerra de partidas* (war of irregular partisan bands) was a spontaneous creation of the Spanish peasantry and may have involved 200,000 or more combatants. The French found themselves a beleaguered island in a hostile ocean, controlling no more than the main towns. The simplest communications became major problems of military logistics, and the French dared move through the countryside only in great force. Small detachments and stragglers were relentlessly cut down. In the long run, the bulk of the French army of occupation was limited to garrison and supply duties. Most French casualties—possibly as many as 180,000 over a five-year period—resulted from the work of the *guerrilleros,* who probably lost no more than 25,000 of their own activists.

The main suffering, and the main heroics, of the war belonged to the Spanish civilians. French occupation policy was harsh, and savage reprisals were exacted in cities that resisted or in areas closely associated with guerrilleros. Whole towns were sacked, riot and rape by the French soldiery were not uncommon, and thousands of civilians were shot merely as examples. In turn, the most vivid symbols of the Spanish will to resist were given by the populace as a whole, highlighted by the two spectacular sieges-to-the-death of Zaragoza in 1808 and 1809. Popular resistance in Spain served as an inspiring example to other peoples held subject under Napoleonic imperialism, most notably in Germany, where the post-1809 patriotic awakening was directly stimulated by the Spanish revolt.

The War of Independence was in the long run a struggle of attrition in which the French were ground down by constant harassment and, from 1812, by the commitment of Napoleon's main strength to eastern and central Europe. The depletion of French forces in that year made possible a strategic counteroffensive by the regular Anglo-Spanish-Portuguese field army, but Wellesley's overweening caution wasted the opportunity. The final victorious campaign of 1813 brought a steady retreat by the shrunken French forces, no longer able to contest major battles in the main part of the peninsula.

Though the final outcome was complete victory, the cost was heavy. To the destruction of the Spanish state was added the devastation of the peninsula's economy. No other country in Europe suffered so heavily from the *francesada.*

The Cádiz Cortes and the 1812 Constitution

Collapse of the Spanish monarchy under the pressures of French imperialism opened the way for the first breakthrough of modern Spanish liberalism. This was not the product of French intervention, for the proponents of drastic reform and a more or less representative system of government had slowly been gathering strength for twenty years. Rather, the breakdown of the Spanish system under French dominion gave reformers the opportunity to put their ideas into practice.

When the royal family crossed into France to meet Napoleon in the spring of 1808, Spanish affairs were left in the hands of a small Regency Council that refused to recognize the abdication of the Spanish throne subsequently wrung from Carlos IV and his heir D. Fernando. Conversely, the Regency Council was unable to function as the government of Spain, for the popular revolt of May–June 1808 resulted in the formation of town and regional juntas in almost every major district. The juntas were composed of local notables, with the nobility predominant, but they also expressed the conviction of the middle- and upper-class elite in most of the country that government rested upon the sovereignty of the people as well as of the crown, and that after the collapse of monarchist government, representatives of the people had the duty to take charge of affairs. On the one hand there was concern to prevent the situation from degenerating into anarchy, and on the other, widespread expression among elite elements of the need for representative leadership to provide necessary reforms while guiding popular resistance. Representatives of the principal juntas in turn delegated authority to a national Junta Central in September 1808.

The scene of the greatest social ferment during the reign of Carlos IV had been Valencia, and in this region the most revolutionary outbursts of the War of Independence occurred. Within the span of a few years, Valencian political society moved from the traditional bread riots of the urban poor, an intermittent phenomenon since ancient times, to organized modern revolutionary conspiracies. Social revolutionary riots broke out in both town and countryside, and several revolutionary local juntas were formed before the authority of the captain general and the more moderate regional junta could be reimposed over the district.

The national Junta Central meanwhile fled south in 1808–1809 to escape the French advance, and found itself increasingly hard put to establish executive authority on the existing ad hoc basis. Reformist leaders in local juntas demanded throughout 1809 that a representative national Cortes assembly be summoned to reorganize the government and restructure national institutions. At the end of January 1810, the Junta Central resigned its executive authority to the Regency Council but at the same time called for the selection of representatives to a new Cortes—a potentially revolutionary act of political representation.

This was not merely a spur-of-the-moment attempt to fill the gap left by captivity of the royal family in France. It was the result of the predevelopment of Spanish liberalism that had been taking shape during the reign of Carlos IV, based on political ideas derived from Locke, Montesquieu, and other theorists. It was a liberalism derived from a somewhat romanticized conception of Spanish history that tended to exaggerate the achievements of the medieval Cortes, positing a parliamentary "Spanish tradition of liberty" that had been cut short by the imposition of Habsburg despotism after the defeat of the *comuneros* in 1520-1521.

The seat of Spanish government during the greater part of the War of Independence was Cádiz, the country's leading Atlantic port, separated from the mainland by a narrow peninsula easily defended from French assault, protected and provisioned by the British and Spanish fleets. The liberal Cortes and its resulting constitution could probably have taken the shape they did only in Cádiz, the most liberal city in the peninsula at that time. Open to foreign influence, living off the American trade, led mostly by a middle class that had made its money from commerce and not landed dominion, the Cádiz environment gave a decisive thrust to constitutional reformism.

Deputies to the Cádiz Cortes were nominally to have been chosen by a system of indirect universal male suffrage in which the votes of twenty-five-year-old heads of households were channeled through district electoral councils. Since part of the country was under French occupation, it was impossible to carry out elections in a number of districts. These districts, as well as the American colonies, were represented by substitutes, *suplentes,* appointed from Cádiz by local authorities, giving disproportionate voice to Cádiz liberalism. Suplentes, however, accounted for only 53 out of 300 deputies. Priests numbered nearly twice as many—97—almost one-third of the total. The most striking thing about the social composition of the Cortes delegation was the overrepresentation of the clerical and lay intelligentsia, to the exclusion of representatives of concrete social and economic interests, a situation rather similar to that of the German assembly at Frankfurt nearly forty years later. Only 14 of the deputies were titled aristocrats. What had happened was that amid the civic breakdown and confusion of 1808-1810, activists among the intelligentsia had come to the

Table 2.   Composition of the Cortes of Cádiz, 1810

Clergy	97
Lawyers	60
Gov't employees	55
Military	46
Intellectuals	20
Landowners	15
Miscellaneous	10
	303

Source: M. Fernández Almagro, *Orígenes del régimen constitucional en España* (Madrid, 1928), p. 82.

fore and asserted themselves in a society in which most elements lacked explicit political consciousness. The regions most heavily represented were Galicia, Valencia, Catalonia, and Andalusia, while the conservative north-central part of the country, mostly under French occupation, was underrepresented.

The deputies immediately rejected the idea of forming a traditional three-estate Cortes and met as a unicameral assembly. Liberal elements seized the initiative and set the pace of deliberations from the start. They dominated press and propaganda and included most of the eloquent spokesmen in the chamber. The Cortes immediately set to work to provide a progressivist written constitution for Spain which would embody both the social and economic ideals of eighteenth-century monarchist reform and the political norms of parliamentary liberalism. At that time the only written representative constitution anywhere in the world was that of the United States, and the Cádiz deputies were proudly aware that they were taking the lead in continental European liberalism.

The new constitution, completed in 1812, was based on the principle of national sovereignty rather than royal authority. It established a unicameral legislature with general control over legislation, leaving the crown only a suspensive veto. Electoral provisions for universal male suffrage by householders' votes on an indirect basis made this theoretically a more democratic constitution than that of either the United States or England. Local administration was placed under central control, but provision was made for provincial councils, half of whose members would be appointed and half elected, to deliberate on provincial affairs. Uniform regulations for municipalities were created and the archaic guild system abolished. Sweeping social reforms were established, as all aristocratic legal privileges, seigneurial jurisdiction, and the right of entailment were abolished. In subsequent regulations of 1813, the highly uneven and indirect provincial tax structure was replaced with a series of direct taxes on business and property. Catholicism was recognized as the official religion of the state and of the people, but the Inquisition—in part an arm of the government—was officially abolished. Church censorship was still upheld, and heresy in religion remained a nominal crime.

The constitution contained 384 articles, nearly three times as many as any subsequent Spanish code of government, and represented an attempt to work out a thorough new liberal scheme of government and society in harmony, as much as possible, with traditional Spanish values. It was the most advanced document of its time in Europe, and, while drawing on both English and French ideas, it tried to form a uniquely Spanish synthesis of old beliefs with new rights and liberties. For the next quarter-century it stood as the classic document of constitutional liberalism in western continental Europe, and influenced liberal aspirations in Italy and Portugal particularly.

The constitution of 1812 was the work of the middle-class political intelligentsia, supported by most of the middle and part of the upper classes. The degree of support in the country at large is uncertain. Scarcely more than 10 percent of the population were literate at the beginning of the nineteenth century, and the lower classes lacked political consciousness. On the other hand, it was clear enough that in a number of regions the peasants stood directly behind liberal reforms insofar as they brought the abolition of seigneurial exactions, against which there was increasing protest.

Conservatives were outnumbered, outmaneuvered, and outtalked at Cádiz. They had not expected an institutional revolution of such dimensions, but opposition to the new constitution grew rapidly. It was led by the officeholders of the government of the old regime, by aristocrats who feared the loss of seigneurial dominion, by senior members of the military hierarchy (who felt their authority was being undermined), and by most church leaders, opposed to loss of church seigneurial jurisdiction (*abadengo*), growth of state control, and the danger of renewed attacks on church property. In the electoral campaign for the first regular Cortes in 1813, most of the clergy swung into the ranks of the antiliberal opposition. In turn, advanced anticlerical liberals demanded that priests be excluded from sitting in Cortes. By the time the last French troops had deserted the peninsula, Spain was an arena of sharp political strife between supporters and opponents of the constitution.

The Fernandine Reaction, 1814-1820

The immediate future of the Spanish political system depended on the attitude of the heir to the throne, who returned from French exile in April 1814 to begin his reign as Fernando VII. He proved in many ways the basest king in Spanish history. Cowardly, selfish, grasping, suspicious, and vengeful, D. Fernando seemed almost incapable of any perception of the commonweal. He thought only in terms of his power and security and was unmoved by the enormous sacrifices of Spanish people to retain their independence and preserve his throne. At a time when other, more enlightened west European rulers strove to forget past grievances and come to terms with change, Fernando VII thought only of returning to the situation as it had been before 1808. Though originally required to swear loyalty to the constitution, he found as his triumphant homeward journey led him nearer Madrid that powerful forces in the army, society, church, and former bureaucracy would support a return to absolutism. Hence he gave his blessing to the first direct military intervention in modern Spanish government, the overthrow of the constitutional system by the army command in April 1814. The Madrid rabble was aroused to paroxysms of enthusiasm for its restored sovereign, giving vent to cries of "Long live the absolute king" and even a few of "Long live chains!"

Absolute monarchy was restored on the terms of 1808, and all the changes wrought by the Cádiz Cortes were swept away. A decree of 1814 restored seigneurial domain, although it withheld all juridical rights that had formerly been attached, recognizing only territorial and economic (but not judicial) jurisdiction. Thus absolute monarchy reached its height under Fernando VII between 1814 and 1820. The liberals were persecuted, and though executions were largely avoided, many were imprisoned or harried out of the country.

The regime was not at first bloody, but it was tyrannical, suspicious, and above all, administratively inefficient. Fernando VII's only trusted association was with a narrow and capricious court camarilla, and he regularly failed to back up his own government appointees. Between 1814 and 1820 the average length of tenure for cabinet ministers was approximately six months. The treasury lay in a state of total disarray and the debt increased steadily. There was one attempt at tax reorganization in 1817, when provision was made for a simplified single contribution on land by all classes, cutting across seigneurial dues and rents, but it was not effectively implemented. Absolute monarchy proved completely unable to meet its own obligations.

Meanwhile, during the decade 1810-1820, most of Spanish America was lost to the independence movements that had emerged in major areas throughout the colonies at a time when the Spanish government was suffering virtual atrophy amid war and reactionary absolutism. The Cádiz Cortes had wanted to extend parliamentary representation to the colonies, but insisted on continued centralization of government and administration while refusing further de jure liberalization of trade. In most regions the Spanish-American independence movement was limited mainly to a Spanish creole or Spanish-mestizo minority of the landed upper classes and commercial elite who insisted upon the right to conduct their affairs independently. With certain exceptions, the lower classes in America tended to be neutral or even pro-Spanish. Only the collapse of the Spanish state under the weight of the French invasion had made it possible for the revolts to achieve success. After 1814, Fernando's corrupt and incoherent regime was incapable of a major effort to restore Spanish control. The empire was lost mainly by default. Just as the sixteenth-century conquest had been a largely private enterprise that received only marginal assistance from the royal government, so the nineteenth-century independence movements met only marginal opposition from the Spanish homeland. At one point even that was almost enough to thwart them, for the one notable expedition dispatched under General Pablo Morillo restored Spanish control over the northern part of South America, while an imperial viceroy held fast the Spanish bastion of the Andean regions. Their efforts eventually failed in a struggle of attrition that drew no further support from the mother country, whose government was exhausted by financial deficits and, after 1820, renewed political conflict. Despite the long association and the importance of the empire to national commerce in the eighteenth century, Spanish people were not actively identified with the empire. Most classes and regions had never had direct contact with America, and one of the more notable things about its loss was how little attention it attracted in Spain. After 1825, all that remained of the empire was Cuba, Puerto Rico, and the island possesions in the Pacific.

The Liberal Triennium of 1820-1823

Between 1814 and 1820 the liberal opposition was limited mainly to the small middle-class intelligentsia of the provincial capitals. Active opposition, however, was led by a new element—dissident sectors of the army officer corps. This was a radically new development, for the eighteenth-century army had been a well disciplined if not always efficiently trained military force. It had, however, been swamped by the War of Independence, which brought in a whole new cadre of middle class officers, many of whom were demoted or left without assignment when the old hierarchy was restored in 1814. Accustomed to great power and respect during the war, young officers could not resign themselves to secondary status and miserable pay, or none at all, under the ramshackle Fernandine regime. Their discontent was given an ideological and moral content by vague notions of liberalism and constitutionalism. Moreover, elements of the senior command had already set the example of political revolt by the overthrow of the constitutional regime in 1814. During the next six years a series of minor, abortive counter-revolts by nominally liberal officers in various provincial garrisons was finally climaxed by the rebellion of the major expeditionary corps that was painfully being assembled at military camps outside of Cádiz.

The success of this revolt, whose chief leader was Major Rafael del Riego, was due not to its own strength but to the general malaise that gripped Spain in 1820. There were several sources of this dissatisfaction: the postwar economic depression, the financial prostration of the government, a yellow fever epidemic in the south, and the dismay felt by a large part of the politically conscious over the capricious, inept rule of D. Fernando. At first, Riego's rebels received almost no support elsewhere—but neither was there any show of enthusiasm for the absolutist regime. As Riego led his detachments in a meandering march northward to rally backing, his forces slowly dwindled, but so did whatever support remained for the regime in Madrid. Several other provincial garrisons came out in revolt, and D. Fernando was finally left with no alternatives save to accede to rebel demands and restore the constitution of 1812.

The rebellion of January 1820 was the first to use the term *pronunciamiento,* and foreshadowed what became the standard tactic of military revolt in nineteenth-century Spain. The pronunciamiento did not rely on careful planning or the unified support of the army. More often than not it was the work of a comparatively small group of senior or middle-rank officers who did not attack the government in a direct coup but simply "pronounced" or raised the flag of revolt against existing government policy. The pronunciamiento then usually had to rely upon support from other quarters or the willingness of the government to compromise. The pronunciamiento of 1820 demanded a complete change of institutions from absolutism to constitutionalism, but subsequent pronunciamientos were often aimed at lesser changes of policy or simply a shift in personnel.

Restored constitutional government was at first placed in the hands of veteran doceañista (1812) liberals who had gained experience at Cádiz. They had profited from the events of the past decade, and proved moderate men eager to conciliate national interests. Indeed, many of the doceañistas were rather uncomfortable with their own

1812 constitution and not unwilling to reform it in order to give the crown somewhat greater authority, add a second chamber to the legislature, and restrict the suffrage to the propertied elements. From the very beginning, however, D. Fernando refused to fully accept his role of constitutional monarch and would not cooperate in the building of a viable moderate liberal system.

The new liberal government repeated the social, institutional, and economic reforms of 1812–1813. Señoríos and abadengo dominion, together with the right of entail, were once more abolished. Separate ecclesiastical legal jurisdiction was done away with, the Inquisition abolished, state control over church orders established, many of the latter suppressed, and most monastic lands confiscated. The government soon began public sale of monastic lands, mostly to monied middle class interests. A beginning was made at monetary reform and the debt was reorganized, though no immediate solution was in sight for the government financial crisis. Finally, the territorial reorganization of Spain which the Cortes of Cádiz had begun was completed in 1821 by the redistricting of the country (including the Balearics and Canaries) into fifty-two administrative provinces.

These changes were accompanied by considerable agitation by the peasants of Valencia and several other regions against the remnants of seigneurial domain. Further plans to divide up village common lands, however, led to signs of hostility particularly among peasants in some southern districts, where loss of community property would deprive the rural lower classes of practically their only source of economic assistance. By 1821, the first violent labor protest broke out in the Levantine town of Alcoy, where unemployed textile workers and artisans engaged in a Luddite type of destruction of new machinery in textile factories.

The doceañistas soon found themselves challenged on both the left and the right. Within the ranks of liberalism, pressure came from the *exaltado* faction of radicals, who were especially strong in the provincial capitals among the middle class intelligentsia and some small businessmen. From the very beginning, their Jacobin style of politics did not scruple at terrorism, conspiracy, or riot. During the six years of the Fernandine reaction, underground liberals had become used to functioning by means of secret organization and conspiratorial societies. Local chapters of Spanish Masonry had become a common conspiratorial vehicle, and the practice of clandestine sectarian plotting was not given up after 1820. The sectors of the army led by exaltado officers were praised as a necessary pretorian guarantee of the liberal system, and exaltados insisted that such sectors be allowed to function almost as an independent institution.

The exaltados rallied support by playing on the local interests of provincialism, reenforcing common hatred of military conscription (and the reluctance to fight the incomprehensible campaigns in America), demanding reduction or abolition of the depised *consumos* (excise taxes), and insisting on direct democratization of the suffrage. These claims formed the basis of the radical liberal program that tended to dominate the politics of many provincial towns (though not the countryside) for half a century, until 1874. A main factor in cementing the factional unity of the radical political intelligentsia itself was the intense desire for more government jobs, particularly on the local and provincial level. This was a major political motive for professional and white-collar elements in a society whose economy could not provide adequate employment. In Madrid, by contrast, the same social elements were less radical, perhaps because employment opportunities were greater, but there the mob could be mobilized on occasion, as the same lower class strata that had cheered D. Fernando were occasionally whipped up to riot for the exaltados.

After the 1822 elections, the exaltados gained control of the government and forced a more radical line, attacking the church issue head on. The Jesuit order was again dissolved in Spain, the other orders brought under strict regulation, and plans were drawn up for a general expropriation of church land. Throughout 1822, hostility between moderate and radical liberals increased, while supporters of absolutism rallied the northeastern countryside and prepared for civil war.

Influence of Spanish Liberalism on Italy and Portugal

Spain had first captured the imagination of patriots and reformers in central Europe with the national rising against Napoleon. Subsequently, the 1812 constitution served as an inspiration to liberals in Italy and in Portugal, and Spain in fact led in the process of political democratization in western Europe until 1843. Conversely, the Fernandine reaction had some effect in inspiring Italian ultraconservatives during the postwar years.

The Spanish pattern of conspiracy and revolt by liberal army officers, in association with Masonic and other liberal secret societies, was emulated in both Portugal and Italy. In the wake of Riego's successful rebellion, the first and only pronunciamiento in Italian history was carried out by liberal officers in the kingdom of the Two Sicilies. The Spanish-style military conspiracy also helped to inspire the beginning of the Russian revolutionary movement with the revolt of the Decembrist army officers in 1825. Italian liberalism in 1820–1821 relied on junior officers and the provincial middle classes, essentially the same social base as in Spain. It even used a Hispanized political vocabulary, for it was led by *giunte* (juntas), appointed local *capi politici* (jefes políticos), used the terms of *liberali* and *servili* (emulating the Spanish word *serviles* applied to supporters of absolutism), and in the end talked of resisting by means of a *guerrilla*. For both Portuguese and Italian liberals of these years, the Spanish constitution of 1812 remained the standard document of reference. All of this was a spontaneous response to Spanish liberalism, for the government of 1820–1823 did nothing to intervene in the affairs of either country. Its own policy in Europe was purely and strictly defensive.

The Second Reaction, 1822–1824

Violent reaction and reprisal as a response to political change was introduced into Spanish politics by Fernando VII in 1814. The doceañista moderates were willing to forgive and forget past excesses against themselves when they returned to power in 1820, but the exaltados demanded revenge and seemed determined to institutionalize a style of reprisal and atrocity in several spectacular political killings. This in turn stimulated the reaction of ultra-conservatives.

Opposition to liberalism during the triennium 1820–1823 was based on the same interests as it had been in 1812–1814. To these were added broad dissatisfaction with the continued economic depression, compounded by protraction of the state financial crisis under liberal rule. Of about equal importance were an increasing hostility in the foral regions of the northeast to political centralization in Madrid, and a broad sense of resentment in some areas against the primacy of urban economic interests. Parts of the countryside had been in a phase of social and economic disturbance since 1808, but direct opposition to liberalism was centered in the conservative north and more especially in the particularist northeast. Landed aristocrats usually resented abolition of seigneuries, while many peasants feared liberal curtailment of traditional peasant communal land rights in favor of middle class, private ownership. One historian has counted a total of 122 local revolts against the liberal regime in these years, and conservative royalist rebel juntas were set up at varying times in three different regions, culminating in a separate royalist "regency" in the hills of northern Catalonia in 1822. By that time the northeastern quarter of Spain was in a state of virtual civil war.

Religious sentiment played a major role in this opposition. The church was at first disposed to accept constitutional government in 1820, just as it had initially in 1810–1812. This transigent attitude was sharply reversed, however, by the abolition of ecclesiastical jurisdiction and the restrictions on orders and their property, with the beginning of the suppression of the monasteries. Exaltados came into power on a flood of anticlerical propaganda, and a number of priests were murdered by liberals in the civil strife of 1822-1823. Even in the elections of 1822 that were won by the exaltados, however, nearly 20 percent of the deputies chosen were clergy. A considerable proportion of these were supporters of moderate liberalism who subsequently had to go into exile, indicating that as late as 1822 the liberal clergy who had played a major role at Cádiz were still influential.

Almost from the start of the constitutional triennium, Fernando VII tried to encourage intervention by the conservative European powers of the Quadruple Alliance to save him from constitutional government. For the first two years there was little disposition on their part to do so. The Spanish king had lost prestige, even among conservative European leaders, by his blindly reactionary and vindictive course in 1814, which had contrased so sharply with that of the restored Bourbon crown in France. The doceañista cabinet of the first part of the triennium did not unduly alarm the conservative powers, and though Austrian troops intervened in Italy to suppress liberal government there in 1821, that was based on general recognition of a distinct Habsburg sphere of influence in the Italian peninsula. There was no similar determination by France to meddle in Spanish affairs. It was not until after the rise to power of the exaltados, attended by new extreme measures, and the outbreak of virtual civil war in Spain, that a French expeditionary force entered the peninsula in 1823. Indeed, it has been suspected that D. Fernando first agreed to appoint an exaltado ministry in Madrid in order to complete the polarization of Spanish politics and invite conservative intervention. At any rate, with the liberals divided among themselves there was little will to resist, and the forces of constitutionalism, beset by 100,000 French invaders and a smaller Spanish "army of faith" of right-wing peasant militia, soon collapsed. There was no resistance to the French in the Spanish countryside, where liberalism was more often than not viewed with hostility.

The reaction of 1823 far exceeded in scope and ferocity that of 1814. During the next two years the army officer corps was temporarily dissolved, thousands of liberals driven into exile, considerable property confiscated, many hundreds arrested, and scores of executions carried out. Fernando VII insisted that French military detachments remain in the country to protect him, yet his behavior embarrassed conservative French military and political leaders, who tried unsuccessfully to moderate the Spanish reaction. Fernando's only program at first was the complete restoration of absolutism, bringing the return of seigneuries, entailments, the ecclesiastical fuero, and nearly all the laws and institutions that had been abolished, save the Inquisition.

Fernandine Absolutism between Ultra-Royalism and Liberalism, 1824–1833

The king's main concern was to preserve absolute authority for himself, yet he had to govern through ministers whom he was rarely disposed to trust and so continued to rely on personal favorites. Hence his alarm on discovering, after the restoration of absolutism, that a strong ultraroyalist faction of rural upper class and church leaders had emerged who insisted on stringent reorganization of government to suppress liberalism totally. They also wanted to place government completely in the hands of their own reactionary ministers. The *apostólicos* or *negros,* as the ultraroyalist reactionaries came to be called, also demanded restoration of the Inquisition as a check on public morality, anticlericalism, and political subversion. Local "Juntas de la fe" (Committees of the Faith) were organized in many districts, particularly in the northeastern regions of the country, and the force of "Royalist Volunteers" that had supplanted the army in 1823 was eventually expanded to 120,000 men. Fernando VII came more and more to fear becoming a prisoner of the *negros* and, in so doing, losing French military backing to sustain his government against the liberals. His reluctance to give complete control of affairs to the *negros* led to several ultrareactionary military revolts in 1824–1825.

More serious was the outbreak of the *guerra dels malcontents* in the western districts of the Catalan countryside in 1827. This revolt among poor peasants in the Catalan backlands, whose economy had been even more depressed than usual during the past twenty years, seems to have been instigated by a coterie of upper-class rural reactionaries and apostólico church leaders. The apostólico faction was absolutely doctrinaire with regard to its reactionary program; the capricious, personal, opportunist absolutism of Fernando VII seemed to them little more than the prelude to another round of liberal rule. Their aim was to spark a general rural insurrection that would demand absolute monarchist rule, nominally under Fernando VII but actually under complete control of the apostólicos, restoration of the Inquisition as a guarantee of true religion, and destruction of all remnants of liberalism. This somewhat artificial uprising never spread beyond rural Catalonia, and was suppressed after several months by the newly reorganized royal army. Nonetheless, the guerra dels malcontents gave voice to the first formal appeal by the *negros* for the leadership of D. Fernando's younger brother and presumed heir, the pious, apostólico D. Carlos María Isidro. The formative elements of the subsequent Carlist movement were taking shape.

To avoid the clutches of the *negros,* D. Fernando relied on a small group of practical absolutists during the last nine years of his reign. This was not, as some have said, a reversion to enlightened despotism, but it did introduce into royal government a sense of the need for economic reform and some concern to conciliate the interests of the more moderate elements of Spanish society. Old state loans were largely repudiated, drying up Spanish credit in the international financial markets, but the government's own financial organization was somewhat improved. Efforts were made through publicity and propaganda to create a positive public attitude toward the royal regime. Domestic production was encouraged, increased tariff protection was provided for Catalan industry, and the first rudimentary stock exchange was set up.

Yet even in its final years, Fernandine absolutism made no genuine concessions to liberalism. This period was marked by the five-year reign of the sanguinary Conde de España as captain general of Barcelona (1827-1832). His repression of dissidents was so savage that it greatly encouraged a new growth of liberalism in the Catalan capital, which had earlier played a major role in the struggles of Spanish constitutionalism during the triennium 1820-1823. Minor border incursions by liberal exiles both from France in the north and Gibraltar in the south were meanwhile turned back with ease. The local security commissions organized by the reaction had internal affairs in most districts well under control.

The Succession Crisis and the Royal Statute of 1834

The apostólico supporters of D. Carlos remained quiet after 1827 in part because it seemed that the succession of their candidate to the throne of the physically ailing, childless Fernando, three times a widower, was almost inevitable. The king's marriage to the young María Cristina of Naples did not alarm them, but the birth of a daughter to the royal couple was more disturbing. Carlists immediately emphasized the Salic Law of the Bourbon monarchy, supposedly brought to Spain with Felipe V, according to which the royal succession could not pass through the female line. The crown had revoked this in 1789, but failed to complete final ratification by the traditional Cortes. Fernando VII, not surprisingly, wanted to be succeeded by his own daughter rather than by a rival and antagonistic brother, and repeated the revocation by royal decree. When he suddenly fell ill in 1832 and was virtually incapacitated, Carlist leaders seized the opportunity to force the royal government to cancel the revocation. Don Fernando, still not quite fifty years old, subsequently recovered and repromulgated the revocation, then early in 1833 forced his ambitious brother into Portuguese exile. The last cabinet appointed by Fernando VII worked to prepare for the succession of the infant princess Isabel by reducing the Royal Volunteers further and eliminating as much of the local administrative influence of the apostólicos as possible.

The death of Fernando VII at the close of 1833 left the throne to a three-year-old daughter under the protection of the youthful queen mother, María Cristina. This Neapolitan regent was a jolly, spontaneous, good-natured young princess lacking in special education or intelligence but determined to hold the throne for her daughter. To accomplish this and beat back the expected assault of the apostólicos, it would be necessary to renounce Fernandine extremes of absolutism and reach a compromise that would gain the support of moderates. At the beginning of 1834, the queen regent appointed a new ministry headed by the most prominent of the moderate doceañista liberals, José Martínez de la Rosa, who had served briefly as prime minister during the triennium.

This resulted in promulgation of the Royal Statute of 1834. The new Spanish document was not a copy of the French Charter of 1814, as has been alleged, nor was it a genuine constitution. It was an attempt by Martínez de la Rosa to replace the Cádiz constitution with a new charter founded on a *juste milieu* between traditionalism and liberalism. The statute was thus a compromise between a real constitution and the mere reform of traditional laws, and was also based in part on the study of the limited post-1815 constitutions of several west German principalities. It provided for a bicameral legislature, the lower house to be chosen by the indirect suffrage in two stages of some 18,000 electors (approximately .15 of 1 percent of the population), and the senate to be composed of grandes, church hierarchs, and royal appointees. The legislature would have little more than a consultative function, for the crown retained absolute veto powers and the government was responsible to it alone. No bill of rights was included and administration was centralized in Madrid, but regional fueros were still recognized.

The elections of 1834 were then "made" from Madrid, initiating what became a common nineteenth-century practice. One objective of government manipulation was to get more of the middle class interests of the country represented, as distinct from clerics, bureaucrats, and the radical intelligentsia. This attempt was to some extent successful, as indicated by table 3.

Table 3. *Professional Backgrounds of Cortes Members*

Year of election	Business and professional	Government and military	Clergy
1820	45	69	35
1822	61	60	28
1834	130	53	5
1836	98	86	4

Source: Fermín Caballero, *El Gobierno y las Cortes del Estatuto* (Madrid, 1837), p. xxxiv.

Yet even under so restricted a suffrage, the deputies in the new Estamento de Procuradores, as the lower chamber was called, did not merely form a safe, progovernment bloc. The debates of an open chamber, full publicity, and freedom of the press were used to discuss issues extensively. By September 1834 the newly emerging Progressive faction, heirs of the exaltados of the triennium, counted 77 of the 188 votes in the lower house and brought up censure votes against the government. Moreover, they were given armed strength in many parts of the country by reorganization of the middle class Urban Militia first formed during the triennium. In most towns the Militia fell under Progressivist control.

Anticlerical violence reappeared almost immediately. In July 1834 several monasteries in Madrid were set afire and a number of monks were murdered by a mob. The rioters were inflamed by the outbreak of a cholera epidemic—apparently blamed on the religious—and by the armed depredations of clerical Carlists in the northern country-side. During the summer of 1835 similar outbursts appeared in Barcelona and several provincial cities.

Carlism and the First Carlist War of 1833—1840

Bands of guerrilleros were formed in the northeast in support of the cause of the exiled D. Carlos soon after receiving news of the death of Fernando VII and the planned Isabeline succession under María Cristina at the close of 1833. During 1834, the struggle took on the dimensions of civil war. The Carlist cause was strongest in the three Basque provinces and Navarre, in rural mountainous Catalonia, and in the more backward and rural areas of Aragón and the Levant.

There was also a following in other parts of northern Spain. The common denominators of the movement were localism, religious and political traditionalism, and to some extent ruralism. It grouped the provincial elements that were most strongly opposed to liberalism, and its keynote was reaction, without a clearly and fully articulated program save return to absolute monarchy. The first Carlist contingents were based on former members of the Royal Volunteers and local patriots of the mountain areas. They were led by priests, gentry, and village notables. In the Basque provinces the regard for regional fueros, partially threatened by liberalism, was a major factor. In Navarre, religious zeal and respect for traditional leadership may have been even stronger in encouraging the movement. In some of the more backward rural areas of the northeast there was general resentment of the new urban-dominated economy and the interests fostered by liberalism. In parts of the Catalan countryside the rebellious propensities of peasants and gentry, resentful of the outside world and given to semi-anarchist outbursts of banditry in an earlier time, were once more revived.

In less than a year Carlist volunteers were formed into regular battalions in Navarre and the Basque country, their stronghold, and a small field army began to take shape. Yet the Carlists were unable to win over the cities, even in that region, and they were always considerably weaker in manpower and supplies than the government forces. Carlist units in Catalonia and the east were more loosely organized, and many of them operated as guerrilla forces. In the Basque core area, conscription was introduced and regular discipline built up. Fighting in or near their home region, their morale was usually better than that of government draftees of south and central Spain, and though they remained deficient in more sophisticated equipment, the bayonet charges of the Carlist infantry proved to be the most effective single tactic in the war. Yet the Carlist army was most successful on the defensive, relying partly on guerrilla units. It never developed much offensive strength, and the climactic expedition to the outskirts of Madrid in 1837 was unable to launch an assault on the capital. That the civil war lasted nearly seven years was due in large measure to the disarray of the nascent liberal regime, unable to generate the considerable resources of money, manpower, and material needed to fight campaigns of attrition against regional forces.

Don Carlos "V," the traditionalist leader, turned out to be destructive to his own cause. Irresolute and incompetent as a military chief, he also lacked political perception and was dominated by a narrow coterie of priests and apostólicos. There were a number of outstanding Carlist military leaders, the best of whom, the professional Guipuzcoan officer Zumalacárregui, was killed in 1835. In the end, as the traditionalists were worn down by attrition and government forces closed in, a split developed between the fanatical apostólico elements and the more practical regional traditionalists. Rafael Maroto, a professional general commanding the main Carlist force, became involved in a death struggle with the clerical and civilian apostólico leaders, termed *brutos* by the professional Carlist officers, and in 1839 accepted a generous peace offer from the liberal General Espartero. The terms of this "Compromise of Vergara" pledged to eschew reprisals, incorporate Carlist officers in the regular army, and respect Basque privileges. The last fighting ended when Carlist forces in the east were run across the border in 1840.

Yet Carlism did not die after its military defeat. Though the dynastic issue of Salic male legitimacy remained the central Carlist claim, what really kept the movement alive was the strength of religious traditionalism and the insistence on regional identity and privileges. The so-called Second Carlist War of 1846-1849 was no more than a rising of the Catalan back country, not yet integrated into the liberal social and economic system. However, the frustration and relative failures of representative government during the middle decades of the century made it difficult to create real unity and overcome the tug of localism and cultural traditionalism. A more dynamic society than that of the Spanish middle classes might have been able to integrate the interests of various parts of the peninsula, but the halting development of the country left archaic interests intact. The liberal regime in Madrid tended to usurp local privileges without offering the advantages of a modern central government. The excesses of Spanish radicalism in a later generation also contributed to the revival of traditionalism after it had seemed to be losing much of its support. Though the Carlist movement lay largely dormant until after 1869, it kept much of its latent appeal in the conservative rural areas of the northeast.

The Triumph of Liberalism, 1835-1840

By the mid-1830s, Spanish liberalism had become distinctly stronger than during the triennium. The beginning of economic recovery during the last years of Fernando VII, the spread of liberal ideas and a growing revulsion against Fernandine absolutism, which swung key regions such as the urban districts of Catalonia on the liberal side, all played a part in this. The need for allies to support the Isabeline succession had provided for a smooth governmental transition under the Statute of 1834, but during 1834 and 1835 the Carlist reaction gathered strength in the Basque country and other northeastern regions.

The moderate government of Martínez de la Rosa soon found itself between two fires, just as its predecessor had during the triennium. A wave of radical revolts in many of the leading provincial towns broke out in July 1835, exceeding anything in 1822-1823, and the government had little choice but to strengthen itself by moving to the left. In September, the financier Juan Alvarez de Mendizábal replaced Martínez de la Rosa as prime minister, and his cabinet was charged with the task of amending the Statute in a more liberal direction. During the ensuing debate the split between Moderates and Progressives became clearer than ever. For new elections that were held in March 1836, qualifications were lowered so as to double the suffrage, raising it to between 30,000 and 50,000 electors. With the assistance of a degree of government manipulation from Madrid, the Moderate elements were almost completely eliminated and a strongly Progressive chamber was elected.

Meanwhile Mendizábal moved to solve two problems simultaneously: financing of the civil war against Carlism and the disposing of monastic properties (restored to the church by the Fernandine reaction). In March 1836 the government declared all monastic lands to be national property and began their sale immediately at public auction. During the following year plans were made for the confiscation and sale of all church lands, though so sweeping a measure was not immediately enacted into law. The aim of this broad disamortization of formerly entailed church property was not simply to dispossess the church and finance the civil war; it was meant to strengthen the middle classes economically, and it was hoped by some that it would create a stable, liberal, lower-middle-class, property-owning peasantry.

The beginning of the great disamortization of church land completed the total estrangement of the Spanish Catholic Church from liberalism. Though a few bishops supported the Moderates, most church leaders became completely committed to Carlism, and legal sanctions were taken against some groups in the clergy for political reasons. As a result of this tension between church and state, thirty-two of the sixty-two sees in Spain were vacant by 1840.

Though nearly all Spaniards remained nominal Catholics, and religious or spiritual anti-Catholicism, as distinct from political anti-clericalism, was almost unknown, the middle decades of the century marked the nadir of Spanish Catholicism's public position and influence on the elite. Middle class Catholic businessmen saw no spiritual contradiction in despoiling the church of its lands, and even the Moderates protested the way it was done more than the act of disamortization itself. Many monks and priests of uncertain vocation left the clergy, and it has been estimated that during the first decades of liberalism approximately one-third renounced their vows altogether.

The queen regent, María Cristina, who functioned as head of state, was a comparatively simple woman but by no means lacking in common sense. She realized that the Moderates were much more interested than the Progressives in preserving strong royal prerogatives in Spain. After more disorders and much intriguing by the Moderates, she dismissed Mendizábal in May 1836 and replaced him with a Moderate leader, Istúriz. For the elections to be held in July the suffrage was broadened by decree, lowering property qualifications to enfranchise approximately 50,000 of the wealthy and 15,000 educated men and officials qualified as *capacidades* (those who are specially qualified), of whom about 6,000 were army and national guard officers. This total of 65,000 amounted to .5 to .6 of 1 percent of the Spanish population, and was actually a greater proportion than were enfranchised at that time in France, which had no provision for capacidades. In the elections of July 1836 some government influence was no doubt employed, but the Moderate factions also relied on more effective organization, forming an alliance with nonradical Progressives. Approximately two-thirds of the new electorate made use of the ballot. In the first round of voting, the government alliance won about eighty seats, to fifty-six for the opposition, which carried most of the larger cities.

The radical sectors had no intention of being eliminated from power. Before the second round of voting could be held, the Progressives began a series of revolts in provincial capitals, starting at Málaga on July 25. These culminated in a pronunciamiento by noncommissioned officers at the royal summer palace of La Granja in August, forcing the queen to restore the Cádiz constitution of 1812. A Progressive ministry took power under José María Calatrava. It mobilized new military and financial resources for the civil war, and then held elections—the third in less than a year—in October 1836, on the basis of the 1812 system of universal male householders' suffrage in a three-stage indirect process. By that time the bulk of the public were growing weary of turmoil, and the more moderate elements of the Progressives gained control of the Cortes.

The year 1837 was a crucial one in the First Carlist War, as the government forces were nearly paralyzed by mutiny and the traditionalist army came close to seizing Madrid. At the same time, the Cortes was occupied with preparing a new constitution to supersede that of 1812. The resultant constitution of 1837 was a conciliatory and balanced document. Though the principle of national sovereignty was restored, government authority was shared by crown and parliament, with the former retaining major powers. The new constitution stated that the crown could not rule without the parliament, but government ministers were to be summoned and dismissed by the crown alone. The legislature was made bicameral, with the senate to be appointed by the crown from among names proposed by wealthy electors. Finally, municipal governments were placed under local control through popular elections by a broad suffrage and were also given jurisdiction over local units of the reorganized National Militia.

The semidemocratic voting provisions of 1812 were dropped in favor of a censitary suffrage only slightly broader than that of 1836. Approximately 78,000 voters were enfranchised directly, but provision for capacidades was considerably reduced by comparison with the 1836 law. Yet the suffrage provisions in general were much broader, for there was also concern to enfranchise peasant smallholders who paid little in the way of direct taxes. Hence a secondary provision gave the vote to any peasant farmer who owned a yoke of cattle. In some provinces of the northwest this included many comparatively poor peasants, resulting in 22,000 qualified voters in Pontevedra and 18,000 in Asturias. Altogether, the suffrage list for the country as a whole was increased to 265,000 (2.1 percent of the population). This amounted to 1 voter for every 48 inhabitants, compared to 1 for every 200 under the 1831 electoral law in France.

The Moderates denounced the 1837 constitution as too radical. In the campaign for the next elections (September 1837), they developed the first approximation of a regular political organization in Spain by forming coordinated committees of journalists and other activists to promote their propaganda. Under the broader suffrage, there was only 56 percent participation. Moreover, radical Progressives abstained in many of the larger cities in protest against the government leadership of the more moderate Progressives, whose constitution they denounced as too conservative. The Moderates gained primary support from the larger landowners of central and southern Spain and benefited both from the radicals' abstention and from a general rightward swing among the middle and upper classes after the recent series of revolts and mutinies. They won 200 seats to the Progressives's 60 in one of the fairer elections to be held in nineteenth-century Spain.

The Moderates held power for nearly two years, but on increasingly poorer terms with the liberal leaders of the regular army. The latter finally brought the crown to dissolve the Cortes once more and hold new elections in 1839 that, coupled with the abstention of the Moderates, resulted in a radical Progressive victory. This coincided with the end of the primary phase of the civil war and the triumph for the liberal cause, but brought new tension and drastic polarity to liberal politics. The Progressive Cortes was then in turn dissolved, and the Moderates organized a Central Commission to give them official leadership in new elections at the beginning of 1840. These may not have been so relatively free of governmental interference as the preceding contests of 1837 and 1839. At any rate, they resulted in a new victory for the Moderates, who then prepared to safeguard the triumph of moderate liberalism by new institutional changes that would eliminate the bases of Progressive strength.

The Military in Politics, 1834-1840

It was during the First Carlist War that the basic pattern of military intervention and leadership in politics was established, a pattern that persisted for at least forty years. This intervention was expressed in a variety of forms, ranging from outright mutiny, particularly in 1837, through direct pronunciamientos in 1835 and 1836, to more indirect forms of suasion behind the scenes, begun in 1834 by moderate army liberals who became spokesmen for a more representative policy.

That military leaders played such crucial roles was due first of all to the institutional vacuum in which liberalism was reintroduced after the final decade of Fernandine absolutism, and to the poor organization of the liberal forces and the relative weakness of the interests on which they were established. The two main rival factions, the Moderates and Progressives, could not even agree upon rules of the game, and the Progressives, particularly, felt justified in summoning both civilian mobs and armed intervention by sympathetic military elements. Equally important was the fact that liberalism was being established during a major civil war in which the military leadership was of crucial significance and hence played a disproportionately influential role.

Most of the army and its officers remained aloof from politics, but of the minority who became involved, the greater number reinforced either Moderate or Progressive liberalism. This proliberal orientation can be explained by a number of factors. Most officers felt a patriotic responsibility to support the liberal cause with which the established national government was becoming identified. Most were of middle class background; they leaned toward liberalism because of its mystique of modernization and new opportunity. Thus they played the role of a modernizing middle class elite in a society in which the core of the middle classes were not yet ready to take full charge. More mundane factors were also involved, such as poor pay (and after the war, unemployment), personal rivalries, and the fact that the liberal government was so ill organized during the war that commanding officers sometimes had to intervene in government administration simply to care for the needs of their troops.

Espartero and the Failure of Progressivism, 1840-1843

The dominant figure in the Spanish army at the close of the First Carlist War was General Baldomero Espartero, who commanded the government forces in the north during the climactic campaign that concluded with the compromise peace of Vergara in 1839. He had become identified with Progressive interests in opposition to rivals in the military who supported the Moderates, and his influence was in large measure responsible for the dissolution of the Moderate Cortes and the brief return of the Progressives to power in 1839-1840.

The Moderate government that regained control in 1840 then passed legislation raising property qualifications for the vote, and moved to cut the base from under Progressive strength in the provincial towns. Though the principle of popular election of provincial assemblies and municipal councils was retained, a new law stipulated that the ministry of interior in Madrid would alone have the right to appoint mayors and other officials of provincial capitals from among all those local councilors elected, and that the appointive *jefes políticos* in charge of provinces would choose all officials for smaller towns from among those elected in them. These laws were in fact constitutional amendments, however, and could not be instituted simply by majority vote of parliament. Their imposition amounted to a civilian pronunciamiento, and the Progressives threatened revolt.

At this point the queen regent tried to gain the support of the commander-in-chief of the army, Espartero, who was in Barcelona. But Espartero was even more vehemently implored by the Progressives to be their savior, and he refused to sanction the new laws, while stressing his support of the queen regent and the young queen. Hence María Cristina offered to appoint Espartero prime minister as the only hope of finding a compromise that would support the throne. When she refused to sanction annulment of the municipalities law, however, the Progressives broke into two months of protracted street demonstrations and minor disorders in provincial capitals all over Spain. This forced appointment of Espartero as prime minister on the Progressives' own terms, and ultimately drove María Cristina to abdicate the regency.

Espartero then became interim regent in October 1840, and de facto head of state, the first and only time that a military figure held that position until 1936. New elections in 1841 naturally brought an overwhelming Progressive victory and ratification by the new Cortes of Espartero as regent for life. The Progressive caudillo was the son of a Castilian wheelwright. He had little education and scant political understanding or talent, and was given to bouts of indolence alternating with periods of activity. He had not sought a political career but had been eagerly pressed into service by the Progressives as the only means of assuring their triumph. His political ideas were limited to vague notions about the current of the times and popular sovereignty, later expressed in his popular catchphrase "Let the national will be fulfilled"—a slogan without content adopted in lieu of a program. He was gratified to be hailed by Progressive crowds and enjoyed the status which politics had brought him, but he had little in the way of purposeful leadership to offer. The only significant initiative of the government in 1841 was to begin to put the lands of the secular clergy as well as monasteries on the market for private purchase.

The only way in which Spanish politics became more liberal under Espartero was in the suffrage. Thanks to the *yuntero* (cattle owner) clause of the 1837 constitution, the number of electors had risen to 343,000 in 1839 and 424,000 in 1840 (3.5 percent of the population). This amounted to 1 voter for every 13 inhabitants of Alava, 1 for every 14 in Guipuzcoa, 15 in Zamora, 16 in Orense, and 17 in Pontevedra—the broadest European suffrage of the period. By 1843, the voting lists had increased to 500,000 or more.

The response of one group of the Moderates to the Espartero regime was a counter-pronunciamiento by a handful of military and civilian figures in the Basque country in October 1841. This was easily quashed, for it drew no support from the temporarily exhausted Carlists. It did bring the elimination of Basque fueros. Provincial governments were established in place of the traditional juntas, Basque tariff privileges were abolished, and regular conscription was introduced.

Reaction to the attempted Moderate pronunciamiento served as catalyst in a new Progressive outburst in Barcelona. There a Junta de Vigilancia was set up to defend against the danger from the right, but within a month it had been converted into a Junta Popular that demolished the Ciudadela, Barcelona's fortress built by Felipe V as a symbol of centralist sovereignty in the Catalan capital. The Junta Popular represented a broad mobilization of elements of the middle and also the lower classes. Before it was forcibly suppressed, it demanded government protection for domestic industry and collaborated with the first significant efforts to organize trade unions in Spain.

One year later, in November 1842, the structure of government in Barcelona broke down altogether. The possessing classes were alienated by Espartero's free-trade policy, while the workers were disgruntled over the *quinta* system of general military recruitment—a compulsory draft for certain elements of the poor—and over the high level of excises. Within forty-eight hours a tax riot of sorts had flamed into a broad popular revolt, and a new Junta Directiva Popular took over the government. When Espartero dispatched an army to reduce Barcelona by force, the more restrained middle class elements formed a Conciliation Junta to work out a compromise solution. After the government insisted on unconditional surrender, it was supplanted by a new radical junta of the lower classes. The rebels raised the first black flags of total defiance seen in Barcelona, as Espartero bombarded the city, then occupied it by military force and carried out a severe repression.

By this time Espartero's honeymoon with Progressive opinion had long since ended. Incapable of governing effectively himself, he was dominated by a clique of military associates (nicknamed Ayacuchos by their enemies, since some of them had been present at the final Spanish defeat of Ayacucho in South America in 1825). He paid little attention either to the Progressive Cortes or to the wants and demands of the provinces, and suppressed newspapers to protect himself from criticism. Spanish Progressivism had proved invertebrate and ineffective. Not strong enough or sufficiently united to govern through civilian politics, it had relied on a military strong man who was incapable of providing leadership. By 1843, many of the Progressives themselves were looking for an alternative solution.

The strongest opposition to Espartero was being coordinated by a group of Moderate senior officers in exile, led by General Ramón María Narváez. Their conspiracy drew support from the more moderate Carlists, from much of the clergy, and from the French government of Louis Philippe, which feared that affairs in Spain were getting out of hand. It was also supported by a significant number of the Progressives, who found themselves unemployed under the current scheme or out of favor with the ruling clique. Some of these Progressive conspirators did not necessarily want to overthrow Espartero, but they did want to force a change in policy and get rid of the Ayacucho group, whose hands were on the levers of power.

The Cortes elections of 1843 were won by a coalition of Moderates and "pure" Progressives (as the anti-Espartero sector of the Progressives called themselves). Finding himself unable to control the new assembly, Espartero dissolved it, but this merely served as the spark to touch off the joint Moderate-"pure" Progressive pronunciamiento that overthrew the regency. It was a snowballing revolt that started late in May in several of the Andalusian provincial capitals. After winning major military support in June, it was climaxed by a skirmish outside Madrid between a rebel force and a few units still loyal to Espartero. By that time his power had melted away; he was defeated and forced into retirement, replaced by a temporary compromise ministry faced with the task of restructuring liberal government in Spain. The last round of this conflict was fought by the radical left in Barcelona, where the popular militia refused to disband after the new government had been formed. The third popular revolt in Barcelona within two years occurred during September 1843, when the city was dominated by a new radical junta representing artisans, factory workers, and the unemployed. It lacked clear leadership or program but made demands for greater democratization and for social and economic concessions from both the government and property owners. The revolt acquired the slang name of the *Jamancia,* from the gypsy usage *jamar* meaning "to eat," indicating its identification with the lowest social strata. Like its predecessors, the Jamancia was suppressed by force (November 1843), but this time there were no fearful reprisals.

Foreign Affairs, 1815-1843

During the decade that preceded the War of Independence, Spain had sunk into the humiliating role of a Napoleonic satellite. The heroic resistance of the Spanish people preserved national independence, but the resulting economic prostration, the revolt in America, and the total ineptness of the Fernandine regime placed the country in a position of diplomatic impotence after 1814. Spanish representatives played no role at the Congress of Vienna and were almost completely ignored, nor did Spanish diplomacy fare better in subsequent years. The petty, vengeful, extraordinarily narrow-minded Fernando enjoyed no esteem even among other conservative rulers. The major effort which his government exerted in 1818 to elicit help from other European powers to repress the Spanish American revolt was a complete failure. In addition, the British government stood ready by 1823 to block any marshalling of support for the Spanish repression in America, and the United States adhered to this position in its Monroe Doctrine. The weakness and dependency of the first half of the Fernandine regime was then climaxed by reliance on French troops to restore absolute monarchy.

During Fernando's reign, Spain became a debtor nation for the first time in its history. This was the almost inevitable result of being deprived of the bulk of Spanish American resources and the trade and revenue accruing from them, especially at a time when the country was suffering from heavy war losses and the administrative system had fallen into decay. There was some improvement in the handling of the national debt during the second half of the reign, insofar as it was better administered and new loans were negotiated, but as a result of these loans the foreign debt doubled between 1824 and 1834.

After the death of Fernando VII, the Spanish government was able to enter a phase of more fruitful diplomatic relations. Between 1830 and 1834, France, Spain, and Portugal all joined the ranks of constitutional monarchy alongside Britain, and in the latter year the four powers signed a Quadruple Alliance. This was not an association of equals, however, and merely inaugurated a phase of British and French tutelage. Ambassadors of these two powers tried frequently to intervene in domestic affairs during the 1830s and 1840s, the British government leaning toward the less radical of the Progressives and the French toward the Moderates. The domestic division resulting from civil war and political stalemate was such that the principal effort to secure more humane treatment of prisoners during the First Carlist War was not arranged by Spaniards but was negotiated through British intermediaries in the Elliott Convention of 1835. Britain supplied much of the equipment and money for the government triumph, which also represented victory for the policy of the two main western powers and was viewed unfavorably by the conservative governments of central and eastern Europe. Though British influence seemed predominant for a time, French diplomacy assumed a stronger role after the overthrow of the Progressives in 1843, and government reliance on foreign loans accentuated this relative dependence.

Economic Development, 1815-1843

The political cleavages and failures of the quarter-century that followed the War of Independence would undoubtedly have been much less severe had the period not been one of economic doldrums. The years 1814-1820 were a time of unrelieved postwar depression. A brief revival began during the liberal triennium, then was choked off by international depression. Revival of Catalan manufactures was hampered by the flow of French textile exports that undersold Catalan production inside Spain. General recovery in Spain did not get under way until 1827, and Catalan textile production increased markedly after about 1830. The general upswing owed comparatively little to government policy: the program of hard money and general deflation that was followed in 1814-1820 reenforced depression. This financial policy was reversed during 1821–1823 but was restored under the second Fernandine reaction. Much of the money brought in by foreign loans between 1823 and 1827 was simply stolen by the court camarilla. Beginning in 1827, the state began to work in greater cooperation with private finance, achieving a higher level of honesty and coherence in its financial operations, and this assisted the importing of machinery for textile production. The policy of liberal government during the triennium and after 1834 also stressed bringing in money through foreign loans, but included a degree of monetary devaluation, which apparently stimulated production.

By 1834 those with social and economic power were in fair agreement on the desirability of liberal constitutionalism, but disagreed among themselves about the exact form. Large landholders and proto-industrialists favored the Moderates, while commercial interests and smaller entrepeneurs and shopkeepers supported Progressivism. Nevertheless, many of the rural districts of Spain still lived largely outside the orbit of the commerce and industry of a new and developing nineteenth-century economy. Self-contained regions of local artisan production were still almost more the rule than the exception in the geography of Spanish manufactures, and this was yet another factor that made the social and economic mobilization of a cohesive liberalism quite difficult. In turn, economic distress encouraged the drift of marginal elements to the towns, where they formed a subclass easily stirred up by Progressive agitation.

Seigneurial jurisdiction over rural properties was not definitively eliminated until after 1836, and the new settlement of property rights was at first not fully clear. Seigneurial territorial jurisdictions were often transferred into private property rights, an enormous boon to the landholding aristocracy, for they henceforth held in absolute title what had previously been restricted by a kind of condominial relationship. Nevertheless, property titles to small towns under former seigneurial domain, and land from which only marginal dues were collected, remained bones of contention. Dues and rights had been confused ever since the start of the War of Independence and in some cases were not entirely settled until decades after the actual abolition of seigneuries in 1836. Though some aristocrats who formerly held extensive domains were recognized as private owners of these huge tracts, such ownership normally could not be extended over small towns, villages, and mountain areas. Some nobles lost the economic benefits of most of their seigneuries almost entirely. Lawsuits went on for years, and certain dispossessed lords were eventually awarded pensions or other compensations.

Table 4. *Sales of Church and Common Lands, 1836–1856,*
valued in reales (5 reales equalled one peseta)

Years	Lands of secular clergy	Lands of regular clergy
1836–44	399,258,967	503,571,422
1845–54	45,380,906	22,465,745
1854–56	354,912,492	80,593,951
Total cost of church lands sold, 1836–56		1,406,183,483
Cost of common and wastelands sold, 1836–56		519,168,728
Grand total		1,925,352,211

Source: L. Sánchez Agesta, *Historia del constitucionalismo español* (Madrid, 1955), p. 463.

The transfer and sale of church lands was not completed for several decades. All church properties were not thrown on the market until the new rulings by the Espartero regency in 1841, and the sale of the properties of the secular clergy was not fully consummated until the 1850s. The most valuable lands transferred to private ownership were in New Castile, Extremadura, and Andalusia, the regions of the great thirteenth-century endowments.

The disamortization was a comparative political success but a distinct economic failure. The first phase was carried out in 1836–1837 amid great haste to complete the first rounds of sales to Progressive supporters before the Moderates could intervene. Lands were sold at little more than 10 percent down, with ten years to pay. Rates were often well under the fair market value. Though the state gained the support of a new elite, its finances deteriorated. Concentration of landholdings accelerated after 1836. Land rents from peasants rose, while *bracero* wages remained stagnant. The heavily unbalanced agrarian structure of modern Spain, particularly in the center and south, had assumed its full dimensions by the 1840s.

Since the new liberal elite was fundamentally land-based, one of the first acts of restored constitutional government in 1820 had been to contradict its nominal doctrines of the free market by setting rigorous import restrictions on grain. This violated Spain's centuries-old tradition of cheap food imports, guaranteeing higher grain prices that lowered the standard of living but maintained the principal source of income for the new elite.

Spanish Romanticism

For the first time in more than one hundred years Spanish esthetics, expressed in the romantic art of the early nineteenth century, gripped the European imagination. The central figure in this was Francisco Goya y Lucientes (1746-1828), whose finest achievements were his later paintings done in the nineteenth century. Change in the perception of the Spanish esthetic was also the result of a revaluation by art critics and historians of western Europe, who began early in the century to project the image of a "Romantic Spain." Foreign writers who tavelled in Spain—Théophile Gautier, Prosper Merimée, Washington Irving, and others—elaborated this image in the literary world of the 1830s and after, contributing to a mystique based on one-sided glimpses of gypsies, bandits, flamenco dancing, and Moorish residues which in its extreme form was more Andalusian than Spanish. Yet with this there came, for the first time in modern European culture, an appreciation for the positive as well as the negative qualities of the uniquely Hispanic.

There was a romantic generation in Spanish literature and criticism as well, headed by the essayist Mariano José de Larra and linked with the liberal political movement in Madrid and the provincial capitals of the south. In Catalonia, on the other hand, the sense of romanticism was more conservative and was associated with historical themes and influenced by English and German writers, particularly Scott. A sense of the individuality of Catalan society was intensified.

The development of Hispanic romanticism had the effect of reviving regional languages and quickening their literary use; the hegemony of Castilian that had endured for three centuries was challenged. By mid-century there were also evidences of more popular cultural forms in the Catalan-speaking regions, with working class choral groups in Barcelona and popular theatricals in both Barcelona and Valencia. This reawakening of popular culture was reinforced by the *costumbrista* trend in the literature of the next generation, devoted to capturing regional styles and mores. The growth of regionalist culture did not at first challenge Spanish unity or the broader hegemony of Castilian Spanish culture. By the end of the nineteenth century, however, it helped to inspire dissociative regionalism, compounding the difficulties of integrating a liberal system.

20

The Isabeline Regime and First Democratic Interlude

The Rule of the Moderates

The overthrow of Espartero led within a year to the establishment of a new regime of oligarchic liberalism under the hegemony of the Moderates, led by the *espadón de Loja,* Ramón María Narváez. The Moderate party that took shape in the 1840s was based essentially on the wealthy and talented, but above all the wealthy, of the upper and upper-middle classes. It stood for a government built on property **and** rational administration. It was interested in representative government and constitutionalism mainly because royal absolutism was capricious and inefficient. Its liberalism was limited, however, to representation of those with economic power in the country, and the basis of Moderate rule was extremely narrow.

The position of the Progressives differed mainly in degree. The Progressives were not democrats, but believed that suffrage, to be effective, had to represent a broader cross-section of society. The Progressives stood for fiscal reform and a somewhat more equitable tax system. They were much more anticlerical. Moderates wanted a modus vivendi with the church, allowing it to keep many of its privileges and part of its property. The Progressives wanted to strip the church of all its property and privilege, and tended toward disestablishment and absolute freedom of religion. Both supported central administration to encourage uniformity, efficiency, and moderniza-tion. The Progressives, however, were emphatic about local self-gov-ernment, especially because their support lay in the lower-middle and middle-middle classes of the provincial towns. The Moderates in-sisted upon central regulation of local affairs, to keep political power under control.

Neither group was effectively organized as a modern political party and neither could operate as an efficient unit. Both were split by a variety of personal, ideological, and provincial factions, and the lines between them tended to blur. The official Moderates tended toward extreme oligarchy, but a *puritano* group stood for "pure" constitu-tionalism and reasonable civil guarantees. Radical Progressives were often willing to call down the mob on their side, but moderate Progressives feared violence and extremism and were willing to work with liberal elements among the Moderates.

The movement that overthrew Espartero had been a loose coalition of Moderates and anti-Espartero Progressives with the nominal aim of restoring genuine representative government under the compro-mise constitution of 1837. The coalition ministry broke down after two successive prime ministers had to resign within a few months. An attempt by the moderate Progressive Olózaga to force the adolescent queen to hand power to a Progressive ministry that would hold new elections backfired, and brought an all-Moderate government to power at the close of 1843.

Elections were held in 1844 under fairly rigorous central control, and the Moderates then moved to write a new constitution and consolidate an almost exclusively Moderate regime. Lacking strong organization or internal unity, their main rallying point was Narváez and his personal domination of the army. With three comparatively brief interruptions, Narváez was premier from 1844 to 1851. He was a man of moderately liberal ideas and authoritarian temperament. A constitutionalist in his youth, Narváez had been expelled from the army in 1823 and did not regain his commission until the Carlist war, during which he rose to prominence as commander of the reserve forces in central Spain. A strong leader, determined and energetic, he possessed the force of personality and will needed to establish a degree of order in the army and hold the factions and cliques of the Moderates together. Narváez was a genuine supporter of constitution-alism and parliamentary government but also a ruthless advocate of law and order. He was not given to capricious persecution, but imposed maximal sanctions against rebels. More than two hundred radicals in revolt against the new regime were executed in 1843 and 1844, and the Moderate government began to establish rural security by the formation in 1844 of a special constabulary called the Civil Guard, modeled on the French rural gendarmerie.

Under Narváez's direction, the Moderates drew up a new constitution in 1845. Most of the seventy-seven articles of the 1837 constitution were transferred unaltered into the eighty articles of the new document, but several fundamental changes were made. The concept of national sovereignty was ignored, and the power of the throne was greatly increased. It was empowered to convoke, suspend, and dissolve the legislature and was given absolute veto power over all legislation. Freedom of the press was guaranteed, but jury trials for offenses were eliminated. The Senate was transformed from an elected body into a lifetime appointive oligarchy composed of the elite of the government administration, army, church, aristocracy, and property owners. Moreover, the Senate was made equal to the Cortes in legislative power. Under an 1846 law, the property qualification for suffrage was drastically raised, reducing the electorate to 100,000 of the most wealthy (and a tiny minority of the best educated) citizens. Even these were not always allowed to cast valid ballots unhindered during the elections of the next twenty years (save in 1854), since general control was exercised from Madrid. Electoral units were organized by single-member districts rather than by bloc voting for whole provincial lists, as the Progressives would have preferred. By 1860 the suffrage had expanded only slightly, to include about 160,000 of the elite, or approximately 1 percent of the total population of Spain.

Moreover, the Moderate regime restored central control over provincial government by repromulgating the local government law of 1840. A central financial system was created for the first time after the Bank of Spain was established in 1847. Four years later it was given authority to issue money for all of Spain. A uniform commercial legal code had already been worked out in 1829, and the Moderates established a common criminal code in 1848. The only regions excepted from it were Catalonia, which retained its own civil and commercial codes, and the Basque provinces (including Navarre), whose fueros, recently suspended by Espartero, were partially restored. A new protective tariff was established in 1849, and a unified tax system for Spain (again excepting the Basque provinces) was finally created. The principal sources of income were taxes on land, urban rents, and industry and commerce, and the consumos (local excise taxes), that weighed heavily on the lower classes. The national debt was finally amortized and brought under control, but the collection of consumos and some other taxes was still not effectively centralized. Control of the collection of district consumos became a central factor in local politics. Much of the proceeds were drained off, and only a comparatively small proportion reached the national government.

A major goal of the Moderate government was to reach an understanding with the church. Sale of church lands was suspended, and a concordat was finally signed in 1851 recognizing Catholic supervision of the moral content of education and providing for financial support of the clergy and the election of bishops by the state. The church in turn recognized the loss of most of its lands, but was to be indemnified with government bonds. The Moderates also created the legal basis for a centralized university network and national educational system. This was eventually completed by the 1857 Moyano law on public education, though the state achieved little in the construction of a public school system.

Thus the Moderate regime in the generation after 1843 managed to establish the legal and institutional framework of a modern, centralized, parliamentary state in Spain. It did not rest upon a social basis sufficient to sustain it, nor could it achieve a viable political structure, but it laid the basis of modern national Spanish administration.

A new social oligarchy quickly emerged under the Moderates, a fusion of some of the old aristocracy and a new monied elite of middle class background. Ten new grande titles and fifty-three lesser titles were created between 1845 and 1850; this was six times as many as had been created between 1835 and 1840 and more than Fernando VII had granted between 1815 and 1820.

The chief theoretician of the Moderate regime was the Extremaduran noble Juan Donoso Cortés, who endeavored to provide a philosophical basis for oligarchic liberalism by stressing the moral authority of a properly constituted society and government. This, he said, should be based on the claims of superior intelligence and of religion. The rights and legitimacy of government so constituted became overriding, and Donoso Cortés urged no hesitation in converting that government into temporary dictatorship if necessary to meet the threat of subversive revolution.

The queen, Isabel, was thirteen years of age when Espartero was overthrown and had been in no position to exercise personal initiative in the establishment of the Moderate (subsequently Isabeline) regime, whose constitution devolved such weighty responsibilities upon her. Good-natured, poorly educated, alternately frivolous and pious, she was of only average intelligence and completely lacked the discipline, constancy, and understanding required of a constitutional monarch. Her marriage in 1846 at the age of sixteen was a disaster; the new consort, Francisco de Asís, a conservative Spanish aristocrat and cousin of the queen, was pious, effeminate, given to intrigue, and probably sexually impotent. The match had been arranged to harmonize with French diplomatic interests, since the French government supported the Moderates while England inclined toward the Progressives. The French vetoed a German prince, and a domestic marriage seemed the best compromise. Isabel's younger sister was wed at the same time to a younger son of the French constitutional monarch, Louis Philippe. The sensuous queen, her consort proving a hopeless husband, drifted away into a series of scandalous liaisons that resulted in seven (probably all illegitimate) children. As the years passed, the queen's political relations and favor became increasingly capricious, so that she compounded, rather than neutralized, the factionalism of the Moderates.

The Moderates were divided into three main factions: 1) the official or government Moderates, who clung to the court and government power and became increasingly arbitrary in political practice; 2) the puritanos, who held to "pure" constitutionalism, urged broader civil guarantees including the right to jury trial for press offenses, and opposed the conservative influence of France as well as the French marriage of Isabel's sister; and 3) on the other extreme, the ultraconservative Moderates, who were ultra-Catholic, in some cases ex-Carlist, and stood for a hyperoligarchic form of government with strengthened royal authority.

French and British influence was very important in Spanish factional politics between 1844 and 1850, as it had been during the Carlist war. Diplomatic pressures, added to the resentment against Narváez among other Moderate factions and the court circle, were instrumental in forcing Narváez from power for the second time in April 1846. During the next eighteen months four different ministries were formed, the last two of them puritano cabinets (between March and October 1847) whose main support was the most liberal of the Moderate generals, Francisco Serrano. But the puritanos, aside from British backing, had only forty votes in parliament to back them and could not gain approval for new elections. The only alternative was Narváez. After four years in power, the Moderates had become hopelessly divided by personality, faction, as well as philosophy. The reorganization of government and administration had not yet taken hold, and the new liberal elite was too small and too divided by region and by interests, and too uncertain of its political program to govern coherently.

Narváez held power firmly during 1848-1849, years of revolution in much of the rest of Europe. He suppressed two minor revolts and ended the Carlist insurrection of 1846-1849 in Catalonia (sometimes called the Second Carlist War). The stability of Spanish government during those years of turmoil in continental Europe won the respect of the other powers and completed the rehabilitation of the Spanish constitutional monarchy internationally, with recognition finally forthcoming from the crowns of central and eastern Europe. Narváez dispatched an expedition to Rome to help defend the sovereignty of the papacy in 1849.

The main elements of the Moderates and in the court circle were determined to avoid any broadening of political participation that might include the Progressives—or British influence in politics or free trade—but they also wanted to be rid of the strong personal authority of Narváez. After the danger of revolt passed in 1849, he was forced from power for the third time to make way for an ultraconservative general, the Conde de Clonard, but this roused such protest that Narváez was able to form another government within twenty days. The main period of his rule was finally ended at the beginning of 1851, not by revolt of Progressives, for they were impotent, but at the initiative of the conservative elements of the Moderates. The ultra-conservatives remained in control of government from January 1851 until overthrown by popular revolt in mid-1854.

The new prime minister was a capable civil servant and former finance minister, Antonio Bravo Murillo, who was determined to establish the institutional basis for stable elitist government. After Louis Napoleon's coup d'état in France at the end of 1851, Bravo Murillo felt strong enough to close the Cortes and rule by decree. His goals were to guarantee strong central authority, suppress popular representation, eliminate army influence in politics (which he detested), and reform the administration. He began to reorganize provincial administration and outlined a new road, canal, and railway construction program. The new constitution that he projected in 1852 would have reduced the Cortes to an advisory role and pared the electorate to a mere 7,000 citizens of wealth and status.

This was too much even for the Moderates, who feared that Bravo Murillo would return Spain to domination by crown, church, and aristocracy. Bravo was forced from power at the end of 1852, to be replaced in quick succession by several, only slightly less conservative, Moderate splinter cabinets. By that time it was clear that the Moderates as a functional alignment had completely disintegrated. During 1853 some of the puritanos began to work with the Progressives in the hope of broadening participation and civil rights. In addition to being weakened by the hopelessly narrow basis of the political system, the Isabeline regime was further undermined in the early 1850s by a series of government financial scandals involving the royal family. The first Spanish railroad concessions contained the usual lucrative financial arrangements found in other countries. Much corruption was involved, including perquisites for the queen mother and her new husband, a former army sergeant ennobled by the crown. When the Cortes was presented with a new railroad regulation bill at the end of 1853, it rejected the measure in a fit of opposition, even though the new draft made some attempt to reform the system of concessions. Parliament was then closed by the government and not reopened until after the regime was overthrown. There was a temporary economic downturn in 1853-1854, compounded by the government's effort to collect new taxes in advance. By that time even the upper middle classes were turning against the corrupt and cliquish regime, which had excluded a broader leadership from power.

The Progressive Biennium of 1854-1856

The Spanish revolution of 1854 began with the *vicalvarada,* a small-scale military revolt of sectors of the Madrid garrison led by several of the more liberal Moderate generals. Its limited aim, encouraged perhaps by the moderate liberal Saldanha coup in Portugal in 1851, was to force a slight broadening of the government. The vicalvarada was defeated, but was seconded by a series of risings in provincial capitals, and then by a revolt of Madrid's lower classes in July that brought four days of street fighting in the capital, the only significant Madrid revolt of the nineteenth century. The government clique was not exactly overthrown but it saw its support disintegrate. The queen found it prudent to recall Espartero from retirement in order to head a provisional government that would hold new constituent elections for constitutional reform. The elections of 1854 were conducted on the basis of an expanded suffrage that enfranchised nearly 700,000, about 5 percent of the population. Electoral participation was about 70 percent, and returned a chamber dominated by Progressives and composed primarily of landowners and lawyers. The 1854 revolt was in a sense the Spanish "1848," though its only expression of national-ism was a growing interest in Iberian union with Portugal under a dynastic marriage. Despite some popular disturbances, its general tone was quite moderate and compared with the explosions of 1835-1837 seemed to indicate civic acculturation.

The new Cortes proceeded to write a new Progressive constitution in 1855. The charter declared sovereignty to rest "essentially in the nation," broadened the sphere of civil liberty, retained the greatly reduced property qualification, but maintained the principle of elitist liberalism with a Senate restricted to the wealthy. The main thrust of the new legislation of the biennium 1854-1856 was to open up Spain more fully then ever before to business enterprise. Disentailment was carried even further; common and waste lands were placed on sale to private owners, together with the lands of the military orders, hitherto exempted from the church disamortization. New corporate laws were enacted for business expansion, along with new regulations to foster banking and credit. The revolution of 1854 thus marked the breakthrough of the middle-middle and upper-middle classes.

There were three principal political factions in the new parliament: the Liberal Union, a reorganization of the more liberal Moderates under General Leopoldo O'Donnell, who had led the vicalvarada; the moderate wing of the Progressives, who were willing to cooperate with the more conservative O'Donnell; and the *progresistas puros*— the "pure" or more liberal Progressives, who would not work with the Liberal Union or other remnants of the Moderates. To their left was the small Democrat Party, formed several years earlier by a left-wing split from the Progressives. The Democrats were also split between those willing to work within the legal order and radicals who preached insurrection to achieve universal male suffrage and an end to conscription and excise taxes.

The biennium 1854–1856 also marked the direct entry of the social question into Spanish politics. The urban lower classes supported the revolt actively in most of the larger towns. In general, their demands were vague and their ranks unorganized; their most precise demand was for the abolition or at least reduction of the consumos. Only in Barcelona was there a significant nucleus of organized labor. There thousands of workers joined new syndicates, and some 30,000 participated in a great demonstration in 1855 demanding "Association or Death!"—that is, full legalization of trade union activity. This the Progressive government under Espartero steadfastly refused.

The leading political groups in parliament remained firm in their monarchism and in their elitist liberalism. Internal division and the specter of popular revolt increased their uncertainty. The main danger from the left was the National Militia, an official paramilitary force first organized during the Carlist war, dissolved in 1843, then reorganized in 1854. It was made up of the urban lower-middle and lower classes, and leaned strongly toward the progresistas puros and somewhat less toward the Democrats. Even many of the Progressives became apprehensive about the danger of popular revolt, particularly after the economic downturn of 1856 and food riots in Valladolid and other towns. The only real leader the Progressives had was Espartero, but he refused to lead, crippled by memories of how a combination of "advanced" policies and personal rule had united the center and right of the political spectrum against him in 1843.

Amid the growing tension of 1856, O'Donnell seized the initiative by getting the queen's backing for a new cabinet. The O'Donnell government was nonparliamentary, for Espartero and the Progressivist factions retained their parliamentary majority, but most of the moderate Progressives were not disposed to resist. The only real conflict in Madrid was with the National Militia, put down after several days fighting. This was paralleled by struggle in other cities, particularly Barcelona, where 400 were killed before the army imposed control.

The Liberal Union

O'Donnell offered the only hope for the system by attempting reconciliation rather than exclusion, by offering an authentic compromise and an attempt at "pure" constitutionalism. Hence after the victory in 1856 and derogation of the new constitution, he realized that he could not merely return to that of 1845, and he passed an "Additional Act" to install an elective senate and jury trials for press offenses, two long-standing Progressive demands, reminiscent of Saldanha's Acto Adicional of 1852 in Portugal. This was unacceptable to the ultraconservative remnants of the Moderates and the neoclericals of the court circle, who also wished to reverse terms of the economic and political settlement with the church.

Within a few months Narváez returned to power; he derogated the Additional Act, stifled the opposition press, and repressed several bloody riots by Democrats in provincial capitals. Yet the experience of this ministry, like that of Narváez's final cabinet nine years later, showed that even an ultraconservative and semi-authoritarian government was impossible under the Isabeline regime, for lack of a unified, systematized base of ultraconservative support. Without social backing, it had to rely on the army and the court circle, but both of these were congeries of factions, and the queen was capricious and personalistic. Only an absolute puppet would have retained the support of the court circle, yet the degree of political mobilization in the country was such that stronger leadership was needed even to manage a fake parliamentary system. Narváez was Isabel's only real strong man but had the temperament of a manic depressive; he resigned over the most trivial of issues—royal insistence on promotion of a military favorite.

Hence after two more temporary cabinets the crown had to revert to O'Donnell's attempted compromise. The resulting "long ministry" of O'Donnell (June 1858–February 1863) was the most successful in the history of Spanish liberalism to that date, yet it too ended in failure. O'Donnell had formed the Liberal Union from a coalition of puritano (and some formerly "official") Moderates and moderate Progressives. Under his government the Cortes was kept open much of the time. Though elections were managed by the minister of the interior, Posada Herrera, this was done with discretion, allowing a minority of both radical Progressives and ultra-Moderates to win seats in congress. Gross fiscal irregularities were avoided and relative freedom of the press maintained. O'Donnell hoped to achieve workable consensus through compromise and also through economic development, which would reconcile broader groups with the system. He governed during the height of railway expansion and the economic boom of the 1850s. His government stressed road-building—a prime national need—coastal installations, and development of the navy. It compromised over the final reduction of church properties, but incurred clerical wrath by proposing recognition of the new united (and anticlerical) kingdom of Italy.

O'Donnell also placed emphasis on an aggressive foreign policy and on refurbishing Spain's image abroad, hoping to encourage national unity. Spanish Filipino troops participated in the French conquest of Cochin China (southern Vietnam) beginning in 1858, and Spanish forces formed part of the international expedition to collect debts from Mexico in 1861. The Spanish navy was active off the coast of South America and ultimately involved in the minor naval "War of the Pacific" off the Peruvian coast in 1865 and the temporary "reannexation" of Santo Domingo. The grandest moment for O'Donnell's policy was the Hispano-Moroccan war of 1859–1860 which grew out of a minor border incident at Ceuta and resulted in a complete, if discreetly limited, Spanish victory—the only clear-cut victory for Spanish arms against a foreign foe in the nineteenth century.

O'Donnell's government failed because its sources of support were too heterogeneous to remain unified and because it was ultimately subjected to strong pressure from both left and right. The fulcrum was too weak to hold the weight; some of the leaders of the puritano elements refused to back O'Donnell's priorities, and after two or three years, personal differences became extreme. The court circle detested the Liberal Union, and the radical Progressives were unrelenting in their assaults, using press freedom to hasten destruction of the only effective government that had upheld press freedom. The royalist right emphasized pure privilege and the radical left pure doctrine; O'Donnell was ground between the upper and nether millstones.

Paralysis of the Isabeline Monarchy

In 1863–1864 a new prime minister, the Marqués de Miraflores, went through the motions of establishing a two-party compromise, but the ground had already cracked beneath him. If pure constitutionalism would not be permitted under O'Donnell, it would not function under a personal government. Narváez returned briefly in 1864-1865 but could offer only a holding action.

A parliamentary system cannot operate on the basis of a single party. This was the final weakness of O'Donnell's program. Unable to elicit a loyal opposition, he tried to unite all the main factions, but the coalition was too unwieldy and it splintered. In this sense the responsibility for the collapse of the Isabeline regime belonged to Isabel and the palace crowd. The parliamentary monarchy would never work unless the parliaments were allowed to represent most of the responsible interests in the country. The moderate Progressives had fully demonstrated their loyalty to the crown in 1854, but that had made next to no impression. So long as more than half of Spanish liberalism was permanently excluded from direct political power, there was no hope for more than a return to Fernandine despotism. Even the upper classes would not accept that; hence the absolute futility of the regime's policy in the 1860s.

By 1865 the die was cast. O'Donnell's last government came too late, for almost none of the Progressives were willing to go along with the government game. O'Donnell proposed once more a program of pure constitutionalism. He reestablished press freedom, carried through recognition of the new anticlerical Italian state, and reformed the electoral law, reducing by half the property qualification and extending the electorate to a total of approximately 420,000. This had no effect; it was met by the Madrid artillery sergeants' mutiny of San Gil in June 1866, the most subversive military movement in thirty years, for the officer-conspirators lost control of the movement and it became a rising of noncommisioned officers. The revolt was harshly suppressed and forty sergeants were shot.

Narváez then returned for the seventh and last time. As in 1864, he made brief conciliatory gestures, indicating willingness to work with a loyal opposition, but his reluctance to take broadly generous measures and the doctrinaire hostility of the left frustrated such intentions. He governed for a year and a half until his death in April 1868, O'Donnell dying in exile a few months before him. Narváez was the last leader capable of governing within the system, and his demise was followed by a form of political dictatorship under Luis González Brabo, who manipulated a handpicked parliament.

The Revolution of 1868

General disgust with the arbitrary government of the Isabeline regime might not have come to a head when it did, despite the death of Narváez, had it not been for the economic depression of 1866-1868.

This brought a collapse of the Barcelona banking system, a major trade decline, and severe budgetary problems. González Brabo was forced to cut spending, including the new naval program, and raise taxes. There was already much unemployment by 1867, and the highest wheat prices of the century, bringing new stirrings among the lower classes.

Successive minor military revolts had failed since 1864, but a victorious one was made possible by the union of the center and left opposition between 1866 and 1868. First the Progressives and Democrats made a pact in exile, then the more liberal of the Unionists joined them after the final crackdown by González Brabo. Their sole agreement was to depose a futile queen and let the structure of the new regime be determined by a constituent parliament based on universal male suffrage. The resulting revolt of September 1868 was the only one in which the navy played a significant role. Only a portion of the army actually defended the crown. After a pitched battle near Córdoba, the rebels victoriously entered Madrid, having accomplished Spain's "glorious" democratic revolt of the nineteenth century.

The leader of this first effort to establish a representative monarchy was Don Juan Prim, chief military hero of the Moroccan war, head of the Progressive party and the most popular public figure of his generation. Prim was the outstanding figure of nineteenth-century Spanish liberalism. The most tenacious, and the most skillful, of the military rebels of the age of pronunciamientos, he had by far the most public appeal and the greatest political talent and insight. Only Prim possessed the peculiar combination of firmness, vision, and political tact to lead a serious effort at implanting functional democratic constitutional monarchy.

In deference to rank and unity, the head of the provisional government was General Francisco Serrano, leader of the Liberal Unionists. Prim became prime minister only in 1869 after the new constitution was drawn up. Elections were held at the end of 1868 on the basis of universal suffrage for all males twenty-five years of age or over, swelling the suffrage lists at one fell swoop from the 418,000 voters of 1865 to more than 3,800,000 and making Spain for the second time in the century the country with the most democratic suffrage in the world. The elections were conducted with comparative freedom and order. Approximately 70 percent of the voters participated, producing a parliament of 130 Progressives, 90 Unionists, 70 Republicans, 45 Democrats, and 17 Carlists.

The constitution of 1869 established universal male suffrage, retained the monarchist form of government, granted the crown a suspensive veto and the right to dissolve parliament, created a bicameral legislature, retained official recognition of Catholicism as the religion of Spain and state support of the church, but for the first time in modern Spanish history guaranteed a vague toleration of other religions in public worship. Its preamble was based on that of the American constitution and it established a broad and comprehensive framework of civil liberties, including freedom of association (bringing the right to form trade unions) for the first time in Spanish history. Provincial assemblies and municipal councils were made elective, though they divided local government power with appointive provincial civil governors. It was a model document and, save for its silence on the issue of Cuban slavery, one of the two or three most advanced in the world at that time.

The Revolt in Cuba

Overthrow of the Isabeline regime was followed within one month by a major revolt in Cuba, the principal remaining Spanish colony in America. Cuba had been extremely quiet during the generation of Spanish American independence struggles before 1825. At that time it lacked a strong autonomous creole class, and the existence of a slave society discouraged radical political ideas among the local elite. Rise of sugar and tobacco production during the nineteenth century made the island much more important economically than it had ever been before, and gave it a leading place in Spanish commerce and in the tax system. By the 1860s there had developed considerable support in Cuba for reform, looking toward some type of autonomy and relief from Spanish tariffs. Negotiations on the latter issue had however been broken off in 1867, and taxes were raised.

The revolt that began in backward, semi-isolated southeast Cuba in October 1868 drew only scattered support in the island, in the main from a few middle class rebels, some poor peasants (*guajiros*), and numbers of runaway slaves. Prim was inclined to be conciliatory and would have favored tax relief and some form of partial autonomy, but the government's hand was forced by conservative landowning, slave-holding interests in Cuba. There had been considerable Spanish emigration to Cuba the generation before, and the immigrants were the basis for a large *españolista* sector in the Cuban towns that opposed concessions. The government embarked on a policy of military repression but found it almost impossible to come to grips with irregular forces in the mountainous and tangled countryside.

The Elective, Democratic Monarchy, 1869–1873

The new regime immediately began to fall prey to the same divisions that had ruined the Progressivist biennium of 1854–1856. During the 1860s there had developed to the left of the Democrats a Republican movement that opposed any form of monarchy and advocated extreme federalism, complete political democracy, and the broadest possible civil liberties. The Federal Republicans collaborated with Progressives and Unionists only in order to overthrow Isabel II, and then launched a direct political assault on the elective monarchy, even though the elections of 1868 were generally fair and some form of monarchy was the political preference of the great majority of Spaniards. The Federal Republicans emphasized anticlericalism, which was winning popularity among a certain section of the lower middle classes, and they advocated civilianism and were the first liberal party to reject appeals to military leaders for support. Opposition to the draft was one of their most popular planks among the lower classes in the cities. Their other great appeal was the demand to reduce or abolish the consumos. The principal following of the Federal Republicans was among the lower middle classes, and to some extent the lower classes, of the provincial towns of southern and eastern Spain. Their organizational infrastructure was built from the unemployed or semi-employed local intelligentsia eager for positions in local government.

Prim had hoped to be able to reduce the military draft, but the Cuban revolt made that impossible. The government had to face two major Republican revolts in 1869. One was occasioned by the decision to disband the newly formed popular militia, the Volunteers of Liberty, which had been granted a kind of political dole for its unemployed members. The second took the form of an organized Republican insurrection at the end of 1869 after the new monarchist constitution had been completed. The rebellion was strongest in Valencia and Zaragoza, but was suppressed by the army. Meanwhile, civic order was undermined further by the revival of large-scale banditry in the southern provinces.

By 1870 Prim had lost popularity with both the left and right. His main concern was to choose a new candidate for the throne who would make an effective constitutional monarch and provide political balance. Two of the leading candidates were Isabel's brother-in-law, the French Duc de Montpensier, and Don Amadeo, a younger son of the reigning Italian House of Savoy. Montpensier was supported by conservatives, while D. Amadeo was the candidate of anticlerical liberals. Prim was seeking a compromise center liberal candidate, and thought he had found one in a younger son of a collateral branch of the Hohenzollern dynasty. But before a secret Cortes election could be arranged, an administrative slipup let word of the proposal leak out. This roused French fears of a German king in Spain and precipitated the Franco-Prussian war. The Hohenzollern candidacy was withdrawn, and Prim accepted the liberal Italian prince as the best alternative. Over strong opposition, Don Amadeo was elected king by a margin of only one vote. Political factionalism had reached white heat, and D. Juan Prim, the only effective liberal leader Spain had yet seen, was struck down by shotgun-wielding assassins in the heart of Madrid on December 27, 1870, and died three days later. Prim's murderers were never apprehended, perhaps because they might have implicated others. The main evidence points to Republican radicals, possibly encouraged or assisted by conservative elements in an unholy alliance to be rid of the centrist Progressive leader.

The arrival of the new constitutional monarch coincided with the death of Prim. In 1871 Don Amadeo's government was supported by three main groups: the Unionists, henceforth called Conservatives, of Serrano, the Progressives, and the *cimbrio*, or moderate faction of the Democrats (the radical Democrats having gone over to the Republicans). The elections of 1871 were, like the preceding ones, comparatively honest and free of government pressure, returning a majority for the democratic monarchist coalition. Don Amadeo's first cabinet, led by Serrano, lasted only a little over six months, then succumbed to factionalism. Meanwhile the Progressives had split in two. The more practical and moderate followed Práxedes Mateo Sagasta, who favored continued collaboration with the Conservatives. The more doctrinaire and extreme under Manuel Ruiz Zorrilla formed a new Radical party, joined by the cimbrio Democrats. Ruiz Zorrilla gained the confidence of the crown and formed the next cabinet, but could not obtain parliamentary support and had to adjourn the Cortes. When it reopened three months later his government was brought down and was replaced by a new ministry under Sagasta.

The Sagasta cabinet rested to a considerable degree on the Conservatives and stood for a moderate, evolutionary policy of democratic constitutional monarchy. The Radicals insisted that Conservative influence could not be tolerated and that all proclerical elements must be excluded from government. New elections were held early in 1872 to try to find a more workable majority. The Sagasta ministry used a great deal of government pressure in certain provinces and was accused of creating *lázaros* (reviving the dead in order to use their names for false ballots). The Conservatives and *sagastinos* (or Constitutionalists) held a majority in the new Cortes, but revelation of the use of a two-million-peseta fund for unexplained political purposes, together with the Radicals' adoption of the tactic of *retraimiento* (withdrawal from parliament), forced the Sagasta ministry from power in May 1872. Serrano then formed a new government based on the nominal parliamentary majority but, faced by Carlist insurrection and left-wing disorders, insisted on the need to suspend constitutional guarantees temporarily.

Don Amadeo, a scrupulously conscientious constitutional ruler, refused this and granted his confidence to Ruiz Zorrilla, who returned to power and quickly held new elections. These were conducted fairly and honestly, but all the conservative elements abstained because the first Cortes of 1872 had been dissolved before completing the minimum four months specified by the constitution. The result was 54 percent abstention in the balloting of August 1872—the largest abstention yet in Spanish electoral history—and an overwhelming victory for the Radicals. They received 70 percent of the votes cast (though their share was only 32 percent of the nominal electorate) and a correspondingly heavy majority of the seats in the second Cortes of 1872.

Yet the Radicals' complete control of the new parliament was merely the prelude to their own downfall and that of the constitutional monarchy. They carried out a number of notable reforms, severely restricting the budget of the church and abolishing slavery in Puerto Rico, but the absence of any cooperation with moderates and conservatives left the government a prey to extremes. A major Carlist rebellion flared in the north, and the Federal Republicans came out briefly in revolt at El Ferrol. The final crisis of the regime developed after General Hidalgo de Quintana was named captain-general of the Basque region, center of the Carlist rising. Quintana had participated in the mutinous artillery rebellion in 1866, and appointment of a liberal officer with this background led to mass resignations by his former comrades of the artillery corps, whose standards he had betrayed. The conscientious Italian king found himself snubbed and hated by aristocratic society, beset by crippling political factionalism, harassed by Radicals and Republicans, faced with a continuing revolt in Cuba and a Carlist civil war in Spain, and then finally frustrated by the disobedience of the army and a military impasse after Ruiz Zorrilla made the decision to dissolve the artillery corps. Don Amadeo abdicated his seemingly hopeless Spanish throne in February 1873.

This crisis reopened the question of the regime. The Republicans were themselves split between *benévolos,* still willing to cooperate with the Radicals (who were still nominally monarchist), and the *intransigentes,* who insisted on the immediate establishment of a republic even if armed revolt were necessary to accomplish it. That was not required, for Ruiz Zorrilla was now discredited, leaving the

Radicals without a leader. After his resignation, dexterous maneuvering by a minority of pro-Republican Radicals and the benévolos resulted in a Cortes vote to immediately establish a parliamentary republic.

The First Republic, 1873–1874

The establishment of the Republic resulted from a flaunting of the democratic constitution, abstention by the conservatives, and the precipitous abdication of D. Amadeo. New elections were held by the Republican government in May 1873. These were the fourth in slightly more than two years, and amid general public alienation, only 40 percent of the electorate, perhaps the smallest proportion in all Spanish history, participated. Since even most of the Radicals abstained, the result was an all-Republican assembly. Yet the nominal Republican monopoly did not mean unity of spirit or purpose, for as Benito Pérez Galdós later wrote,

> the composition of the new chamber was astonishingly divided. The right was formed by various castes of *benévolos*; the left by *intransigentes* split into heterogeneous groups: federalists, pactists, organicists, simple autonomists or decentralizers, procollectivist federalists, and others who were motivated by the most extravagant ideas. The center was a rainbow composed of all the colors of the solar spectrum of republicanism.*

While a new constitution was being prepared, the reductio ad absurdum of Federalist localism began in the summer of 1873. Federalist city and provincial governments began to declare complete autonomy—in effect, independence—all over southern and eastern Spain. These were essentially localist political revolts by officeholding cliques, town radicals, and the local mob. Though a small Spanish affiliate of the Workingmen's International had been organized since 1868, there was little social revolt during these years. Save for freedom of association, protection of individual rights, and the elimination of consumos, the Federalists scarcely had any more of a social program than did the anticlerical Radicals. The only exception was in the small Levantine textile town of Alcoy, temporary site of the council of the Spanish Federation of the International, where the localist revolt turned into social revolution. Other incidents occurred in a few parts of the Andalusian countryside, where minifundists and rural proletarians staged comparatively bloodless *jacqueries* against landlords.

* *La I* República* (Los Episodios Nacionales) (Madrid, 1953), p. 87.

Government in Spain seemed to dissolve during the summer and autumn of 1873, while the Carlist threat gathered momentum in the Basque country. Three Republican presidents resigned within four months before Emilio Castelar assumed power in September 1873. The most moderate of the Republican leaders, he was essentially a constitutional democrat who had little faith in the Federalist norms. Castelar suspended constitutional guarantees and restored authority to the army, which then without delay put down most of the local revolts. Only the "canton" of Cartagena, which operated its own pirate navy in the west Mediterranean, held out a little longer. But the Federalists were infuriated with Castelar for using government and military authority to repress rebellion, and voted him out of office at the beginning of January 1874.

Restoration of the Bourbon Monarchy

At that point the captain general of Madrid intervened and closed down parliament. A coalition "national government" was formed which declared a unitary (i.e., centralized, nonfederal) Republic, but it developed into a veiled Conservative Republican military dictatorship under Serrano. By the end of 1874 Spain had reached the point of political exhaustion. Serrano's unitary Republic, without a stable base, had no future. At the end of 1874 it was overthrown by a military revolt aimed at the return of constitutional monarchy under the legitimist heir, the twenty-year-old D. Alfonso, son of Isabel II. The political wheel had turned full circle, but the new leader of the moderate constitutional monarchists, Antonio Cánovas del Castillo, had made careful plans to give the restored monarchy a broader base than that of the defunct Isabeline regime.

The Second Carlist War, 1869/1872-1876

Carlism, which had never died in the foral regions and hill country of the northeast, was revived by the overthrow of the Bourbon monarchy, by anticlerical excesses in some parts of the country during 1869, and by the 1869 constitution that granted religious freedom, civil marriage, and termination of Catholic moral control of public education. For three years the new Carlist revolt sputtered and was nearly extinguished, but the exclusion of Carlist candidates by Sagasta from the first elections of 1872 sparked a second revolt, which also ended in failure.

The real opportunity for a Carlist resurgence was provided by the advent of an anticlerical republic which proposed separation of church and state and in many places was accompanied by assaults on church people and property. The revolt gathered momentum during 1873, and by the beginning of 1874 the Carlists had organized a local government in the Basque country and Navarre which collected taxes and operated a postal system. The current pretender, D. Carlos "VII," was the most dynamic and attractive leader that the dynasty produced, and took personal command in the field. Moreover, Carlism began to develop a coherent ideology, based on advocacy of a corporative form of Cortes organization and a degree of administrative decentralization, on behalf of the foral regions that supported the movement. It received some new blood near the top by the adherence of conservative Catholic elements and remnants of ultraconservative Moderates who had backed Isabel II.

By the 1870s, however, Carlism seemed too anachronistic even for most Spanish conservatives. The movement rallied almost no support outside of the northeast. Its only organized base was Navarre and the Basque country, and in most of rural Catalonia it was limited to local guerrilla bands. Though the Carlist field regiments won several impressive victories over the regular Spanish army in 1873–1874, the Carlists could not develop a truly national movement as they had seemed on the verge of doing in the 1830s. Restoration of the Bourbon monarchy deprived them of much potential conservative support, and their military nucleus in the Basque country was worn down steadily throughout 1875–1876. The localized revolt in southeastern Cuba suffered the same process of attrition two years later, bringing to an end the long, slow Ten Years' War (1868–1878) in the sugar island.

The Frustration of Spanish Liberalism

The first half-century and more of Spanish liberalism was a period of repeated frustration. In a broad sense, persistent political breakdown can be explained by the extreme dissidence among the Spanish elite, unable to achieve a functional consensus on political structure. More concretely, a number of factors should be kept in mind when trying to account for the failures of the nineteenth century:

1. The precipitation of liberal political structure in Spain. Liberal leadership seized the initiative to introduce advanced, protodemocratic systems in Spain on various occasions (1812, 1820, 1836–1837, 1854, 1868–1869) when Spanish culture and society had not even achieved the level of other societies still functioning under more

restrictive systems. In no other west European country were such advanced forms introduced at such relatively early stages of social and cultural development.

2. The low caliber of Spanish monarchs throughout most of this period. It is almost impossible to make constitutional monarchy work without a constitutional monarch. Fernando VII did everything within his power to frustrate political change. His daughter Isabel II was only slightly better, more often than not subverting the representative process. By contrast, D. Amadeo was a model constitutional ruler, but labored under abnormally severe handicaps.

3. The chronological lag in carrying out the disamortizing agrarian property revolution, compared with the northwest European countries and France. A difficult phase of socio-economic and institutional development was thus added to the difficulty of introducing parliamentary government.

4. The extent and nature of middle-class liberalism. Not only were the Spanish middle classes proportionately smaller than those of France and northwest Europe, but they were less active, less educated, and showed less initiative and motivation overall. The proportion of those who were really effective was thus even smaller.

5. The weakness of the economic base of middle class reformism. Not only was industrialization barely beginning, but the technological renovation of agriculture, begun in the most advanced countries in the eighteenth century, had in Spain started only in Catalonia.

6. The persistence of regionalism in Spain. Whereas regionalism had been largely overcome in France by the end of the eighteenth century and in Britain before that, it continued in Spain, a country with natural barriers, poor transportation, and an economic and cultural lag.

7. The increasing geographic imbalance in Spanish economic, social, and cultural development. Spain's development continued to be concentrated along the peripheries, and provided relatively scant stimulus to national integration.

8. The failure to achieve a modus vivendi with the church, a failure for which the religious and the anticlerical were about equally responsible. Though liberal churchmen helped take the lead in introducing liberalism, they were not supported by most of the church, which swung over to a strongly antiliberal position after assaults by anticlerical radicals. The church refused to concede complete freedom of worship until 1869, and often rendered compromise difficult.

9. Destructive effects of the radical intelligentsia, cesantes (ex-officeholders), and hangers-on in the provincial capitals, who persisted in demanding unrealistic changes and, rejecting orderly constitutionalism, never hesitated to call out the mob to serve their ends. They

persistently subverted parliamentary liberalism, from the exaltados of the first triennium, through the progresistas puros, to the absurdities of Federal Republicanism.

10. The failure to develop education and other acculturative facilities more rapidly. Though the Moderates made progress in this regard, it did not compare favorably with other countries at similar stages.

11. The continued burden of empire, which added to the problems of the democratic monarchy, making it more difficult to conciliate radical opinion.

The Social Basis of Politics

The liberal regime in Spain was not based primarily on an expanding commercial and industrial bourgeoisie, as in northwestern Europe, but on a new upper-middle-class oligarchy of large landowners. As late as the 1870s there was very little in the way of a genuine Spanish bourgeoisie of the entrepreneurial, industrial variety. Those elements that did exist were confined to Catalonia and a few other peripheral regions and they largely avoided politics.

In general, the mercantile classes of the coastal cities were more inclined toward progressivism than were financiers and industrialists. This more liberal sector of the middle-middle and upper-middle classes was particularly enthusiastic about the revolt of 1854, but twenty years later, after the excesses of 1869–1874, they had become more conservative. The politically active elite under the Isabeline regime consisted mainly of the court circle, the army leaders and the front rank of parliamentary politicians, a select group of Madrid bureaucrats, and the large landowners.

Opportunity for participation in the electoral process varied greatly with the political changes of these decades, as indicated by the variations in the suffrage shown in table 5. Before 1845, the Spanish suffrage was distinctly more liberal than that of France under the July Monarchy, and much more so than was conceivable for any other country at Spain's stage of development. Under the Moderates, the suffrage was cut back sharply. By the early 1860s Spain had the most restricted suffrage in western Europe. O'Donnell's reform in 1865 raised it only a hair's breadth above Italy and Belgium, where 2.3 and 2.1 percent of the population, respectively, were enfranchised.

The Spanish electorate of the nineteenth century was basically an electorate of large landowners. Between 1836 and 1867 landowners made up between 84 and 95 percent of all voters. The urban middle classes not only enjoyed less representation, they also participated

Table 5.   Variations in the Spanish Suffrage, 1836-1867

Date	Eligible voters	Percent of population	Percent of eligible voters casting ballots
July 1836	65,067	.52	69.74
1837	257,984	2.09	55.43
1839	342,559	2.78	63.66
1840	423,787	3.44	75.85
1846	97,100	.79	66.47
1850	121,770	1.11	67.64
1851	122,700	1.11	70.34
1857	157,725	1.01	58.13
1858	157,931	1.02	69.33
1863	179,413	1.14	62.66
1864	166,291	1.06	61.70
1865	418,271	2.67	53.36
1867	396,863	2.38	51.75

Source: Diego Sevilla Andrés, *Historia política de España (1800-1967)*. (Madrid, 1968), p. 234.

less regularly in politics. The level of participation among the enfranchised elite was lower in Madrid, Barcelona, Valencia, and the other three Catalan provinces than nationally; the highest degree of involvement was found in the Andalusian provinces and in some of the other rural provinces of central and northern Spain. The pattern changed during the Progressivist biennium of 1854-1856, but after its failure the urban elite tended to withdraw from politics once more.

Under the Isabeline regime, about 5 percent of those on the suffrage lists were capacidades—intellectuals and professional men lacking the financial qualifications to vote but deemed worthy because of their education or training. O'Donnell increased this proportion to nearly 15 percent. Yet the capacidades always had a higher abstention rate than the *contribuyentes,* indicating either an aversion to politics or a more specific disgust with the Isabeline regime.

An average of about 5 percent of the population were eligible to vote for municipal councilmen—twice as many as could vote in national elections—but in the years 1860-1866 voter participation averaged only 43 percent. This may have been due to a general feeling that no matter what, local affairs would be managed by the minister of the interior and his appointees as provincial jefes políticos and mayors, in conjunction with the chief established local politicians or *caciques.*

Demography and Social Structure

Population increase was rapid during the middle decades of the nineteenth century:

1833	12,286,000
1860	15,645,000
1877	16,622,000

This increase of slightly more than one-third in forty-five years was the most rapid in Spanish history up to that time, both proportionately and absolutely. During the first half of the century Spain's population growth was 10 percent greater than the European average. Before 1860 there was little emigration, for the traditional outlets in Spanish America seemed less attractive during the first two generations after independence. Toward the end of this period, however, there was noticeable Andalusian emigration to French Algeria. The last major afflictions of severe hunger that could be blamed on poor credit and food transportation occurred in 1857 and 1867–1868, and the last major epidemics, in the form of cholera, ravaged the country in 1833–1835, 1853–1856, and in 1865, when 237,000 died within six months. Though the marriage rate in Spanish society was not particularly high, the birth rate in the 1860s was approximately 39 per 1,000, one of the highest in Europe, and fell very little during the latter part of the century. In 1910 it stood at 33. Only in Catalonia was there a significant diminution of the birth rate; there it fell to 27 at the end of the century and continued to drop. The highest birth rate was in the Canaries.

After 1860, however, Spain fell considerably behind the general European rate of population expansion, in part because of a failure to reduce mortality. General hygienic conditions in Spain remained rather poor. As late as 1900 the death rate stood at 30, compared with a central and west European average of 18.

The pattern of distribution of population set in the eighteenth century continued. Catalonia's percentage of Spain's total had been 8.1 in 1797, rising to 10.5 by 1857 (and later stood at 11.6 in 1950). The populations of most of the other peripheral areas remained proportionately about the same. The major losers were Aragón, Navarre, and León–Old Castile. Over a 150-year period, Old Castile's share of the Spanish population declined from 9 percent in 1800 to 5.8 percent in 1950.

The first reasonably accurate census to divide Spanish society into social and economic categories was taken in 1860 and showed the following numbers for occupational categories:

Rural laborers	2,354,000
Landowners of all categories	1,466,000
Servants (male and female)	818,000
Artisans	665,000
Small businessmen (20 percent of them women)	333,000
Factory workers (1/3 of them women)	150,000
Middle class professional men	100,000
White collar employees	70,000
Clergy	63,000
Factory owners (including small producers)	13,000
Miners	23,000

At the beginning of the century, the lower classes in the towns and cities were mainly artisans and servants. Only in Barcelona did an industrial working class begin to take shape, and even then a direct breakthrough into political life was made only partially during the democratic quinquennium of 1869-1874. The urban lower classes were not, however, completely inactive in public affairs, for mobs were persistently aroused by exaltados and Progressives, Democrats and Federalists, from 1820 on. Yet the lower classes were only sporadically mobilized and then mostly for middle-class goals: constitutional liberalization and broadening of the suffrage. Before 1873 their only class interests were opposition to the draft and consumos, and in Barcelona, the struggle for freedom of organization. Random urban violence can be traced to some extent to the existence of a significant stratum of underemployed lumpen, unskilled or unemployable ex-peasants, not integrated into the urban economy and society and never mobilized for systematic political action.

Economic Development

The principal economic change in Spain during the middle years of the nineteenth century was the disamortization. Sale of church lands had begun under Carlos IV in 1798, but the main period of sales was 1836-1845. By 1845 58 percent of church lands had been sold, and most of the remainder were disposed of in the two decades that followed. The sale of common lands and the territories of the orders, which began in 1855, was carried on rapidly during the next decade but continued until the end of the century. Whereas nearly all church lands were turned over to private ownership, a large minority of common and municipal lands were retained by the local institutions. Church land placed on the market amounted altogether to at least 20 percent of the arable land in Spain, to which the common lands added at least 5 percent, plus a sizable amount of waste and forest land. Thus in the space of two generations, some four million hectares of land were placed on the market, and their new owners broadened the base of the landowning oligarchy of southern, central, and north-west Spain, helping to form the new interest group that served as the main fulcrum of Spanish politics for the remainder of the century.

In many parts of León and Old Castile the commons were retained and in some districts were still as much as two-thirds of the land. In Galicia and Catalonia commons had never been important, but their sales were felt keenly in much of the center and south and in Aragón, ruining peasants who were living a marginal existence and had been partly sustained by their use. Loss of these lands also greatly reduced local government resources for education and social services. Whereas disentailment and transfer of church lands might in the abstract—disregarding the way it was done and the manner of estab-lishing new title—be considered socially and economically progres-sive, the effect of the sale of common lands in regions where such losses were most severe was to strip society of its framework in the very areas where its structure was weakest. In much of the north and center, however, reaching as far south as parts of La Mancha, the post-1855 disamortization of common and corporate lands, like the earlier sale of church lands, was of broader benefit to medium- and smallholders. In those areas it also provided greater opportunity for stable family-rental farms. Almost all the new land in Navarre, for example, went to the peasantry, so that there, liberal land legislation reinforced the balance and stability of a traditional, antiliberal peas-ant society. Meanwhile in many regions the land of smallholders was being steadily subdivided into ever smaller units, for the new nine-teenth-century Spanish civil code, like that of France, encouraged equal subdivision among heirs.

Between 1800 and 1860 the area under cultivation in Spain in-creased greatly, from 8,500,000 to 13,000,000 hectares. Whereas less than 3,000,000 hectares of grain were cultivated at the beginning of the century, more than 5,000,000 were sown in 1860. This extension was prompted in part by the rapid growth of population, as during the preceding century, but was also due to the large acquisitions of land by semibourgeois proprietors, eager to put their new property to market use by cultivating the more marginal strips of soil. Since most of the new land sown was of inferior quality, the introduction of a few modest improvements in farming technique did not prevent the aver-age productivity of grain per hectare from declining approximately 10 percent during the first half of the nineteenth century. Prices also declined somewhat because of the increase in absolute volume of production. Increased output made it possible for Spain to export grain in twenty-five of the thirty-two years between 1849 and 1881. A change occurred after about 1860, when more and more marginal land was retired. Between 1860 and 1880 approximately 1,500,000 hectares were taken out of wheat cultivation, but this period also saw more important improvements in technique. Consequently productivity rose somewhat, as for other reasons did prices.

There was a great increase in Spanish vineyards during the nineteenth century; the area devoted to grapes expanded from 400,000 hectares in 1800 to nearly 1,500,000 hectares by 1900. Moreover between 1800 and 1860, productivity per hectare doubled. Overall, Spanish grape and wine production increased six and a half fold during the course of the nineteenth century.

The only really important industrial development during the mid-century period was the expansion of Catalan textile production, particularly in cottons, which carried out the conversion to steam power after 1845. A fourfold increase in Catalan cotton goods output took place during the ten years 1839-1849. Production of woolens increased considerably in the 1850s. Henceforth Catalan industrialists would be among the wealthiest, though not necessarily among the most politically influential, people in Spain.

Corporate investment and concentration of industrial capital first began to reach notable dimensions after the Spanish company acts of 1848 and 1856 simplified procedures and established limited liability. Corporate investment inside Spain tripled between 1857 and 1865. The concentration of capital in the Catalan textile industry reduced the number of producing firms from 4,500 in 1850 to 3,600 in 1860.

The mining industry also began to develop from mid-century, mostly on the basis of concessions to foreign enterprise, since the initiative, skill, and capital for modern mining was lacking in Spain. The chief fields were copper at the Río Tinto mines in Andalusia, zinc in Asturias, and lead in Cartagena. Only the iron ore of Vizcaya and the nascent coal mines of Asturias remained largely under domestic control.

One of the main achievements of the Isabeline period was construction of a national transportation system. Railroad contracts were a major object of politico-financial manipulation in Madrid, and the key period of development was the five years 1855-1860. For the next decade and after, Spain achieved one of the highest per capita rates of railroad construction in the world. By 1868 5,000 kilometers of track had been laid. The basic road network expanded from 9,500 to 18,000 kilometers under the Isabeline regime (and doubled again during the remainder of the century, reaching 41,500 kilometers by 1908). It was also improved slightly in quality and a considerable number of durable stone bridges were built, but many of the existing roads were so

Table 6. *Mineral Exports, 1850–1875*

Year	Tons
1850	3,908
1855	16,224
1860	107,130
1865	144,127
1866	136,460
1867	215,998
1868	264,386
1869	203,017
1870	509,020
1871	734,783
1872	1,151,103
1873	1,154,491
1874	1,130,094
1875	784,006

Source: N. Sánchez Albornoz, *España hace un siglo* (Madrid, 1968), p. 139.

poor and geographical barriers so formidable that parts of the country were still left poorly connected.

In the economic thinking of the time, railroad building was considered the key to general economic development, the vital stimulus that would inject the capital and opportunity for development. Major railroad building accompanied, if it did not exactly prompt, a period of rapid economic development in England, France, Germany, and the United States, and this was also true at the end of the century in Russia. In Spain, as in Portugal under the program of *fontismo* (see p. 536), railroad building had much less effect in stimulating economic growth, and its effect was also somewhat diminished during the following generation in Italy.

The basic barriers of distance and terrain that have always hampered communication in the peninsula made railroad development more difficult and expensive than in most countries. The railroads could not stimulate an almost nonexistent modern metallurgy; nearly all rails had to be imported. Despite low labor and operating costs, it long proved difficult to move traffic and passengers at a profit: there was not enough of either to move, and distances between major centers were great.

Railroad building could have a broad stimulative effect only when it was part of a general pattern of complementary development in several key sectors of the economy. This was not the case in Spain, even though the period 1854–1866 was one of modestly sustained growth. Investment in Spanish industry suddenly dropped off after

1857, despite the fact that sales and profits in the stronger enterprises remained rather high. The reasons for this may be in part an entrepreneurial mystery, but alternative investments probably had much to do with it. Nearly 40 percent of the capital for railway construction was raised in Spain, and this presumably diverted investment from other industries. The economic structure was still too weak to provide the complementary factors of development necessary to sustain major growth. Heavy investment in one area alone thus achieved relatively little in the short run.

The two leading fields of Spanish investment were neither industry nor railroads but land and the government debt. The state budget increased 70 percent between 1855 and 1860 and doubled during the decade 1856-1865. The main item was a huge increase in military expenditures to support O'Donnell's neo-imperialist foreign policy. The outlay on the army and navy increased more than 115 percent between 1857 and 1860. State subsidies to railroads came a very poor second to the military. Interest payments on the national debt rose from 89,000,000 pesetas in 1860 to 328,000,000 in 1870. To make matters worse, the disorder of public finance, coupled with the government's tendency to default on foreign bonds, resulted in the closing of the London (1851) and Paris (1861) stock exchanges to standard long-term Spanish loans.

The main source of foreign capital throughout this period was France, 35 percent of whose mid-nineteenth-century foreign investment went to Spain. French interests were particularly important in mining, railroads, the founding of new joint-stock corporations (save in Catalonia), and funding the national debt through short-term loans at steep interest rates. French engineers and skilled workmen played a major role in developing railroads and mining.

Indeed, the Isabeline regime rather than the eighteenth century was probably the high point of *afrancesamiento* in Spain. French political and economic ideas accompanied the intensified aping of French styles and culture and a snobbish disdain among many upper-class Spaniards for Spanish styles, mores, and even physical appearance. The attitude of the Isabeline elite, like that of France under the July Monarchy and the Second Empire, was that economic development was inconsonant with full political liberty and would more than compensate for its absence.

The Bank of Spain, with a monopoly of monetary issue, was established by the Moderates in 1847/56 as an institution of private shareholders. Private banks, centered in Madrid, began to develop in the 1850s but did poorly and made little headway. The first regular Spanish stock exchange was set up at Madrid in 1831. A second was later established at Barcelona and, after 1890, a third in Bilbao. The first full-scale modern stock-market crash was that at Barcelona in 1866, caused by overspeculation and some faulty political manipulations. It marked the beginning of the brief economic decline of 1866-1868.

Foreign trade increased considerably after mid-century, doubling between 1852 and 1862. It doubled again between 1870 and 1897, after which it temporarily fell off. At mid-century the Spanish merchant fleet had begun to reach respectable dimensions and showed considerable initiative in the introduction of steam-powered vessels, but after 1870 foreign competition became too severe and the fleet went into a rather sharp decline.

As a basically agrarian system, the Spanish economy remained in semicolonial status vis-a-vis foreign finance and commerce throughout the nineteenth century. Of the forty years 1860-1900 the trade balance was favorable for only eleven. The difference was made up by foreign investment, a growing national debt, money remittances from abroad by the increasing number of Spanish emigrants after 1860, and sale of part of the considerable stock of gold and silver bullion that was still in the country.

In Spain, as elsewhere, the main economic issue in politics during the nineteenth century was the tariff. The government of Fernando VII had established a fairly strong protective tariff in 1825. The Progressives under Espartero instituted a new tariff in 1841 that was much more precise as well as lower, with rates ranging from 15 to 50 percent compared with the 50 to 200 percent norms of the Fernandine tariff. Even under the Progressives, however, certain types of competing goods were excluded. The Isabeline regime was dominated by large landed interests who wanted cheap industrial goods and low reciprocal duties for their agrarian exports. Hence the 1849 tariff of the Moderates was lower, with no exclusions, which increased the pressure on nascent Spanish industry. Catalan producers organized major protests. Despite this, when the Progressives returned to power with a free-trade ideology the new tariff of 1869 (introduced by a Progressive Catalan finance minister, Laureano Figuerola) set the lowest Spanish rates of the century and came close to free trade. During the next four years the internal market expanded and Spanish exports increased, thanks to generally favorable conditions. The cycle was completed, however, by the Bourbon restoration, which returned to a fairly strong protective tariff in 1875.

Despite the emphasis in Madrid on money-making under the Isabeline regime, there was no Spanish Friedrich List and never any clear concept of integrated national economic modernization. Government resources were not placed behind any major efforts at national development, but were used to support established agrarian interests and provide opportunity for special financial groups backed by foreign capital. Since critical analysis was wanting, it was assumed that sufficient injections of credit would naturally produce expansion. The main overseas resource, Cuba, was not fully opened for free entry of Spanish grain and textiles until the very last years of the Isabeline regime.

As of 1875, Spain had still not begun to develop a real industrial platform, and its economic growth rate was well below that of the industrializing countries. The distance between the Spanish economy and those of the northwest European countries was probably proportionately greater in 1875 than in 1845.

Cultural Change

Educational development was one of the most pressing needs of nineteenth-century Spanish society. The Isabeline regime established a national educational system for the first time in the country's history, but did not commit the money and energy to build it. Some of the old church and village schools were actually eliminated. Though new public schools were opened in many towns, they made only limited progress. Literacy doubled between 1840 and 1860 but only reached the level of 25 percent. Very little progress was made in higher education, despite the attempt, with the Moyano law of 1857, to coordinate the entire university system under state aegis. French cultural influence here was strong, also, and many Spanish university courses were based on poor translations of French textbooks and ideas.

Spanish literature of the first half of the nineteenth century was absolutely second rate. Though romanticism did not dominate Spanish literature until the 1830s, its themes persisted past mid-century,

Table 7.   *Educational Development, 1803-1860*

Year	Percent of literacy	Number of schools	Pupils
1803	5.96	11,553	400,000
1841	9.21	15,805	653,738
1860	19.27	22,753	1,000,974

Source: Sánchez Agesta, *Historia del constitucionalismo español,* pp. 465-66.
Note: Though these are the most reliable literacy figures for the period, they are apparently based on the percentage of literacy for the entire population. The figures for adult literacy would probably be at least 5 percent higher.

along with *costumbrismo*—novels, stories, and sketches devoted to capturing the distinctive manners and mores of the regions of Spain. Most of the new reading public, on the other hand, sought more escapist literature, which increased greatly in volume after mid-century. There were some examples of moralistic realism—the comedies of Manuel Bretón de los Herreros, the vignettes of Ramón de Mesonero Romanos, or some of the *costumbrista* novels of "Fernán Caballero"—but none of it equaled the criticism in Mariano José de Larra's essays and sketches of the 1830s. Theaters in the larger towns were well attended, though the theatrical writing was inferior. The zarzuela, the native Spanish form of operetta, was also developed during the middle of the century.

The rise of the periodical press began in the 1830s. Its centers were Madrid and Barcelona, though in the 1850s some key provincial newspapers were founded that outlasted the leading organs of the metropolises. The basis of journalism was the sectarian political newspaper, which pullulated on the most marginal financing. During the 1850s in Madrid there were nine Moderate and conservative newspapers, six representing the Liberal Union, three the Progressives, and two the Democrats.

The only new Spanish philosophical school of the century was a domestic variant of Krausism, the transplantation and reformulation of the ideas of Karl C. F. Krause, an obscure Austrian idealist philosopher. Julián Sanz del Río, professor of philosophy at the University of Madrid, disseminated his interpretation of Krause's ideas through the newly centralized university system. Krausian idealism in Spain meant a vague pantheism and a creed of tolerance, education, free inquiry, physical and artistic training, religious skepticism, the blossoming of innate natural harmony, and the development of a rounded personality. Though the Krausists strove to avoid conflict they clashed directly with Spanish Catholic culture, and in 1867 the Krausist professors were temporarily expelled from their chairs in Madrid. Restored in 1868, they advanced the chief intellectual rationale for the anticlericalism of the democratic interlude. The principal leader of Spanish Krausism was Francisco Giner de los Ríos, a charismatic, fatherly little pedagogue who trained a new generation of independent secular teachers and scholars. One of his primary goals was the elimination of Catholic influence in education. The gentle, simplistic teachings of Krausism exerted considerable appeal in an environment where formal intellectual culture was weak and students were seeking new cultural norms.

During the mid-nineteenth century Spanish science was almost nonexistent. The work of the universities in the sciences was backward in the extreme; rather than making up ground, more was lost.

The only achievement in applied science worthy of note was the "Ictíneo" of the Barcelona inventor Narciso Monturiol, an experimental submarine developed in the 1860s.

In popular spectacles the nineteenth and early twentieth centuries were the golden age of the *corrida de toros*. The first modern bullfight rings had been built in Madrid (1754) and Zaragoza (1764) and many new ones were added in the early nineteenth century. By 1886 the provincial town of Murcia had one that seated 18,000. Though bullfights were temporarily suppressed from 1805 to 1807, their major development came after 1830, and modern bullfighting was at its height between 1875 and 1950. Yet bullfighting was never unopposed. Progressivist elements were quick to mount strong criticism of the supposed moral effects of the spectacle, and complaints were constant down to 1936.

The middle decades of the nineteenth century saw the full establishment of the myth of romantic Spain, fixed in foreign literature especially by Prosper Mérimée's novel *Carmen* (1846). This idea, as we have seen, was an essentially esthetic one built around exotic, unmodernized mores—gypsy dancers, *bandoleros,* music, passion, and honor, the *chiaroscuro* of Andalusian exoticism. Such images might have little or nothing to do with the Spain that was slowly developing in Madrid, the north, and the east, but they set the vogue in foreign ideas of a country reduced in imagination essentially to the Andalusian and the gypsy.

The domestic equivalent was the spread of Andalusian gypsy flamenco music, so different from northern Spanish folk music, that first gained favor among the upper classes at the end of the eighteenth century. The high point in domestic (as distinct from tourist) flamenco was reached in the late nineteenth century, which also witnessed the development of modern stylized Spanish dance, or *ballet español.*

The Crisis of Spanish Catholicism

Spanish Catholicism suffered severely from the onset of liberalism, though at first there was little in the way of a spiritual or philosophical assault on the church. The church suffered economically when it lost nearly all of its landed property. It also suffered spiritually and professionally. The number of religious vocations declined steadily during the eighteenth century, and after the delayed, confused impact of liberal political and social ideas, they declined even more drastically during the first half of the nineteenth century. As noted earlier, it has been estimated that as many as one-third of the clergy renounced their vows between 1800 and 1840. The monastic orders

were reduced by legislation and confiscation. By 1860, in a population of 15,645,000, there were only 63,000 religious, proportionately
less than one-sixth as many as in the seventeenth century. There was
only 1 priest for every 300 inhabitants, and only 1,683 monks in the
entire country (but approximately 19,000 nuns).

Early-nineteenth-century Spanish liberalism was not for the most
part anti-Catholic but merely moderately anti-clerical. Nearly all the
early liberals were believers. After having enriched themselves by
expropriation of church land, the liberal elite was eager to effect a
rapprochement with religion. The Moderates strove to reach a new
modus vivendi, and the Isabeline regime ultimately became rather
proclerical (the court circle extremely so). The hold of the Catholic
moral imagination on the minds of the great mass of Spaniards was
still strong, even among the unchurched. Early democratic and radical demands in Spain were not infrequently couched in terms of the
morality of Jesus and the gospels, while opposing Catholic ecclesiasti-
cism.*

The only Catholic thinker worthy of note in the early nineteenth
century was the Catalan priest Jaime Balmes (1810–1840). Balmes
hoped to modernize Catholic philosophy, introduce social reform to
re-Christianize society, and reconcile the two branches of the dynasty.
He wrote several basic popular works of Catholic philosophy. The
principal, almost the only, exemplar of evangelical work among the
unchurched lower classes was another Catalan priest, Antonio María
Claret.

The second quarter of the century made it clear that in the larger
cities all over Spain, and in large parts of the southern countryside,
the lower classes were living outside the direct social and spiritual
network of the church. Some of these areas had always been poorly
endowed with religious services, and the effects of the disamortization
reduced church work even more. The de-Christianization of the working classes—a category in which the peasant farmers of north and
north-central Spain should not in this sense be included—progressed
steadily during the remainder of the century. On the other hand,
direct philosophical assaults on Catholic religion itself became significant only in 1869.

By that time the nadir of the Catholic decline, reached between

* Enrique O'Donnell, brother of the Liberal Union leader, commented: "Ask our
absolutists about the basis of their principles, and they will not say thirty words
without mixing in religion and divinity thirty times. Inquire of our democrats and you
will hear them speak only of Jesus and the Gospel. Neither group knows how to act
politically without dressing up as monks." *La democracia española* (Madrid, 1858), p.
13.

1835 and 1860, had passed. From about 1860 a slow resurgence of Spanish Catholicism began, first with a revival of Catholic piety among the upper and upper-middle classes. Significantly more respect was shown for the Carlist clergy by government forces in the mid-1870s than in the 1830s. The Catholic revival among the upper classes continued during the 1880s and 1890s with liturgical and educational reform and the expansion of church education. The result, however, was a religious split in society between the Catholic upper classes and stable peasantry on the one hand, and an increasingly radical anti-Catholic intelligentsia and de-Christianized working class on the other.

Foreign Affairs

Internationally, Spain during the nineteenth century was in very much the same situation as Holland and Portugal—a comparatively weak country still possessing far-flung and important overseas domains. In addition to Cuba and Puerto Rico, Spain retained the African presidios, the Philippines, and three chains of islands in the west Pacific (the Carolines, Marianas, and Palaus). During most of this period, Spanish foreign policy was absolutely static and defensive, seeking only to retain the overseas possessions.

In the 1840s the primary foreign influence on Spain was that of France, whose July Monarchy backed the Moderates against the British-supported Progressives, and pressured Spanish leaders into the disastrous marriage of Isabel with the dismal Francisco de Asís—a match that had destructive consequences for the Spanish polity—to prevent the possibility of her marrying a British-connected German prince. The Spanish government itself intervened once in Portuguese affairs for the same political ends: a Spanish military expedition in 1847 helped put down a progessivist revolt in Porto, opening the way for the return of the Chartists (the Portuguese equivalent of the Moderates). French policy supported Spain fully, while the British were inclined to back the other side in Portugal.

The stability of Narváez's government in 1848 marked a kind of coming-of-age for nineteenth-century Spain in the concert of nations. Narváez even managed to expel the British ambassador for meddling in internal politics, and relations with Britain were not regularized until 1850. The Moderate regime then enjoyed very friendly relations with the French Second Empire, which tried to give some support to Spanish interests just as it did to Italian nationalism, on the theory of fostering amity among the Latin powers and a kind of Romance-speaking bloc. The Spanish expedition of 5,000 troops to Rome on behalf of the papacy in 1849 was in support of a French initiative.

The Hispanic version of the national unification drives of the period 1848–1870 was the idea of Iberian union between Spain and Portugal, backed up by the peninsular railway construction of the 1850s. The ideal of Spanish and Portuguese union did not have deep roots in either country but received strong support from some groups, particularly the Progressives. It was usually associated with the goal of a dynastic union, first seriously broached in the 1840s when Isabel was married, then again after 1868. The Federalists hoped ultimately to include Portugal in a broad peninsular federation, but the ideal of Iberian union faded after 1874, partly because it had been supported most strongly by the more radical and was viewed with suspicion by conservatives as a revolutionist's scheme.

Spanish political leaders continued to be reluctant to concede the independence of Spanish America. That of Mexico was officially recognized in 1836, but thirty years were required before the same recognition was given to all the new states. Reform in Cuba was persistently ignored, and after 1837 the Antilles were denied further representation in the Madrid Cortes. Spain's defensive policy, virtually restricted to the peninsula, changed only once during the period, and that was during O'Donnell's long ministry, which endeavored to foster unity and stability by an active, not to say aggressive, foreign policy. The high point of this orientation was the Moroccan war of 1859–1860, in the settlement of which Spain was granted titular possession of the territory of Ifni, along the southwestern Atlantic coast of Morocco. Between 1858 and 1863 small Spanish forces, mainly Filipino, served in Indochina in support of the French occupation and conquest. In 1861 the O'Donnell government accepted a request from the nominal president of strife-torn Santo Domingo to re-extend Spanish sovereignty over that area. This infelicitous effort was officially canceled by Narváez in 1865 after four years of frustration and limited military occupation. The fourth incident was the so-called War of the Pacific off the western coast of South America between 1862 and 1866, a series of absurd, intrinsically unimportant naval encounters mistakenly calculated to enhance Spanish prestige.

The advent of the Republic in 1873 was received with great hostility by other governments. Only the United States and Switzerland granted recognition to the new Spanish regime, and the restoration of the monarchy in 1875 was accepted abroad with a sense of relief.

21

The Restored Constitutional
Monarchy, 1875-1899

The reorganization of the Spanish polity in 1875-1876 was largely the work of one man, Antonio Cánovas del Castillo, who headed the regency council brought to power by military coup. Cánovas was a professional politician as well as a noted amateur historian. His political career and thinking had been formed in good measure by helping to develop O'Donnell's Liberal Union, and his goal was to establish a workable constitutional monarchy, the bases for which he conceived to be a responsible constitutional crown and a parliament capable of genuine authority. This would require a liberalization of the Isabeline system, which had failed because the crown was capricious and authoritarian and the political system too narrow and exclusive.

The restoration of constitutional monarchy was assisted by the political exhaustion of the country in 1875. Republicanism was discredited and moderate opinion was willing to accept a tolerant monarchist regime, abetting the legal institutionalization of the new government. Cánovas had, however, opposed the monarchist coup by the military, preferring a legal transition, which subsequently had to be worked out by a new constituent Cortes elected in 1876. These elections were held under the democratic suffrage of the 1869 constitution, restored temporarily as the law of the land. The Cánovas government, however, distinguished sharply between legal and illegal activity. Only those parties, groups, and newspapers that accepted the principle of constitutional monarchy under the Bourbon dynasty had the right to free activity. Elements which did not, such as republicans and Carlists, were largely suppressed. The government used a great deal of pressure against antidynastic groups in the 1876 elections, forcing most of them to withdraw. This resulted in large-scale abstention, officially announced as 45 percent. The new parliament contained an overwhelming government majority based on Cánovas's Liberal Conservative party (the first adjective having been chosen to indicate that it did not propose a simple reversion to the Isabeline regime). There was considerable continuity between the new chamber and its predecessors before 1873, nearly half the deputies having sat under the democratic monarchy of D. Amadeo.

The main work of the Cortes was adoption of a new monarchist constitution, a draft of which had already been prepared by a commission of notables. It reduced the suffrage to adult males who paid twenty-five pesetas annual land tax or fifty pesetas annual industrial tax. The new document declared that sovereignty resided "in the Cortes with the King"—a somewhat ambiguous compromise—and gave the crown the rights of permanent veto, appointment of ministers, and calling of elections. Once appointed, however, ministers were responsible to the Cortes, not the crown. The 1876 constitution reestablished full central control over local government and administration and abolished trial by jury. A Senate was restored, with half its members to hold lifetime seats and be appointed by the crown, the other half to be elected indirectly and corporatively.

The new constitution recognized Catholicism as the official religion, while granting toleration, though not the right of public announcement and proselytization, to adherents of all other religions. Catholic supervision of public education was restored, including a degree of censorship over publications and over curricula in higher education. Nevertheless there were strong Catholic and papal protests against the toleration of other religions and the retention by the state of general control over schools, especially colleges and universities.

Despite the dissatisfaction of clericals, Carlism went into serious decline after its defeat in 1876. This was accelerated by urbanization, social and economic change, the nominal success of the new system, and the attraction of most Catholic opinion to the regime. The Carlists developed serious personal divisions, and a struggle over party leadership led to the secession of many of the ultraclericals led by Ramón Nocedal. Rejecting the Carlist dynasty for supposed liberal deviations, they organized a faction called Integristas, propounding a radical doctrine of pure theocracy, integrating invertebrate modern society under the "reign of Jesus Christ." The Integristas thus restricted themselves to a small fringe of Catholic ultras.

Orthodox Carlists survived as a small minority based on regional and family tradition. By the end of the century their leader was a Galician orator, theoretician, and organizer, Juan Vázquez de Mella. He was an ardent propagandist who helped to develop a slightly more empirical political philosophy, based in part on regional rights and the adoption of a system of Catholic corporatism somewhat similar to the doctrines of Mun in France and Vogelsang in Austria.

Caciquismo and the Structure of Restoration Politics

The political system of the Restoration rested on oligarchy, articulated through the alliance of provincial political factions and boss control. This latter aspect—domination of local affairs and elections by district bosses and oligarchs—gave rise to the general label *caciquismo* that was later used to describe the structure of local politics. Yet criticism of boss rule, fraud, and coercion reached its peak only after the turn of the century, when such practices were already diminishing significantly. It is now appreciated that something in the nature of caciquismo was almost inevitable in a country which, according to the 1879 census, still registered only 28 percent general literacy. Not dissimilar systems had functioned in England at the beginning of the century, in France under the July Monarchy, and in parts of the United States during the years of the Spanish Restoration, though the nominal level of literacy and civic culture was higher in these countries during the years in question.

The new governing system was intended to benefit the possessing classes, but not in such exclusive fashion as the Isabeline regime, which had been based primarily on Madrid finance and the big landed interests. Cánovas intended to make the Restoration regime sufficiently flexible and comprehensive to represent all significant economic interests, giving it greater breadth and solidity than its predecessor.

The major fraud in the regime's economic administration was the tax collection system, which despite the reforms of the 1840s and the existence of a centralized state system remained in fact largely decentralized. Registration and assessment were in the hands of local boards subject to all manner of pressure and manipulation. In 1883 it was discovered that 35 percent of the arable land in Seville province had simply disappeared from the local tax rolls.

Cánovas's Liberal Conservative party was set up hastily in 1875 on a rather centralized basis through administrative appointments in the provinces. Cánovas exercised general personal control over the affairs of five southeastern provinces (Málaga, Granada, Jaén, Almería, and Murcia) and paid particular interest to patronage in most of the rest of the south. Other Conservative foci were Aragón and Old Castile (with the exception of Madrid). Catalonia, on the other hand, was at first occupied by what was almost an administrative dictatorship. Catalans had played an active role in Republicanism (in 1873 thirty-two of the forty-nine provincial governors had been Catalans), but in the quarter-century after 1875 only 1 percent of the top regional administrators named to positions in Catalonia were Catalans.

One of the salient figures of the new regime was Cánovas's minister of the interior, Francisco Romero Robledo, an ex-Radical who emerged as the most notorious electoral manipulator of late-nineteenth-century Spain. It was he who engineered the Cortes balloting of 1876 in which the number of opposition seats was held to 58 compared with the 333 for the Liberal Conservatives. Three months later, in April 1876, he established an administrative sub-section, the "Dirección General de Política y Administración," primarily to handle elections and patronage.

Cánovas resigned the leadership of the government after three years in order to allow new elections to be held. He was succeeded very briefly by General Martínez de Campos, the savior of the dynasty in 1874 and pacifier of Cuba. Martínez de Campos was a national hero to whom government might briefly be trusted; his prestige helped to serve as a guarantee of orderly elections, and as prime minister he could obtain parliamentary ratification of the peace terms he had negotiated earlier in Cuba.

The elections of 1879 were the first conducted under the restricted censitary suffrage of the new constitution. Originally the vote was given to approximately 850,000 people, or 5.1 percent of the population, which compared favorably with other west European countries at similar stages. (In Italy only 2.2 percent could vote at that time.) Representation was broadest in the regions where land was most widely distributed—Old Castile, Aragón, Navarre, Madrid, and Galicia, and much more restricted in latifundist districts and in the larger towns. During the early 1880s, for reasons that are not entirely clear, the suffrage lists contracted approximately 7 percent.

In 1879 the ministry of the interior was occupied by a conscientious younger Conservative luminary, Francisco Silvela, who reduced considerably the government pressure in elections. Thus even under restricted suffrage the Conservative majority dropped by forty seats. The main opposition, Sagasta's Constitutional party, while flailing against what it termed "an egoistic and exclusivist oligarchy," strengthened its position as second most powerful by more than doubling its representation to fifty-six seats.

Cánovas then returned to power at the close of 1879 and governed for fourteen months more. The major achievement of this ministry was passage of a law in 1880 abolishing slavery in Cuba. All the while, opposition to the Conservatives' monopoly of political power was growing. Cánovas was willing to accept the principle of a two-party system but continued to doubt the reliability of Sagasta's Constitutionalists. The latter, however, expanded their base in 1880 by joining with a dissident faction of some of the more liberal of the Conservatives led by Martínez de Campos to form the Liberal Fusionist party. The Fusionists were pledged to accept the rules of the game, and the regime, as a loyal opposition, and demanded an opportunity to share power.

The beginning of the two-party system in Spanish politics in 1881 was expedited by the political discretion of the new king, Alfonso XII. He had grown up as an exile in England and had learned much from the errors of his mother. From the very moment of his coronation in 1875 the slight, tubercular Alfonso XII proved a model constitutional monarch. Within months of the formation of the first significant loyal opposition group, D. Alfonso called them to power by appointing a Fusionist ministry under Sagasta in February 1881.

The outstanding achievement of the first Sagasta government was abolition of censorship, leading to the extremely liberal Press Law of 1883, which largely governed freedom of speech in Spain until 1936. Complete freedom of ideas was also introduced in higher education, and de facto permission was given for trade union and working class organization, resulting in the first major proletarian activity since the Restoration began.

The immediate goal of the Fusionists was new elections. Those of 1881 returned a heavy majority for the Fusionists, almost identical in size to that of the Conservatives two years earlier and the result of a similar government manipulation. There was one notable difference, however: Sagasta wanted to attract the more moderate and reasonable of the small democratic and progressive groups to loyal participation in the system. Government pressure in the larger towns, which tended to vote for the more "advanced" candidates, was lessened, and the representation of the democratic groups increased from fourteen to thirty-two.

During the two and a half years of the first Sagasta government the Fusionist administration worked to set up a broader, more effective political organization. In 1881-1882 the government annulled the election of more than 700 municipal councils in Spain in order to bolster party strength at that level. This was not, however, merely a matter of arbitrary interference but part of an attempt to open up local and provincial affairs, which had been almost completely dominated by the Conservatives for six years. A new law of 1882 greatly broadened male suffrage for municipal and provincial elections, so that nominal electoral democracy for males henceforth existed on the local level. As a result, the major electoral contests of the 1880s and early 1890s took place in municipal and provincial politics.

Conversely it was later charged at times that the Liberal Fusionists were in fact more corrupt than the Conservatives because they catered to a wider variety of interests. Some of their reforms merely broadened the scope of caciquismo. A new court law of 1882 provided that nearly half the local and provincial judges be appointed by local administrators. No professional qualifications were placed on these offices, and during the next two or three decades there were numerous complaints of the corruption or incompetence of the local judiciary. Protest against malfeasance in elections and in government administration was common throughout the Restoration period. Between 1883 and 1890 more than thirty-five hundred cases, great and small, were examined by the courts. Nearly four hundred convictions resulted, an indication that the nominal caciquismo was not entirely immune to the rule of law.

Though the Sagasta government began to lay the basis for a broader Liberal party and a program of moderate reform, it accepted the rules of the Restoration system and did not attempt major constitutional or institutional changes. Bound by obligations to the regime and keeping in mind the experience of the Republic, Sagasta resisted demands from the left to immediately institute universal male suffrage. This brought the splitting off in 1881–1882 of the most liberal wing of the party, which formed the Liberal Dynastic Left under General Serrano and Francisco Posada Herrera, former lieutenant of O'Donnell. On the other hand, the Conservatives still distrusted Sagasta and the Fusionists and stood ready to block further reforms. Beset by foes on both sides, harassed by several minor republican armed revolts and a rash of anarchist activity among the lower classes, Sagasta resigned in October 1883. The king then granted power to a Dynastic Left ministry, headed by Posada Herrera, which proposed to institute universal male suffrage and reform the Senate. A government Commission on Social Reform was promptly established, but on the key issue of universal suffrage the Fusionist majority brought down the government within three months.

Cánovas returned to power at the beginning of 1884 and immediately conducted new elections, with Romero Robledo exerting maximal pressure for votes from the ministry of the interior. Official abstention was only 28 percent, but in fact many of the Fusionists themselves failed to contest the elections. The Conservatives claimed 318 of the 392 Cortes seats, the republican and democratic groups were almost completely eliminated (5 seats), and the Dynastic Left and Fusionists were left with 36 and 31 seats respectively. Meanwhile Cánovas had succeeded in bringing the Catholic Union party, representing ultraclericals, and the moderate fringe of the Carlists to join the Conservatives, who for the first time were able to present a united front of Spanish conservatism.

Cánovas's political leadership seemed stronger than ever in 1884-1885, but the illness and death of the scrupulous Alfonso XII in November 1885 threatened crisis. Tubercular and somewhat debauched, the king died prematurely without a male heir, though a son, also named Alfonso, was born posthumously several months later. The Conservative oligarchy stood little chance of governing alone, whereas a strong and reliable two-party system of loyal opposition had not yet been firmly established. The day before the king's death, Cánovas visited Sagasta and an agreement was reached for cooperation in a two-party system of constitutional monarchy. The Conservative leader realized that in a politically still unsettled country, a reliable Liberal government stood a better chance of consolidating a constitutional regency under the queen regent, Alfonso's Habsburg widow María Cristina, until the regular succession could be resumed. The day after Alfonso's death Cánovas resigned and María Cristina appointed Sagasta prime minister.

Sagasta's Reform Ministry, 1885-1890

Without delay, Sagasta completed negotiations to bring in most of the Dynastic Left and several other small liberal factions, and it was in the winter of 1885-1886 that the broader Liberal party finally emerged. The new elections of 1886 were controlled by government manipulation only slightly less than those preceding. The Liberals did, however, content themselves with 278 deputies, the fewest for any government party since the Restoration, and the Conservatives were allowed 56, more than any opposition party had yet been permitted.

During the next four years Sagasta's long ministry completed the official liberalization of the constitutional monarchy. Between 1887 and 1890 it restored trial by jury, established a formal law of associations that legalized trade unions, completed a new Civil Code (a Criminal Code had been adopted in 1882 and a new Commercial Code in 1885), and crowned its reforms by restoring universal male suffrage in 1890. Sagasta himself was not enthusiastic about the latter step, but went along to maintain harmony with the more liberal elements of the party.

The nominal success of the Liberals helped to complete the ruin of republicanism. Castelar officially espoused democratic reform under the monarchy in 1888. For the next generation republicanism was reduced to regional and personal factionalism. Only the exiled Ruiz Zorrilla maintained a militant banner, still trying vainly to excite the army to rebellion against the monarchy.

The army had ceased to function as a special political force since the Restoration. Such had been the case whenever a coherent political system managed temporarily to achieve civic stability. This did not mean that the military leadership played no role in politics, for leading generals were given Senate seats and exercised a small degree of influence. Moreover, as an institution the army remained largely immune to civilian regulation. The officer corps was reduced slightly, several new academies and technical journals were established, and some effort was made to professionalize the military, but these changes went only halfway. Most of the army budget still went for officers' salaries, while equipment and training were abysmal. Major reforms were blocked by vested interests.

By 1890 a two-party parliamentary system had been institutionalized in Spain. This corresponded to the earlier English experience, to the "rotativist" system in Portugal, and to the contemporary *destra* and *sinistra* under "transformismo" in Italy (though the Italian groups did not function as organized political parties). The Spanish *turno* system has frequently been denounced as a sham for corrupt oligarchy, but in fact it was a major civic accomplishment. There were noteworthy differences between Liberals and Conservatives, and their achievement of a system of cooperation and alternation was leading to a period of genuine constitutional monarchy that combined order with liberty and could carry out basic reforms.

Sagasta's long government lasted slightly more than four and a half years. It came to an end because it had completed its main program and because the Conservatives were restive to return to power. The immediate cause of Sagasta's resignation was an intrigue by the dissident Conservative Romero Robledo (at the time head of a small, personalistic Reformist party) to spread rumors of a major financial scandal in which the prime minister's wife was supposedly involved. The queen regent, María Cristina, was extremely grateful to Sagasta for having stabilized affairs after the death of Alfonso XII and was eager to spare him what she feared might be major embarrassment. She asked for the government's resignation, and Cánovas returned to power in July 1890.

Stagnation of Restoration Politics in the 1890's

It was in accord with Cánovas's doctrines of order and equilibrium that the first elections under the new provisions of universal male suffrage would be conducted by a Conservative government. The new minister of the interior, the high-minded Francisco Silvela, number-two leader of the party, relaxed some of the customary government pressures, and in the larger cities the elections were conducted fairly honestly. The Conservative victory of 253 seats in the 1891 elections was the lowest yet for a government party under the Restoration. The Liberals were allowed to come up to 74—a new high for the loyal opposition—and the republicans won 31 seats, mainly in the cities. The opposition margin would have been higher save for abstention among illiterate southern peasants and even more among urban workers influenced by anarchist doctrines, together with the influence of caciques in rural districts and the practice of buying votes directly, which was apparently initiated in 1891.

The new Conservative government passed a strongly protectionist tariff (1891) and initiated a few modest measures of social reform, but broke down over intraparty politics. Cánovas finally came to a parting of the ways with the right wing of the Conservatives, the former Catholic Unionists, whose leader left the government. He then broadened his base, however, by bringing the Romero Robledo faction back into the Conservative fold, but to his dismay this soon led to a complete split. After the prime minister continued to back certain of Romero Robledo's henchmen who controlled an extremely corrupt municipal council of Madrid that was involved in a major financial scandal, the fastidious Silvela walked out of the government and the party, carrying many Conservatives with him. The government lost half its votes and failed in a parliamentary test of confidence. Sagasta returned to power in December 1892.

By that time public esteem for Cánovas (never a popular figure) had dropped considerably. In 1892 there were protests against central domination in parts of Catalonia, Andalusia, the Basque region, Asturias, and Galicia. The question of local government—its honesty and autonomy—was now becoming a paramount issue. In Catalonia economic expansion, a revival of vernacular culture, and expanded middle-class wealth and power were giving rise to a regionalist movement. This drew strength from localism, the remnants of federalism, vestiges of Catalan Carlism, but most of all from new Catalan economic and civic development. The first concrete expression of political Catalanism was the "Bases de Manresa" of 1892, a program drawn up by intellectuals and professional men calling for regional autonomy.

The question of local government came to the forefront not simply because of centralization or corruption—one or the other or both were evident in nearly every other government of the time—but even more because of the gross inadequacy and inefficiency of local services. In matters of sanitation, communication, housing, roads, and education, Spain was falling farther behind than it need have, even in terms of comparative economic strength. This was not altogether the fault of government; lack of mobilization among the middle classes brought a lack of civic impetus for reform and development. What was done in the larger cities was done mainly by private enterprise, and it was insufficient. In turn, rigid centralization meant that the major decisions had to be taken on the national administrative level, and the modest share of taxes returned to local government was insufficient to meet needs.

Many of the dissatisfied elements in the middle classes were not opposed to the basic structure of government per se but simply wanted more attention to their local interests. They, in turn, greatly distrusted the swelling notes of radicalism in lower class affairs and sometimes looked on local self-government as a surer instrument of control. Most of the twenty or so local government reform plans presented between 1892 and 1907 proposed devolution of partially corporate—not strictly inorganic mass democratic—suffrage upon the local middle classes and economic groups to enable them to handle their affairs more efficiently. The essentially conservative tint of many of these projects deprived them of support by liberals and republicans, splitting potential reform interests.

After the two-party turno system had become established in the 1890s it faced a temporary impasse. The two alternating parties were both associations of more or less entrenched interests—though the interests varied somewhat—while Spanish society had not developed sufficiently vigorous new autonomous elements to sustain major reform in the decade after 1890. Social and civic development was highly unbalanced geographically, with the most active regions on the northern and northeastern seaboards, a stable, self-contained agrarian society in the north-center, and a static, backward, socially unbalanced, acivic region in the south. Proponents of further reform were divided by region, ideology, and personality. Thus the two main parties were able to bargain and manipulate their way through government for another decade and more with little change.

The most liberal feature of the Spanish parliamentary system was not the democratic suffrage—which simply was not going to function in a still illiterate peasant society—but the organization of parliamentary operations. The Standing Orders of the Cortes provided for minority representation on all legislative committees, with rights that came close to a veto of all proposals. This assured legislative influence for the parliamentary minority, not in the interest of reform but of opposition to change. It had been arranged in 1876 in order to conciliate the minority excluded from executive power, and was one of the principal concessions designed to avoid the exclusiveness of the Isabeline regime that had made representative government impossible. Yet this very structure of the parliament tended to make it immobile. Oligarchic parliamentarianism tried to avoid total exclusiveness but made genuine parliamentary reform by the majority more difficult. Narrowly participatory immobilism would not in the long run substitute for authentic representation, yet majoritarian reform was feared as too one-sided or radical.

The Cánovas-Sagasta oligarchies, for all their limitations, did represent the main social and economic interests of the country, at least of the 1870s and 1880s. Their real insufficiency lay not in their original nature but in their failure to expand and reform themselves, incorporating new goals and interests from the 1890s on. Yet the society was still insufficiently educated beyond local personalism and amoral familialism to generate broadly based reform interests. The first of the genre of "disaster" reformist books, Lucas Mallada's *Los males de la patria,* published in 1890, labeled caciquismo correctly as not a cause but an effect of the social, economic, and educational backwardness of the country.

Social and educational development were necessary to reform the political system, but it was the task of the government to encourage social, economic, and educational improvement. Something was accomplished in economic development between 1875 and 1890. Foreign capital was attracted for industrialization, Catalan production expanded, and agrarian exports rose considerably. The greatest failure was in education, where Spain had the lowest per capita budget in Europe. This was mainly compensated for by the church, which, with state support, provided much of the country's basic education. Altogether, the literate proportion of the population rose from perhaps 35 percent in 1877 to 44 percent by 1900, putting Spain just ahead of Russia, Portugal, and the Balkans.

Disproportionate expenditures on the army and navy to maintain Spain's security have been frequently pointed to as the major example of sterile employment of state funds. The point here is not that Spain did not need relatively as much or as good a military establishment as it possessed—what it possessed was extremely weak, and it undoubtedly needed some form of national protection—but that what it had was grossly inefficient and cost several times its worth. Internal conflict had resulted in the creation of a partly autonomous military

Table 8. Illiteracy in Spain, Italy, and Portugal, 1860-1911

Country	Year	Age group	Percent of illiteracy
Spain	1860		76
	1877	All ages	72
	1887		68
	1887		61
	1900	Over 10 years	56
	1910		50
Italy	1871		69
	1881	6 years and over	62
	1901		48
	1911		38
Portugal	1890		76
	1900	7 years and over	74
	1911		70

Source: Carlo Cipolla, *Educación y desarrollo en Occidente* (Barcelona, 1970), pp. 157-58.

establishment, and nearly half the state budget was perforce wasted on fruitless expenditures.

When he formed a new government at the close of 1892, Sagasta found himself momentarily popular as a result of the general reaction against Cánovas. His ministry called new elections early in 1893. In their first opportunity to administer universal male suffrage the Liberals differed little from the Conservatives. The same sort of government pressure was used against opposition candidates in the countryside, and the government Liberals gained the customary topheavy majority—281. After the split in their party, some Conservatives abstained; Cánovas's group returned only 44 deputies, and Silvela 17. The moral victors, however, were the deputies of the newly formed Republican Union. The government followed what was now becoming the standard practice of more or less keeping hands off the elections in the larger towns, and the Republican Union gained about one-fourth the urban seats, or 33. Together with the 14 deputies of Castelar's Possibilists (ex-republican reformists), this amounted to well over 10 percent of the Cortes seats and victory for more than 60 percent of all the republican or Possibilist candidates who ran. The republican groups were still poorly united, however, and were unable to follow up on this victory for the remainder of the decade. Most of the Possibilists joined the Liberals and thus gained a seat in the Sagasta government.

A major factor in blocking change during the 1890s was the Cuban problem, which had a paralyzing effect on Spanish affairs. The final Cuban rebellion started in January 1895, and its consequences drove the Sagasta ministry from office. Cánovas's last government, from 1895 to 1897, was probably his most corrupt—not because interference and fraud were worse than ten or twenty years earlier but because the society had made cultural, economic, and educational progress and was less willing to tolerate abuses. Because of the Cuban crisis and because the Cortes was only two years old, the customary calling of elections by an incoming government was postponed, after the Liberals had agreed to support temporarily, or at least to refrain from upsetting, the new Conservative cabinet. In domestic affairs Cánovas no longer had any policy save to try to cement the remaining power of those Conservatives more or less loyal to him. The Romero Robledo gang was brought into the new ministry, while Cánovas concentrated his ire on the "disloyal" Silvela. Silvela's Constitutional Union party of opposition Conservatives was gaining much support among the ordinary Conservative following on the basis of its stand for honest government and a degree of decentralization, along with the usual calls for national unity and support of Catholicism. The group did well in the May 1895 municipal elections, resulting in wholesale cancellation of results in some districts. Sagasta had recently done the same thing, but the Conservatives' falsification of municipal elections was carried out on a broader scale and gave control of key cities to representatives of the Romero Robledo spoils apparatus. This led to an informal protest union of *hombres honrados* ("honest citizens") supported by Liberals, Silvelists, and republicans, climaxed by an attempt on the life of the protest leader.

The agreement with the Liberals having broken down, Cánovas conducted new elections in April 1896. These were the most dishonest in twelve years. Many republicans abstained, so the main target of government persecution was the Silvelists, whose leader was probably now more popular than Cánovas among rank-and-file Conservatives. The government party then won the customary overwhelming victory. This enabled the Cánovas ministry to dominate parliament, but it still had no other policy than to repress the Cuban revolt and maintain the status quo in Spain. These final years of Cánovas's career were a time of growing tension and uncertainty, marked by increased restiveness among the lower classes and gory anarchist atrocities in Barcelona that led to police repression and the beginning of a polarization of society.

Economic Development, 1877–1900

The Restoration period was a time of notable, though by no means spectacular, economic development. The basis for a modern industrial system finally emerged, though Spain was still far from a "take off" or "long spurt" phase of industrialization. There was considerable growth in the general economy during the decade 1877–1886, but the 1890s were relatively depressed, a slow but fairly steady expansion following during the years 1900–1913. The greatest commercial expansion came in the period 1880–1891.

The country's number one industry was still Catalan textiles. Spain was already nearly self-sufficient in textiles, and from 1886 on became a net exporter in that sector. Catalan production tripled between 1868 and 1889. Cottons benefited especially from the complete opening of the Cuban market after 1882, but there was also a boom in woolens; by the 1880s Catalonia had the third largest regional woolens industry in Europe. After 1890 the main problem would be overproduction. This was due not merely to the narrowness of the Spanish domestic market, but also to the fact that the Catalan textile industry never completed its managerial and technological transformation. It could not compete on the major world markets, and its export trade relied in large measure on the protected preserve of Cuba. Fearing open competition with foreign industry, Catalan mills produced at high prices mainly for the greater Spanish market, whose absorptive capacity was limited. The resulting imbalance resulted in intermittent crisis from the 1890s on.

Spain played a major world role in mining exports. The principal item was iron ore, production of which nearly tripled between 1880 and 1900. The peak year was 1899, in which nearly nine and one-half million tons were sent abroad. Copper was also important, and Spain became the leading copper exporter in Europe. There was a great increase in domestic coal production, which tripled between 1870 and 1900.

If wine and agriculture had stimulated the capital formation behind Catalan textiles a century earlier, iron ore exports did much the same for Basque metallurgy. Production of iron and steel began to achieve significant proportions in the 1880s. Injection of British capital (belatedly following the reform of investment regulations in 1869) also played a role, but the chief factors were Vizcayan entrepreneurship and the initial profits of massive ore exports.

Railway construction increased once more after 1875, and during

Table 9.   Spanish Railway Construction, 1856–1901

Years	Kilometers of track laid	Annual average
1856–60	1,441	288.2
1861–65	2,912	582.4
1866–70	652	130.4
1871–75	746	149.2
1876–80	1,354	270.8
1881–85	1,453	290.6
1886–90	1,090	218.0
1891–95	1,293	258.6
1895–1901	1,854	370.8

Source: J. Vicens Vives, *Manual de historia económica de España* (Barcelona, 1959), p. 616.

the next quarter-century the track network doubled. By the 1880s an expanding economy was providing a greater volume of traffic and making a more rational use of the system possible.

The Restoration was a boom period for wine and olive oil exports. After French vineyards were ravaged by phylloxera, Spain temporarily dominated the international wine market. Wine export reached its height in the ten years 1882–1892, but in the 1890s the same disease began to afflict Spanish cultivation. Exports declined by more than 40 percent and never regained their previous importance. The increase in olive oil exports was less pronounced, but reached a temporary high point after the turn of the century.

This was a period of declining grain cultivation and production. The marginal lands pressed into tillage during the earlier part of the century were relatively unproductive, and their yield could not compete with cheap foreign imports after 1882. Grain acreage declined 20

Table 10.   Changes in Agricultural Tillage and Productivity, 1800–1900

Crop	Thousands of hectares sown			Annual production (thousands)			Average yield per hectare			National per capita production		
	1800	1860	1900	1800	1860	1900	1800	1860	1900	1800	1860	1900
Wheat	2,900	5,100	3,700	18.3qm*	29.6	25.7	6.31qm	5.8	6.92	174kg	188	138
Cereals	6,100	9,000	7,000	29.5	55.75	51.54	6.47	6.2	7.06	371	355	336
Vineyards	400	1,200	1,450	3.85hl	10.8	21.6	9.62hl	9.	14.88	36hl	68	116
Olives	—	859	1,360	0.69	1.44	2.09	—	1.67	1.8	6	9	11

Source: Vicens Vives, *Manual de historia económica*, pp. 578–79.
   *One quintalmetrico equals one hundred kilos.

percent between 1860 and 1900 as marginal land was retired. Yield per hectare increased by approximately the same percentage, but the Spanish average of 6.92 quintales of wheat per hectare compared very poorly with other parts of western Europe. Even in Italy the yield had stood at 9 quintales as early as 1870.

The first Restoration tariff, in 1876, maintained the general level established by the liberal tariff of 1869, but struck out the clause it had contained limiting the import tax on any kind of goods to 15 percent of value. The Conservatives became more and more a high tariff party, while some Liberals, supported by large merchants and the main commercial interests, were still free-trade advocates. The first Sagasta government of the Restoration negotiated a more liberal commercial treaty with France in 1882, but the Conservatives sealed the controversy with the steep protective tariff of 1891, which united both urban industrial and rural grain-producing interests. By 1906 Spain had the highest tariff barriers in Europe.

Population Trends

The population continued the expansive trend normal to the period, rising from 16,622,000 in 1877 to 18,594,000 in 1900. As in many of the poorer regions of Europe, the level of growth was reduced by a comparatively high rate of emigration, for in absolute figures the late nineteenth and early twentieth centuries were the greatest period of emigration in Spanish history. Between 1882 and 1914 approximately one million emigrants left the country. The heaviest rate of departure was from the Canaries and the northern coastal regions, and the two main goals of emigration were Argentina and Brazil.

Social and occupational change in this period was slow but fairly continuous. Occupation ratios were altered as follows:

	1877 census	*1887 census*
Primary sector (agriculture)	70 percent	66.5 percent
Secondary sector (industry)	11	14.6
Tertiary sector (services)	19	18.7

Culture

Serious thought about law, institutions, and government during the second half of the eighteenth century in Spain was increasingly dominated by varieties of organicist theory which sought to harmonize and correct or reform the ideology of doctrinaire individualist liberalism that had reigned during the first half of the century. The best known of these organicist doctrines was the Krausist philosophy of pantheism, harmony, and balanced development that had taken root in the 1850s and 1860s. In 1876 the pedagogical leader of this movement, Francisco Giner de los Ríos, was able with his colleagues to officially establish an Institución Libre de Enseñanza, and it became the most influential teacher-training school in Spain. By the end of the century Krausism dominated the academic intelligentsia, and Krausist professors were influential among Liberal party and moderate republican leaders.

The two other major branches of organicist thought were Neo-Thomist philosophy and the Catalan "historical school" of law and institutions. Catholic Neo-Thomists, influenced by the Neo-Thomist revival in Italy, occupied key chairs of philosophy and endeavored to make Catholic policy in Spain more flexible and effective within liberal society, playing a key role in the late-nineteenth-century Catholic revival. The Catalan historical school, influenced by Herder and Savigny, stressed the importance of tradition and historic balance in legal institutions, defending what remained of the Catalan legal system.

The period's greatest polymath was Marcelino Menéndez Pelayo (1856–1912), whose three principal multivolume works were *La ciencia española* (1876–1879), *Historia de los heterodoxos españoles* (1880–1882), and the *Historia de las ideas estéticas en España* (1883–1884). Menéndez Pelayo's voluminous writings were marked by an accomplished literary style, broad documentation, and a fervently Catholic spirit. He stood as the champion of Catholic traditionalism in Spanish culture and, while often polemical in manner, was always concerned with humanist studies, strove for comprehension of other positions, and was accessible to dialogue.

Modern science slowly began to register some slight accomplishment in Spain toward the end of the century, with the work of Santiago Ramón y Cajal in histology and Eduardo Torroja in geometry. Historical study made important advances, particularly in Eduardo Hinojosa's work on the history of law, and in the investigations of Julián Ribera into Hispano-Muslim society and of Antoni Rubió i Lluch into medieval Catalonia.

During the late nineteenth century, naturalism became a dominant motif in Spanish literature, as the Spanish novel moved from the *costumbrismo* of the preceding generation through the thesis novel that emphasized psychology (Juan de Valera, Pedro Antonio de Alarcón) to the naturalist themes of Emilia Pardo Bazán and, above all, Benito Pérez Galdós. Pérez Galdós was one of the two or three greatest social and historical novelists of nineteenth-century Europe.

His multivolume *Episodios nacionales* recreated successive stages of nineteenth-century Spanish life, while his major works were rivaled only by those of Balzac as treatments of society. There was also noticeable a more genuine cultural self-consciousness in Spanish letters and a more direct debate about common European cultural trends on the one hand and the specifically *castizo*, or native Spanish, on the other.

Spanish music was quite feeble during these years, despite the fact that Spanish themes were being used by leading composers in Germany and Russia. The most important development was the rise of the national operetta form, the zarzuela, in the work of such composers as Barbieri, Bretón, and Chapí. Spanish painting revealed no significant achievements until after the turn of the century. The Restoration period was highlighted by the rediscovery of the landscape and after 1900 by naturalistic forms. The chief artists of the period were from the north and northeast: Darío de Regoyos, the Catalans Santiago Rusiñol and Ramón Casas, and the Valencian Joaquín Sorolla.

Discovery of the Region

During the second half of the century there developed a growing cultural and political self-consciousness in the major regions of Spain. It stemmed from the cultural romanticism of an earlier generation that had stressed the historical and the particular, from new historical study that was bringing out regional differences and identities, and from an esthetic awareness of the quality of the countryside and the physical environment. The rediscovery of the region was part of the general nineteenth-century awakening of cultural, regional, ethnic, and national identities. As in all other parts of Europe, it began by taking a cultural and specifically literary form. The first great movement of regional culture was the Catalan *Renaixença,* beginning slowly with a revival of literature in the Catalan vernacular in the 1830s and 1840s. In 1859 Catalanist litterateurs officially restored the *jocs florals* (poetry contests) of the late Middle Ages, and in the following generation Catalan literature began to blossom. The term *renascence* for the cultural revival was derived in part from the newspaper *La Renaixenç,* founded in 1871, that became its principal spokesman. The great strength of modern Catalan literature has been its poetry. By the end of the nineteenth century the outstanding lyric, epic, and dramatic poets in Spain were writing in Catalan, not Castilian—the canon Mossen Jacint Verdaguer, author of the great epic poems *L'Atlàntida* (1876) and *Canigó* (1886), the dramatist Angel

Guimerá, whose outstanding plays were *Mar i Cel* and *Terra Baixa,* and the lyricist Joan Maragall. A late figure of unique achievement was the expressionist architect Antoni Gaudí, the outstanding Spanish architect of the early twentieth century.

There was a similar revival of regional self-consciousness and vernacular literature in Galicia, but on a lesser scale. In Galicia, as in Catalonia, there emerged during mid-century a school of romantic regionalist historians who tended to exaggerate the accomplishments of and the injustices done their native region. Galician poetry contests were inaugurated at Santiago de Compostela in 1875, and a "Biblioteca gallega" began publishing a new series of fifty-two titles in 1885. As in Catalonia, the brightest facet of the Galician literary revival was its poetry. A number of poets of varying literary and ideological orientation emerged; the only one of outstanding literary value was the lyricist Rosalía de Castro, whose work was filled with Galician *saudade,* sadness, longing. Galician regionalism began to assume modest political dimensions with the publication of Alfredo Brañas's *El regionalismo* (1889), which proposed a new system of regionalist federalism.

There was also a minor Valencian *renaixença* during the late nineteenth century, producing a new generation of writers in the Valencian dialect of Catalan. Valencia also brought forth a regional literature in Castilian, mainly in the series of novels published by Vicente Blasco Ibáñez between 1894 and 1902. In general, however, regional feeling was less strong in the Levant than in Catalonia, the Basque country, or even Galicia. The major Valencian writers of the turn of the century—"Azorín" and Gabriel Miró—wrote in Castilian and in the mainstream of all-Spanish culture.

Literature in the Castilian language expressed a more moderate regionalist culture that was not directed toward any potentially political concern. Prime manifestations of this were the novels of José Ma. de Pereda about the land and people of Old Castile, the Galician novels of Pardo Bazán, and Armando Palacio Valdés's Asturian novels.

The Emergence of Political Catalanism

Catalonia had played no special role in Spanish politics during the first quarter of the nineteenth century. Regional political self-consciousness burst forth in the 1830s, provoked by the three-way split in Spanish affairs between Carlists, Moderates, and Progressives. The struggle for and against the new liberal system and the issues of centralization versus local self-government led to a high degree of effervescence in Catalonia between 1835 and 1843, but during the Isabeline regime there was little or no sense of Catalanist political particularism. Key regional issues—mainly economic concerns and the question of local self-government—were fought out in the framework of all-Spanish problems. During the mid-century years, specifically Catalanist feeling had been concentrated on cultural activity, and the literary renaixença was the work of a small elite of the middle and upper classes. The first book to appear on what would become known as the Catalan problem was Juan Illas Vidal's very moderate *Cataluña en España* (1855). Juan Cortada's subsequent *Cataluña y los catalanes* (1860) was more particularistic, with a degree of romantic nationalist inspiration.

The struggle for local self-government that had been pressed by Progressives and Democrats since the 1830s and 1840s took on a more distinctly regionalist character under the democratic monarchy of D. Amadeo and the First Republic. Catalan ultra-liberals were especially active in the Federal Republican movement, and it was a former Republican, Valentí Almirall, who founded a Centre Català early in the 1880s to support regional political as well as cultural interests. Almirall's *Lo Catalanisme* (1886) was the first clear exposition of Catalan political nationalism, though it was couched in terms of close federal association with the rest of Spain.

The wealthy upper-middle and upper classes in Catalonia provided little support for either local self-government or the cultural renaixença, so that no daily newspaper was published in Catalan until Almirall established one in 1879. At that time, however, Catalonia was the richest region in Spain in terms of the number of voluntary associations. Some of these, such as the workingmen's choirs of Josep Clavé, helped popularize Catalan culture among certain sectors of the lower classes. A link with the upper classes was forged by the newspaper editor and critic Mañé Flaquer, one of the most influential commentators in Catalonia during the 1870s and 1880s. Mañé Flaquer publicized a form of conservative regionalism, based on tradition, culture, and the protection of established local interests, which he called *fogueralisme*. The need to provide greater shelter and encouragement for Catalan economic development was expressed in the *Memorial de greuges* (complaints) presented to the government by Catalan business leaders in 1885 in protest against proposals for reducing the tariff.

By the late 1880s a new political orientation was emerging among moderate and conservative political and economic interests in Catalonia. This can be explained by the difference in economic structure between semi-industrial Catalonia and a still largely rural Spain. The Restoration regime, despite its accomplishments, was unable to pro-

vide local government and administration at the level required by a
rapidly modernizing society. Though Catalan industry lived off the
domestic market for the most part, the feeling grew that the disparity
between the social, economic, and cultural development of Catalonia
and most of the rest of Spain was holding Catalonia back. Active
middle class elements in the cultural revival and in the business
community were reaching the conclusion that middle class interests in
Catalonia must take full control of their destinies in order to achieve
complete development. In 1887 some of the more conservative and
practical members of the Centre Català split off to form a separate
Lliga de Catalunya. Two years later a major campaign was waged to
win concessions for Catalonia in the new Spanish commercial code.
New support was drawn from ultra-Catholic and post-Carlist elements. Carlism had been very strong in the less-developed, rural parts
of the region, and in the last years of the century ultra-Catholics
began to look toward the regionalist movement in opposition to their
main enemy, the centralized liberal state. This attitude was best
expressed by the bishop of Vich, Torras i Bages, whose *La Tradició
catalana* (1892) praised the greater religious fidelity of Catalan society.

Political Catalanism finally emerged in the 1892 "Bases de Manresa," the manifesto of regionalist intellectuals and professional men
that called for political and adminstrative autonomy and greater
support for Catalan economic development. The movement was socially moderate and rejected the democratic republicanism that had
been associated with Almirall's group. It acquired an official theoretician in Enric Prat de la Riba, whose "Catechism" of 1894 defined
Catalonia as the fatherland of Catalans and Spain as merely the state
system operating as the enemy of the fatherland. The Catalanist
movement was not separatist, but demanded regional autonomy on
the basis of a corporate suffrage, complete control over regional civil
and criminal affairs, and a specific limit on the military obligations of
Catalans within the Spanish system.

Foreign Affairs during the Restoration Period

Government leaders after 1875 avoided involvement in the major
diplomatic and military issues of Europe, while demonstrating extreme touchiness at any point in which other powers impinged on
Spanish interests. Cánovas defined his policy as one of "contraction"
(*recogimiento*)—by contrast with O'Donnell, or even Prim—but emphasized that it was not one of isolation. The three main concerns of
Spanish government abroad were the overseas empire in both the

Caribbean and the Pacific, relations with northwest Africa (primarily Morocco), and with increasing vagueness, relations with Portugal. After 1875 there were still a few surviving voices that advocated a policy of "peninsularism" (some sort of union between Spain and Portugal), but this was more or less associated with subversion or revolution, and the very mention of union was carefully avoided by the two governments.

After O'Donnell's "long government," Spain had shown little active interest in Moroccan affairs, but under the Restoration a handful of *africanista* advocates slowly became more vocal. The Real Sociedad Geográfica, founded in 1876, devoted considerable attention to Africa. The Sociedad Española de Africanistas y Colonistas was formed in 1883 and was complemented to some extent by *La Estrella de Occidente,* a bicultural revue in both Castilian and Arabic published by a circle in Granada. Several small groups of Franciscans did a little missionary work in Morocco during those years, as well. The territories of Río de Oro (later called the Spanish Sahara) and Río Muñi (Spanish Guinea), south of Morocco down the African coast, had been granted to Spain earlier by treaty and during these years were formally occupied. The goals of the africanistas were to build on these territories and on the existing Spanish *presidios* on the north Moroccan coast to establish a special relationship between Spain and Morocco, upholding the *makhzen* (the current Sultanate) as a client of Spain while keeping other European powers out. Little interest was generated in Spain, however, and Spanish policy remained basically passive.

It was understood that the only vital concern was the overseas colonies. Spanish policy made no attempt to build agreements or alliances with other powers to protect them, however. It was felt that such association would cause more harm than good, and that the remainder of the Spanish empire would be most secure if Spain remained diplomatically contracted within its own little sphere. Intermittent pressure from the United States over Cuba was a source of anxiety, but after the end of the Grant administration Spanish leaders believed that overt American intervention in the Spanish Antilles was unlikely. During the 1880s the only incident was an incursion by the German navy into the Spanish-held Caroline islands in the western Pacific in 1885. This aroused great resentment among Spaniards and was settled by arbitration in favor of Spain.

There were Liberal party leaders, however, who felt that Spanish diplomacy must be more active and associate itself with major powers. Spain's only potential enemy in Europe was judged to be France, because of the French record of intervention in Spanish affairs during the past two centuries. The Third Republic was a source of apprehension that it might subvert the monarchy, while conversely French monarchist legitimists had made themselves objects of hostility because of their support for Carlism. The restored monarchy cultivated good relations with Germany as a counterweight to France, but Bismarck had no interest in becoming involved in the affairs of southwestern Europe. The Liberal Segismundo Moret, foreign minister under Sagasta's long government, did arrange a Mediterranean defense pact with Italy in 1887, thus hoping to associate Spain indirectly with the Triple Alliance, but the agreement has been termed a model of vagueness and involved no concrete obligations.

The Cuban Disaster

Spain's only significant overseas possession was Cuba. Control of the island was deemed important partly for economic reasons but even more as an article of prestige. It was genuinely feared by Cánovas and other key leaders that final loss of empire would produce so grave a trauma that it would bring the collapse of the regime and of the dynasty. The peace settlement that ended the Ten Years War in 1878 had promised Cuba the same system of municipal autonomy that existed in Puerto Rico. A reform party had been formed in Cuba during the 1860s, seeking commercial freedom and local autonomy, and the subsequent Autonomist party sent a small delegation to the Spanish Cortes under the Restoration system. Though all slavery was ended by 1886, the promised municipal autonomy was never instituted. The Autonomists finally withdrew from the Madrid parliament after flagrant electoral fraud and manipulation in Cuba.

It has been observed not inaccurately that Cuba was to Spain as Ireland was to England during this period. Control of both islands dated from the "old," sixteenth-century empires of the two powers. Just as the "Irish lords" formed a powerful imperial interest group, so there were important Spanish social and economic concerns in Cuba. Considerable money was invested in the plantation economy, and Catalan commerce, particularly, benefited greatly from the protectionist system, 60 percent of Catalan exports going to Cuba. The Cuban "Orangemen" were the españolistas, the "Spanishist" elements, swollen by emigration from the peninsula in the nineteenth century, that had built the Cuban middle class. These immigrant lower-middle-class bureaucrats and shopkeepers were the backbone of the Unión Constitucional dedicated to keeping Cuba Spanish. For most people in Spain, however, the key issues were neither social nor economic, but the patriotic and emotional appeal of sustaining the Spanish flag.

Despite the españolismo of much of the Cuban middle classes, one of the main problems was that Cuba's natural market was the United States. The Spanish economy, on the other hand, could neither absorb exports nor provide necessary imports at the right prices. To this economic conflict was added the growing sentiment of Cuban patriotism among at least a large minority of the local population. Cubans charged that Spain exploited the island through taxes, the tariff system, and an undeniably corrupt administration. Spanish government spokesmen insisted that after military and administrative costs were reckoned Cuba was actually a financial liability to the Spanish government, which may well have been true.

Sagasta's colonial minister in 1893, Antonio Maura, introduced a proposal that would have given Cuba a single-chamber representative assembly for the entire island to legislate on internal affairs, an advisory council to assist the captain-general, and a system of genuinely autonomous municipal government. Even Sagasta, however, refused to support the measure, and other interests were unalterably opposed, forcing Maura's resignation. A more moderate autonomy law was finally passed at the beginning of 1895, ten days before the final Cuban revolt began, but by then it was too late.

The Cánovas ministry of 1895 to 1897 adopted an intransigent hard line under pressure from the Romero Robledo gang and various patriotic, ultraconservative elements. The *silvelistas,* alone among major domestic political groups, urged concessions, but they were ignored on factional grounds. Martínez de Campos, victor in 1878, was sent as captain general to repeat his earlier feat, but found support for independence in Cuba much broader than twenty years before. He urged conciliation and compromise, and so was replaced in 1896 by Valeriano Weyler, who had a reputation for being the toughest, most efficient general in the Spanish army. By 1897 nearly a quarter million troops had been poured into Cuba; they faced not an ordinary military conflict but one of the first of modern colonial guerrilla wars. Weyler accepted the situation for what it was, cordoned off areas of the island, and began to relocate part of the rural Cuban population in *reconcentraciones* where they were safe from the rebels. Within Spain, public opinion generally supported a hard line, in the country's principal outpouring of patriotic feeling during the late nineteenth and early twentieth centuries. The Cuban rebels were viewed as traitors, and it was generally felt that any negotiations or concessions should be preceded by a military victory that would make Spanish sovereignty clear.

The victory was slow in coming. Weyler penned the rebels within the eastern half of the island but could not destroy them. Much of the Cuban economy was systematically wrecked by the insurgents in a scorched-earth policy, and the suffering of part of the civilian population became extreme. The racial antagonisms between blacks and whites that were expected to split the rebel movement never became especially serious. By mid-1897 the more liberal Spanish political opinion was growing restive. Just as the "yellow press" in the United States harped on Spanish atrocities (most of which were in fact committed either by rebels or by Cuban españolista volunteers), the Spanish liberal press grew increasingly critical of the slowness of Weyler's program. In July 1897 Moret, one of the three top Liberal party leaders, came out for immediate autonomy.

In the following month Cánovas was murdered by an Italian anarchist at a Basque summer resort. The assassination may have been encouraged by Cuban agents, but it was primarily a protest against the repression of anarchist terrorism within Spain. It led to a change in policy, for no Conservative could replace Cánovas. After a brief transition ministry, Sagasta returned to power in October 1897. His government replaced Weyler with a less vigorous commander and finally passed the old autonomy bill, but by that time Cuban dissidents would accept nothing short of independence.

Pressure from the United States mounted steadily, and the mysterious explosion of the USS *Maine* in Havana harbor in February 1898 made war between the United States and Spain almost inevitable. The Sagasta ministry did everything it could to avoid the conflict, even granting the unilateral armistice to the Cubans that the American government demanded. Its only salvation would have been to relinquish Cuba completely and immediately, but no Spanish government would capitulate under pressure. The Sagasta ministry accepted the conflict as an ineluctable test of honor. Though Spanish opinion rallied almost completely to the national cause, creaking, obsolescent Spanish warships were easily blasted out of the water in both the Caribbean and the Pacific by the sleek, powerful new American fleet. Cánovas had once vowed that Spain would fight "to the last man and the last peseta," but after the destruction of the navy the war was over. The United States, whose government was determined to settle the Cuban problem once and for all, deprived Spain of all its Caribbean and Pacific possessions, but it did not solve the Cuban problem. Puerto Rico and the Philippines passed under American sovereignty, while the lesser Pacific islands were transferred to Germany. The struggle for Cuba had cost Spain its navy, 50,000 military deaths (nearly all from disease), and its national self-respect. The Spanish disaster of 1898 was part of the series of humiliations suffered by the weaker states of southwestern Europe in the increasingly rugged imperial competition of that decade; it corresponded to the British Ultimatum to Portugal in 1891 and the Italian disaster at Adowa in 1896. Each of these precipitated a domestic crisis, and in Spain the Restoration regime sank to its nadir.

22

Portugal under the Nineteenth-Century Constitutional Monarchy

By the end of the eighteenth century the weight of Portuguese society had begun to shift for the first time since the Middle Ages. Though the traditional peasant structure remained almost unchanged, a new upper middle class of wealth and potential influence was beginning to emerge. It was made up of elements of the commercial bourgeoisie in the coastal towns, an elite of educated bureaucrats and officeholders, and some of the nonaristocratic and petty noble landholders in central and south-central Portugal. The traditional aristocracy was already in decline. However, the incipient shift in the weight of Portuguese elites had no immediate political consequences, for the preeminence of the virtually absolute Portuguese monarchy remained unquestioned. The reforms of an elitist enlightened despotism fulfilled nearly all the ambitions of the new upper middle class.

With the beginning of the French revolutionary and Napoleonic wars, Portugal entered a period of more than fifty years in which major issues were decided largely by the influence and pressures of foreign powers. Portugal continued faithful to its alliance with Britain during the French wars, and sheltered by geography, was able for a time to remain largely independent of French imperialism. In 1801, a petty border invasion by Spanish forces acting the role of French satellite seized the Portuguese border district of Olivença in what was called somewhat derisively the War of the Oranges. Under French

SPAIN

Rio Minho

Rio Lima

Bragança

Viana do Castelo

MINHO

TRAS- OS- MONTES

Braga

E

Guimarais

ALTO DOURO

ATLANTIC

DOURO

Porto

LITORAL

Rio Douro

OCEAN

BEIRA ALTA

Viseu

Aveiro

Rio Dão

Guarda

BEIRA

Rio Mondego

Coimbra

LITORAL

BEIRA BAIXA

S P A I N

Rio Tejo

ESTRE-

Santarém

RIBATEJO

MADURA

ALTO

Lisbon

ALEMTEJO

Setúbal

Evora

BAIXO

Beja

ALEMTEJO

Silves

ALGARVE

0   50 Mi

GULF OF CÃDIZ

0   50 Km

Modern Portugal

UWCL

pressure the Portuguese crown was forced to pay an indemnity to Spain and make commercial concessions to France. The Olivença district has been a part of Spain ever since.

Nevertheless, the Portuguese crown still endeavored to maintain its neutrality in the European wars, intermittently shielded by the British fleet. By the time that Napoleon's continental power reached its height in 1806–1807, Portugal was the only state outside his control. Under overwhelming French pressure the crown finally agreed to declare war on Britain in the autumn of 1807, but this move came too late to stave off invasion by a French army, operating with Spanish assistance. The royal family fled with all the court to Brazil, leaving a virtually inoperative regency council behind.

The French "conquest" was a mere walkover. Most of the Portuguese elite did not seem willing to resist the Napoleonic variant of enlightened despotism, but patriotism was stronger in the lower classes. The sparks for revolt came in 1808 from a British naval blockade in the Atlantic and the beginning of the great Spanish uprising against French imperialism. With the small French garrisons in Portugal depleted, rebellions broke out in the principal towns of the north and spread throughout the kingdom. Municipal and regional juntas were formed in a manner somewhat parallel to the Spanish.

The Portuguese resistance was, however, less independent and spontaneous. Militarily it relied on British assistance. The expeditionary force under Wellesley, together with Portuguese contingents of equal size (though not equal strength), repelled three successive French invasions from Spanish territory (1808, 1809, 1811). Britain bore much of the expense and provided nearly all the equipment for the Portuguese military forces, which were placed under the command of a British general, Beresford. Moreover, the leading elements of the Portuguese resistance did not demonstrate the same degree of localist and reformist zeal that marked much of the Spanish defense. Subordination to the center was much greater in Portugal, where British military and diplomatic influence was predominant. Only a score or so writers and journalists supported a radical Portuguese brand of liberalism, and in 1810 they were deported to the Azores and Britain. Altogether, the war may have cost the lives of a quarter-million Portuguese. It ravaged portions of the countryside and depleted what was already the most antiquated transportation system in western Europe. The aftermath was scarcely more promising, for Portuguese commerce was wrecked, the treasury empty and more deeply in debt. Portuguese representatives were virtually ignored at the Congress of Vienna. Very little compensation could be expected for war destruction, and in Britain, sentiment was building for intervention to close the Portuguese slave trade.

The royal family remained in Brazil, which now exceeded the mother country in population and greatly surpassed it in commercial importance. In 1815 Brazil was raised to the nominal status of kingdom, making it theoretically equal in juridical right with the mother country. An independence movement was building among the upper classes of Portuguese America as among those of Spanish America, yet the settlement of the royal family in Rio de Janeiro in 1807 had given Brazil much greater attention from the royal government, making it the temporary center of the empire, and so checked rebellious feelings. Mad Maria I finally died in 1816 and the prince regent ascended the throne, still in Rio, as João VI (1816–1826). As a ruler he was irresolute, wanting in willpower and insight. In Pernambuco a republican revolt broke out in 1817 and lasted for ten weeks, until it was put down.

At home in Portugal discontent spread among influential elements after the end of the war. Commerce, which had remained fairly strong until 1807, did not recover, and the trade of Brazil was increasingly controlled by Britain. The crown was far away, providing no leadership and leaving the government of Portugal under a royal junta and more particularly under the British general, Beresford, who remained commander-in-chief of the Portuguese forces. There were two foci of liberal reformism, largely paralleling those in Spain. One was among the proto-bourgeois of the port cities and the middle class intelligentsia. The exiles of 1810 had generated a great deal of publicity abroad and stirred up a following among the very small politically conscious minority. Some of the political intelligentsia had assumed a radical Jacobin orientation, but most thought in terms of a moderate representative system. The second focus was among the officer corps of the Portuguese army, which had become much more important during the war. A minority of the officers had been influenced by liberal ideas, and some had joined Masonic lodges. Finally, among the local notables and aristocrats in some rural areas there was support for conservative, semitraditional reformism, aimed at achieving an attentive national government more concerned with local needs, but eschewing drastic reform or change in political representation.

One conspiracy was discovered in 1817 which led to the arrest and execution of Gomes Freire, ranking active general in the Portuguese army and head of Portuguese Freemasonry. The repression made Beresford's rule even more odious, and the first effective liberal group was organized by a secret society called the Sinédrio (from a Greek word for assembly), founded in Porto in 1818. It was not a Masonic lodge, and of its thirteen leaders eight were bourgeois, three were officers, and two were aristocratic jurists. Porto had remained throughout the early modern period the economic center of northwestern Portugal, drawing on a large hinterland in the Douro-Minho regions.

The Sinédrio's opportunity came after the successful Spanish revolt early in 1820. The Portuguese rebellion broke out at Porto in August. The towns of the northwest and center rallied to it, and liberal juntas were formed in Porto and Lisbon. At first the only goal clearly agreed upon was the elimination of Beresford and return of the monarchy from Brazil. But the crown showed no interest in returning to an uncertain welcome, and in November the liberal leadership was reconsolidated. Army commanders were disgruntled at the command of the new civilian Junta that had been set up, and planned a coup to increase their own influence. Liberal opinion was strong among junior officers, however, and the pronunciamiento of senior commanders on November 11 (the *Martinhada,* since it was St. Martín's Day) imposed on the Junta acceptance of the voting norms of the Spanish Constitution of 1812, while balancing this with the appointment of conservative members to the Provisional Junta. Eight days later a counter-pronunciamiento by some of the most liberal officers reduced conservative influence, and elections for the constituent Cortes of 1821 were held under the Spanish three-tier system of semidemocratic but indirect suffrage. The Portuguese clergy split on the issue of parliamentary government; the cardinal-patriarch and most of the hierarchy were intransigently opposed, but many of the lower clergy showed rather strongly liberal sympathies.

The constituent Cortes of 1821 was the first representative assembly to meet in Portugal since 1689. The composition of its membership by professions is shown in table 11. The characteristic that the deputies had most in common was that the great majority of them

Table 11. Composition of the Portuguese Cortes of 1821

Magistrates and jurists	39
Teachers and liberal professionals	21
Clergy	16
Military	10
Physicians	6
Landowners	5
Merchants	3
	100

Source: Fernando Piteira Santos, *Geografia e economia da Revolução de 1820* (Lisbon, 1962).

represented the rural and landholding upper middle class and were especially interested in advancing the position of that class. The most conservative deputies were those chosen from the Beira region, seat of the country's only university (Coimbra).

The Portuguese constitution of 1822 was not merely the first modern constitution of Portugal, but in some ways was the most radically democratic political charter the country has ever had. Even the Republican constitution of 1911 was less democratic, because of its sectarian anticlerical provisions. The goal of the drafters of the new constitution was to limit the power of the crown, establish a representative system, guarantee individual rights, and create a rational, unified legal system. Their chief inspiration was the Spanish constitution of 1812. The new Portuguese document, declaring that "sovereignty resides essentially in the Nation," established a unicameral legislature to which the executive would be responsible, independent of the crown. Parliaments were to be elected biennially by direct universal male suffrage, excluding only women, illiterates, and friars. Equal constitutional rights were posited for all male citizens, and separate legal jurisdiction of seigneurial and church domains was abolished. The Inquisition and special ecclesiastical courts were done away with. Yet despite this drastic reordering of Portuguese legal principles, the new constitution tried not unsuccessfully to reach a compromise with traditional institutions, safeguarding a monarchy that would reign but not rule, preserving the religious and economic interests of the church, and not imposing social and economic reform on landholders.

Meanwhile a liberal rebellion had broken out in Brazil at the beginning of 1821, encouraging João VI to return soon afterward to Portugal, leaving his son D. Pedro regent of Brazil. His attitude was much more cooperative than that of his Spanish contemporary Fernando VII, and he was ready to accept a system of constitutional monarchy. However, a primary aim of the Portuguese mercantile class was to reassert sovereignty over Brazil and regain control of Brazilian commerce. This was unacceptable to the dominant elements in Brazil and was strongly opposed by British policy.

Rather than allow himself to be removed by the new Portuguese regime, the Brazilian regent, D. Pedro (heir to the Portuguese throne), rejected the demands of Lisbon in his "grito do Ipiranga," the Brazilian declaration of independence. Dom Pedro was a romantic and rather idealistic prince who was also unstable and afflicted with epilepsy. He was capable of outbursts of energy, but his behavior was marked by sharp personal contradictions and occasional acts of highhandedness. With British encouragement, he was acclaimed constitutional emperor of Brazil by Brazilian representatives before the close of 1822.

The attitude of Portuguese constitutionalists paralleled almost exactly that of Spanish liberals in 1810-1812 and 1820-1823; they were willing to grant representation to colonial spokesmen in the parliament of the mother country but rejected autonomy. The difference lay in the continuity of unified legitimate government in Brazil—a constitutional monarchy under the younger branch of the Portuguese dynasty, established without violence—and the special protection and interest of Great Britain, which had been guaranteed a favored status with Brazilian commerce in a wartime treaty. Hence the Portuguese crown liquidated its obligations to its American colony in 1825, officially recognizing Brazilian independence, whereas hostilities and recriminations between Spain and Spanish America dragged on another forty years.

Meanwhile the course of Portuguese liberalism in 1822-1823 roughly paralleled that of Spain during those same years. Radical proto-Jacobin elements came to the fore, broadcasting incendiary propaganda hostile to the interests of the church, the aristocracy, and the upper middle class. At the opposite extreme were the Portuguese traditionalists, led by elements of the aristocracy and supported by most of the rural nobility and the clergy, especially the hierarchy. The traditionalists represented the old elite and the liberals the new; in numbers they were approximately equal, though the traditionalists had the potential of arousing the conservative, illiterate, essentially apolitical peasant masses behind them in support of religion and the accepted norms of life. Just as Portuguese liberalism was encouraged to seize power by the Spanish liberal pronunciamiento of 1820, the Portuguese reaction was given its chance by the Spanish civil war of 1822-1823 and the French intervention restoring the absolute regime of Fernando VII. An "absolutist" junta was established by the traditionalist aristocracy in the Tras-os-Montes, the most rural, backward, traditional, and inaccessible part of the country, where medieval communal systems still prevailed. In May 1823, one month after French forces entered Spain, a military revolt, later known as the *vilafrancada,* began at Vila Franca de Xira, just north of Lisbon, and toppled the government.

Complete power was once more placed in the hands of João VI, but that indulgent, uncertain monarch lacked the neo-absolutist ambitions of Fernando VII and instead was influenced by British and French ideas of moderate constitutional monarchy. In Spain, even Fernando VII was criticized by traditionalists for his centralist ambitions, somewhat anticlerical policies, and concessions to wealthy liberal moderates. Spanish traditionalists and neo-absolutists later turned to D. Carlos, the king's younger brother, as their champion, but in Portugal, support of traditionalist forces for a separate candidate, the king's second son, D. Miguel, crystallized more rapidly. That Portuguese *miguelismo* emerged two or three years before Spanish *carlismo* was a consequence of the greater liberality of the Portuguese ruler as well as of the split in the royal family between the easygoing king and his ambitious, ultraconservative, and authoritarian Spanish queen, D. Carlota Joaquina, sister of Fernando VII and D. Carlos. The young D. Miguel was his mother's favorite son and he identified fully with her. He too was ambitious, clerical, and authoritarian, given to violent physical exercise and a rural, military, traditional style of life. By 1824 the traditionalists had begun to close ranks behind D. Miguel in opposition to João VI. Dom Miguel was not in the direct line of succession, but if his elder brother Pedro I of Brazil remained in his American kingdom, D. Miguel would inherit the throne. To encourage this and establish more conservative rule, the traditionalists seized control of the government in April 1824 (in a coup known as the *abrilada*) to force João VI to institute a fully absolute and reactionary policy and presumably to have D. Miguel proclaimed heir. This maneuver was foiled by the energetic reaction of the British and French ambassadors, and D. Miguel had to leave the country.

The next phase began with the death of João VI in 1826. Dom Pedro was still reigning as emperor of Brazil, which he was reluctant to leave. Prompted by the great powers, he tried to settle the dynastic-constitutional issue through an imaginative but unrealistic compromise. His first step was to promulgate immediately a new constitutional charter to take the place of the original constitution abrogated three years earlier. The Portuguese Charter of 1826 was based on the Brazilian constitution of 1823, the French charter granted by Louis XVIII in 1814, and the constitutional ideas of Benjamin Constant. It became the basic document of constitutional monarchy in Portugal and, undergoing a series of amendments, remained in effect until 1910. It made no mention of national sovereignty but gave control of the executive to the crown. A two-chamber legislature was established, a chamber of deputies chosen by indirect suffrage and an upper chamber of peers, both lifetime and hereditary members, selected by the crown, which appointed all ministers and held an absolute veto over legislation. Guarantees of civil rights were much more limited than in the constitution of 1822. Even so, the Charter might not have received the allegiance of the princess regent (Pedro's sister) and other authorities in Portugal had it not been for the resolute action of the military governor of Porto, the liberal Gen Saldanha.

Having thus rendered felicitous the kingdom of Portugal, the second part of D. Pedro's plan was to abdicate his right to the Portuguese throne in favor of his seven-year-old daughter, Maria da Glória, so that he might remain emperor of Brazil. The heiress would be betrothed to her uncle, D. Miguel, provided that the latter swore allegiance to the Charter. There were several precedents for uncle-niece marriages within the Portuguese dynasty; after Maria da Glória came of age and the two were married, they could rule jointly and heal the politico-dynastic schism. This proposal was based on the supposition that D. Miguel might be held faithful to the Charter by his oath and by joint international guarantees from Great Britain, patron of D. Pedro, and from the Austrian Habsburg crown, chief supporter of D. Miguel.

Dom Miguel snatched at the chance and was made D. Pedro's lieutenant in Portugal. Returning to Lisbon early in 1828, he swore allegiance to the Charter and took command of the Portuguese armed forces. A division of British troops, stationed in Portugal since December 1826 to safeguard the constitutional succession, was then withdrawn. Encouraged by the hard-core traditionalists, D. Miguel appointed an absolutist ministry that revoked the Charter, revived the traditional three-estate Cortes, purged liberals in the government, and crowned Miguel king with Cortes approval in July 1828. A liberal, pro-Pedro revolt in Porto collapsed and Portuguese liberals, like their Spanish counterparts five years earlier, began a mass exodus. More than 14,000 were arrested, and property was theoretically confiscated from 80,000 families, more than 10 percent of the kingdom. For three years D. Miguel ruled without significant resistance, yet most of the middle and some of the upper classes remained hostile to his regime.

Nevertheless, active liberals formed only a small minority, and Dom Miguel would probably have consolidated his rule had it not been for the change in the international situation after 1830 and events in Brazil. Establishment of the constitutional July Monarchy in France stimulated the forces of west European liberalism, while in Rio de Janeiro Pedro I reached a complete political impasse as emperor of Brazil. Again with British and French encouragement, he abdicated the Brazilian throne in favor of his eldest son, Pedro II, early in 1831, and resolved to win back the Portuguese crown. Thanks in part to British assistance, a small force of volunteers and foreign auxiliaries established themselves in 1832 in the Azores, the only portion of Portuguese territory that had never recognized D. Miguel.

There D. Pedro reestablished constitutional government under the Charter of 1826. His new minister of justice and finance, an exiled jurist and reformer from the Alemtejo, Mousinho da Silveira, proceeded immediately to the abolition of the traditional structure of

economic relations and property laws. All church and many seigneurial tithes and dues were eliminated, and the abolition of entailment
of estates was begun, beginning with the smaller ones. Monopolies
were prohibited and excise taxes and duties reduced. The administrative system was reorganized along modern French lines; juridical and
administrative offices were separated, the equality of all citizens before the law established, and the jury system set up. The final victory
of the liberals made these reforms effective, and they constituted the
beginning of civic modernization—much more sweeping than anything attempted by Pombal.

Yet the Miguelista regime still occupied Portugal and increased its
army to 80,000 men, albeit largely illiterate, poorly trained, ill-equipped peasant draftees. Dom Pedro raised an expeditionary force of
7,500 with British assistance and in mid-1832 landed at Porto. This
city, with its important commerce and comparatively large middle
class, was the focus of liberalism, and its inhabitants were strong
supporters of the constitutional restoration. Dom Miguel's greatly
superior forces invested Porto and held it under siege for thirteen
months but lacked the means, and perhaps the determination, to
conquer it. Failure to take the city was fatal for the traditionalist
cause, for it revealed the determination of the liberals and the limitations of the absolutist regime. Many of D. Miguel's nominal supporters began to waver, and in 1833 another small expedition to the
Algarve took the traditionalists in the rear and began to rally support
in southern Portugal. With British help, the traditionalist fleet was
largely destroyed, and as the liberal offensive from the south gathered
momentum, Lisbon was abandoned and the siege of Porto raised.

With the Miguelistas forced on the defensive, their fate was sealed
by the death of Fernando VII in Spain (who, however, had himself
protested D. Miguel's usurpation) and the espousal of constitutionalism by the Spanish queen regent. Signing of the Quadruple Alliance
by the four western constitutional monarchies in April 1834 provided
further British naval and financial backing. Together with direct
Spanish military assistance, that completed the final defeat of Portuguese traditionalism in May 1834. Miguelism had preceded and to
some extent inspired the rise of Spanish Carlism, not least through the
influence of D. Carlos's Portuguese wife, a sister of D. Miguel. Support for traditionalism was proportionately as great as in Spain, but
the regional identities that provided such strong redoubts for Carlism
were lacking in Portugal. The outcome of the civil war was determined in part by pressure and assistance from abroad, but the bold
and energetic leadership of D. Pedro was also vital, as well as the
action of those in the middle class who fought for constitutionalism.

Liberal victory brought the establishment of full constitutional government under the Charter and implantation of the legal and economic reforms of Mousinho da Silveira. The new administrative system divided Portugal into seventeen districts, each of them named after its chief town, and this further increased the influence of the urban middle classes and intelligentsia. Suffrage for the chamber of deputies was semidemocratic but indirect. Males of twenty-five years of age or older, all heads of families, officers, priests, and graduates with higher degrees were entitled to vote for provincial electors. The electors, however, were required to have at least 200,000 reis annual income, and it was they who chose the deputies.

Religion

The institution that paid the heaviest price for the defeat of traditionalism was the church. There were approximately 30,000 of the clergy in Portugal at that time, one-third of them in the orders. This was nearly 1 percent of the population, a percentage half again greater than that in Spain and larger than in any other nominally Christian country. Nearly all the hierarchy and the great bulk of the clergy had supported D. Miguel. The victorious liberal monarchy carried out a general purge of clerical ranks, expelling all of D. Miguel's appointees in the hierarchy and evicting many of his supporters among the lower clergy. For nearly a century, animosity toward the monastic establishments had been building up among reformers and liberals, who claimed that these were otiose, parasitical institutions that monopolized vital wealth. In 1834 all convents and monasteries were abolished and all their lands, together with much of the remaining property of the church, confiscated. Members of religious orders were guaranteed a lifetime pension.

The Portuguese disamortization thus preceded Spain's by two years, and it was at once more radical and less severe: more radical in that all orders were dissolved, but less severe in that a little land was left in the hands of the church, at least somewhat more than in Spain. The greater radicalism came from the more directly liberal, anticlerical sentiments of the Portuguese crown and from the stronger central power existing in Portugal. As in Spain, the disamortization was also prompted by the financial strain of the civil war that had left the crown with a heavy debt. Accurate statistics are not available, but the sale of church lands and most of the royal lands (especially those of the former military orders) in the 1830s and 1840s probably resulted in the transfer of ownership of nearly one-fourth the cultivated land in Portugal. The resulting profit had only a slight effect on the treasury balance, but the sales helped to establish a new upper middle class of landowners who exercised increasing political influence and whose social and economic interests were tied to the constitutional monarchy.

As in Spain, the disamortization was anticlerical, but despite its greater radicalism it was not anti-Catholic. There was no question of separating church and state, and the regime continued to be officially Catholic. In subsequent concordats of 1848, 1857, and 1886, the papacy officially recognized the crown's right of nomination. According to the letter of the law, the Portuguese church hierarchy could not receive bulls from Rome, make appointments, or even ordain priests without the crown's consent. As the century wore on and the regime was pressed by demands for greater liberalization, constitutional conservatism established closer identity once more between government and church. After 1848 the Portuguese hierarchy fully accepted the regime, and in the latter decades of the century there was often a fairly close relationship between local church authorities and the leaders of the established parties. The association of church and crown met increasing hostility from radicals in later decades.

In general, the Portuguese church had no more success than that of Spain in adapting to the cultural and social changes of the period, and its educational achievements were even fewer. The customs and behavior of the clergy had still not been fully brought into accord with formal standards, and a certain amount of concubinage persisted. These shortcomings were not such liabilities as they would have been in other areas, for Portuguese society as a whole was changing only slowly and remained rural and conservative, and also more respectful of the traditional place and structure of religion.

As in Spain, there occurred a Catholic revival at the close of the nineteenth century. A law of 1901 legalized the return of monastic orders that engaged in educational or charity work. When the monarchy was overthrown nine years later, 160 monastic houses had been reestablished, though their population was small. A lay association, the Apostolado da Oração, was formed in 1909 and soon claimed a nominal two million members—more than one-third of the country's population.

Like its Spanish counterpart, the Portuguese intelligentsia became increasingly anti-Catholic, particularly at the close of the century. This mood was heightened by the Catholic revival and by the continuing influence of religion in a semitraditional rural society. By the beginning of the twentieth century, the fixation of middle class radicalism on anticlericalism as a political and cultural panacea was distinctly stronger than in Spain.

Portuguese Masonry

Members of the Masonic lodges played a major role in the rise of Portuguese liberalism and anticlericalism. Freemasonry entered Portugal from England before the middle of the eighteenth century and spread slowly there and in Brazil. By 1812 there were thirteen lodges in Lisbon alone. Brazilian Masons were active in the riots of 1801 and 1817, but in Portugal Masons were found on both sides of the Gomes da Freire revolt in 1817. By 1820, however, Masons were devoted almost unanimously to the liberal cause in politics, and their secrecy and cohesiveness enabled them to play a vital role in mobilizing support in a society in which there were few effective associations. Portuguese Freemasonry was middle class, especially upper middle class, with some aristocratic support. At the behest of leading Masons, D. Pedro himself joined the order. By the 1830s the Masons had become, by and large, the principal promoters of anticlericalism.

After the triumph of constitutionalism, Portuguese Masonry split in accordance with the main cleavages in liberal ranks, dividing into more radical and more conservative groups. A united Grand Orient was not established until 1869, but by that time, Masonry was ceasing to play a catalytic role. The upper middle class, established in power and wealth, were less attracted to it, and by the late nineteenth century Masons were drawn mainly from the lower middle class ranks of white-collar employees. Its place in radical politics at the turn of the century was taken over largely by secret republican radical political societies, especially the Carbonária, with more than 40,000 members; by 1912 the Masons had fewer than 3,000.

Septembrism

Pedro IV* (1826–1834) died of tuberculosis within three months of his final triumph and was succeeded by his fifteen-year-old daughter, Maria da Glória, as Maria II (1834–1853). She played the role of constitutional monarch as well as Portuguese conditions permitted and more responsibly than her equally youthful Spanish contemporary, Isabel II.

Under the new parliament of 1834 Portuguese affairs were dominated by upper-middle- and upper-class liberals who had come to power with D. Pedro. This new liberal oligarchy was quite compara-

* To clarify dynastic chronology, it should be explained that Pedro III was never king in his own right. He was the husband and uncle of Maria I, ruling jointly with her during the first years of her reign until his death in 1786.

ble in social composition and economic interests to the Spanish
Moderates of the 1840s. It was represented by a political intelligentsia
of lawyers, and its wealth was based on land, much of it newly
acquired. The Portuguese liberal oligarchy was, however, proportionately narrower than that sustaining the Moderate regime in Spain, for
the church and royal lands divided up at the beginning of this period
were distributed among only 623 new owners. Terms of sale were
usually below market price, and 60 percent of the cost was paid for
with state credits. Thus though sales continued at a lower rate for
several decades, they did little to attentuate the state fiscal crisis,
which grew increasingly severe. The treasury building itself burned
down.

The liberal oligarchy was opposed by democratic elements who
wanted direct suffrage, more complete civic freedom, and greater
attention to the interests of the middle and lower classes. A spirit of
revolt was encouraged by economic depression and a new fall in
prices, which provoked hunger riots in Porto. Dissidence in the chamber prompted new elections in 1836, won by the government though
the oppositon triumphed in the districts of Douro, Beira, and the
Algarve. The opposition's focus was the Porto district, where it gained
twenty-seven of the twenty-eight seats. Oppositon leaders then planned a popular demonstration in Lisbon to coincide with the arrival of
the opposition deputies from Porto in September 1836. This resulted
in the "Septembrist" revolt, in which the opposition brought out a
demonstration by the Lisbon mob that was given prompt support by
the Municipal Guard (a special constabulary established for Lisbon
and Porto). The outburst was the equivalent of the Spanish Progessive
revolts and followed on the heels of the sergeants' mutiny at La
Granja (August 1836) that temporarily reimposed the constitution of
1812 in Spain.

The crown had to give way and appoint a new compromise ministry led by a former general and leading Freemason, the Marquês de
Sá da Bandeira. The resulting Septembrist government was not a
direct representative of the lower-middle- and lower-class rebels, but
rather an effort to establish a more moderate and flexible policy that
could uphold the regime while conciliating broader interest groups. It
was also willing to represent the interests of the proto-industrial
sectors of the middle class, which had been thoroughly subordinated
to the landowning and commercial bourgeoisie. For eight months the
ministry of the interior was occupied by Manuel da Silva Passos
("Passos Manuel"), who carried out a whole series of reforms. The
government made improvements in the administrative and judicial
systems, initiated a protective tariff, encouraged commerce, and stimulated manufacturing and the importation of machinery (the first

Portuguese industrial exposition was held in 1838). It imposed new penal reforms, abolished the slave trade, and created a system of specialized and secondary schools, including an institute to train skilled workers.

The Septembrist ministry reinstituted the constitution of 1822, but this led to an attempted counter-coup by the throne: the *belenzada* of November 1836, supported by British and French diplomacy, which was resolved by an agreement to hold elections for an assembly that would write a new constitution. These were boycotted by upper class liberals and produced a strong Septembrist victory, but meanwhile economic conditions worsened. Several traditionalist guerrilla bands took up arms in eastern Portugal in emulation of the Carlists. The upper-middle-class leaders of Septembrist reformism, who never formed an organized group, were badly split by personality, principle, and status rivalry. Though the Septembrists themselves rejected radical measures, the oligarchic supporters of the old Charter were eager to be rid of the new government. A reaction was encouraged by the economic depression, by British diplomacy, which combatted the new policy of protectionism, and by Belgium, interested in making inroads in Portuguese Africa. The "marshals' revolt" of mid-1837, led by the moderate generals Ericeira and Saldanha, however, met resolute resistance from the Lisbon lower classes despite initial success in the provinces, and it ultimately collapsed.

This left the way open for the drafting of the new Portuguese constitution of 1838, which turned out to be a compromise between the Charter and the more democratic constitution of 1822. The new document was influenced by the recent Spanish Progressive constitution of 1837 and the Belgian constitution of 1831. A moderating influence was also played by French diplomacy, which supported the moderate faction of the Septembrists (the reverse of the French alignment in Spanish politics). The constitution instituted an elective senate of the wealthy but retained the absolute veto power of the crown as well as the royal right to name ministers and dissolve parliament. It also specified more clearly the separation of powers and introduced a measure of political and administrative decentralization (though the centralist-localist controversy never became as important in Portugal as in Spain).

By the time the new constitution was written the Septembrist leaders had become more conservative, fearing radical pressures from below and eager to protect the established interests of which they had become a part. The traditionalist revolt in the east had been put down by 1838, and the prime minister, Sá da Bandeira, labored to conciliate conservatives by trying to establish an understanding with the church.

Rivalries within the Septembrist parliament became increasingly severe, and he resigned in April 1839.

Chartism

The trend away from the Septembrist compromises accelerated after the close of 1839. From that point conservatives were in continuous control of the government. Hostility to the new constitution among the upper classes and major economic interests had never slackened, and their political representatives exerted growing pressure for a return to the Charter of 1826. Chartism became the doctrine of conservative liberalism, opposed to a broader suffrage, wider civil guarantees, local self-government, and decentralization, and in general favoring the suppression of what was sometimes dubbed *canalhocracia,* government by or for the lower classes.

The initiative was seized at the beginning of 1842 by the minister of justice, an opportunistic Septembrist moderate, Costa Cabral. When elections in Porto indicated a conservative trend, he proclaimed restoration of the Charter. Joint pressure from other pro-Chartist forces resulted in the reorganization of government in February 1842, and the replacement of the constitution of 1838 by the Charter of 1826 in a kind of joint civilian-military pronunciamiento. A leading general, the duke of Terceira, took office as the new Chartist prime minister, to some extent foreshadowing the role of Narváez two years later in Spain. The main figure in the Chartist government, however, was the civilian politician Costa Cabral, who became minister of the interior to manage the politics of the new regime.

Like the July Monarchy in France and the Isabeline regime in Spain, Portuguese Chartism was designed to institutionalize the rule of the new social and economic elite. Under its suffrage regulations only 36,400 citizens—.7 percent of the population—were eligible to vote, and only 4,500 eligible to sit in parliament. Thirty new Chartist peers were created to staff the once more appointive senate, and the new parliamentary elections of 1842 were to a considerable degree manipulated by the government. A pro-liberal revolt by part of the army in 1844 was put down, and the next elections in 1845 were conducted in an even more arbitrary fashion.

The Chartist government proceeded to carry out political and administrative reforms similar to those of the French July Monarchy in the preceding decade and of the Moderate regime in Spain a few years later. A new administrative code was drawn up, municipal government was reformed and thoroughly centralized, and the National Guard, at first expanded under the Septembrists from the previous Municipal Guard, was further reduced and placed under professional discipline. Relations with the papacy were finally regularized. Taxation was reformed, making fiscal administration more efficient but leaving excises with the main burden of supplying income and assigning costs of nearly all local services to local government. A road-building program was begun, and some new measures taken to advance education.

In 1846-1847 the Chartist regime had to face new challenges from both the right and the left. Liberalism in Portugal as elsewhere was essentially an urban and elitist movement. It was almost completely dissociated from the peasants, nearly 80 percent of the people, who were further alienated by local government domination and an increased tax burden. Liberal legislation had abolished seigneurial legal jurisdiction but had left the peasants still subject to many feudal economic dues, to which the new excises were added. In the spring of 1846 the peasants of the Minho reacted in what became known as the Maria da Fonte movement. Peasant women were aroused by a new sanitation decree of Costa Cabral forbidding the traditional practice of free burials in churches, and under the nominal leadership of a local peasant woman, Maria da Fonte, they marched against civil authorities. Miguelista elements encouraged the reaction, which began to protest local government and tax oppression. Radical Septembrists from the opposite extreme joined in, and the protest movement spread somewhat amorphously through Tras-os-Montes and Beira, supported by priests, aristocrats, and in some areas town radicals. Imposition of martial law and attempted military repression only increased opposition; part of the army began to defect. Costa Cabral and Terceira were forced out, and in May 1846 some of the offending local regulations were abolished.

The new government was a more liberal ministry under the veteran Duque de Palmela. It soon encountered opposition from the court circle and the Chartists, encouraged by Costa Cabral from exile. D. Maria's German husband, Ferdinand of Saxe-Coburg (who was influenced by the authoritarian royalist notions of his uncle, Leopold of Belgium), urged its ouster and the formation of a more conservative government. In the so-called *emboscada de Belem* of October 1846, D. Maria forced the Palmela ministry to resign in favor of a new government under the war minister, Gen. Saldanha. The whole tactic was reminiscent of the first attempt to oust the Septembrists in the belenzada exactly ten years earlier.

The result was a revolt of the middle and lower classes in Porto, dubbed by their enemies the *patuléia* (rabble), who formed a rebel junta under the somewhat mistaken notion that the Cabral faction had reimposed itself and was usurping the royal prerogatives. The revolt was encouraged by a new financial crisis and price downturn that brought temporary unemployment and misery to many. It spread throughout northern Portugal and to the extreme south and the Azores. Saldanha assumed de facto powers of dictatorship and a state of civil war existed for eight months. Some miguelista elements joined the neo-Septembrist forces led by the Patuléia junta of middle class leaders in Porto. The government forces gained only limited successes and were ultimately victorious in June 1847 only because of British naval and Spanish military intervention on their behalf. Saldanha remained in office for two more years, carrying out reprisals against those active in the Patuléia. He then retired to an honorary post at court, and Costa Cabral returned to power in mid-1849.

Regenerationism and the Establishment of Rotativism, 1851–1878

Costa Cabral as prime minister was even more overweening than in his earlier tour as minister of justice. He became increasingly arbitrary, attempting to establish semiconstitutional government on the narrowest of bases. In this respect, Costa Cabral's government in 1849–1851 was somewhat like that of Bravo Murillo in Spain during 1851–1852, though the former was probably more corrupt. Like Bravo, he made the mistake of alienating key military politicians, overreaching himself in a grab for full power by trying to have his chief Chartist competitor, Marshal Saldanha, removed from his honorary position at court.

Thus it was the Chartist general Saldanha, restorer of orthodox Chartism in 1846, who finally led a wavering revolt that overthrew Costa Cabral and the Chartist regime in May 1851. Saldanha, the leading political general of nineteenth-century Portugal, played a role analogous to that of O'Donnell in Spain. O'Donnell's goal was to liberalize the Isabeline regime slightly through more attentive and conciliatory government. He later joined liberal Moderates and moderate Progressives in a new Liberal Union and tried to encourage a loyal opposition. He eventually failed, and the Isabeline regime collapsed, but O'Donnell's politics foreshadowed the Restoration system of Cánovas that functioned for half a century after 1875.

Saldanha and his colleagues were more successful than O'Donnell. The Chartists had never been a regular, coherently organized political party, and in 1851 Saldanha tried to organize a more liberal group composed of the most flexible Chartists and moderate ex-Septembrists and Patuleians. The group became known as the Regenerator party, and to widen its support, in 1852 amended the Charter by the first "Additional Act," introducing direct elections on the basis of a broadened but still minority suffrage. It also increased the powers of parliament slightly and abolished the death penalty for political crimes. Yet the Regenerator government of Saldanha did not intend to give up the powers of electoral manipulation. The elections of 1851 had been the freest in nearly fifteen years; those of 1852 were more carefully controlled to return a strong Regenerator majority. A *fornada* (baking or confection) of twenty new aristocratic titles was carried out, as later happened during O'Donnell's long government in Spain, and the Regenerators were given a safe majority in the senate. Despite mounting protests, however, the political opposition did not reject the system but joined to form a new liberal group, the Historical or Progressive party, that succeeded Saldanha when the first Regenerator government came to an end in 1856. This was the beginning of *rotativismo*—the alternating in power of conservative and liberal parties willing to accept the rules of the regime and play the role of loyal opposition. It preceded the establishment of the turno system under the Spanish constitutional monarchy by nearly a quarter century.

There were three primary differences between Spain and Portugal that explain the earlier stabilization of a functional parliamentary system in Portugal. a) The Portuguese monarchy possessed greater political discretion and responsibility. In Spain the crown consistently refused power or participation to the major opposition party, driving it to revolution. This did not happen in Portugal after 1851. Maria II died in childbirth at the age of thirty-four in 1853. She was succeeded by her sons Pedro V (1853-1861), who died tragically of an undiagnosed illness at the age of twenty-four, and Luis I (1861-1889). Pedro V was the most precocious ruler in Portuguese history, a dedicated progressive and probably the most brilliant European prince of his generation, and his younger brother was a model constitutional monarch. b) In a small country such as Portugal, with a tiny political and economic elite, it was easier to conciliate the leading interest groups and coordinate them behind two main parties. c) In Portugal, the regional problem scarcely existed and the lower classes were culturally and politically even more backward than in Spain. Hence Portuguese society did not face such radical and divergent political pressures as did the Spanish.

The strongest figure in Saldanha's first Regenerator cabinet was the minister of finance, Fontes Pereira de Melo, chief proponent of a policy of economic development that became known as *fontismo*. This was the Portuguese equivalent of the Spanish economic expansion and railroad building of the decade 1855-1865. Fontes consolidated the national debt at 3 percent and created a new ministry of public works, building more roads, beginning telegraph construction, and encouraging railroad expansion. New credit was obtained, foreign investment stimulated, and taxes both increased and reorganized, while tariff duties were lowered. In general, the program was aimed at laying some of the foundations, particularly in communication and transportation, for a more modern economy. There was little attempt at direct industrialization, however, and the costs were born mostly by the lower classes in the form of excise taxes. Property taxes, as in Spain, tended to be rigged in favor of the largeholders to the detriment of small property owners. This general orientation characterized the economic policy of Portuguese government for the next generation. Bad economic conditions in 1855-1856, however, together with criticism for too-generous concessions to foreign investors, played a major role in the erosion of Saldanha's political support, leading to his resignation in 1856.

The Regenerators were succeeded for the next three years by a ministry of the Historicals under their chief, the Duque de Loulé. The Historicals had organized themselves loosely in 1854 as a more liberal opposition group, but neither they nor the Regenerators formed a fully structured political party. Political boundaries blurred rather easily, and both factions were little more than loose coalitions based on outstanding personalities and local interests. Differences between them did exist, but they were more of emphasis than of ideology. The Historicals stood for a slightly broader suffrage and more honest elections, but they were less democratic than many of the former Septembrists, and politics was still restricted to a small elite. The Historicals naturally won the next election, conducted by their own ministry, after which the government negotiated the new Concordat of 1857 and a few Catholic orders were allowed to reenter Portugal.

When the Regenerators returned to power under the Duque da Terceira in 1859, they inaugurated an electoral system of individual candidate constituencies in place of provincial lists. This, with some manipulation, facilitated the election of notables, and the Regenerators won a large majority. The death of Terceira, however, deprived the Regenerators of effective leadership (Saldanha had withdrawn), and after an interim ministry the Historicals formed a new government that lasted from 1860 to 1865. After that it became difficult for a leader of either of the two factions to hold a majority, and the first "fusionist" (coalition) ministry was formed in 1865.

Portugal escaped almost completely any influence by or involvement in the turmoil of Spanish radicalism and republicanism in the years 1868-1874. Republican propaganda in Portugal began at this time, however, and a republican party with Marxist overtones was organized in 1872 but made little progress. The only potential point of contact between Spanish and Portuguese affairs during these years was in the question of dynastic union. In both countries there were liberal proponents of Iberian union, some vague sort of federative association between the two countries, but in view of numerous obstacles the only practical issue was that of dynastic union or alliance. One of Prim's leading candidates for the Spanish crown in 1869 was Ferdinand of Saxe-Coburg, father of the Portuguese king and former consort of Maria II. Such a succession would have provided for a union of the Hispanic crowns under Luis I after the death of the elderly Ferdinand, but when the Portuguese objected, Ferdinand agreed to accept the offer only subject to Portuguese government approval and a Spanish guarantee of Portuguese independence. This undercut the very idea of Iberian union, and the Portuguese candidacy was dropped.

By the 1860s the center of attention in public affairs was taken by the financial question, which bedeviled Portuguese government to the end of the monarchy in 1910 and throughout the history of the parliamentary republic that followed. The government debt mounted rapidly, nearly doubling between 1854 and 1869, when it hit a level of almost fifty dollars per capita, a crushing burden for so poor a country. There was no end in sight. The royal jewels were sold and the royal estates mortgaged, but the main problem was poor government management, waste and corruption, and above all extremely low revenue from an unproductive economy. All entailment of estates was abolished in 1863, opening up the market for agricultural production, but the effects of this were slow in coming. Fontismo relied mainly on foreign investment and the raising of loans, while encouraging free trade (to the detriment of national manufactures) and maintaining high excises.

A new opposition movement among radical intellectuals began after 1865, and in 1867 a small element of middle class progressives joined with the more liberal of the Historicals to form a loosely organized grouping known as the Popular or Reformist party. Protests among the lower classes over excises and among businessmen over foreign competition and taxes mounted steadily. An attempt by the government to raise excises further was blocked by a merchants' revolt in Porto and several other cities on the first day of 1868 (and hence termed the *janeirinha*). The Fusionist cabinet was forced to resign and was replaced with a Reformist ministry that hoped to reduce the budget and balance the tax structure. Lacking organized support, internal unity, and a clear-cut program, it accomplished little. A heterogeneous semi-Reformist ministry under the aged ex-Septembrist Sá da Bandeira and the bishop of Viseu that took office in 1869 did fire employees, lower salaries, abolish subsidies, and reduce state operations, but it still did not balance the budget and lasted only a month. Short-lived heterogeneous ministries followed for two years, while 55 percent of the state budget went to service the debt. In 1871 the Regenerators returned to power in a ministry led by Fontes.

Portuguese Reformism never took coherent form and did not seriously try to develop a popular base. The Reformists' disagreements with the Regenerators proved less profound than they had originally seemed, and in 1876 the Reformists merged with the Historicals to form the new Progressive Party. After six years in power the Regenerator ministry resigned in 1877, and regular rotativismo was resumed at approximately the same time that the system of the turno was being established in Spain and trasformismo was beginning to operate in Italian politics. After an interim eight-month government led by a conservative independent, Fontes returned to power in 1878, then gave way to a Progressive government the following year. The Regenerators took over once more in 1881, and after two brief ministries led by colleagues, Fontes headed the government for five more years. The Progressives then governed under their chief, José Luciano de Castro, from 1886 to 1890. Thanks to the narrower circle of Portuguese politics and the smaller range of interests in Portugal, rotativismo in those years functioned more smoothly than the Spanish turno.

Economic Development

The first effects of modern economic development began to be felt by the beginning of the nineteenth century, not so much in terms of Portugal's domestic expansion but as a consequence of foreign competition and imports. Industrializing Britain had begun to produce so many goods—primarily textiles—so cheaply that they cut deeply into the domestic market in Portugal and also into Portuguese exports to Brazil. As harsh in its effects as British competition was the closure of markets by war and the independence of Brazil, which in the decade 1796-1806 had accounted for three-quarters of all Portuguese commerce, re-exports from Brazil totaling from 60 to 80 percent of all Portuguese exports. Most of this valuable trade was lost. Altogether, using the level of the year 1800 as 100, Portuguese manufactured exports, while never very extensive, declined to 66 in 1805 and 10 in 1810 and recovered to only 27 in 1820.

The period from 1808 to 1826 was a time of general price deflation, with a particularly sharp decline in prices and commerce between 1817 and 1820. These economic pressures were of great importance in encouraging the coastal bourgeoisie to support a revolt for representative government that might provide more stimulus for economic development. Similarly, the loss of Brazil, coupled with the general problem of reviving commerce in a deflated market, encouraged the first real effort to increase Portuguese manufactures since Pombal. The first two waves of Portuguese pre-industrialization were the Ericeira program of 1675-1690 and the Pombaline efforts of 1769-1778. The third occurred after the triumph of liberalism in 1820: between 1820 and 1822, 177 new manufacturing establishments were set up, an increase of 15 percent, bringing the total to 1,031 shops, most of them very small. In the following eighteen months from mid-1822 to the end of 1823 the number rose by 20 percent, the main beneficiary being the Porto district.

During the following decade of reaction and internal turmoil there was little advance, but a new wave of industrialization developed after 1835. The Septembrist movement of 1836 was to some extent an industrialists' movement, for some of its leaders were industrialists and small merchants, and it drew support from artisans and workers. Certain Septembrist leaders, especially Sá da Bandeira, were the first to conceive of the economic development of Portuguese Africa to complement the expanded commerce and industry of metropolitan Portugal. In general, the mechanization of Portuguese industry began around 1835, but depending as it did on the importation of steam engines and other machinery the process was very slow. By 1845 only 30 of 634 manufacturing plants (only a few of which could be called factories) possessed steam power. In the post-1835 phase of mechanization, the Lisbon region progressed more rapidly than did Porto.

The basis of the Portuguese economy, agriculture, began to change but also very slowly. At the beginning of·the nineteenth century only about one-sixth of the surface of Portugal was under cultivation, and it is doubtful if the proportion had ever been any higher. The economic reforms of the liberal regime—selling church and some royal lands, beginning the breakup of aristocratic entailed estates, and abolishing many seigneurial obligations—greatly enlarged the land market and the opportunities for agriculture. Though many *foreiro* and emphyteutic rights were swept away, the reforms rallied most of the wealthier elements to the liberal regime. The extent of land under cultivation increased, though not as dramatically as in Spain during the same period. Among the peasantry, subsistance cultivation of corn and potatoes also rose. Market production increased somewhat, and between 1839 and 1855 Portugal actually exported grain for the first time in centuries. (It is not entirely clear, however, whether this was due to greatly increased production or to a shift in commercial and transportation patterns, for considerable grain was also imported from Spain.) There was no significant improvement in agricultural technique, which was scarcely as advanced as Spain's. Thus the changes in Portuguese landholding and agriculture between 1834 and 1855 were not in any drastic productive reform but simply in the consolidation of a new class of middle and large landholders, drawn from the upper middle class and the aristocracy, which now controlled the primary sources of wealth. This class was able, together with major commercial and financial interests, to largely control Portuguese government for nearly seventy years after the return of the Charter in 1842.

Fontismo as practiced in the 1850s and 1860s stressed commerce, finance, and transportation. The first bona fide Portuguese bank, the Bank of Lisbon, had been founded in 1821. The number of banks increased to three by 1858, thirteen by 1867, and fifty-one by 1875. Deposits increased eight-fold between 1858 and 1875. The first Portuguese bankers came primarily from wholesale commerce, since this was the major source of profit and capital formation in the traditional Portuguese economy. Some large landowners also became involved, but nineteenth-century Portuguese banking showed little interest in trying to finance industrial development. Its resources were limited, and it preferred easy, high-interest earnings through short-term loans, state bonds, transportation projects, and real estate mortgages.

Portuguese railroad construction was begun soon after that of Spain and on much the same financial terms, but the rhythm of its development was considerably slower. Foreign capital and technology dominated, and political favoritism played a major role. The first short line out of Lisbon was built in 1856, and the kilometers of track increased as shown in table 12.

The new Portuguese tariff of 1853 moved in the direction of freer trade, providing protection only for a few favored items such as cotton textiles, and the low tariff policy was not reversed until 1889. Correspondingly, after 1852 there was a decline in the rate of importation of steam engines and machinery for the development of Portu-

Table 12. Portuguese Railroad Expansion, 1877-1912

Year	Kilometers of track
1877	952
1885	1,529
1894	2,353
1902	2,381
1907	2,753
1912	2,974

Source: Dicionario de História de Portugal, 1:450.

guese industry. Higher commercial prices after 1850 made this emphasis on commercial and financial interests possible. Yet the government's opening of maximal commercial opportunities did not benefit all branches of export. In 1852 the salt producers' *Roda* (corporation) was dissolved. It had tried to maintain quantity production at even prices and fair sales terms. With commerce unregulated, individual salt merchants tended to price salt out of the international market, leading to a great decline in production.

Taxes were raised significantly during the second round of fontismo in the 1870s, and government revenue rose by a startling 50 percent between 1871 and 1876. There was much new construction and the biggest wave of speculation the century had seen. During the early 1870s new banks were set up in all the major provincial towns. Portugal attracted considerable investment from Brazil, and in turn, Portuguese financiers invested in Spanish money and state finance between 1871 and 1875. Cutting of the Spanish interest rate by the Restoration government in 1876 helped to burst the Portuguese financial bubble and to provoke the third major financial crisis of the century in Portugal (others occurred in 1836–1837 and 1846). The next financial cycle lasted fifteen years; when the crisis of 1891 struck, the bondholders affected most were French and German investors in Portuguese state finance and transportation.

The gravest financial problem throughout was that of the state budget, operated at a perpetual deficit. The actual deficit was highest just before the crisis of 1890–1891, after which it was reduced, but the national debt mounted steadily. Despite the heavy load of excises borne by the lower classes, the Portuguese economy as a whole was probably undertaxed. Between 1820 and 1920 the per capita tax burden increased by about 100 percent, but the growth in income and production was somewhat higher than that. Given the determination of dominant political and economic interests to avoid direct taxation as much as possible, the fiscal burden in Portugal, as in most other countries, was shifted to indirect taxes. Fluctuation of the budget deficit, the rise in the national debt, and the increase in the proportion of indirect taxes are shown in tables 13–15.

The major development in the Portuguese economy of the late nineteenth century was the expansion of agriculture, which got underway around the middle of the century but accelerated only in the 1890s. There were at least three main factors involved. Population increased steadily, and despite emigration the demand for food steadily mounted. Secondly, all *morgados* (entailment of estates) were finally abolished in 1863, completing the opening up of the land market. Third, the first tariff of the century that provided real protection for grain was adopted in 1889. Altogether between 1874 and

Table 13.   Portuguese Budget Deficit, 1822-1910

Year	Contos*
1822	1,607
1828	3,868
1835-36	4,453
1839-40	2,152
1849-50	2,261
1859-60	1,444
1869-70	14,590
1879-80	10,149
1889-90	13,297
1899-1900	6,413
1909-10	6,896

Table 14.   Portuguese National Debt, 1822-1910

Year	Contos
1822	38,000
1827	45,000
1834	61,000
1840	72,000
1855	94,518
1865	201,207
1890	592,613
1910	878,590

Table 15.   Percent of Portuguese Taxes Indirect, 1840-1910

Year	Percent
1840-41	52.0
1845-46	71.4
1864-65	66.0
1909-10	61.3

Source, tables 13-15: Dic. Hist. Port., 2:193-94.
  *A conto equalled 1,000 mil-réis.

1934 the extent of land under cultivation in Portugal increased by 70 percent, as indicated in the following figures:

	1874	1902	1934
Crops and fallow	21.3%	35.1%	37.9%
Forest	7.0	22.1	28.4
Uncultivated but productive	23.4	21.7	15.0
Cultivable but not under cultivation	44.3	17.3	14.9
Land unfit for cultivation	3.8	3.8	3.8

The new land inheritance law after 1863 provided for equal division of property among heirs, and the average size of Portuguese cultivation units remained uneconomically small. In 1868, five years after the final extinction of morgados, there were 5,678,385 agrarian properties averaging 1.55 hectares. In much of the Minho, minifundia were even more the rule than in Spanish Galicia. Some landlords owned many small properties and renting was still common, but there may have been a slightly higher percentage of small peasant proprietors than in Spain generally. Many renters retained long-term emphyteutic rights. Expansion of peasant agriculture was encouraged by the decline in fixed rental costs under the slow inflation of the later nineteenth century. The cultivation of corn was extended, and some improvement in technique was made possible by increased use of fertilizer, mainly manure, and new sources of water. The greatest extension of cultivation occurred not in the heavily populated, already heavily cultivated Minho, but in the southern two-thirds of Portugal, where the Alemtejo was finally repopulated by the close of the century.

In part because of the agricultural expansion, the 1890s were a decade of rapid growth in commerce. This occurred despite the tariff of 1892, which marked Portugal's swing, though in lesser degree, toward the general trend of heavier protectionism in Europe during the late nineteenth century. There was also a new wave of industrialization around the turn of the century, yet it was modest and hardly served to take up the slack in the extremely slow growth of domestic manufactures. Portugal still suffered from the main deficiencies of underdeveloped countries: lack of capital for productive investment, lack of skilled labor, lack of technology (there were only 150 qualified engineers in Portugal in 1870), and lack of industrial raw materials. There was a notable increase in corporate investment during the second half of the century, as shown in table 16, but it was quite small by comparison with the industrialized countries. Even during the first decade of the twentieth century, corporate investment in commerce exceeded that in industry.

Table 16. Corporate Investment in Portugal, Excluding Transport

	To 1849		1900-1909	
Total	106,652		470,194	
Industry	1,800	1.7%	192,532	40.9%
Commerce	103,502	96.9%	220,171	47.0%

Source: Armando de Castro, *Introdução ao estudo da economia portuguesa* (Lisbon, 1947).

Portuguese Society

Despite the institutional revolution and half a century of political turmoil, there was less change in Portuguese society than in anywhere else in Europe save the Balkans. The principal changes occurred at the top, for the chief consequence of the establishment of Portuguese liberalism was formation of a new oligarchy of "bourgeois nobility." This was made up of an increasingly fluid fusion of chief descendants of the old landed aristocracy and members of the new economic and political elite, who were given new titles in recognition of their wealth or services. Hence the generic term *barões* that was often used to define the new upper class oligarchy. This formation of a new nine-teenth-century aristocracy *embourgeoisée*, closely associated with large-scale landowning and commerce and finance, exactly paralleled a process going on at the same time in Spain.

By 1856 the Portuguese nobility had increased to 315 titles, distrib-uted as shown in table 17. Of the seven ducal titles, one dated from the seventeenth century, one from the eighteenth, one had been given the British hero Wellington, and the other four had been given to upper class liberal leaders since 1832: Terceira (1932), Palmela (1833), Saldanha (1846), Loulé (1862). In 1820 there had been only 5 barons;

Table 17. Distribution of Portuguese Titles, 1856

Dukes	7
Marquises	21
Counts	79
Viscounts with rank of *grandeza*	33
Barons with rank of *grandeza*	13
Viscounts	69
Barons	93
	315

Source: *Dic. Hist. Port.*, 3:160.

by 1856 there were 106. Between 1826 and 1856 108 titles of marquis, count, and viscount were granted, more than double the 84 that had existed. The process continued at this rate until at least 1880, reaching its height in the Reformist interlude and reestablishment of rotativismo between 1868 and 1876. During those eight years 15 new titles of baron and 55 new titles of viscount were created. The abolition of morgados in 1863 struck a blow to aristocratic landholding, but by that time much of the neo-aristocracy was tied in to diversified economic interests.

The major source of prestige created by the liberal regime for the traditional hereditary aristocracy was the chamber of peers in the Portuguese legislature, as established by the Charter of 1826. The Second Additional Act (1885) suppressed hereditary membership in favor of royal nomination and indirect election, but elections were abolished and hereditary membership restored by the Third Additional Act of 1896, which also retained provisions for royal nomination. This was part of an effort to maintain the leadership of the official aristocratic elite, which by that point was clearly waning. After 1870, the proportion of cabinet ministers with titles steadily declined, and by the beginning of the twentieth century the nobility, whether embourgeoisée or not, had lost its actual place of dominance.

Population increase was steady, thanks to the maintenance of a moderately (though not extremely) high birthrate and the decline of the death rate in the later nineteenth century. An estimate of the increase in population is shown in table 18, the first systematic census

Table 18. *Portuguese Population, 1801–1920*

Year	Population
1801	2,931,930
1821	3,026,450
1835	3,061,684
1838	3,224,474
1841	3,396,972
1854	3,499,121
1858	3,584,677
1861	3,693,362
1864	3,829,618
1878	4,160,315
1890	4,660,095
1900	5,016,267
1911	5,547,708
1920	5,621,977

Source: *Dic. Hist. Port.,* 1:799.

being that of 1864. The rate of increase was approximately equal to Spain's during that period but less than in most other parts of Europe. Between 1886, when adequate records began to be kept, and 1925, the birthrate oscillated between 29 and 33 per thousand. This rate was at first not as high as that of most other similarly underdeveloped countries, and in 1901, for example, was lower than that of Spain (35) and even of industrialized Germany (35.7). The comparatively moderate birthrate was the result mainly of heavy emigration of young males, a rather low marriage rate, and a relatively high average age of marriage. On the other hand, it showed little sign of declining in the early twentieth century as did that of other western countries, mainly because in Portugal social conditions changed so slowly. The decline in the death rate in the late nineteenth century was almost greater than average, dropping from 25 per thousand in 1886 to 18 in 1925. During the years 1901–1905 the Portuguese average of 19.9 was lower than those of Spain (26) and Italy (22), equal to that of Germany (19.9), and scarcely above that of France (19.5). During the first quarter of the twentieth century, however, there was little improvement; significant progress was not made until after 1925.

As far as division by social classes is concerned, in 1821 the nobility and upper bourgeoisie numbered 1 percent of the population, the clergy nearly 2 percent, the middle classes approximately 9 percent, and peasants and town laborers 88 percent. As late as 1890, when the first accurate censuses of economic activity were made, the middle classes had scarcely expanded to 15 percent. In 1890, 61 percent of the labor force was engaged in agriculture, declining to 57 percent in 1911. Industrial employment accounted for 18.4 percent in 1890 and 21 percent in 1911. During that period the proportion of tertiary or service employees rose from 20.6 to 22 percent.

Accurate statistics on the proportion of peasants employed as laborers compared with the proportion who owned or rented land are not available. It has been calculated that early in the nineteenth century about 75 percent of the men in the Alemtejo worked as hired laborers, but the percentage was not so great elsewhere.

One of the salient characteristics of the Portuguese lower classes in the nineteenth century was their general illiteracy, which explains in part why there was so little interest in broadening the suffrage. Terms of enfranchisement varied as shown in table 19. Even with the restricted suffrage, electoral participation was low and rarely exceeded 60 percent.

Emigration reached sizable proportions in the latter part of the century. It had begun to increase after closing of the slave trade to Brazil led to a demand for non-slave labor in Portuguese America. From 1861 to 1872 the emigration was modest, 50,000 people in

Table 19. Terms of Enfranchisement, Portugal, 1864-1915

Year	Requirements for voting	Number of eligible voters	Percent of population
1864	Males over 25 and with 100 reis annual income	344,173	11.1
1878	Literate males and male heads of families	580,214	13.9
1890		874,528	18.7
1910	Literate males over 21 or with 500 reis income	650,341	11.6
1911	Literate males over 21 or heads of families	782,292	13.9
1913	Literate males over 21	379,714	6.7
1915		450,322	8.0

Source: Adapted from Souza Junior, *Censo eleitoral da metrópole,* in Bento Carqueja, *O Povo portuguez* (Porto, 1916), pp. 233-34.

twelve years. In the forty years 1873 to 1913, nearly 1,000,000 people left Portugal—994,813 according to the statistics—and only 50,000 of them ever moved back. The peak year was 1912, when 77,000 left. The bulk of the emigration came from the heavily populated Minho-Douro region, and it represented a cross section of Portuguese society, illiterate peasants predominating. The great majority emigrated to Brazil, though in the early twentieth century nearly 15 percent went to North America. The emigrants left not because of lack of employment in Portugal, for in most of these years there was a shortage of farm laborers, but because of the extremely low wages and lack of any genuine opportunity for advancement at home. Though only 5 percent of the emigrants ever returned permanently (a somewhat lower figure than for Spain and much lower than for Italy), a large proportion did send money to their families, boosting domestic income and assisting the sorely pressed Portuguese balance of payments. The modest Portuguese economic expansion of the late nineteenth century and the great increase in the number of individual agrarian properties owed more than a little to the investment of emigrants.

The urban working class lacked size, importance, and even organization in nineteenth-century Portugal. The absence of industrialization meant that urban growth lagged behind that of much of Europe. There were only two cities of any size, and most manufacturing was done in small shops. Only toward the end of the century did city workers achieve a certain degree of organization and visibility, primarily in Lisbon and Porto. Their numbers increased as follows:

1890	860,825	18.5 percent of the population
1900	977,583	19.5
1910	1,169,542	21.3

Even as late as 1910, however, only 20 percent of the workers engaged in manufacturing were industrial workers employed by factories with more than ten workers.

An organized workers' movement was slow to develop under these conditions. The first workers' syndicate was created in Lisbon in 1838 but was short-lived. Trade union organization did not begin in earnest until the Regenerators took office in 1851. During the next few years a number of syndicates were formed, mainly in Lisbon. Several strikes that were held in 1852 led to disorder, and a new law was passed making labor stoppages illegal. This legislation remained effective until 1911, but depending on the circumstances it was often not enforced. The right of association was itself eliminated in 1862 but restored in 1870. The new civil code of 1867 also made provision for cooperatives, the first of which was formed in Portugal in 1871. By 1889 there were 44 worker cooperatives and 392 worker associations of all kinds (194 in Lisbon, 109 in Porto) with a total of 138,870 members.

Between 1872 and 1899 there were more than fifty strikes in Portugal, most of them more or less tolerated by the authorities, but the major phase of strike activity did not begin until 1903. As in Spain, there were both socialist and anarcho-syndicalist labor movements, as well as smaller individual syndical groups. In general, the labor movement was numerically weak, internally divided, and on shaky legal ground. Its achievements were few, and available statistics indicate that the real wages of urban workers actually declined, or at least failed to rise, during the half century from 1860 to 1910. Despite emigration, the pace of economic development was so slow that population growth more than kept pace, and there were always enough surplus unskilled and semiskilled workers to keep wages down. Working conditions were poor; in the few small Portuguese mines the accident rate was three or four times greater than in German mines. About 1890 there began a trend toward more intensive organization in Portuguese manufacturing in the direction of greater specialization, a shorter working day, and less employment of women. The percentage of women among industrial employees declined slowly from 34.8 in 1890 to 28.3 in 1910. As late as 1917, 16.2 percent of all employees were minors. The state did pass reform legislation between 1889 and 1893. Arbitration tribunals and labor exchanges were set up in the larger towns, and the first major labor regulations, in 1891, attempted to meliorate conditions and regulate night and underground work and the labor of women and children. In general, however, the conditions of Portuguese workers were in some respects even poorer than those of their Spanish counterparts.

Culture and Education

The establishment of Portuguese liberalism coincided with a cultural revival among the Portuguese elite that was primarily associated with the romantic movement in literature. The two chief figures were the poet Almeida Garrett and the historian Alexandre Herculano. Almeida Garrett, the greatest Portuguese romantic poet both in epic and lyric forms, also labored to revive Portuguese drama, which had been virtually dormant since the pioneer labors of Gil Vicente in the sixteenth century. Herculano was the greatest historian in either Spain or Portugal in the nineteenth century and may be considered either the Portuguese Ranke or Michelet. His histories of medieval Portugal and of the Portuguese Inquisition are both historiographic and literary classics, and are also noteworthy for attempting to develop the previously untouched field of social history. In general, Portuguese liberalism leaned heavily on the romantic spirit, and the liberal state established several new cultural institutions—a new art institute and a national theater, for example.

In the 1860s there was a movement toward realism and social concern among leading intellectuals, partly identified with the Reformists. The leading literary figure of the latter part of the century was the quasi-naturalist novelist and diplomat Eça de Queiroz, among the half dozen best west European novelists of his time. By the 1890s, however, a neoromanticist trend was setting in which stressed nostalgia, estheticism, irrationalism, a form of nationalism and also of national pessimism.

Aside from small circles of literati, there existed a small political intelligentsia from 1820 on, associated with political activism and journalism. An enormous number of newspapers were founded in nineteenth-century Portugal, nearly all of them the mouthpieces of political factions, backed by extremely scanty resources, and short of life. Even the largest newspapers rarely printed more than two thousand copies, and prices were rather high. In 1821, the first full year of liberalism, 39 newspapers were founded. The press suffered from the reaction after 1823, but journalistic agitation and pamphleteering was a significant factor in the victory of 1833–1834. The years 1834 to 1851 were in some ways the golden age of political journalism in Portugal, at least as far as polemical and literary style were concerned. Between 1835 and 1837 170 newspapers were founded,

Table 20. Percent of Illiterates in Portuguese Population over
Seven Years of Age, 1890–1911

Year	Males	Females	General
1890	67.6	83.5	76.0
1900	65.0	82.1	74.1
1911	60.8	77.4	69.7

Source: *Dic. Hist. Port.,* 2:51.

though the Chartist regime imposed censorship after 1842 and there was a certain amount of repression in the next nine years. After 1851 journalism continued to expand, and the founding of newspapers reached its height in the 1880s, when an annual average of 184, mostly very short-lived, papers were established. Only a few, such as Lisbon's *O Século,* achieved any distinction. In general, Portuguese press regulations were quite liberal. The right of jury trial for press offenses was abolished in 1890, and there were further restrictions in 1898 and 1907, but there was no effective libel law, and journals were normally free to print all manner of scurrilous accusations, even against the royal family.

Schools fared more poorly than newspapers. Abolition of the Catholic orders was a major blow to Catholic education, which operated the only system of primary schools in the country. The government was hard pressed to take up the slack, but public educational facilities were expanded at a steady if rather slow rate. In 1820 there had been approximately 2.5 primary schools (all Catholic) per 10,000 population. In 1870 there were 6 and in 1900 9. Between 1845 and 1870 the number of state schools doubled, reaching a total of 2,359. By the end of the century the figure increased to approximately 4,000, and the percentage of state schools among all schools rose from 62 percent in 1868 to 74.2 percent in 1900. Catholic orders were not officially permitted to teach again until a new law of 1901, and by that time the status of Catholic education had declined greatly. In general, the record of nineteenth-century Portuguese liberalism in education was poor, even considering the country's limited resources. Two efforts were made, in 1859 and 1890, to establish a separate ministry of public instruction, but neither lasted more than a year or two. Proportionately less was spent on education than in any other European state save the Ottoman empire.

The popular culture of the Portuguese peasantry was altered very little during the course of the nineteenth century. Despite the anticlericalism of the intellectuals, the ordinary Portuguese remained among the most religious in Europe, and even many of the younger esthetes of the late century became fashionably Catholic. Superstition among the peasants remained extreme into the twentieth century. The Portuguese language was the only tongue in Europe in which religious blasphemy was not a popular form of speech, just as Portuguese had been the only western vernacular to adopt neutral terminology for names of the days of the week instead of pagan-derived words. The influence of clerical styles would still be seen in the form of peasant women's dress in the second half of the twentieth century. Of all regions, the Minho—heartland of Portugal—was the most deeply religious, and, characteristically, the most dechristianized of the lower classes were in Lisbon and to a lesser extent Porto.

It was during the nineteenth century that the feeling of saudade was recognized as characteristic of the emotional tone of much of Portuguese society. Variously translated as "yearning," "longing," or "nostalgia," the melancholy moods of saudade became the keynote of people for whom a sad lyricism had long since replaced the epic tones of the expansionist age. In the Minho, the predominance of saudade may also be traced to the high rate of emigration and the sadness attendant on loneliness and separation. Much the same atmosphere was found in Spanish Galicia, where similar conditions prevailed.

During the later nineteenth century a major popular song form developed in Lisbon and several other towns—the *fado* (lit. "fate"). The first important fado was the "Fado da Severa," celebrating the star-crossed loves of a gypsy singer, Maria de Severa, and a nobleman, after Severa's death in 1849. Such melancholy, lyric "fates" were probably sung before, but after mid-century became more popular in tavern and demimonde night spots of Lisbon. A police crackdown in the 1850s on taverns, gambling, and other vice centers restricted the spread of fados, but the classic period of fado singing was the decade 1865–1875, when the form was made more respectable and acquired a broader following. Fados have remained the dominant form of Portuguese popular song ever since.

Portuguese Africa in the Nineteenth Century

The Portuguese coastal possessions in Africa, mostly forts and trading stations, had attracted little attention during the eighteenth century aside from their usefulness in the slave trade. The Charter of 1826 made everyone born in the Portuguese dominions a citizen, equal under the law, and the subsequent liberal victory in 1834 meant the eventual end of the slave trade. By that time slaving did not mean very much to the economy of Portugal. Just as the Portuguese Asian trade had become by the seventeenth century an increasingly intra-

Asian business, so the Portuguese African slave trade had become by the nineteenth century an increasingly intra-African business. It was more important to those African chiefs and tribes who sold other Africans to the traders than it was to the Portuguese, for it was the major African export to pay for goods sought from European traders.

Portuguese Africa first drew the attention of other powers because of the determination of Britain, and to a lesser extent of several other governments, to stamp out the slave trade. At that point Portugal actually lacked the naval strength to patrol its African waters effectively. During the 1820s part of its small fleet was sent to Brazil to help form the nucleus of a Brazilian navy, and more ships were lost in the Portuguese civil war. Under pressure from the British government, the Septembrist regime officially abolished the slave trade in 1836, but at that time there were insufficient government forces along the coast of Angola and Moçambique to enforce the order. This situation led to a famous directive by Lord Palmerston in 1839 authorizing searches of Portuguese vessels which the British fleet suspected of slaving. Deep resentment was aroused in Portugal. The slave trade from Portuguese Africa was not completely ended for thirty years, however, and though it was soon staunched in Guinea and Angola, the trade from Moçambique actually increased during the 1840s.

It was the Septembrist regime of 1836-1842 and more concretely its key leader, Sá da Bandeira, that first envisioned a program of African expansion for Portugal. This was a part of the Septembrist vision of developing the energies and possibilities of Portugal, creating a new kind of empire in place of Brazil. It was also stimulated by French expansion in Algeria, but Portugal lacked the resources to move more directly into Africa at that time and was fortunate to keep the toehold it had. By mid-century most of the Guinea coastal region staked out by the Portuguese had been lost to France and little attention was paid to the remainder. The Regenerator government of the 1850s and early 1860s had little interest in the African territories, in contrast to the overseas emphasis of the Liberal Union government of O'Donnell in Spain between 1858 and 1863.

Interest in overseas development remained stronger in the Historical-Reformist-Progressivist sector of politics than among the more conservative Regenerators. After 1870, however, with the unification of Germany and Italy and the beginning of a new wave of west European imperial expansion, there was a growing feeling in Portuguese politics that retention and development of the overseas territories was an indispensable guarantee of Portugal's own independence and success as a small country. Portuguese Africa consisted of little more than dominion over the coastal territories of Portuguese

Guinea, Angola, and Moçambique. Effective control did not extend very far inland. In Moçambique a series of *prazos* (lit. "terms" or "limits") had been staked out far inland by overlords from Goa and Portugal in the seventeenth century. The prazos formed large plantation districts, sometimes with a sizable native population, and battened on the gold-mining economy of the seventeenth century but subsequently went into decline. The *prazeiros,* increasingly African in racial composition, had become a separate intermediate kind of overlord.

During the 1860s the government slowly increased the money spent on overseas territories. Angola received twice as much as Moçambique, however, and the remaining districts of Portuguese India more than Angola. Several badly arranged expeditions of exploration and conquest farther inland were carried out in Angola and Moçambique during the 1860s and 1870s. In Moçambique it was as much a task of conquering as of incorporating the local prazeiros and their lands, for even in the decadence of the prazo system the district overlords strove to maintain their semi-independence. In 1864 the Banco Nacional Ultramarino was established, and in 1867 a steamer line was set up in the Luanda region of Angola, financed by British capital. During the next six years the Angolan river trade increased seven times over.

In Moçambique 70 percent of local commerce was concentrated on the off-shore island of Moçambique itself, and ivory remained the chief article of trade. Completion of the Suez Canal in 1869, however, opened up the direct European route to the east coast of Africa and the Indian Ocean, somewhat increasing Moçambique's commercial importance. Some years later gold and diamonds were discovered to the southwest in Boer territory. The discovery led to a major expansion of the old trading fortress of Lourenço Marques on the southern coast of Moçambique, and it became the most direct outlet for part of the Boer territory.

The chief figure in Portuguese policy during the 1870s was João de Andrade Corvo, foreign minister from 1871 to 1877 and again from 1878 to 1879. Corvo also held the ministry of the navy and overseas affairs for most of this period. He was a liberal expansionist, looking to the occupation of large inland territories. He encouraged international cooperation and freer trade, lowered duties, and fostered communications building, economic development, and exploration. The most dramatic achievement of those years was the trek led by an army captain, Alexandre Serpa Pinto, across southern Africa from Luanda on the west coast to Durban on the east, in 1877-1878. In 1879 Corvo separated Portuguese Guinea from the Cape Verde islands, establishing it as a separate province of Portugal. In general, however, he lacked the support and facilities to realize his major plans.

Portuguese claims were later shunted aside at the Berlin Congress of 1885, summoned by Bismarck to draw clear lines of demarcation among competing colonial powers in Africa. They were completely excluded from the greatest prize, the Congo territory, though the Portuguese had been in that region for four hundred years. Over half the stations in the Congo at that time were operated by Portuguese, who more nearly fulfilled the stipulated requirement of "effective occupation" than did any other power, but a small, weak, unindustrialized country stood little chance of winning its case.

On the other hand, progress was made in delimiting the boundaries of the greater Angolan region, and by 1886 Portuguese expansionists had begun to talk enthusiastically of a *mapa côr de rosa* ("rose-colored map," for the Portuguese emblem). This sketch, drawn up in Lisbon, showed Portuguese territory stretching all the way across southern continental Africa from Angola to Moçambique. In 1888, however, British ambitions were voiced for creation of a "Cape to Cairo" route of British-controlled territory through east Africa from north to south, which among other things would block the proposed route of Portuguese expansion. A military expedition through western Moçambique under Serpa Pinto in 1889 roused British hostility, resulting in a famous ultimatum from the British prime minister, Lord Salisbury, in January 1890, demanding that the Portuguese withdraw from the disputed territory. The Portuguese diplomatic and military situation was absolutely hopeless. Britain was the nearest thing to an ally that the Portuguese government had, and no support could be expected elsewhere. Capitulation was inevitable, despite loud and bitter protests from middle class patriots. In the following year, after relations were patched up, a new Moçambique Company of private investors was licensed by the Portuguese government to undertake the economic development of that region. British economic interests were now predominant there and the new company, chartered for fifty years, functioned as a virtual state within a state to do what the Portuguese government was unable to accomplish in developing communications and exploiting the raw materials of Moçambique.

Decline and Collapse of the Constitutional Monarchy, 1890–1910

After the successful reestablishment of rotativismo in the 1870s, Portuguese politics was free of radical pressures of any kind for nearly a generation. The established oligarchy governed unchallenged for two decades, and during the twelve years 1878 to 1890 rotativismo worked with efficient parity, the Regenerators holding office for eighty-one months and the Progressives for sixty-nine months. Tranquil alternation was interrupted by the Ultimatum crisis, which forced the Progressivist ministry to resign. The subsequent Regenerator government was unable to get the Cortes to approve a new African treaty worked out on British terms, and had to give way to the first of several nonparty coalition ministries that governed for more than two years.

The official settlement with Britain was worked out in January 1891, helping to precipitate the first overt republican rebellion against the constitutional monarchy. Portuguese republicanism had emerged in the aftermath of the radical intellectuals' enthusiasm for the European revolutions of 1848. In the 1850s and 1860s nascent Portuguese republicanism had been doctrinally amorphous but inclined toward federalist, cooperativist, social reformist positions. In the 1860s it won the allegiance of much of the new intelligentsia, reacting against the "putrid peace" of Regenerationism and the oligarchic rotativist system. A divergence developed in 1871, when the Portuguese Socialist party was founded, carrying the left wing of the tiny republican movement with it. It soon became clear, however, that the potential support for radical movements was extremely limited. Though the Socialist party won the support of much of the small organized working class movement in Lisbon and Porto, it could not advance beyond this narrow base and was badly split by internal quarrels. The main current of republicanism became more moderate and was organized as the Unitary Republican party in 1880, strongly influenced by the democratic, middle class, but nonradical Third Republic in France. The main goals of Portuguese republicanism in the 1880s and 1890s were complete political freedom and equality, guarantees for the rights to association and to strike, separation of church and state, and the elimination of most indirect, regressive taxes. Its proponents relied almost exclusively on propaganda, invoking the symbols of past Portuguese greatness and calling for a rebirth of the nation and a new place for it in the world, under democratic institutions. The first republican deputy was elected from Porto in 1878, and overthrow of the monarchy in Brazil in 1889 served as a stimulus to republican agitation in Portugal.

The national humiliation of the Ultimatum and the government's acceptance of British demands provided the first opportunity for republicans to mobilize a broader national protest. They insisted that under the monarchy Portugal would soon lose its independence. A conspiracy of pro-republican noncommissioned officers developed in the Porto garrison, and after the government attempted to transfer dissidents, erupted in an abortive Spanish-style revolt on January 31,

1891. Led by three junior officers, it relied on NCO's but was quickly smashed by Municipal Guard and loyal army units.

The republican revolt was more a sign of changing times than an immediate threat. The real problem was the national financial crisis precipitated by the diplomatic humiliation and political uncertainty. A banking moratorium had to be declared, and the state neared bankruptcy in 1891–1892. Foreign creditors demanded international control of Portuguese customs and the German government urged a naval demonstration off Lisbon similar to that recently brandished against Venezuela. The outstanding cultural historian and political critic Oliveira Martins took office as minister of finance in a new nonparty government in 1892 but failed to win passage of effective financial reforms.

The pressure eased by 1893, however, and a regular Regenerator ministry took over under the party chief, Hintze Ribeiro. It dissolved the businessmen's association that had helped block tax reform, but could not restore political tranquillity and normal rotativismo. Even regular party members and supporters were losing confidence in the oligarchic system. The scope of politicization was increasing. Whereas the politicized had included only 5 to 10 percent of the population in the early and middle decades of the century, by the end of the century economic and cultural change was broadening this to 15 or 20 percent. The new demands on government required new programs, but the established factions were opposed to basic reform and democratization, for fear of losing power.

In these circumstances the weight of rivalries and status jockeying could not be borne as easily as in earlier decades, and the Regenerator government began to break up. Consequently Hintze Ribeiro postponed the 1894 elections and ruled by decree under emergency powers, sharing leadership with his minister of the interior, the energetic João Franco. A new electoral system was established restricting representation of minority parties, and the opposition for the most part withdrew from the 1895 election. A new constitutional measure, the Third Additional Act, was then passed in 1896 to strengthen royal executive power. Eleven years earlier, in more tranquil times, a liberalizing amendment (the Second Additional Act) had made the senate mostly elective and deprived the crown of moderating powers. The new act of 1896 abolished senate elections and restored the moderating powers of the crown, including the right to dissolve parliament.

The Regenerator government was thus relying on a kind of constitutional authoritarianism under the crown to retard the process of political erosion. The new king, D. Carlos I (1889–1908), was reluctant to endorse this strategy completely. An oceanographer of some distinction and also a painter, the blond, robust, increasingly portly

D. Carlos maintained the cultural distinction of the royal family established by his late father and uncle. He had a similar sense of scruple, but found it hard to chart a constructive course amid increasing factionalism, republican criticism, and the mutual discrediting of Regenerators and Progressives among themselves. After the Regenerators handed him increased power, they insisted that he use it in 1897 for another fornada of peers, to give them a safe majority in the senate. He refused, the Regenerators resigned, and a Progressive ministry assumed power, governing from 1897 to 1900.

By the end of the century the status of Portuguese Africa was slightly more secure, thanks in part to growing rivalry between Britain and Germany. In 1898 there was discussion between representatives of the two powers over a possible partition of Portuguese territories, since Portugal was supposedly too weak to control or develop them. A secret clause in an Anglo-German treaty of that year provided for the potential division of Portuguese Africa into German and British spheres of economic interest, a possible prelude to outright partition. The outbreak of the Boer War the following year, accompanied by German hostility, led the British government to an abrupt change of position. In October 1899 the British and Portuguese governments signed a secret declaration of friendship and pledged to help maintain each other's interests and possessions. In December 1900 the Anglo-Portuguese alliance was publicly reaffirmed, thanks at least in part to the helpful diplomatic assistance of the Portuguese king, who realized that the frustrations of the years 1885–1890 had come from a hopeless effort by the Portuguese government to play what was in effect a major power role all by itself.

Despite the humiliation of the Ultimatum and the inability to ever make the *mapa côr de rosa* a reality, Portuguese expansion in the great age of European imperialism was quite considerable, in view of the meager resources of the home country. Spain, which was much larger and slightly more wealthy, was much less successful; Italy, larger still and more industrial and powerful, achieved no more— hardly as much—as small, weak Portugal. Yet the slowly growing republican opposition made of the failures and supposed disgrace of the monarchist regime abroad one of its most effective propaganda themes. Even the agreement of 1900 was vociferously denounced by Portuguese ultras as another capitulation.

The Regenerators returned to power in 1900 but soon had to face a serious defection by the most important of their younger leaders, the forty-five-year old João Franco, who walked out with a minority of nominally reformist Regenerator deputies constituting themselves the Liberal Regenerators. The prime minister, Hintze Ribeiro, had no reply to political opposition other than further manipulation. The republicans had recently managed to elect three deputies in Porto where, despite fraud, their votes could not be ignored. Therefore in 1901 the government carried out an elaborate electoral gerrymander, reorganizing the country into thirty-three special electoral districts and in the resulting elections shutting out the republicans and reducing Franco's parliamentary representation to a single deputy. Otherwise the government's only achievement was to convert and consolidate the foreign debt with a new loan agreement. Beyond that it had no program. Like Cánovas and Sagasta in Spain after 1890, Hintze Ribeiro's only goal was to preserve the status quo.

João Franco became the most controversial politician of the period and an increasingly formidable rival. His high cheek bones and slanting eyes gave him a somewhat exotic appearance, and his energy and aggressiveness were second to none. He loomed in Portuguese politics as the kind of loyal conservative reformist that Antonio Maura was in Spain, denouncing fraud and electoral corruption with great vehemence. In a series of public rallies and speeches—the sort of campaign that was not common in the Portuguese system of minimal mobilization—he promised honest government and elections, limitation of the budget, educational expansion, and a degree of local government autonomy. He had also shown in the last elections that he would not scruple to collaborate with the republicans if that were deemed useful, and he obtained revenge on the Regenerators by helping to force the resignation of Hintze Ribeiro in 1904. The next ministry was organized by the Progressive chief, José Luciano de Castro, who was in poor health and could keep a government together only two years. Hintze Ribeiro was then reappointed to make the elections of 1906, but as in Spain, government control no longer worked so well as in earlier years. A compromise with Franco was necessary, and Hintze could not govern effectively.

In an effort to revitalize the political system, Dom Carlos then appointed João Franco prime minister. Since Franco lacked anything approaching a parliamentary majority he tried to create a "liberal concentration" with the Progressives. The leader of the Progressives, Castro, accepted and thereby undercut the rotativist system, not because his colleagues really supported Franco's ideas but because of a new rivalry between Castro and Hintze Ribeiro, whom the former accused of trying to undermine his leadership within the Progressive party. As a consequence, the Progressives also split between Castro and the supporters of his bitter personal rival, José de Alpoim, whom Ribeiro was trying to establish as a counterweight to Franco. The new prime minister's announced goals of reforming the budget and the electoral system and of making ministers responsible to parliament alone were intensively combatted by the regular Regenerators, who doubted their capacity to survive in a reformed system. Thus the established leaders and factions all strove to cancel each other out.

Meanwhile the republicans, who had won four seats in Lisbon in the 1906 elections, began to come forward. They capitalized on Franco's reformism and advanced new demands, creating disorders in parliament. The principal target of their propaganda was the fat, personable sovereign, D. Carlos, who was accused of squandering illicit financial advances secretly tendered by the government. The problem here was that the royal list had been set at a fixed figure decades before and was inadequate for the rising prices of the twentieth century, but because government expenses and electoral corruption had been the chief domestic issues for years, no ministry dared officially raise the royal budget. There was no real evidence that the queen was a spendthrift, as charged, and the royal family had already sold or pawned most royal properties. The real issue was the ideological and moral revolt of the radical intelligentsia, who sought to make the royal father-figure a symbolic sacrifice to expiate the miseries of twentieth-century Portugal. After insisting on an inquiry, the republican deputies were expelled from parliament, and a prorepublican strike at normally conservative Coimbra University led to its closing.

All the while Franco had been unable either to achieve basic reforms or to generate effective parliamentary support. In the spring of 1907 he imposed a new press law to muzzle republican propaganda and obtained royal authorization to close parliament and rule by decree, though at the beginning of his ministry he had sworn publicly "to God" to preserve liberties and refrain from dictatorship. Decree powers had been used before from time to time and had always been sanctioned by subsequent bills of indemnity from parliament. This was, however, the most overt use of decree power in half a century and was a recognition of the inefficacy of the existing parliamentary system. In the long run, Franco's "dictatorship" had the same effect as the Primo de Rivera regime in Spain. It alienated all the established political factions and left the government standing on thin air. Having done more than any other leader to destroy the Regenerator party and the rotativist system, Franco was unable to implement a clearcut program or capitalize on the reform sentiment that undeniably existed among part of the small body politic. His publicly invoked norm of *Pouca política, muita administração* (little politicking, much administration) echoed the "practical" line of critics of the parliamentary system all over Europe, but what Portugal faced was a political crisis and he was incapable of devising means to handle it.

Meanwhile the republican movement gained ground among the urban lower middle classes and among elements of the elite. A secret activist association known ordinarily as the Carbonária, organized in

1896, had expanded to include several thousand members. Carbonarism had a long history in Portuguese liberal politics, parallel to but not identical with Free Masonry. The first secret activists had been organized in 1822–1823 under the influence of exiled army officers belonging to the Italian *carbonari*. Until about 1864 all major political groups had their own secret *carbonária*, often joined by people of the highest social rank. Under the rotativist regime, secret political societies had faded away. The new republican Carbonária of the early twentieth century was based on lower-middle-class nationalist radicalism, stimulated by the protest over Portugal's international position, motivated by intense anticlericalism and hatred for religion, which was considered the root of Portugal's backwardness, and increasingly grounded on hostility toward the king himself.

In September 1907 D. Carlos made the grave mistake of publicly identifying himself with the Franco dictatorship, which in turn proceeded to write off the large royal debt and increase the rather small civil list by about 50 percent. By that time the great majority of "monarchist" politicians, that is, representatives of two formerly established parties, had come out in opposition to the dictatorship. Franco promised elections at the end of a year (in April 1908), but the republicans seized the initiative by attempting a military revolt in January 1908. This led to a general crackdown, and preparations were made to impose exile on those guilty of "political crimes." Removal of the republican leaders would have had a severe effect on the still numerically small movement, so the Carbonária changed the terms of struggle. On February 1, 1908, both the king and the heir to the throne were shot as their open carriages crossed one of the main squares in Lisbon. It was an unprecedented act, the first regicide in Portuguese history, and opened the era of twentieth-century radicalism in Portugal.

The murder of D. Carlos doomed the monarchy. The only surviving male member of the royal family was his second son, the eighteen-year-old prince Manuel, who was not ready to assume the responsibilities of government. Even more debilitating was the fact that he had no loyal political leaders or groups on which to rely; all the parties and personal cliques had been alienated by Franco. The Council of State was convened, and an attempt at compromise was decided upon. Franco resigned and never returned to political life. A new coalition cabinet was formed under an admiral, Ferreira do Amaral, foreshadowing the *dictablanda* of Berenguer and Aznar two decades later in Spain. No attempt was made at a thorough investigation of the royal assassinations. The physical authors were executed, but their accomplices were given a tacit immunity, in the hope of establishing some kind of truce. Unlike the later Spanish successors to

Primo de Rivera, Amaral held elections on schedule in April 1908. They did not reveal any profound shift; out of more than one hundred seats, the republicans won only eleven (eight of them in Lisbon). The government's main problem was not republican opposition but the extreme factionalism of the nominal monarchists. Julio Vilhena, new chief of the Regenerators, tried to subvert the Amaral ministry, which was then succeeded not by a Vilhena cabinet but by a government of Campos Henriques, head of the most conservative faction of Regenerators.

During the first seventy-one years of liberalism, from 1834 to 1905, there had been fifty-four cabinets, with an average life of one year and four months. Between 1905 and 1910 there were ten, averaging six months each. In a period of thirty-two months between February 1908 and October 1910 there were six cabinets, changing more rapidly still. Until 1870 most government ministers had some sort of aristocratic title; during the decade 1900-1910 only four of sixty had titles. Political leadership had become more middle class, but this had not led to greater continuity or deeper roots. Quarrels over status, faction, and personality had destroyed political cohesion. By the beginning of 1910 the Regenerators had split into three main groups and the Progressives into two. Outside the larger towns, there was little popular support for the republican movement, but inside the parliament the monarchist politicians had lost all faith in the regime and seemed to have little hope or interest in maintaining their own system.

The main phase of modern labor unrest had begun in Portugal in 1903, as the workers were caught in an inflationary price scissors. During 1910 strike activity reached an all-time high, as shown in these figures given by Armando de Castro:

Year	Number of Industrial Strikers
1903	1,225
1904	1,108
1905	2,107
1906	9,137
1907	6,181
1908	2,681
1909	2,038
1910	10,538

Rural laborers remained much more quiet. During the ten years 1903-1912 only 14,200 farm workers, all in the south, were listed as having been on strike. Altogether, these numbers are very modest compared with those of many other countries in this period, but the protest they reveal was unprecedented in Portugal and added another element of unrest.

The main strength of the republicans was in Lisbon, where they won control of the municipal council in November 1908. Until that point their official leadership had been moderate, but at the end of 1908 it fell under the control of the radicals. In most of the country the movement's following remained scattered and amorphous. Its main thrust lay in the semisecret Carbonária groups and among the intelligentsia, particularly journalists and students, giving the republicans disproportionate publicity, a major factor in their rise. They were also strong among noncommissioned officers in the army, and among naval officers, who were impressed by republican propaganda about the monarchy's failure to win Portugal a proper place overseas. Finally, the republicans also received financial and other support from dissident monarchist politicians, especially Alpoim's faction of the Progressives, who may even have had a hand in the regicide.

In the elections of August 1910 the republican minority was increased from eleven to only fourteen (eleven of them from Lisbon). If the movement were to wait upon the organization of representative public opinion, it would apparently be waiting for some time, so more direct tactics were once more decided upon. Meanwhile the government made more and more concessions in a vain effort to placate the left. It capitulated to virulent anticlerical propaganda by officially dissolving the Jesuit order in Portugal for the second time, at the beginning of October.

Since the monarchists had virtually conceded the ground to republican doctrine, there was no reason to delay a direct seizure of government. On the next day, October 4, 1910, a revolt was begun in Lisbon by the crews of two rebellious warships and a few companies of dissident troops rallied by a group of naval officers. The rebels lacked the strength to take the capital, but loyal forces proved totally irresolute. As the rebels began to win over some of their opponents, the government, with almost no one willing to fight for it, collapsed. The political system was thoroughly exhausted and had given no sign of new ideas, programs, or mobilization of energy. Most of the politically active were alienated, and the monarchy fell by default. As the remnants of the royal family went into exile, the old upper class oligarchy was replaced by a radical new middle class elite.

23

The Portuguese Parliamentary Republic, 1910-1926

On October 5, 1910, as the king was leaving Portugal, a Republican provisional government took office. It was composed of the top leaders of the Portuguese Republican party (PRP), which had engineered the overthrow of the monarchy, under the interim presidency of Teófilo Braga, a cultural historian and leading Republican ideologue. The man who stood out, however, was the minister of justice, Afonso Costa, for it was he who directed the assault on the Republicans' remaining bête noire, the Portuguese Catholic Church. The majority of Republicans took the position that Catholicism was the number one enemy of individualist middle class radicalism and must be completely broken as a source of influence in Portugal. A pastoral letter by the church hierarchy protesting the new antireligious policy was suppressed by the government. When the bishop of Porto insisted on the right to free speech he was forcibly deposed, and other high church officials were subsequently forced to follow him into exile.

Church and state were officially separated in April 1911 by a law patterned on recent French legislation, though the Portuguese was more extreme in its terms. Church properties were placed under the control of secular *associações cultuais* (derived from the French *associations cultuelles*). The church was prohibited from acquiring property through wills or donations, and one-third of all subsequent church offerings were to be confiscated for secular charities. The number of seminaries was reduced from thirteen to five, and all religious instruction in Portuguese schools was abolished. Religious oaths and the wearing of religious clothing in public were prohibited. All Catholic orders in Portugal were abolished, and to encourage priests to renounce their vocations, clergy who apostatized were offered preference in government employment. According to one report, 800 of the 6,800 priests in Portugal left their calling during the first years of the Republic.

The new government also announced major changes in social policy. All titles and nearly all decorations were abolished and a program of school expansion was begun. The right to strike was legalized in 1911, and some changes were made in tenancy laws that benefited peasant renters and sharecroppers. Tax reform was begun; certain onerous excises were abolished and others reduced.

The Republican regime thus swept in as a fresh new radical force promising freedom, progress, and greater social justice. It was essentially urban and middle class, though supported by radical aristocrats, some city workers, and a few groups of peasants. Yet it was better defined by what it opposed—the monarchy and the church—than by a concrete program to realize its loftier but somewhat abstract goals.

The first elections under the new government were held in May 1911 on a basis approximating universal male suffrage. Monarchists abstained and the voting was swept by the Republicans. The social and professional background of the members of the first Republican parliament is shown in table 21.

An indication of the elite elements behind the new regime is given in these figures. The middle class intelligentsia and official bureau-

Table 21.   Composition of the First Parliament of the
Portuguese Republic, 1911

Physicians	48	Magistrates	5
Army and Navy officers	47	Solicitors	3
Government employees	25	Commercial employees	2
Lawyers	24	Students	2
Landowners	18	Priests	2
Professors	11	Farm manager	1
Teachers	12	Engineer	1
Merchants	8	Veterinarian	1
Journalists	8	Barber	1
Pharmacists	6	Worker	1

Source: As Constituintes de 1911 e os seus deputados (Lisbon, 1911), in Marcello Caetano, Constituições portuguesas (Braga, 1968), p. 99.

cracy predominated, and there was little representation of economic interests. Very few of the deputies had sat in parliament before. Preparation of the new Republican constitution was completed in August 1911. It established a parliamentary system of government with a president as nominal head of state, to be chosen by parliament for a four-year term. The legislature was made bicameral, with a lower house, called the assembly, to be selected by direct election. The constitution provided for full civil liberties, save for the Catholic church, and instituted the right of habeus corpus. A new red and green flag was substituted for the old blue and white banner of the monarchy. The constituent assembly then elected one-third of its members as the new senate, the remainder becoming the first regular assembly.

It was during the voting for the first president in August 1911 that major splits in the Republican party appeared. Three factions emerged: the Evolutionists under António José de Almeida, the Unionists under Manuel Brito Camacho, and the Democrats under Costa. The Democrats stood for radical and intransigent republicanism. The Evolutionists urged a policy of moderation and conciliation, providing for proportionate representation, revision of the intolerant anticlerical laws, and amnesty for those charged with political offenses. The Unionists, led by moderate intellectuals, stood somewhere between the two. The presidential election was settled by compromise, resulting in the choice of a venerable octogenarian and romantic old-style Republican, Manuel de Arriaga.

Presidents of the Portuguese Republic

Teófilo Braga	1910-1911
Manuel de Arriaga	1911-1915
Teófilo Braga	1915
Bernardino Machado	1915-1917
Sidónio Pais	1917-1918
João do Canto e Castro	1918-1919
António José de Almeida	1919-1923
Manuel Teixeira Gomes	1923-1925
Bernardino Machado	1925-1926
António Oscar de Fragoso Carmona	1926-1951
Francisco Craveiro Lopes	1951-1958
Américo Tomás	1958-

The first cabinet appointed by Arriaga was a moderate ministry of Unionists and Evolutionists headed by the veteran Republican journalist João Chagas. Opposition came from three sources: the monarchist right, the anarchist working class left, and the Democrat faction of the Republican party itself. Portuguese anarcho-syndicalism, weak in numbers and largely limited to Lisbon and Porto, greeted the coming of the Republic not as a new era of freedom but as another phase in the revolutionary struggle against the "bourgeois state" in which the latter had suddenly become more vulnerable. Successive strikes in Lisbon by trade and transport employees during the first weeks of the Republic had been met as early as November 1910 with a mass middle class demonstration in Lisbon, organized by the Republican Carbonária, calling for greater discipline and order.

The monarchist reaction was weak. Contrary to Republican propaganda, relations between monarchist politicians and church leaders were not—or were no longer—close, especially after the former had shown themselves completely ineffective in protecting religious interests. The peasantry, a mass conservative force, was unmobilized by any political faction, and there was no love among the peasants for professional monarchist politicians. The nominal aristocracy, whose titles had been abolished, was completely unable to function as a pressure group, for it lacked organization and was politically divided. Nevertheless, a petty attempt at rousing monarchist revolt in the conservative Minho was made by the former cavalry officer, Paiva Couceiro, with a raid from across the Spanish border. This was easily thwarted and led to a crackdown by the government.

The first year of the Republic was marked by intermittent outbursts of city mobs against churches and monarchist centers. After formation of the Chagas government, such disorders were whipped up by Democrats against the conservative Evolutionists. The Democrat leader Costa gained the support of the largest body of deputies in the assembly and forced the Chagas government out of office within two months of its formation.

It was succeeded by a coalition ministry of all three Republican factions, with the Unionists predominating, under a physician, Dr Augusto de Vasconcellos (November 1911). Rather than attempting national conciliation, this administration resumed an intense anticlericalism, forcing more church leaders into exile. While hatred grew on the right, opposition became more intense on the left; a strike wave unprecedented in Portuguese history broke out in the spring of 1912. On the one hand a minor mutiny in the army sputtered and died; on the other a general strike was attempted in Lisbon. At that point the Vasconcellos government was replaced by a coalition ministry under the historian Duarte Leite (June 1912). Its main priority was repressing the strike wave, but it also had to contain a more serious "invasion" attempt from Spanish Galicia by Paiva Couceiro's small band of monarchist exiles. After the government cracked down on a march of farm workers from Evora, Costa and the Democrats took the side of labor leaders and overturned the Leite government in January 1913.

The Democrats then took complete control of the Republican government in a ministry headed by Costa. The new prime minister had become the most influential and also the most feared and hated of the Republican politicians. He was a lawyer by profession, lacked oratorical skill, but was an excellent political organizer, a capable administrator, and a skilled parliamentarian. He was idolized by followers, but his ruthless sectarianism aroused intense enmity in other groups. The great achievement of the Costa ministry was to balance the budget for 1913-1914, the first time that this had happened in nearly a century. To that extent it was efficient, but it was also high-handed. State appointments were made with little regard to the new constitution. A new electoral law of 1913 deprived illiterate heads of families of the right to vote, halving the electorate from 850,000 to 400,000.

The anarcho-syndicalists declared war on Costa's government when it took office. In April 1913 it had to suppress a revolt by a clique of ultraradical army officers who thought the ministry too dictatorial. More political arrests were carried out. Disorders increased during the course of the year, and the Democrats lost control of the Lisbon mob. Strikes grew more frequent, and a railway shutdown at the beginning of 1914 temporarily paralyzed the country.

Costa was then replaced by the moderate Bernardino Machado, who governed on the basis of a coalition ministry for the remainder of 1914. Machado's major policy innovation was to attempt a truce with the church; he granted amnesty to all clergy convicted of opposing the government. The main pressure came not from the right, however, but from the left. Though Machado was one of the Republicans' few elder statesmen, he could not calm the factional strife and finally resigned after one major cabinet reorganization and eleven months in office. He was succeeded at the close of 1914 by a new Democrat ministry under Azevedo Coutinho.

The First Reaction: The Pimenta de Castro Government, January-May 1915

The reaction was ultimately spearheaded by the military, beginning with a veteran officer of the African campaigns who publicly protested Democrat favoritism in army promotions. After he was arrested and reassigned, discontented officers turned to the army's most senior general, the retired seventy-nine-year-old Pimenta de Castro, a lifelong liberal who had served briefly as minister of war in the

Chagas government. Arriaga appointed Castro prime minister in January 1915 and Castro formed a largely military government (save for two seats) supported by the Evolutionists. Parliament was closed in March, and the new ministry functioned as a de facto dictatorship. It stopped the attacks on the church, abolishing the associações cultuais, and restored civil liberties to monarchists. Castro proposed to introduce a multicandidate list system of voting and widen the suffrage to include more of the semiliterate and illiterate peasantry, but his government lacked internal unity and was strongly combatted by Democrats and Unionists. It was overthrown on May 14-15 by a revolt of liberal army and navy officers, supported by some elements of the National Republican Guard, the citizens' militia that under the new regime replaced the old Municipal Guard.

Return of the Democrats; Portuguese Entry into the First World War

After the successful revolt, Arriaga resigned and was replaced as president by Teófilo Braga, who appointed a new Democrat ministry under José de Castro, later succeeded by Costa. With other groups largely abstaining, elections were swept by the Democrats. Rigid anticlerical policies were reimposed, a series of government scandals occurred, disorders were frequent throughout the summer, a monarchist rising had to be suppressed, and there were assassination attempts on national leaders, one of them blinding the prime minister in one eye and breaking his arm.

Rather than pacifying the country and constructing a progressive government that could meet Portugal's needs, the ambition of the main faction of Democrats was to bring Portugal into the First World War on the side of the Entente. One of the sharpest criticisms of the monarchy was that Portugal had faded to insignificance internationally, and the Republican leaders believed that the country had to enter the war to gain status and protect its interests in Africa. The British government was interested in the support of the Portuguese artillery, the least inadequate branch of the Portuguese military, but knew that the army of its small ally was of scant value and made it clear that the diplomatic alliance did not require Portugal's entrance into the war. However, as the Entente became sorely pressed and the Democrat government made clear its eagerness, the wartime government of Britain indicated that it would provide broad economic and material assistance if Portugal aligned itself against Germany. Minor German border aggression against Portuguese African territory a year earlier helped provide a vague *casus belli,* and Britain's first request was that the thirty-six German ships blocked in the Tejo estuary at the outset of the war be impounded. This was done in February 1916, and the vessels were handed over to Britain. Germany declared war on Portugal the following month.

The Democrats and Evolutionists then formed an *união sagrada* on the French model, and the Evolutionist leader Almeida became leader of a coalition government with Costa as minister of finance. Mobilization for war brought extreme hardship. Over a period of two and a half years more than two hundred thousand men were called up, a considerable social and economic strain for a poor country of little more than six million. The "sacred union" government fared no better than its predecessors. In 1916 there was another wave of strikes, with bomb explosions and a series of major arson attempts, leading to the restoration of the death penalty that had been abolished by the monarchy. Government administrative scandals continued; a minor army plot at the end of the year was foiled. Conditions grew more difficult in 1917 after two bad harvests in a row. Price inflation, strikes, and inevitable wartime shortages led to assaults on shops; the government in turn mobilized several key industries and was met with a one-day general strike.

Costa replaced the sacred union with a new Democrat ministry under his leadership, focusing resentment from all sides and making him the most hated man in Portugal. To some extent his regime modeled itself on the new Clemenceau government in France, save that it was more corrupt and that the Portuguese had less reason for patriotic sacrifice in the war. The peasants as usual bowed submissively to wartime mobilization, but popular rumor had it that the French government paid the Costa ministry by the head for every Portuguese sent to war. By April 1917 the Portuguese army had placed two reinforced divisions (40,000 men) in France and had strengthened the units in Africa.

During the course of 1917 the war became a key issue, and many of both the Unionists and Evolutionists turned against the Democrats. Toward the end of the year a "center" conspiracy was developed under Sidónio Pais, an army major and former professor of mathematics at Coimbra and a leading Unionist who, significantly, had also served as the last Portuguese ambassador to Germany. The revolt was built around army officers, but pro-Republican naval commanders had also to be brought in, apparently purchased by the bribes of a wealthy Alemtejano Unionist. The coup was initiated in Lisbon on December 5, 1917, though three days of intermittent fighting were required before the Democrat government was overthrown.

The Second Reaction: The "República Nova" of Sidónio Pais, 1917-1918

The resulting "Decembrist" government was headed by Pais and was based on the Unionists and the Centrist party, an alignment, formed two months earlier by the physician Egas Moniz, that combined the right wing of the Evolutionists and the more liberal wing of the old monarchist Progressives. However, the anti-Costa Unionists became more hesitant about backing Pais all the way, and he relied increasingly on the Centrists, organizing his followers into a new National Republican party. The Democrats were proscribed, along with the left wing of the Evolutionists who had cooperated with them. Bernardino Machado, who had replaced Braga as president two years earlier, was deposed, and the associações cultuais were abolished for the second time, while the Monarchist Commission, representing the Portuguese right, was allowed to reorganize. A new revolt in the navy in January 1918 proved abortive and was easily crushed.

Sidónio Pais was a slender, handsome, courteous man of early middle age, extremely attractive to women and appealing to much of the public at large. He was perhaps the only figure of the parliamentary republic who had genuine charisma, traveling about the country and drawing enthusiastic ovations from crowds. After witnessing harsh prison conditions when visiting Porto at the beginning of 1918, he decreed amnesty for all political prisoners. Pais was brave, generous, and idealistic, but he lacked a clear and fully articulated program. His main goal was a stronger government, which he called a República nova, based on a presidential system of executive power. He had been a lifelong liberal, and his new concept of a stronger executive was in part derived from his four years' experience as ambassador in Berlin. In May 1918 parliamentary elections were held, accompanied by a plebiscite on Pais's elevation to the presidency. Universal male suffrage, enfranchising illiterates, was instituted for the first time in Portuguese history. The opposition parties abstained; Pais was elected president with a total of approximately 500,000 votes, the sidonista National Republicans gained full control of the assembly, and the monarchists won more than one-fourth of the seats in that body.

After the electoral triumph, however, Pais found it difficult to give concrete form to his vaguely conceived República nova. While reconciliation was achieved with the church, opposition grew on the left. The president had long believed in the certainty of military victory by the Central Powers, and he reduced Portuguese forces on the western front. Thus he was blamed by critics for the collapse of an overwhelmingly outgunned and outnumbered Portuguese division in the second phase of the great German *Friedenssturm* of the spring of 1918. In fact, the German breakthrough in that sector was almost inevitable, and the frontline troops resisted tenaciously. Meanwhile, the National Republicans were unable to function as a disciplined party, and the Centrists balked at the new presidential system. The parliament of 1918 was as turbulent as its predecessors and political unity was still not to be found.

The domestic political situation degenerated in the autumn of 1918. In October a pro-Democrat revolt by liberal sectors of the army momentarily seized Coimbra, and a similar abortive rebellion occurred at Evora, along with a separate minor uprising of armed farm laborers. There followed another brief general strike in Lisbon, marked by bomb explosions and terrorism against anti-anarchist workers. To combat the leftist opposition, two military juntas, one in the north and one in the south, were set up by conservative officers. Pais planned a trip to Porto on December 14, 1918, to straighten out the resulting confusion. Before boarding his train at the Lisbon railway station he was murdered by a lower-middle-class Carbonarist radical.

A senior admiral, Canto e Castro, was elected by the assembly to succeed Pais. He appointed a sidonista army captain, Tamagnini Barbosa, as prime minister, and the Portuguese system reverted from sidonista presidentialism to a parliamentary executive form of government. The new ministry tried to steer a middle course but in mid-January 1919 had to put down a revolt by army liberals in Lisbon and Santarem. Nine days later, on January 19, a major monarchist rebellion broke out in Porto led by Paiva Couceiro. This was met by an outburst of liberal Republican enthusiasm at Lisbon, where a collateral military revolt was smothered. The rebellion was confined to the northern half of the country, then to Porto itself, where the "monarchy of the north" was crushed after an existence of twenty-five days.

The revolt had led to the formation of a more liberal centrist government in Lisbon and, after the defeat of the right and popular agitation by the left, to the establishment of a pro-Democrat coalition government under a Democrat, Domingos Pereira. The sidonista group found itself impotent and divided after the death of Pais. Lacking an ideology or a leader, without strong organizational roots, they were unable to resist the return of the liberal factions and the regular parliamentary system.

In the meantime, the conclusion of the war ended the heavy drain on Portuguese resources. Out of 200,000 men mobilized, 8,367 had died of battle wounds and many others were disabled. In the postwar settlement, Portugal won the Kionga border region of Angola, seized

by Germany in 1894, and was awarded 3/4 of 1 percent of future
German reparations.

Last Phase of the Parliamentary Party System, 1919–1926

The return to the earlier parliamentary party system was accompanied by new restrictions on the right to vote, excluding illiterates once
more, and was completed by elections in May 1919. These were swept
by the Democrats, who had the largest and most effective political
organization in the country, particularly strong in some of the larger
provincial towns. In Lisbon, by contrast, the majority of the qualified
electorate always abstained; a high point was reached in 1919, when
80 percent of the voters in the capital stayed home.*

Colonel Sá Cardoso, one of the most reliable Democrat officers,
became head of a new Democrat ministry. The assembly then elected
the Evolutionist chief, Almeida, president of the Republic in place of
Canto e Castro. Return of constitutional "normalcy" and international peace resulted, however, in a new outburst of disorders. The
spring of 1919 was full of strikes, arson attempts, and petty heterogeneous outbursts. The anarcho-syndicalist movement, first organized
on a national basis in 1914, was reconstituted in 1919 as the General
Confederation of Labor. The more violent anarchists, in Portugal as
in Spain, were inspired by the Russian Revolution to plan an offensive against the "remnants of bourgeois society" and notably against
the Democrat government. In Lisbon middle class extremists formed
a communist group and vied with anarchist terrorists in promoting
what was later known vaguely as the Red Legion. A government
decree in May 1919 provided for summary prosecution of terrorists.

The Democrats lost unity and cohesion soon after returning to
power. Afonso Costa had little desire to re-enter the Portuguese
cockpit. He headed the Portuguese delegation at Versailles and lived
on a generous income as state financial representative in Paris. Cro-
nyism, porkbarreling, and payroll padding got completely out of
hand, and the budget deficit leaped upward. During the latter part of
1919 the moderate and conservative Republican factions joined together in a Liberal Republican party to form a loyal opposition to the
Democrats. Sá Cardoso's government was brought down at the beginning of 1920, but when a new Liberal ministry was appointed it was

---

* Abstention in Lisbon declined to 53 percent in 1922 and 60 percent in 1925.
Participation was much higher among the rural and small-town middle class. Total
national voter participation was 60 percent in 1915 and rose to 71 percent in the last
regular elections of 1925.

forced to relinquish power after riots by the Democrat street mob. Three short-lived Democrat ministries alternated during the next six months amid a tumult of strikes, riots, and bomb explosions. These disorders were highlighted by street fights between strikers and the lower-middle-class Republican Guard, which had been reorganized, expanded, equipped with surplus French material, and invested with broader powers to combat the syndicalists.

A Liberal government under António Granjó finally succeeded in taking power in July 1920, but lasted only four months. Its successor was a supposedly tough Democrat ministry headed by the chief of the Republican Guard, Lt. Col. Liberato Pinto. After three months, Pinto's government fell under the weight of its own corruption (March 1921). Eighteen days were required to find a successor, which deposed Pinto as head of the guard and sentenced him to a year in jail, but this ministry was in turn forced to resign by a rebellion of part of the Guard in May 1921.

After two years of kaleidoscopic parliamentary politics, a truce was worked out between the Liberals and the main faction of the Democrats under António Ma. da Silva. A new Liberal government held elections that sought to restore a semblance of the old rotativist system, but a workable majority could not be found. New government scandals forced a reorganization of the Liberal government, bringing in Granjó as prime minister once more in August 1921.

Two months later the party-factional system reached an all-time low, with another revolt by Carbonarist elements of the Guard in October. They kidnapped and murdered the prime minister and several leading supporters of Pais's defunct República nova. Another colonel, their leader, headed a new coalition cabinet for fifteen days but was forced to resign, in part because of a joint Anglo-French-Spanish naval demonstration; foreign governments had found the course of events in Lisbon too much to tolerate. Two more short-lived ministries limped through until elections were again held in January 1922. The Democrats, controlling the key ministries and strong provincial machines, returned a strong majority.

This enabled the Democrat leader, Silva, to form a "stable" government that lasted more than twenty months, from February 1922 to October 30, 1923. Its stability was of course only nominal; only a few days after it was formed the new ministry was almost overthrown by a revolt of the Lisbon units of the Republican Guard. The government hastily retreated to Cascais outside Lisbon and called in the army to save it. After the revolt was put down, an effort was made to draw the Guard's teeth by reducing its size from 12,000 to 3,500. This in turn handicapped the maintenance of public order, as strikes and bombings continued. The Silva ministry finally collapsed, partly because of the administrative and financial corruption that it engendered. With Silva discredited by the autumn of 1923, the only man who might have held the party together was Costa, but he steadfastly refused to return from his gilded exile in Paris. An alternative was a brief thirty-five-day government by notables of the newly formed Nationalist party (a fusion of the Liberals and an earlier moderate offshoot of the Democrats, the Reconstituents, who had separated in 1920). This was met with an abortive pro-Democrat naval revolt, then was voted down by the Democrat majority in the assembly.

The irresolvable divisions of the Republican political elite had made it impossible to form a government without considerable reliance on military authority, and for the next eleven months Portugal was governed by two successive ministries headed by officers. These were succeeded by a ninety-day government of the newly formed Democratic Left (or *zurdo*) group, followed by a succession of more moderate Democrat ministries during 1925. There were the customary disorders and scandals, with mounting antileft activism among the military.

The syndicalist confederation (CGT) began to weaken in 1925, as moderate workers dropped out in opposition to destructive strikes and pseudorevolutionary agitation. Several small, hard-core anarchist groups had refused ever to associate themselves; others who wearied of the CGT's "apolitical" orientation left to join new lower-middle-class radical parties, the Radical party proper (founded in 1922 by liberal elements of the old Evolutionists who still opposed the Democrats), and the Democratic Left party. A tiny Portuguese Communist party had been organized in July 1921 under the Third International but never developed any following under the parliamentary Republic.

The main opposition to a functioning parliamentary system came from within, not from without. The last regular cabinet was formed by Silva near the close of 1925 and lasted approximately six months. By 1926 the Democrat party was nearly as exhausted politically as the monarchists had been sixteen years earlier. Rent by factionalism, it could not govern, yet the several arms of its political machine represented and mobilized the largest and most active (largely middle class) political strata in the country, dominating elections and parliaments.* The Democrats thus constituted a political majority, but not an effective governmental party. The ministries of the 1920s had tried

* The results of the 1925 elections, which were probably as fair as any, were:

Democrats	80	Zurdos (Democratic Left)	6	Catholics	4
Nationalists	36	Monarchists	6	Syndicalists	2
Independents	18	Union of Economic Interests	4		

to broaden their social programs on the one hand, while adopting a more conservative position in beating back pseudorevolutionary syndicalism on the other. Extreme corruption, porkbarreling and highly irresponsible political management together resulted in spiraling deficits and the most severe inflation in modern Portuguese history. Inflation affected the lower middle class and sections of the peasantry and urban workers in particular. In 1925 there broke open the infamous Portuguese bank note case, the largest state finance swindle in the history of modern western capitalism. Discontent mounted in 1925-1926, but the monarchist right and the working class left remained small and ineffective minorities, and there was little challenge from within the official political system.

The main source of outside political intervention were the armed forces. The Republic had been established by military revolt and it was rarely free of such interference for more than a few months at a time. Praetorianism under the Portuguese parliamentary regime has never been studied, but apparently stemmed from several obvious factors. In a system dominated by bureaucrats and intelligentsia, military officers were the most powerful single force in the bureaucracy. The narrowness of political life made it easier for officers to see themselves as leaders of a sort of special modernizing elite, while the frustrations of Portugal's international situation and its military policy always left some of the army and navy disgruntled. The victorious end of the World War, coupled with the assassination of Pais and collapse of the República nova, temporarily discouraged military intervention. Army and navy officers were themselves almost as divided over political outlook and goals as were civilians, but the negative features of the restored parliamentary regime stimulated discontent and encouraged renewed intervention. Salient factors in this situation were the increase in disorder and terrorism at home, mounting ministerial instability, the murderous intromission of the Republican Guard into government, the need for successive ministries to rely on "special relations" with key military or paramilitary leaders, and increasing discontent over an inflation from which privileged politicians were protected. Altogether, 46 percent of the prime ministers between 1919 and 1926 were members of some branch of the military. Two antileft revolts at Lisbon in April and July 1925 were foiled, but when the ringleaders, headed by Gen. Sinel de Cordes, were brought to trial, they were absolved by the courts. Such impunity accorded "respectable" conspirators against the regime by leading functionaries was a clear indication of the government's lack of moral authority (and foreshadowed the indulgence shown republican conspirators by monarchist authorities in Spain in 1930).

A more serious anti-Democrat military conspiracy was initiated in

Table 22.   Democrat and Opposition Deputies, 1915-1925

Year	Democrats (PRP)	Total Opposition (Largest Opposition Party)
1915	103	25 (22 Evolutionists)
1919	85	75 (38 Evolutionists)
1921	56	106 (73 Liberals)
1922	74	83 (33 Liberals)
1925	80	76 (36 Nationalists)

Source: A.-H. de Oliveira Marques, "Revolution and Counterrevolution in Portugal," *Studien über die Revolution* (Berlin, 1969), p. 416.

conservative Braga early in 1926. It was begun by a restive and disillusioned former liberal navy officer, Mendes Cabeçadas, but drew on the prestige of the commander of the wartime Portuguese Expeditionary Corps to France, General Gomes da Costa, by making him its figurehead. The resultant military rebellion of June 1926 that overthrew the Silva government was the eighteenth pronunciamiento in the history of the Republic. Its success was hailed by spokesmen of a half dozen different political groups, ranging from the revolutionary left to the monarchist right, each of whom expected to receive favor from the ambiguous goals of national salvation announced by the victorious rebels. Few realized at the time that this was not to be an interim dictatorship of temporary reorganization on the classical model, as attempted by Castro and Pais, but the end of the parliamentary Republic.

The sixteen-year parliamentary regime of the Portuguese Republicans was the most turbulent and unstable in modern European history. This is the more remarkable in view of the fact that the various Republican factions enjoyed a virtual political monopoly throughout. Democrats, Evolutionists, and Unionists and their subsequent subfractions and regroupings differed comparatively little in their broader ideological beliefs. The only major difference had to do with treatment of the church, and after nine years even that was largely resolved on a more moderate, nonradical, basis. The major sources of discord, aside from the war issue in 1917, were personalism and status rivalry. Elimination of the moderating power of monarchy was not replaced by internalized concepts of responsibility and cooperation. Drawing of sharp personalistic and factional lines precluded growth of larger cooperative political groups that might have achieved tolerance and stability. Hostility of Republicans toward Catholics, and the rejection of middle class parliamentarianism by the small revolutionary left, assured a narrowing political spectrum and removed the need for Republican factions to unite to face broader political contests as distinct from revolutionary threats that were merely suppressed by force. This encouraged a somewhat artificial monopoly and left its oligarchic participants free to concentrate on continuous quarreling over spoils. Republicanism had been generated as a doctrinaire force at the turn of the century. Modeled on the most sectarian features of French radicalism, the Republican factions did not represent broad interests in society but narrow political ambitions. Thus they established a unique but unenviable record in the annals of modern European representative government.

Social and Economic Change Under the Parliamentary Republic

The rate of social change and involvement increased under the Republic, but the basic configuration of Portuguese society was only slightly altered. Public affairs were still primarily the preserve of the population of Lisbon, Porto, and Coimbra, and to a lesser extent a few other medium-sized cities. The peasants were still little involved and viewed affairs in Lisbon with suspicion. The rural population largely supported the final overthrow of the Democrat regime.

Population increased fairly rapidly:

1900	5,423,132
1911	5,960,056
1920	6,032,991
1930	6,825,883

The urban proportion of the population, however, grew very slowly, from 16 to 19 percent during the first three decades of the century. Lisbon expanded to nearly 600,000 by 1930 and Porto to more than 230,000. The late-nineteenth-century trend of heavy emigration continued, increasing down to the World War and then diminishing. somewhat in the 1920s:

1900-11	300,000
1911-20	450,000
1920-30	270,000
	1,020,000

As late as 1890, approximately 84 percent of Portuguese society could be classified as lower class, about 15 percent middle class, and 1 percent upper class. Under the parliamentary regime there was a shift away from agrarian employment, but also a proportionate drop in industrial employment, as shown in table 23. The increase of nearly 70 percent in service employment seems to have stemmed from

Table 23.   Percent of Employment in Sectors of the
Portuguese Economy, 1890–1930

	1890	1911	1930
Agrarian	61	57	46
Industrial	18.4	21	17
Service	20.6	22	37

Source: *Dic. Hist. Port.,* 3:462.

three main sources: a substantial growth in public employment (creating much of the steadily worsening fiscal problem); increases in the size of the army and Republican Guard (also weighing more heavily on the state debt); and a considerable growth of the middle classes between 1890 and 1930, from approximately 15 to 29 percent of the total population, stimulating the demand for domestic servants. Though most of this was growth of the marginal lower middle class, there were many more households employing full or part-time domestics in 1925 than in 1900.

The "people" were not much better represented than under the monarchy, since the illiterate half of society was still denied the right to vote. The elements that gained most from the parliamentary Republic were the radical urban intelligentsia of central and southern Portugal. The conservative north was underrepresented on that level; the number of parliamentary leaders from the region was 25 to 50 percent less than its population warranted. The new elite nationally was younger than its predecessor; cabinet ministers under the Republic were on the average in their forties, whereas under the monarchy they had been in their fifties.

The parliamentary Republic did represent an advance in women's rights. Equal rights of divorce for both husband and wife were established in 1910, followed by a second law providing for equal legal rights in marriage. The Republican electoral law, however, was clarified in 1913 to exclude all women from voting.

The Republic had no concerted economic program. In agriculture the remaining common lands were divided up between 1910 and 1923, mostly to the benefit of the upper middle class. Subdivision of peasant plots continued, and the number of holdings steadily increased. Portuguese commerce continued to rely on agricultural exports such as wine, cork, and fruit. Despite further increase in the amount of land cultivated, food production did not keep pace with population growth. Shortage of bread was persistent; between 1919 and 1923 the state subsidized millers to keep prices down.

A profile of Portuguese industry was provided by the industrial survey of 1917: There were only 130,000 industrial workers, of whom 35 percent were women and 15 percent minors. There were 2,500 industrial establishments in Lisbon employing nearly half the country's industrial labor force, and 364 in Porto employing about 20 percent. Nearly all Portuguese industry was still in the small-shop phase of organization. Of 5,647 establishments, the majority (3,757) employed 10 workers or less, and 865 employed between 11 and 100. There were only 25 large factories, mostly in textiles and other light goods, that employed 500 workers or more.

The small organized sector of the working class improved its economic position under the parliamentary regime. The right to strike was legally recognized in 1910. In 1915 the maximum work day was set at varied limits of from seven to ten hours, depending on the kind of work, and in 1916 a ministry of labor and social welfare was created. In 1919 the maximum work week was lowered by decree to a range of forty-two to forty-eight hours, and obligatory sickness and accident insurance was organized under an institute of social security.

These reforms were carried out under heavy pressure from the small but increasingly radical ranks of Portuguese organized labor. The first great strike wave occurred in 1910-1913, followed by a second in 1917, a third in 1919-1920, and a fourth in 1922-1925. The first was the most successful, since 44 percent of the strikes in 1910-1911 ended in victory.

The first major national organization of Portuguese labor was the National Workers' Union, formed in 1914 and more or less socialist in orientation. As in Spain, however, the anarcho-syndicalists became the dominant influence in organized labor. The General Confederation of Labor, which succeeded the Workers' Union in 1919, was under their influence and represented the bulk of Portuguese syndicates. In 1924, 104 of its 115 member syndicates voted to join the anarchist international. Meanwhile, worker organization was followed by employer organization. In 1919 the first general Owners' Confederation was formed, flanked by a broader Union of Economic Interests in 1925.

In general, the wages and living standards of industrial and white collar workers rose somewhat under the parliamentary regime. Conditions for the peasants did not improve, but those who lost most proportionately under the heavy inflation and tax increases of the regime's last years were the middle and upper middle classes. This helps to explain the willingness of many of them to accept the coup of 1926.

The parliamentary republic achieved some improvement in education. Two new state universities were opened at Lisbon and Porto. Compulsory secular primary education for all children was decreed in

Table 24.   Strikes in Portugal, 1910-1925

Year	Total	Results		
		Victory	Defeat	Compromise
1910	85	36	66	36
1911	162	73	21	43
1912	35	1	7	13
1913	19	5	3	8
1914	10	2	1	4
1915	15	4	2	9
1916	7	3	-	4
1917	26	14	2	10
1918	11	3	3	4
1919	21	7	3	8
1920	39	9	4	26
1921	10	2	2	4
1922	22	10	2	6
1923	21	4	3	7
1924	25	5	4	11
1925	10	4	-	3
	518	182	63	196

Source: A.-H. de Oliveira Marques, *A Primeira República Portuguesa* (Lisbon, 1971),
            p. 161.

1911, and Costa established a government ministry of public instruction in 1913. At that time, one-fifth of the neighborhood districts in
Portugal were without a school of any kind. This proportion decreased to only one-tenth by 1927, though facilities in many areas
remained grossly inadequate. Adult illiteracy declined from 70 percent in 1910 to about 61 percent in 1930, a somewhat more rapid rate
of improvement than under the last decades of the monarchy.

The parliamentary republic failed badly in fiscal management.
From 1911 to 1924 currency was inflated 2800 percent, and after 1914
the budget remained permanently and heavily unbalanced. This provoked great transfers of capital abroad, crippling domestic investment. The exchange value of the escudo steadily declined. So did
government receipts, bringing reductions in the real value of state
expenditures that further exacerbated political and social problems.
During the last decade of the monarchy, the average annual deficit
had been 6,500 contos. This leaped to 77,000 (at inflated prices) in
1919-1920 and to 243,000 in 1924-1925. The national debt, which
had increased from 593,000 contos in 1890 to 879,000 in 1910, nearly
tripled during the first decade of the Republic, reaching 2,236,000 by

1920. This defeated efforts to make the tax system more progressive. Indirect taxes accounted for 61.3 percent of state receipts at the end of the monarchy and were reduced to 58.3 percent by 1912, but under the pressure to raise income were increased again in the early 1920's.* The fiscal situation did improve slightly in 1925-1926, and measures to establish a state tobacco monopoly were part of new efforts to right the balance in the final session of the parliamentary regime. By that time, however, time had run out on the system.

* The proportion of indirect taxes was raised further, to 66.7 percent, in the Salazar fiscal reform of 1928-1929.

24

Climax and Collapse of
Spanish Liberalism, 1899–1931

After the creative, liberalizing decade of the 1880s in Spain, that of
the 1890s brought disillusionment and defeat. The Spanish-American
War, with its subsequent Treaty of Paris, had a shock effect on public
opinion but produced no catharsis. The country had achieved a
degree of economic and cultural development and for the moment, at
least, a stable political system, but still had not made the fundamental
breakthroughs to industrialization, social reform and harmony, and a
functioning democracy. For lack of education, interest, ambition, or
faith, or a combination of several of these, most of the population
ignored political life. In such a situation, reorientation and revitalization of civic energies would be difficult to achieve.

Criticism of corruption, misgovernment, and lack of attention to
real problems had grown throughout the decade, and finally reached
a climax after 1898. The demand was for "regeneration," and regenerationism was for a time the commonly held but disparately and
diffusely defined goal of most political and civic groups. For several
years the central figure of regenerationism was the social and institutional historian and reformer Joaquin Costa. Of humble Aragonese
origins, Costa was obsessed by the problem of Spanish "decadence"
and the ignorance and apathy of the country. He was not a politician
and never achieved a clear-cut program or following, but stressed
education and economic development. Fully conscious of the trauma

inflicted by nineteenth-century liberalism, he urged a new agrarian reform that would emphasize technology combined with cooperative organization. During the 1880s and 1890s chambers of agriculture had been formed in various parts of Spain to advance local interests, and early in 1899 Costa brought them together in a National Producers League. The following year middle class chambers of commerce in Castile and Aragón organized a National Union, led by Basilio Paraíso, which was joined by Costa's group. It soon became clear, however, that Paraíso and his followers were mainly concerned with protecting middle class economic interests and had much less dedication to broad national reform. Costa then broke with them.

Highly critical of *caciquismo* (boss rule), Costa rejected the regular party system and thought in terms of an independent new national movement representing the solid lower middle classes. He stressed social unity and the need to channel regional and social institutions toward a more productive future without maiming traditional usages more than was necessary. His "third force" never took effective form, and at one point he rejected parliament altogether, talking of the need for an "iron surgeon" to mend Spain. Subsequently he looked toward a republican civic breakthrough.

The dissatisfaction of the Spanish fin de siècle gave rise to a new genre of national analysis and critique that became known as the "disaster" literature. This had actually begun about 1890, and bore some resemblance to the writings of seventeenth-century arbitristas. Disaster literature was accompanied by a new spirit of national evaluation and criticism in the next generation of belle-lettrists, the so-called Generation of Ninety-Eight. The result was the most extensive effort ever made by Spanish intellectuals to take stock of the country and its problems.

The currents of regenerationism were manifold, for in a sense nearly everyone was a regenerationist after 1898. They were also divided, fissiparous, and in some instances mutually antagonistic, splitting both vertically and horizontally. The catastrophe gave a strong impulse to regionalism in Catalonia (and to a lesser extent in the Basque country) because it deepened the lack of confidence in the Spanish system and posed economic dilemmas for Catalan industry and commerce. The growth of regionalism further diminished national unity while dividing the forces of middle class progressivism and reform. The Republican minority was still sharply divided. The small Spanish Socialist party was growing slowly but refused to collaborate with other groups and remained an orthodox Marxist party, devoted to class struggle. The anarchist fringe had considerable indirect influence which they exerted toward apoliticism and abstentionism, reducing participation in the system. The belle-lettrists of

Ninety-Eight eventually retreated into esthetics. The new forces of regeneration—or of revolution—were thoroughly at odds with each other, and the resulting triangular and quadrilateral struggles tended to cancel each other out. Most Spaniards still had little desire to become involved.

Silvela

At the beginning of 1899 one political figure stood out as potential leader of a new national orientation: Francisco Silvela. He had differentiated himself from Cánovas's politics eight years earlier, and his program of reformist conservatism gave him a position of moral superiority when contrasted with all other regular Conservative and Liberal party leaders. His dissident Constitutional Union was expanded after the death of Cánovas to a broader Conservative Union that reunited all factions of the old Conservative party save the Romero Robledo gang and a small group of intransigent *canovistas.* Silvela emerged as the most popular politician in Spain and was chosen by the queen regent to succeed Sagasta as prime minister in March 1899.

Silvela was the first leader of the era to speak, in his words, of "a true revolution made from above"; he stood on a platform of dynamic conservatism that proposed reduction of international involvement, reform and purification of administration and elections, economic development, tax and fiscal reform, and the harmonizing of regional interests. His new government included one Catalanist, the jurist and historian Duran i Bas, and a leading hero of patriotic conservatism, General Camilo Polavieja, who was at the time the political focus of a significant current of post-Carlist right-wing opinion and also of moderate Catalanist sympathies. Thus Silvela broadened his government at both the center and the right. The recently elected Liberal parliament of 1898 was dissolved, and new elections were scheduled for April 1899.

Silvela was determined to set a standard of electoral honesty, and consequently the contest of 1899 was the fairest yet held under the 1876 constitution. The government's Conservative majority was the most modest—222 deputies—that the regime had seen, while the Liberals elected 122, an all-time high for the opposition under the turno. Silvela's liberalization of electoral administration was henceforth accepted by both sides, and the flagrant caciquismo of 1876–1898 was never again employed to the same degree under the constitutional monarchy.

Liberty, however, did not bring unity, and as a result the new parliament was more sharply divided than ever. By 1899

> the Conservatives were Silvelists, Pidalists, Romerists, Polaviejists, or partisans of the Holy Sepulchre [Cánovas]. The Liberals were Sagastans, Moretists, Monterists, Gamacists, or Canalejists. There were centralist, possibilist, progressivist, federal, and revolutionary Republicans. The Carlists were divided between the parliamentary faction and partisans of withdrawal, and the Integrists between orthodox and heterodox. To the fierce conflict of these groups between themselves might be added the followers of Costa, Paraíso, the apolitical Chambers of Commerce, the Socialists, anarchists, and regionalists.*

The biggest achievement of the Silvela government was financial reform, associated with the name of its finance minister, Raymundo Fernández Villaverde. Service on the debt amounted to 60 percent of state income, and in recent years the budget had been severely unbalanced. The "Villaverde reform" imposed stringent reductions on expenditure and reorganized and extended the system of taxation. The overall tax load was increased but was also made slightly more progressive, with new direct taxes on corporate and personal income. This reform set the norms of state finance for the next eight years, during which period the budgets were balanced, the national debt reduced somewhat, and a solid currency and stable price level maintained as the Spanish economy continued its modest but steady rate of expansion.

Approval of the Villaverde reform, however, required reorganization of the cabinet. Polavieja resigned as war minister in protest against reduction of military expenditures. There was a brief taxpayers' strike by Catalan businessmen, accompanied by the resignation of the one Catalan member of the cabinet, giving a further boost to regionalist resentment and further dividing national energies. After the cabinet was reconstituted, new social legislation was passed to regulate labor accidents and the employment of women and children. At that point the new minister of war, another general, insisted on imposing his personal choices in the army command. The government reached an impasse, and Silvela resigned before the close of 1900.

After two interim ministries, Silvela returned to power in 1902, but he had already lost confidence in the possibility of effective reform. Local government reorganization was blocked, and further attempts at honest elections brought intense hostility from the established cliques. A wealthy man, Silvela lacked burning personal ambition. He

---

* Sevilla Andrés, *Historia política,* p. 296.

was a devout Catholic who preferred to open cabinet meetings with formal prayer, and he found the political arena increasingly distasteful. Alienated and discouraged, Silvela resigned in 1903 both as prime minister and as leader of the Conservative party. The first regenerationist in power had largely, though not entirely, failed.

Division of the Liberal Party

Of the architects of the Restoration system, only Sagasta survived the disaster of 1898. He was not a regenerationist, for his catalog of reforms had largely been exhausted during the 1880s, nor did his brand of realism induce him to suppose that rapid reform of the country was possible. Sick old man though he was, he remained head of the Liberal party and formed his last government in 1901–1902. It attempted only two things, a minor education reform and a new measure, inspired in part by legislation in France, that would have required government registration of all Catholic orders.

Anticlericalism moved to the forefront of Spanish affairs after 1900. The turning in of the country on itself, an extended spirit of criticism, and the growth of secularist and antireligious attitudes all played a part. More concretely, the privileged position of the church and its control of primary and secondary education roused enmity among liberals and progressives. Antipathy toward the orders was increased as a result of their involvement in the Philippines, the increase of their number in Spain after many French monks and nuns fled government persecution north of the Pyrenees, and especially because of impressions formed, whether correctly or not, of the wealth of the orders. In typically Sagastine fashion, one of the "Old Shepherd" 's last political acts was an effort to reach understanding with the Vatican over the registration of orders, minimizing injury to Catholic interest. This brought the splitting off of the left wing of the party, José Canalejas's Democrat faction.

Sagasta died in 1903, leaving the Liberal party leaderless. It was divided to some extent over policy matters, but even more by factional jockeying for status among would-be successors. None of them had Sagasta's prestige, and after 1903 the Liberals split into several subgroups identified with individual leaders.

The political system thus became much more heterogeneous after 1900. To the succession problem of the Conservatives were added the multidirectional cleavage of the Liberals and the rise of the regionalist movements. The two main Catalanist groups came together in a Lliga Regionalista in 1901, and in Galicia a Unión Galaico-Portuguesa was formed, though with much less support. The republican groups in turn bid to become a major new element by forming an electoral Republican Union in 1903.

Alfonso XIII

In this political atmosphere of uncertainty and cleavage the young Alfonso XIII, posthumous son of Alfonso XII, came of age at sixteen in 1902. He was bright but not well educated, courteous and charming but somewhat wanting in self-discipline. Of an energetic nature, he became a prodigious hunter and was an early lover of sports cars.

The constitutional system of Spain, however, required that the king rule to some extent as well as reign. Sovereignty lay with "King and Cortes," and the crown had to play a discretionary role in appointing and maintaining the unity of parliamentary ministries. Alfonso XII and the queen regent had been able to rely on Cánovas and Sagasta. Alfonso XIII had no such good fortune, dealing with a much more divided and antagonistic—and also more representative and democratic—parliament. Throughout his reign he was faced with a variety of options and with strongly conflicting opinions from varying sources, several of which were often about equally qualified. The crown had to grant confidence to or withdraw it from the leaders and groups with the strongest support or the most viable programs. The parliamentary system was not yet fully self-sustaining, which was not the fault of young D. Alfonso. In the exercise of his constitutional prerogatives he was later accused of being a manipulator and of harboring authoritarian tendencies. That he willingly used them to thwart the majority will was, however, never clear, at least until 1931. When that moment finally arrived, he did not contest the issue but relinquished his royal authority.

Perhaps D. Alfonso's major weakness was that his conception of Spanish affairs was excessively political. He thought in terms of Spain's security, unity, and prestige, but had less knowledge of social, economic, cultural, and religious problems. He was not well acquainted with leading Spaniards. His mother had been an unpopular foreign queen and regent, and he had grown up in a rather restricted family circle. Outside contacts were limited mostly to the upper aristocracy and military and civilian tutors. Even in his mature years Alfonso XIII was not in touch with business, regional, or cultural leaders. He dealt mainly with aristocratic friends, politicians, and a few favorites from the army hierarchy. Indeed, the military was the only other sector of Spanish life with which he had association, and from the beginning D. Alfonso tried to establish himself as an "army king," zealous of the interests of the military and, he hoped, a center of military affection.

During the first ten years of his reign, Alfonso XIII exercised his discretionary powers in government with considerable success. This period developed in four phases: a) a Conservative phase of five separate ministries from 1902 to 1905; b) a Liberal phase of five Liberal ministries from 1905 to 1907; c) the Conservative government of Antonio Maura from 1907 to 1909; and d) the two Liberal ministries of 1909–1912, chief of which was the two-and-one-half-year government of Canalejas.

When Silvela resigned in 1903, D. Alfonso not illogically gave approval to a new ministry headed by Silvela's former colleague, the reformist Conservative Fernández Villaverde. Though a capable lawyer and financial administrator, Villaverde was not a skilled politician. He was groping toward a more progressive policy than that represented by old-style conservatism, but this inspired the opposition of most Conservative forces, who brought him down within five months. Villaverde was succeeded by the former Liberal Antonio Maura, who was in the process of establishing his leadership over the major elements that had made up the Conservative party. Maura was much stronger and more energetic than either Silvela or Villaverde, but at the close of 1904 the government became involved in a contest of wills with the royal family over a minor issue. The queen mother (former queen regent), who exercised considerable influence during the first years of the young Alfonso's reign, opposed Maura for being what she feared was too reformist and too domineering. She was determined that the well-known conservative general and former war minister Polavieja, a particularly devoted friend of the royal family, should be appointed to the key post of captain general of Madrid. The Maura government opposed this for political reasons. Since constitutional authority on such matters was equally divided between the government and the crown, an impasse was reached and the entire ministry resigned. After a brief transition government, the only Conservative alternative, Villaverde, once more formed a ministry, but again only a few months were needed to show that he could never rally either a Conservative majority or a majority of the Conservatives.

Thus in mid-1905, for the first time in his reign, D. Alfonso turned to the Liberals. A general Liberal caretaker ministry was organized under Eugenio Montero Ríos for the purpose of holding new elections and was supported by all factions of the party. The 1905 elections marked another step in the liberalization and regularization of the electoral process and were free of the grosser forms of coercion. Nevertheless, it was still easy to rally a government majority—though not so heavy as in the days of the Restoration—for in nearly one-third of the districts (mostly rural) no opposition candidates presented themselves.

Because of the intensification of the social and regionalist problems, the Liberal phase lasted less than two years. Strikes were increasing, though technically they were illegal, and anarchists in Catalonia and several other regions were more active. Another round of bomb explosions, following that of the 1890's, started in Barcelona in 1906. Regionalist feeling waxed stronger, while the army officer corps, largely though not entirely quiescent for a quarter-century, became uneasy. Officers were disgruntled because of low pay and budgetary restrictions and because of numerous criticisms heaped on the army after 1898. In an age of rampant militarism in Europe, the Spanish army had comparatively little prestige and not too much money; Spain was the only large country in Europe whose armed forces were not expanded during the first decade of the twentieth century. In addition, the army was sometimes used as a police force to quell disorders, a role that many officers found distasteful. Finally, of all the divisive elements in the country, none seemed more insidious to the military than regional nationalism, which threatened to tear Spain apart and was tinged with insults to the Spanish flag and army. A slur against the military in a Catalan humor magazine in 1905 led to a sacking of its press and editorial office by a mob of officers. This violence was followed by a sharp wave of protest from the military all over Spain, demanding satisfaction for the army against subversive attacks.

In response, the Liberals broke in two. Montero Ríos and approximately half of them tried to protect civil guarantees and free speech, while the centralist Moret and others were willing to give the army satisfaction. Hence the crown appointed a minority Liberal government under Moret, early in 1906, that passed a Law of Jurisdictions establishing jurisdiction of military courts over publications or news items that referred to the military. This marked the reentry of the army as a special political force in Spanish affairs. The Law of Jurisdictions was the first, and for a long time the only, major break in the constitutional system of the Restoration. For thirty years the system had become increasingly liberal and democratic, and after a brief interruption it continued to move in that direction during the decade that followed 1906.

Antonio Maura and the "Revolution from Above"

The Moret government was a minority ministry unable to stand on its own feet after the latest split in the Liberal party. During the remainder of 1906 it was followed by three equally short-lived Liberal minority governments, none of which could build viable support. Their main tactic was to try to rally all factions of the Liberals behind an anticlerical program, but this was inadequate as a unifying ploy. Hence early in 1907 the crown summoned a new government under the leader who by that time stood as the undisputed chief of the Conservatives, Antonio Maura.

Maura was the most imposing and charismatic Spanish political figure of his time. He had begun his career as a member of the Gamacist wing of the Liberal party (Gamazo was his father-in-law) and came into prominence as a frustrated reformer in 1893, when he made the only serious attempt to solve the Cuban problem (see p. 511). Maura became a regenerationist sui generis after 1898 and, following Gamazo's final break with Sagasta, joined the Silvelist Conservatives. He inherited and developed the Silvelist program: basic reforms to ensure genuine constitutional government, the establishment of local government autonomy to uproot caciquismo, reform of social legislation, protection of Catholic interests, stimulation of the economy, and strengthening of the nation's defenses, especially the navy. Like Silvela and Costa, Maura was determined to enlist the support of the *fuerzas vivas*—the lower-middle-class "living forces" of Spanish society that often did not bother to vote. In so advanced a city as Barcelona, only 10 percent of the electorate had voted in 1899.

Maura was an intense moralist who often scorned ordinary politicians. He was also the most powerful parliamentary orator of his day. His pride, austerity, and eloquence, along with his ideals and forceful determination, projected the strongest personal mystique of any leader in Spain; he was one of only two politicians whom the king always addressed in formal terms. As early as 1904 he was the most imperious figure in politics, and he was able to attract active new middle class currents to the Conservative party, thus broadening its base slightly. In his first government of 1903-1904, however, he had shown a tendency toward high-handedness and scorn for opposition opinion. In his zeal to eliminate old-style caciquismo, his government had simply kicked out local administrators and put its own men in their place. Maura may have been the undisputed idol of activist Conservatives, but he had become the number-one enemy of the Liberals and the left. If his charismatic qualities elicited support, his arbitrary manner and refusal to compromise also provoked a most intense hostility.

Elections were held in April 1907, within weeks of the formation of the new Maura government. Not suffering from the diffidence of Silvela, Maura was determined to achieve a large and firm majority that would give him a solid base for major reforms without threat of political interruption. Hence his interior minister, Juan de la Cierva, reversed the trend of the decade and exercised considerable government pressure in the balloting. Mayors who had been elected by formal vote kept their seats, but in areas where local officials had previously been named by the central government, new appointments were made in sizable numbers to ensure a Conservative vote. Thus the Conservatives gained 256 seats, giving them firm control of the new parliament, but opposition protests were more numerous and virulent than they had been in years. At the opening of the Cortes, all the opposition deputies boycotted the sessions devoted to the verification of credentials. The other new development of the elections was the emergence of Solidaridad Catalana, a union of Catalan regional groups composed of the nationalist Lliga, Catalan republicans, and Catalan Carlists. These groups coalesced in opposition to the Law of Jurisdictions and in determination to wrest some form of local government autonomy. The Solidaridad alliance gained control of Catalan opinion, prevented electoral manipulation, and swept the balloting in Catalonia.

Maura soon showed that he was not unsympathetic to moderate Catalanism, with which he hoped to achieve an understanding. His first goal, however, was a basic local government autonomy bill which he called "a law for the uprooting of caciquismo." This was the latest of some twenty local government reform measures that had been proposed over the past thirty years. It would have given local governments general autonomy over municipal and provincial affairs, but at the same time tried to guarantee the interests and representation of the fuerzas vivas by providing for the election of municipal governments partly through the corporate suffrage of economic and cultural groups. Moreover, provincial deputies, who were being chosen by direct vote though bereft of authority, would be elected by the councils. Under the parliamentary committee system, the measure was temporarily blocked by the Liberal and leftist minorities.

Maura proposed to face the social question on the basis of freedom under the law. His government legalized the right to strike (and also the use of the lockout) in 1908. It was the first to attempt a modest degree of state regulation of agrarian rents. The first steps were also taken toward a system of labor conciliation tribunals, regulation of labor contracts, and establishment of minimum wages. A National Insurance Institute was created in 1908, marking the beginning of what by the 1920s became a fairly large voluntary insurance system.

The system of municipal justice was reformed so that judges and prosecutors would be named by the judicial system itself rather than by politicians. Another important change was the government's Electoral Reform Law of 1907 improving the methods of registering the electorate and recording ballots, thus diminishing the opportunity for electoral fraud.

The second Maura government lasted more than two and a half years and was one of the two longest parliamentary ministries of twentieth-century Spain. It finally broke down over the issue of disorder and repression. With anarchist outbursts on the rise and the court and jury system encountering difficulty in prosecuting offenders, the government proposed a special Law for the Repression of Terrorism in 1908, giving authorities the right to close anarchist centers and newspapers and deport anarchists.

Though the past generation had been full of anarchist assassinations and attempted assassination of heads of state and government leaders both in Spain and throughout Europe, the opposition seized the opportunity to launch a major anti-Maurist alliance. Maura was a vigorous leader but not a skillful politician. He detested jockeying, backslapping, and compromise, and his supercilious manner infuriated his foes. He scorned the function of publicity and newspaper propaganda, contemptuously dismissing it as the "street rattle." After the government's clear stand on terrorism, the left-wing Catalanists broke with the Lliga and came out in general opposition to his autonomist proposals as too authoritarian. In conjunction with the Liberal leaders Moret and Canalejas, a broad alliance of the left was formed in opposition to the antiterrorist law. Street mobs were brought out against the government, which was forced to withdraw the measure, and the local government reform remained stalled in the Cortes. The cooperation between most republicans and some of the Liberals was then expanded into a Left Bloc against the Maura ministry, proposing to overturn it and combat clericalism. For the first time since 1875 a major part of one of the two chief constitutional parties made a tactical alliance, albeit shortlived, with enemies of the regime.

Maura's downfall was precipitated by the need to send troops across the straits in 1909 to protect the Spanish position in northern Morocco. Sudden call-up of reserves caused much hardship in Madrid and Barcelona, and it was used by trade unions and other leftist elements in the Catalan capital as a pretext for a general strike that mushroomed into the "Tragic Week" of July 1909. Barricades went up in many parts of Barcelona; one-third of the religious buildings in that city were damaged or wholly destroyed, and more than one hundred people killed. In the aftermath, four men were executed in symbolic punishment. One of them was Francisco Ferrer, an anarchist agitator who operated a "rationalist school" in Barcelona and had helped to incite the assassination attempt on the king in 1906, when a score of people were murdered by a bomb in Madrid. In general, the repression that followed the Tragic Week was comparatively moderate, but a few of the individual sentences were excessive. The whole episode provoked almost the entire opposition to demand (with great verbal violence) that Maura resign. The clamor was reinforced by carefully orchestrated protests from the international left in key European cities. Though the government had not transgressed the letter of the constitution, the Liberals made it clear that they would use their tactical alliance with the republicans to wreck the system unless Maura were dismissed. Don Alfonso felt that there was no other prudent course than to give in and appoint a Liberal ministry under Moret.

Canalejas

The Moret government was only a transition ministry. Moret did not have the united support of the Liberals and instead was using the tactical Left Bloc as a means of building personal support outside the regular two-party structure. He could achieve success only by being allowed to dissolve the Cortes and hold new elections, but neither the crown nor all the Liberals would follow his lead. Instead, early in 1910, D. Alfonso appointed a new government under the most vigorous and imaginative of the Liberal chiefs, the somewhat younger politician José Canalejas.

Canalejas presided over the last strong government of the constitutional monarchy, from February 1910 to November 1912. He was in some ways the antithesis of Maura. A politician to his fingertips and a backslapper, he fully understood the importance of publicity and allowed himself no hauteur. Up until 1910 key leaders normally restricted campaigning to their own districts, and parties were built around local notables. By contrast, Canalejas became the first national politician of the century, campaigning nationwide and personally mobilizing support.

Canalejas wanted to continue the liberalization of Spanish affairs that had moved only by fits and starts for the past two decades. This meant social reform and economic stimuli, as well as more understanding of the regionalists' demands than other Liberals were willing to offer. In minor cabinet positions he had attempted several times to deal with the clerical problem, and he believed that Spain required a more vigorous foreign policy. Though he had helped form the Left

Bloc, for him it was only a temporary maneuver to preserve civil and political liberty. A strict constitutionalist and monarchist, he understood the importance of the two-party system and wanted to improve rather than to destroy it. Thus, to the discomfiture of some of his Liberal colleagues, he immediately made overtures to conciliate Maura and the Conservatives. The results of the 1910 elections were the most balanced yet achieved under the regime: 219 Liberals and 102 Conservatives.

The Canalejas government, even more than its Maurist predecessor, became the principal reform ministry of early twentieth-century Spain. It restructured local government finance and a part of the tax system, lowering excises to benefit the poor while raising rents on urban property (a favorite investment of the wealthy). For the first time in Spanish history a government launched a major publicity campaign in favor of social reform. Canalejas made preparations to introduce a wide series of measures, thinking in terms of a national wage arbitration system, expanded regulation of labor conditions, an accident compensation plan, and a modest land reform for poor peasants. Meanwhile, his government carried out a new military reform that reduced somewhat the discrimination against the poor in recruitment. Canalejas also planned to begin a solution to the regionalist dilemma through a bill that would grant partial autonomy to a regional confederation of the four Catalan provinces.

The greatest excitement was engendered, however, by his attempt to deal with the red-hot clerical issue. Canalejas was a devout Catholic and had obtained dispensation to set up an ordained chapel in his family home. As a realistic progressive, however, he believed that the privileges and discriminatory power of the Catholic church in Spain had to be brought under control, or at least regulation, in order to achieve a free and harmonious society. The major objects of anticlerical hostility were the orders, some of which were accused of economic exploitation and discrimination. Consequently the Canalejas government passed the Padlock Law temporarily prohibiting the establishment of further orders in Spain—which now had more than any other Catholic country in the world—until the question of regulation had been settled. Clerical and conservative opinion mounted an allout attack on Canalejas, replete with major demonstrations, that almost equaled the other side's earlier attack on Maura.

Meanwhile, strikes had increased markedly since 1909. Canalejas respected the individual strike as a normal instrument of collective bargaining, but dealt vigorously with coercive general strikes when attempted on the local level. Revolutionary outbursts by small anarchist groups were directly repressed. The government's declaration of martial law in time of crisis drew the customary attacks from the left, and Canalejas was murdered by an anarchist outside the interior ministry building in November 1912.

The tragedy of Canalejas's death was fully appreciated at that moment, but its fatefulness became clear only with the passing of time. He was the last prime minister of the regime who possessed the qualities of prestige, skill, wisdom, and imagination needed to combine reform with political order. In the decade 1913–1923 Spain made considerable social, economic, and cultural progress, but its political life degenerated, even while becoming freer and more democratic.

Breakup of the Party System, 1913–1915

After the murder of Canalejas, the crown delegated authority to the next strongest Liberal leader, the Conde de Romanones, to continue Canalejist reforms on the basis of the existing parliamentary majority, which still had two and a half years to run. This infuriated Maura. The Conservative leader, bitter at having been deposed by an extra-parliamentary alliance, had been willing to respect Canalejas, but like Canalejas himself, he expected the rotation of parties to resume as soon as the Canalejas government ended. The decision of the crown to allow the Liberals to remain in power so long as they had a majority was constitutionally irreproachable, but to Maura violated the unwritten rule that power should be equally alternated. At the beginning of 1913 Maura announced publicly that he would not cooperate in another government or even remain as leader of the Conservative party unless the crown renounced the present ministry and the whole Liberal party, as presently constituted, for having violated the stability and authority of the political system. Thus the Conservative leader responded to the Maura No! campaign of earlier years with a posture of absolute defiance, placing D. Alfonso in the position of either ignoring him or excluding from consideration the bulk of the forces in Spanish politics.

The Romanones ministry lasted eleven months and was broken by its major achievement: presentation of a measure of limited Catalan autonomy under a regional Mancomunitat, or federation of local government of the four Catalan provinces. It was a modest measure that gave the Mancomunitat no new powers other than a concentration of those facilities already in the hands of each of the four participating provincial governments, but it split the Liberals, who saw it as the first step in dividing the unity and sovereignty of Spain. The Romanones government was voted down, leaving the Mancomunitat legislation to be passed by its successor.

With the Liberals unable to govern, the crown had to turn to the

Conservatives. Maura refused to cooperate without authority to ignore the "subversive" Liberals altogether, and the crown could not concede that authority. At this point a majority of Conservatives drew apart from Maura as *idóneos* ("fit"—that is, fit to compromise and form a functioning government). Their leader, Eduardo Dato, was empowered to form the next government and hold elections early in 1914. These revealed the total fragmentation of the political system. Though Dato's interior minister, José Sánchez Guerra, attempted the usual government pressures and manipulations, they no longer sufficed. Political factions were now too experienced and the electorate better educated and more determined. In 1914, for the first time in Spanish history, a government failed to win a majority of seats in an election that it administered. Of the 400 seats, the majority Conservatives of Dato could garner only 188 (and the opposition Maurists-Ciervists another 26). The main group of Liberals under Romanones won 85, and García Prieto's splinter Democrats (heirs to the earlier Canalejist progressives) held 36.

Meanwhile the place of Antonio Maura as a Conservative leader gave way to Maurism as a factional movement, appealing particularly to patriotic middle class youth who wanted unity and renovation within the existing structure of society. Maura continued to insist on "pure constitutionalism," but his intransigence made it impossible for him to function within the actual constitutional system of Spain. The direction of the subsequent Maurist Youth movement with their street propaganda, mass meetings, and overtones of the integral nationalism of Charles Maurras was extraparliamentary and almost extraconstitutional. To conservative middle class Spaniards, the frustration of Maura was, however, symbolic of the frustration and insecurity of the existing system.

After 1913 the old party structure broke up, primarily because of the changes in Spanish society. Its multiple regional and social as well as cultural and religious cleavages could no longer be accommodated within a simple system. Still, there was more continuous tenure among parliamentary representatives in Spain under the constitutional monarchy than under the French Third Republic, and the number of prime ministers was no greater than under the constitutional monarchy in Italy.* Both the Liberal and Conservative factions retained support in many parts of the country, and parliamentary deputies were comparatively young. Nearly half the deputies in Maura's parliament of 1907 had been under fifty. The politicians of Spain

---

* Juan Linz has pointed out that in Spain from 1874 to 1923 there were sixty-two different ministries but only twenty prime ministers. In Italy from 1876 to 1922 there were forty-four ministries but twenty-one prime ministers.

were still, however, predominantly lawyers and intellectuals (that is, writers or journalists). There were very few businessmen or representatives of other professions or interests. Politics was still the work of a special intelligentsia.

The electoral system was slowly becoming more honest, as the experience of 1899 to 1914 testified. True caciquismo functioned only in Galicia and a few other rural districts. Even in the south, elections were sometimes being directly contested. Central government interference in local administration was steadily reduced, and by the early twentieth century local government officials were removed by central fiat as a rule only in the more backward regions of the west and south. Nonetheless, most rural districts were still single-member parliamentary constituencies that could often be dominated by local notables. The real electoral battles were fought in the multi-member "circumscriptions" of the larger towns or more heavily populated areas where a system of semiproportionate representation of majority and minority lists prevailed.

The major problem was that of reconciling differing regional and social interests through the political system. Most of the largest modernizing middle class, that of Catalonia, had split off into regionalism. Basques and others threatened to do the same. In the big cities many had voted for the republican groups since 1893, but in the countryside Liberal and Conservative factions were still secure. Yet after 1913 they were so divided by personality, ambition, and conflicting programs that they could no longer provide stable government or an outlet for reform.

Spain in the Vortex of European Imperialism

The enervation and self-searching that followed the loss of the last remnants of the old colonial empire left Spanish government without great ambition to participate in the final round of modern European imperial expansion that came in the early twentieth century. By that time spheres of influence in most of Africa and Asia were clearly delimited; one of the remaining territories of any importance was the sultanate of Morocco, the northern part of which lay within Spain's historic radius of interest. In 1902 France, with an eye toward the absorption of most of Morocco, proposed an understanding with Spain that would have reserved approximately the northern third of Morocco as a Spanish sphere. The Silvela government rejected the agreement, partly for fear of offending Britain (whose interests were excluded) and partly to avoid becoming involved in new colonial difficulties. Spain did have economic as well as military and diplo-

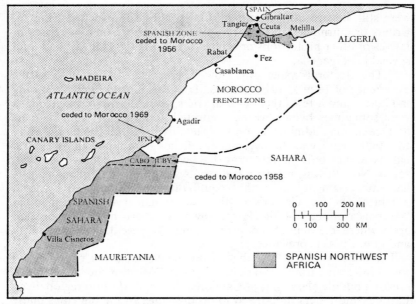

Spanish Possessions in Northwest Africa   *UWCL*

matic interests in Morocco; they were mostly in the form of capital invested in Spanish and Hispano-French mining enterprises outside Melilla, easternmost of the two chief Spanish presidios on the north Moroccan coast. A subsequent treaty of 1904 arranged by France provided for recognition of a smaller Spanish sphere of interest in northern Morocco.

Turmoil within the sultanate, involving attacks on French citizens and interests, gave France its excuse to intervene. Spain was faced with the same issue in miniature in 1908–1909 after assaults by local kabyles against mining works in northeast Morocco. Maura, who up to that point had scrupulously avoided infringing the nominal authority of the sultanate, found himself forced to commit troops to Morocco (indirectly leading to the Tragic Week in Barcelona and his own downfall). Canalejas was subsequently forced to take an energetic stand in order to prevent France from excluding Spain from Morocco altogether. Within the country there was little enthusiasm for a policy of neocolonialism in Morocco, but the Canalejas government felt that it would be too damaging to national self-esteem and Spain's place in the world for France to take over completely what had always been Spain's sphere of interest in northwest Africa. Moreover, it seemed imprudent to permit a foreign power to occupy the other side of the straits, threatening Spain's strategic position. Official protectorates for both France and Spain were set up by treaty in 1913, but the Spanish zone included only the northern 5 percent of Morocco. This was a poor, comparatively barren region inhabited by warlike kabyles rarely controlled even by the sultanate. At first Spanish sovereignty consisted of only a few peripheral military outposts and the establishment of a capital at Tetuán, where a local Moroccan caliph was appointed under Spanish supervision. Almost no effort was made to occupy or directly administer this forbidding, hostile region.

At the beginning of the century Spain's international prestige was again at extremely low ebb. Alfonso XIII's goodwill visits and contacts among foreign royalty were useful, but the international leftist campaign mounted against Maura in 1909 was not unsuccessful in refurbishing the image of a black, inquisitorial Spain. When the World War broke out, no Spanish interests were involved and the official policy of neutrality was the only sane course. The efforts of the crown as an intermediary between civilian relatives and war prisoners in the embattled areas created a more positive image, as did frustrated efforts on behalf of negotiation. Meanwhile, many Liberals and some leftists began to urge Spanish intervention on the side of the Entente, the "progressive" side, and this further added to domestic tensions during the war years.

Economic Development and Social Change

The first third of the twentieth century was an era of significant economic development, raising Spanish income in the late 1920s to a plateau that it would not see again for another twenty-five years. Catalonia continued to lead the way in industrial development, followed by the Basque provinces of Vizcaya and Guipuzcoa. At first the loss of Cuba had a harsh effect on the Catalan economy, whose exports had been based on the Cuban market. Moreover, cotton manufactures had been experiencing difficulty since the early 1890s, and the first years of the century were hard. Barcelona and Valencia provinces between them accounted for 30 percent of all Spanish exports, but Barcelona textile exports dropped off badly after 1900. Conditions improved in later years but only by fits and starts, and the pressures on textile production explain part of the social conflict in Catalonia. By 1913, however, Spanish trade had increased considerably, and the World War provided a greatly expanded export market, stimulating production. The most important development was in

Table 25.   Spanish Orange Exports, 1850-1929
(annual averages for each decade)

Years	Tons	Years	Tons
1850-59	11,898	1890-99	178,289
1860-69	23,482	1900-09	382,926
1870-79	65,975	1910-19	415,571
1880-89	92,378	1920-29	592,831

Source: Plan Nacional de Obras Hidráulicas, 3:133, in El Banco de España: Una historia económica (Madrid, 1970), p. 391.

Valencian citrus production, which by 1930 accounted for 21 percent of exports.

The period 1900-1930 was a time of general industrial expansion. Steel, centered mainly in Vizcaya, Guipuzcoa, and Asturias, benefited from foreign investment; production rose by 263 percent from 1900 to 1913, expanded further during the war, then increased another 235 percent during the 1920s. The starting base was very low, of course, and by 1930 the total was still only one million tons, not yet sufficient for national needs. The major new industry in Catalonia was chemicals. Hydroelectric resources were also developed in Vizcaya and Guipuzcoa, as was an expanded shipbuilding industry, stimulated by the naval programs first of the Liberals (1888) and then of the Conservatives (1908).

Other sectors fared more poorly. By the early twentieth century Catalan shipping had been nearly wiped out because its owners could not finance the conversion to steam. The railway system languished and could not improve its stock and technology for lack of traffic and capital. Mining later declined as well. Exhaustion of the better and more easily worked veins made low-quality Basque iron ore less attractive for export; production dropped by half between 1913 and 1929, and the output of other categories of Spanish ores also dropped during the 1920s.

Simply put, Spain even after the World War had not yet reached the stage of industrial takeoff. The only two regions in which the value of manufactures exceeded that of agriculture were Catalonia and the two main Basque provinces, but even there such a level was not achieved until after the stimulus of the war. All the factors—geographical, economic, and cultural—that had retarded development in the nineteenth century were still present, though to a lesser degree. Progress was being made and the standard of living was rising, but after 1910 Spanish society was living in an era of vastly rising expectations. Political and social ideologies derived from the achievements of the most advanced countries were being advanced in a Spain whose economy was not yet prepared to accommodate their demands. What was by northwest European standards a nineteenth-century rural economy was required to meet the challenge of twenti-eth-century urban and industrial conflict.

Government cannot be entirely absolved of responsibility for this. There was never a serious program to stimulate economic develop-ment, and the failure becomes more significant when contrasted with the attention which Italian government in those same years gave to awarding contracts, subsidies, and other encouragement to Italian industry. Such an orientation was, of course, somewhat more difficult in Spain and was discouraged even more by the nation's quiescent role in diplomatic and military affairs. A pacific country, avoiding competition in the European maelstrom, felt less need to foster strate-gic industries or the nucleus of a military-industrial complex.

The Achilles heel of the Spanish economy was its agriculture, where much of the nineteenth century had been wasted. Structural and technological improvements with which some countries had greatly expanded productivity had still not been introduced in Spain. There was some extension of irrigation, but major hydraulics projects, as preached by Costa, were lacking; what was achieved, as in the Levant, was done by small mechanical pumps and wells. Despite the large olive oil output, producers did not organize well for export, and Italy, for example, cornered most of the market in Argentina. There was a great extension of sugar beet production after the loss of Cuba and the steep protection given by the 1899 tariff, but artificial stimula-tion led to overproduction.

Grain remained the base of the agrarian economy, particularly in the center of Spain. After 1905, the area devoted to wheat cultivation expanded once more; from 3,460,000 hectares in 1903-1907 it rose to 4,200,000 in 1928-1932. A 20 percent extension of tillage was accom-panied by a 33 percent increase in production, indicating only a 9 percent rise in productivity over a twenty-five year period. This very modest achievement was due in considerable measure to greater use of chemical fertilizers. General yield per hectare was still only half that of France, where admittedly the land was naturally more fertile and the climate more beneficent. Though scarcely dramatic, the growth in cereal production enabled Spain to become virtually self-sufficient in grain by 1930.

The trend toward genuine commercial agriculture, begun on some of the larger estates in the eighteenth century, continued, but small producers were ill-equipped to improve their situation. The landless rural population in the south increased, leading to greater social pressure. Equally pressing, however, were problems created by the rental and sharing agreements held by small farmers who cultivated but did not own farms of their own. The first attempt to establish new rental regulations was made by the Maura government in 1907 but achieved little. Resentment among rental farmers was strongest in Galicia, where population increase and subdivision of rental units led to wretched conditions, sustaining a parasitic upper middle class and perhaps the worst system of caciquismo in Spain. Here the government finally intervened, and arrangements were made in the 1920s for compulsory redemption of *foros* (rental contracts) to enable peasants to buy land of their own.

One of the gravest weaknesses in agriculture was lack of rural credit for the small farmer. An effort by the Liberal Santiago Alba to establish a government agricultural bank was largely frustrated. The only significant new opportunities were those created by Catholic cooperatives and rural syndicates; otherwise farmers were largely at the mercy of the village usurer.

Government finance was stabilized at the beginning of the century by the Villaverde reforms of 1899-1900, but after the depression of 1908 fiscal imbalances once more became serious. Spain still lacked a central banking system. The Bank of Spain, founded in 1874, was a privately owned bank of national monetary emission. During its first quarter-century (1874-1898), its primary function had been simply to supply the state with funds. From 1898 to 1914, as the government cut back, it began to invest more heavily in private finance. During the World War the Bank of Spain served mainly to provide increased currency for private banking institutions, promoting inflation. Smaller banks subscribed the national debt—a profitable operation for them, since they could borrow the same funds at a lower rate from the Bank of Spain. At about the same time (the war years), Spanish banks began to play a more direct and creative role in providing capital for industrial development, especially in the Basque country. On the other hand, the region with the largest middle class economy, Catalonia, did not develop strong banking institutions. This was not merely because most Catalan businesses and accounts continued to be comparatively small, but even more because of short-sighted policies. Catalan banks did not emphasize the development of checking account deposits but concentrated on stock securities operations and also on foreign exchange speculation, in which they became overextended and suffered major losses.

The social structure of Spain in the late nineteenth and early twentieth centuries was a comparatively normal one for a country still in the early phases of transition from an agrarian to an industrial economy. Whereas in 1877, 72 percent of active Spanish males were employed in agriculture, a slow but steady increase in employment in other sectors reduced the percentage of agricultural employment to 58 percent in 1910. This was a somewhat slower rate of change than in Italy, but compared favorably with the situation anywhere else outside the industrialized quarter of northwest Europe. In 1910 only 11.5 percent of active Spanish males were employed in industry, half the proportion that existed in Italy.

The population increase, from 18,000,000 in 1900 to more than 23,000,000 in 1930, was checked to some degree by a high rate of emigration. For Spain, as for most of southern and eastern Europe, the peak level of emigration occurred just before the World War. In the year 1912 net emigration mounted to more than 134,000. During the 1920s the annual average was only a fraction of that figure.

Throughout these years commentators in western countries were wont to ascribe the modest rate of Spanish development to the absence of a significant middle class. In fact, the relative size of the Spanish middle classes was about equal to those of Italy and actually larger than in half the countries of Europe. The problem, as in the nineteenth century, was not the existence or even the size of the middle classes, but their characteristics, psychology, values, and ambitions. Spain had a comparatively large noneconomic middle class: a high proportion of army officers (though not of soldiers), a rather large number of people in the liberal professions, and a significant proportion of clergy. Typically "bourgeois" or modernizing, entrepreneurial middle class elements were disproportionately concentrated in Catalonia and the Basque country, partially cut off from the main channels of national life. Industry and innovative or modernizing activity was thus scattered on the periphery. In a somewhat more successful country, Italy, industry, wealth, and modernization tended to be concentrated in a northwestern industrial triangle which played a reasonably united and often decisive role in national affairs.

The Silver Age of Spanish Culture

Literature and the arts in Spain during the first third of the twentieth century achieved such quality that the period has frequently been called the Silver Age of Spanish culture, second only to the Golden Age of the sixteenth and early seventeenth centuries. After 1900 the achievements of Spanish culture began to attract serious attention from abroad for the first time in three hundred years. Its main accomplishments were in esthetics, for despite a few distinguished exceptions, the sciences and other disciplines enjoyed much less attention.

Most of the country's leading thinkers and writers who were concerned with the problems of Spanish culture and values in the modern world have been lumped together as the Generation of '98, the name referring to the new elements who came to maturity after the turn of the century. The men of '98 were not a unified but a diverse group, embracing such figures as Unamuno, Ortega, Azorín, and Ramiro de Maeztu. There was considerable pessimism in their analysis of modern Spain, but also a kind of cultural nationalism and reevaluation of the heartland of Spain, of Castile itself. Yet there was considerable uncertainty over the course which Spanish revitalization should take, with a basic division of opinion between Europeanizers and those, like Unamuno, who protested the "Japanization" of Spain.

Most of the main currents of modern esthetics were felt in Spain during these years, and as a result an increasing dissociation and dehumanization of sensibility. In general, however, Spanish art remained more traditional and humane than that of most European countries. The best Spanish painters—Picasso, Miró, Gris—emigrated to Paris, but the new generation of musical talent finally recaptured Spanish themes for Spanish composition, climaxed by the work of Manuel de Falla. Among the novelists only the personalist, quasi-anarchist Pío Baroja was major, but the best-known of all the Spanish writers have been the poets Federico García Lorca and Juan Ramón Jiménez. In Antoni Gaudí, Catalan culture produced perhaps the most original architect of the early twentieth century.

The dechristianization of the intelligentsia proceeded apace, and the crisis of cultural values eventually became as extreme in Spain as in most other western countries. Catholic thought made little advance during this period and was still largely turned in defensively upon itself. An even greater gulf opened between cultural tradition and the novelties of the age.

The principal new force in education continued to be the disciples and teachings of the Institución Libre. In 1908 a state-financed Committee for the Expansion of Learning was set up to encourage graduate study abroad. The Institución's ideals of broad training in the arts and sciences, including physical education and extensive personal experience, were realized in a few private schools, but it cannot be said that they had much impact on Spanish education as a whole. The university system was improving, but though free compulsory primary education had been a standing law since 1857, no facilities were available for a large minority of the country's children, in city slums or poor villages. Much of primary education and the greater part of the secondary school facilities were under the care of the church, supported by state subsidy, but neither in public nor clerical schools were most services up to the west European norm. In 1900 only 36.7 percent of the people were literate. This indicated adult literacy of about 40 to 50 percent. The situation improved slowly but steadily during the early decades of the century, and by 1930 two-thirds of the adult population was nominally literate. This was not an impressive rate of growth; the proportion of the Spanish state budget devoted to education was one of the lowest in Europe.

The Working Class Movements

Socialist and Fourierist ideas entered Spain in isolated, individual instances as early as the 1840s, and the first labor associations were formed in the thirties and forties. The organized working class movement, however, began with the organization of the Spanish Federation of the First International in 1868-1870. The core of the Spanish Federation was a clandestine, Bakuninist-anarchist Alliance formed in 1870. The Federation was suppressed in subsequent years, though reorganized briefly in 1881 as the Federation of Workers of the Spanish Region. The Federationist movement was avowedly revolutionary from the start, eschewing economic reform and ordinary political action, conceiving of trade unionism as merely the organizational form of revolutionary action.

In the late nineteenth century only a small proportion of workers had been organized, and these mainly in the larger cities of the periphery. Their interests were primarily economic and not political, and the great mass of the workers were not attracted by revolutionary ideas.

Anarchist ideas flourished especially in small cells in Barcelona and a few other towns in the 1890s and found expression in "propaganda by the deed"—bomb-throwing terrorism—during the mid-1890s. It was only after 1900 that the formal idea of anarcho-syndicalism developed, derived largely from French theory but also from the practical example of the older Spanish Federation. The National Confederation of Labor (CNT) was officially organized in 1910 on the theoretical basis of revolutionary anarcho-syndicalism. The CNT expanded into a mass organization only in 1917-1918, and it remained somewhat eclectic in its following. Completely anarcho-syndicalist ideas were espoused by only a minority within the movement. The rank and file were often much less militant, and only constant pressure and terrorism (from both revolutionists and their opponents) converted the major single arm of the working class movement somewhat ambiguously to anarcho-syndicalism. The early movements of the eighties and nineties had petered out, and the major strikes of 1903-1904 were also a failure. The success of the CNT was made possible only by the expanded industrialization of Catalonia during the First World War, swelling the labor force and giving it great bargaining leverage.

Before that, the strongest support for revolutionary syndicalism was found among landless peasants and smallholders in Andalusia, providing the only example of a mass peasant revolutionary movement on a semi-organized basis anywhere in the world. Peasant syndicalism took hold in regions where the upper classes had pioneered individualist political liberalism, but where economic and political changes had left the lower classes almost poorer than before. The provincial appeal of Federal Republicanism also helped create a receptive mood for peasant syndicalism. The evangelical fervor of the anarchist proselytizers stirred a society in which religious appeals and services had been weakened, while the nature of the anarchist message—unity, a general strike, and the revolutionary *reparto* (land-division)—were very attractive for illiterate peasants unprepared to participate in a more organized, disciplined sort of reform or revolutionary movement.

Revolutionary peasant syndicalism in Andalusia hit two peaks. The first came in 1903-1904 when a major strike wave was killed by bad weather conditions and widespread hunger. The second was the so-called *trienio bolchevique* of 1918-1920, involving mass strikes in 1918-1919. The second wave was encouraged by wartime prosperity (in which the poorer peasants did not share) and the excitement brought by the Russian Revolution. But peasant syndicalism was loosely organized and unable to sustain itself. The strikes won some wage increases but did not have revolutionary effects.

Marxist socialism was slower to take root in Spain and did not develop into a mass movement until after 1930. The Spanish Socialist Workers' Party (PSOE) was organized in 1879, and a socialist trade union system (UGT) was begun nine years later. The early history of Spanish socialism is closely associated with the labors of its leader, a Galician typesetter, Pablo Iglesias. The movement which he organized followed the standard lines of late-nineteenth-century Marxism. It was small, thoroughly disciplined, and devoted to practical reforms rather than premature revolutionary efforts. Spanish Socialism encountered extreme difficulty in developing a following. The degree of education and self-discipline that it required did not come easily to Spanish workers. In 1899 the UGT headquarters were moved from Barcelona, leaving the future of the working class movement in Catalonia to anarcho-syndicalism. The anarcho-syndicalist movement surpassed Spanish Socialism in propaganda and education, and its confederative structure was more congenial to Spanish localism and personalism than was the centralized, "regimented" Socialist party. Only after a larger scale of industry developed in regions outside

Catalonia did the UGT slowly begin to develop a following in north-central Spain. The Socialist party at first operated in Marxist isolation but switched to electoral alliance with the republicans in 1910, considerably increasing the Socialist vote. The Socialists began to elect city councillors in the 1890s and won their first seat in parliament in 1910. From that time middle class intellectuals played a greater role in Socialist affairs and helped encourage the party in the reformist collaboration that marked most of its activity between 1917 and 1933.

The Catholic Revival

The expropriation of church lands, nominal restriction of Catholic orders, and concession of limited tolerance to Protestantism had not meant a de-Catholicization of official society in Spain but only a momentary declericalization. The Restoration era carried with it a strong overtone of official piety and the re-Catholicization of government functions.

Loss of local properties, however, had greatly handicapped the work of the Catholic Church in the rural areas and particularly in the southern provinces, where ecclesiastical establishments had always been weak. Moreover, facilities were not readily available to provide for many of the swelling working-class suburbs in the larger cities. The consequence of this situation was a steady de-Catholicization among urban workers and southern peasants.

On the other hand, the church, from the late nineteenth century onwards, endeavored to recoup by its orientation toward the middle and upper classes. Much of the primary education in the country was still operated by the church, and greater attention was given secondary education, particularly among the upper classes. Official piety became quite overt among the possessing classes, and was reinforced by certain internal changes, such as reform of the liturgy, calculated to make religious services more impressive and hold the attention and emotions. Charitable and devotional organizations, particularly for upper-class ladies, increased in number. The number of monks and friars in Spain also increased, particularly after the persecutions in France and Portugal. The most Catholic sector of the lower classes was the landholding northern peasantry, among whom *cofradías,* or lay religious guilds, remained common.

At the same time, a reaction set in against the increased influence of Catholicism among the upper classes and to some extent in the government. A new wave of middle class anticlericalism became a major issue in politics, finally culminating in the left Republican legislation of 1931. The continued hostility of much of official Catholicism to liberalism was greatly resented, as were the privileges granted to it by the state. The clerical issue became one of the major issues dividing liberal from conservative in the middle classes, and encouraged the former to look toward alliance with the revolutionary left to defeat Catholic interests.

Catholic social reform and Catholic trade unions among the lower classes were much less successful than Catholic influence among the upper classes. A series of Workers' Circles organized in the late 1890s were Catholic social societies more than they were trade unions. An organization of Catholic syndicates was formed after 1912, paralleled some years later by a second nonconfessional Catholic workers' syndical federation. These groups were faced with the implacable hostility of the revolutionary movements and were confined for the most part to northern Spain. Their following was only a fraction that of the leftist movements. Another officially Catholic group, however, the Basque regionalist Solidaridad de Trabajadores Vascos, founded in 1911, developed modest worker support in the Basque region.

The most important Catholic social organization was the peasants' confederation (CONCA), founded in 1916 and limited mostly to the northern half of the country. By 1922 it numbered nearly half a million families and represented a greater following than did the CNT. The greatest practical benefit of the CONCA was to provide cheaper credit for many of its members, as well as marketing and purchasing cooperatives.

Catholic Action was formed in Spain during the 1880s, after it had developed in Italy, but it was not mobilized on a broad scale for forty years, until the 1920s. It played no major political role in Spain before 1931. Judging from its membership statistics, the two most genuinely Catholic regions of the country, as far as middle class activists were concerned, were the Basque country and Valencia.

The Republicans

Republicanism made modest advances in the early twentieth century, following a virtual eclipse in the 1890s after the movement had bifurcated between Castelar's possibilism and the tradition of military conspiracy represented by Ruiz Zorrilla. In the late nineteenth century republicanism had dwindled into a congeries of provincial and personalist sects, grouped around local followings or a few key leaders. One of the "historic" Republican personalities, Nicolás Salmerón, took the lead in forming a short-lived Republican Union in 1903. More important was Alejandro Lerroux's Radical Republican party that developed in the wake of the Republican Union. Lerroux followed a course of vulgar demagogy, based mainly on anticlericalism, that rallied a considerable following in urban Catalonia, and he began to reach out in an effort to create a national Republican party. Valencia, one of the most prorepublican regions, was badly split between the factions of the novelist Blasco Ibáñez and a local republican leader, Rodrigo Soriano.

The most constructive of all the republican groups was the Reformist Republican party, organized in 1912 by the Asturian Melquiades Alvarez. The Reformists adopted the banner of Fabian-style social democracy, in which the most important goals were practical social and political reforms, educational improvement, complete religious and cultural liberty, technical development, and a fully free, independent, and responsible parliament. They were less concerned with the question of the regime per se. Yet the Reformists, like the other Republican groups, never became a national party. Their main support came from the Asturian middle classes.

Catalan Nationalism

The organization of Catalan nationalism as a political movement was given impetus by the defeat of 1898, which brought the loss of Catalonia's main export market and prompted a recurrence of industrial crisis. Silvela's first reform government of 1899–1900 included the pro-Catalan General Polavieja as well as one Catalan minister. Frustration of the Silvela government and of Polavieja as a representative led to the formation of a political party, the Lliga Regionalista, that won the four Cortes seats for Barcelona in the 1901 elections, helping to break the established turno in the Catalan capital. For the next five years, however, no further progress was made, largely because of the influence of the demagogic, anti-Catalanist Radical Republicans in Barcelona. Catalan nationalism was essentially middle class in background, and the Lliga stood for a degree of corporate suffrage and the fostering of regional culture and economic development. It was neither subversive nor separatist, but intended to win Catalan autonomy from and within the established system.

Catalanism's first major breakthrough was made possible by reaction to the 1906 Law of Jurisdictions. In opposition to this measure, the Lliga was joined by some Catalan Republicans and by Catalan Carlists in a regional electoral alliance, Catalan Solidarity, that won forty-one of the forty-four Catalan Cortes seats in the 1907 elections. The Lliga's astute political leader, Francesc Cambó, then worked closely with the Maura government of 1907–1909 to try to legislate local government autonomy, and hopefully, a broader regional autonomy bill for Catalonia. However, the left wing of the Catalanists walked out on this tacit alliance in 1908 because the Maura government refused to revoke the Law of Jurisdictions "immediately" and because of provisions for corporate suffrage in the local autonomy bill. Throughout its history Catalanism has been plagued by successive left Catalanist groups splintering apart and reforming.

Despite the failure of the Maura administration, the Lliga regained control of regional politics inside Catalonia after 1911. It was perhaps the only modern, well-organized political party in Spain, and extended its regional influence with the formation of the Catalan Mancomunitat in 1913. This amounted to concentration of the existing limited administrative powers of the four provinces of modern Catalonia in one unit, without devolving new measures of autonomy. Nevertheless, the opportunity was well used by the Catalanists to improve education, roads, and local services and to foster regional culture, giving Catalonia in the second and third decades of the twentieth century by far the most intense cultural life of any region of Spain.

Basque Nationalism

The other important regional movement developed in the Basque provinces. The roots of Basque nationalism lay in regional culture and sentiment and in reaction against the apparent shortcomings of the modern Spanish state. Basque foralism had largely been abolished after the final Carlist war, but the three Basque provinces and Navarre still retained an autonomous fiscal structure (the *concierto económico*) and a greater degree of provincial autonomy than other parts of Spain. Carlist sympathies and ultra-Catholic loyalty remained strong.

The founder of Basque nationalist ideology, Sabino de Arana y Goiri, came from an upper-middle-class Carlist family of industrial entrepreneurs. Arana y Goiri made the Basque language—which he had to learn virtually from scratch—the cornerstone of his movement, but Basque was a primitive, preliterate tongue that was slowly dying out in the Basque country itself and could not provide the cultural platform that the *renaixença* gave Catalanism. The Basque Nationalist party (PNV), founded in 1894, was based upon the concept of an almost absolute regional and racial differentiation between Basques and other Spaniards. Basque nationalism tended toward nearly complete separation, even to the extent of wanting to conduct separate foreign relations. As something of a post-Carlist phenomenon, it was ultra-Catholic and originally advocated a virtual theocracy in government authority. In social background it was essentially lower middle class and never obtained anything comparable to the degree of upper class backing enjoyed by Catalanism. Basque nationalism has continued to be a minority movement within the Basque country.

Like Catalanism, it gained its first political success following the 1898 disaster, electing Arana y Goiri to the provincial assembly of Vizcaya in that year. Yet the PNV remained so weak that it entered no candidates for the Cortes until strongly encouraged by the Lliga in 1918, when it sent seven deputies to Madrid, but by 1923 its parliamentary representation had once more been reduced to one deputy.

The Crisis of 1917 and the Frustration of the Parliamentary System

During the years before World War I the established parties had shown that they were unable to provide vigorous new leadership. This was due to a complex combination of their own disunity, factionalism, and status striving, the opposition of the most important middle class forces in the most active and modern region of country, and not least of all the elimination of the two strongest leaders—Maura by organized ostracism and Canalejas by murder. The minority ministry of Eduardo Dato was unable to introduce any of the social legislation on which he had hoped to base an invigorated reformist Conservative party. Its main concern was to avoid pressures that might push Spain into the World War. When Dato reopened parliament at the end of 1915, he resigned rather than face a petition for economic and military reforms.

The chief Liberal leader, Romanones, then formed a ministry to conduct elections early in 1916. These revealed the extent of apathy and alienation, as well as the difficulties in civic mobilization, of much of the population. In 35 percent of the voting districts of Spain—located in Galicia and the south, west, and center—only one official candidate stood for office, and under the Article 29 electoral reform of the last Maura government was automatically selected without contest. In other districts where anarcho-syndicalists were exerting considerable influence—the antithetical regions of Barcelona province and the extreme south—there was widespread abstention. Somewhat less than half the electorate actually voted. Though the Liberals got a safe majority in parliament, they had received no national mandate.

During 1915 Spain had become the most important neutral country in Europe and hence a chief source of goods. Orders poured in to Spanish producers from the western allies, especially France. Industry expanded rapidly in northern Spain, and for the first time the value of industrial production exceeded 50 percent of the total value of goods and services in Catalonia. Great profits were made. To the capable new finance minister, Santiago Alba (leader of the subsequent Liberal Left fraction of the old Liberal party), this seemed an excellent opportunity to expand state income and begin a broad program of economic stimulation. He put through the Cortes bills reforming aspects of the tax system, establishing an agricultural credit program, and providing subsidies and credit facilities for new industries. However, the Cortes refused to approve his proposals for a surtax on surplus wartime business profits and for modest fiscal pressures on large landowners that would have encouraged moderate agrarian reform.

Meanwhile the industrial labor force swelled greatly. Prices shot upward, while wages fell farther and farther behind in the rate of increase. This brought the CNT and UGT together for the first time in their history, when a unity of action agreement was signed in December 1916 resulting in a twenty-four-hour general strike and threatening much more widespread stoppage in the future.

The middle classes were also restive. The first sector to revolt against the economic squeeze and the political deadlock were the peninsular garrison officers of the Spanish Army, whose meager purchasing power had been reduced to absurd depths by the inflation. During the winter and spring of 1917 infantry and cavalry officers set up a series of Military Juntas in most of the main peninsular garrisons, to protest low pay and favoritism in promotion. The Juntas were formed of junior and middle-rank officers in opposition to the generals, some of whom owed their positions to political influence. The Romanones government was meanwhile succeeded in April 1917 by a weaker ministry under the Democrat García Prieto. An attempt to dissolve the Juntas failed completely; the dissident officers imposed their privilege of sectarian organization and forced creation of a new government in June 1917 under the Conservative Dato. Though the Juntas spoke of reform and national regeneration, their concrete interests were higher pay and other professional perquisites. Nevertheless, their "barracks revolt" was greeted with great encouragement by most republicans, the Catalanists, and even some of the Socialists, who began to draw comparisons between the role that a rebel army might play in Spain and that of the dispirited and subverted Russian soldiery in the radicalization of the revolution that was taking place at the moment in Russia.

Since parliament remained closed and the representative system did not seem to be functioning, Cambó and the Catalan Lliga, together with some of the republicans, seized the opportunity to call a special "Parliamentary Assembly" of reformist deputies in Barcelona, center of the Junta movement. The plan was to use this assembly of a minority of Cortes members as the springboard for an alternate source of legitimacy. It was to call for elections to a new Cortes that would reform the Spanish constitution and limit the power of the crown and established groups. Yet neither Maura nor reformist Liberals from central Spain would have anything to do with this extra-constitutional assembly, which was immediately closed by police.

The initiative then passed to the revolutionary working class movements. The key role was played by the Socialists, but they were supported by Melquiades Alvarez's Reformist Republican party, which had rallied to the regime in 1913 when D. Alfonso XIII seemed to encourage an "opening to the left" but now despaired of further reforms within the system. Yet, though the Socialists had a working agreement with the CNT that vaguely proposed a joint revolutionary general strike, they could not gain the organized assistance of anarcho-syndicalists. The general strike—essentially Socialist in backing—began somewhat prematurely on August 10, 1917, after one railroad company refused to rehire a hundred or so UGT members following a local strike. The first revolutionary general strike in Spanish history was effective only in Barcelona, the Asturian mining region, and a few other centers, and then only partially. Martial law was enforced by the army, still basically loyal to the regime—at least when faced with a challenge from the revolutionary left—and the strike was ultimately a complete failure.

At the end of October, after further pressure from the Juntas, the Dato government was forced to resign. It was replaced by a "government of concentration" under García Prieto. In an effort to broaden representation, this ministry contained two Catalanist members, but it soon began to break down under the weight of internal dissension, strikes by government employees, and general hostility from the organized political factions. In a new effort to gain a workable majority, elections were held at the beginning of 1918. After decades of protest against the lack of full electoral freedom, García Prieto saw to it that the government, in large measure, kept hands off. The result of electoral democracy was complete fractionalization. Abstention was at least 35 percent. Dato's Conservatives, who raised the largest campaign fund, won ninety-eight seats. García Prieto's Democrats, the most popular Liberal group, won ninety-two. No other party or faction returned more than forty. The new Cortes was a political mosaic, as democracy produced a situation of immobility in some respects more frustrating than that of caciquismo. There was nothing uniquely Spanish about this situation. In Italy, where many of the same problems existed, the result of new democratic elections in 1919 was rather similar, though Italy was at that time a more advanced nation.

The only solution was formation in March 1918 of a "National Government" of interparty union led by Antonio Maura, still the most prestigious single figure. It contained all the leading Conservative and Liberal leaders, including the Lliga's Cambó, who as minister of development proved to be the most active member. During an eight-month tenure he prepared a new public works program, the beginnings of major railway reform, a new mining law, new irrigation and hydroelectric projects, and a modest plan of farm credit. Meanwhile the National Government disintegrated from internal dissension. The reformist Liberal Santiago Alba, whose earlier fiscal and development plans had been blocked in 1916, resigned because his colleagues would not support his proposals for educational reform. After yet another resignation, which coincided with the end of the World War, Maura decided that the time had come to present the resignation of the entire ministry.

At that point the crown appointed a strictly minority Liberal government under Romanones, charged with the goal of passing a workable Catalan autonomy statute so as to strengthen the Spanish system by reincorporating the most active middle class forces. At the close of 1918 Romanones appointed a special extraparliamentary commission to prepare a draft. Since nineteen of its thirty-three members had already expressed their public support for some form of Catalan autonomy, a favorable proposal seemed assured. Then the leftist parties—republicans, Socialists, and Reformists under Alvarez—intervened with left Catalanist leaders to urge them to reject any form of autonomy prepared by the constitutional monarchy, on the grounds that a proposal of this government would tend to strengthen the Spanish system rather than weaken it. The left Catalanists pressured the Lliga to join them in walking out of the Cortes in January 1919 to dramatize their rejection of any autonomy statute not prepared exclusively by Catalans. Thus autonomy under the constitutional monarchy, the original goal of the Catalanist movement, was in essence rejected by the Catalanists themselves. Soon afterward the postwar social conflict reached fever pitch, leading the government to close parliament and impose martial law in Barcelona.

What the country desperately needed was a restructuring of the two-party system that would establish a viable, cohesive liberal progressive party on the one hand and a functional, unified conservative party on the other, to achieve reform while maintaining stability. The crown gave the first chance to a minority Conservative ministry under Maura, and it held elections in June 1919 (the third in three years) to try to build a Conservative majority. Though the government did not observe the degree of noninterference followed by its predecessor in 1918, the results of the elections were much the same. After the Maura ministry was narrowly defeated on a parliamentary technicality, another minority government was formed under the independent Conservative reformist Joaquín Sánchez de Toca. It instituted needed social reforms but could survive for only a few months. Yet another transitory Conservative ministry, this time under Manuel Allendesalazar, lasted long enough to pass the first regular budget bill in several years, after which Dato formed his third government in May 1920. In elections at the end of the year, Dato's Conservatives won 185 seats, and with the help of either the Maurist or Ciervist Conservatives (23 seats each) were able to form a working majority.

The Social Crisis of 1919-1923

With much of the public apathetic or having lost confidence in political change, the last four years of the parliamentary system were dominated by two issues—the social struggle with the revolutionary movements, mainly the anarchists, and the disastrous military effort to subdue the native kabyles of the Moroccan Protectorate. As indicated above, the World War helped to produce a social crisis almost as great in Spain as in some of the belligerent countries. A large and rapid growth of the urban working class that pulled in many thousands of illiterate and semiliterate peasants, together with the greatly increased bargaining power of organized labor brought by wartime prosperity, swelled the CNT to 700,000 members by 1919. The multiple cleavages and tensions within Spanish life, the clash of religious and political ideologies, the atmosphere of publicized violence during the war years, and finally, the revolutionary upheavals of eastern and central Europe between 1917 and 1919 all contributed to rapid expansion of the influence of the revolutionary elements within the CNT. By contrast, after 1917 the majority of the much smaller Socialist movement adopted a moderate, reformist attitude.

The CNT's offensive began at Barcelona in the spring of 1919 after a layoff of workers at a power plant known colloquially as the *Canadiense*. The walkout mushroomed into a virtual city-wide general strike that achieved the biggest victory Spanish labor had ever seen. It won wage advances and recognition of the union shop in Barcelona, and helped prompt the government to legislation establishing an eight-hour working day. This merely whetted the ambition of CNT leaders, who attempted another general strike to win release of a dozen imprisoned comrades. That brought a crackdown against the CNT, followed by a Catalan employers' lockout. CNT syndicates

Table 26.   Strike Activity, 1910-1923

Year	Strikes	Strikers	Days Lost
1910	151	35,897	1,408,896
1911	118	22,154	364,178
1912	171	36,306	1,056,109
1913	201	84,316	2,258,159
1914	140	49,267	1,017,889
1915	91	30,591	382,885
1916	178	96,882	2,415,304
1917	176	71,440	1,784,538
1918	256	109,168	1,819,295
1919	403	178,496	4,001,278
1920	424	244,684	7,261,762
1921	233	83,691	2,802,299
1922	429	119,417	2,672,567
1923	411	120,568	3,027,026

Source: Spanish Ministry of Labor.

formed squads of gunmen to murder employers, foremen, policemen, and most of all, dissident workers. Employers' security agents and the police replied, and a vicious circle of violence spiraled upward.

The last Dato government, which came to power in May 1920 when the labor struggle in Barcelona and elsewhere was well advanced, tried to institute a major reform policy. A ministry of labor was created inside the Spanish government and new rent and insurance regulations were established. Most trade unionists under arrest were set free, and the CNT was permitted to resume normal operations. But just as electoral democracy did not bring agreement on reform, so economic adjustments and renewed syndical freedom did not bring labor peace. Employers, particularly in Catalonia, had taken a hard line; by the summer of 1920 the largest strike wave in Spanish history had extended into Andalusia, the UGT was trying to negotiate another joint-action agreement with the CNT, and a small, incendiary Spanish Communist party had been set up. In Barcelona violence escalated rapidly; an anti-anarchist "Free Syndicate" was supported by employers, and finally the local garrison commander, Martínez de Anido, ousted the regular civil governor and seized control himself to restore order by counter-terror. His conciliation policy having failed, Dato accepted the alternative of repression. In revenge, the prime minister was murdered by an anarchist firing from a motorcycle sidecar in March 1921.

By 1922 the CNT was in decline. Some of its syndicates lay in a state of complete disarray, many of the best leaders were arrested or dead, and there were sharp divisions between anarchist and syndicalist (revolutionary and reformist) wings of the movement. No longer supported by the impoverished syndicates, the squads of gunmen robbed banks and other facilities to finance their activities. They maintained a comparatively high level of politico-social disorder in the largest cities, but were in no position to attempt a revolutionary assault on the regime.

The Moroccan Dilemma

In 1921 the Protectorate in northern Morocco blew up in the face of the Spanish government. The mountainous 5 percent of Morocco that formed the Spanish sphere was a largely barren region, difficult to traverse, lacking roads or communications, and at first impossible to govern. The warriors of the kabyles in the Riff and Djebala were superb irregular fighters; they were probably the most difficult foes faced by western forces anywhere in the Afro-Asian world during the 1920s. As long as the World War lasted, the Spanish government had confined itself to occupying a few key centers and bribing native leaders to respect the nominal authority of the Spanish-appointed caliph. A serious program of conquest was begun in 1919. At first the fighting was primarily in the western district of Djebala, with encouraging successes and few casualties. In 1921 a court favorite and veteran officer, General Fernández Silvestre, commander of the eastern Riff district, attempted to push his forces through the virtually uncharted Riff to the center of the Protectorate. His 18,000 troops were poorly trained and equipped and badly led; they were stationed for the most part out of contact with each other in a steadily lengthening chain of makeshift, sandbagged encampments.

At that point the most remarkable figure in the modern history of northern Morocco, Abd el-Krim, emerged. The son of a local tribal leader, Abd el-Krim rallied the disparate kabyles into a semi-unified force that destroyed the Spanish advance unit at Anual in the central Riff and rolled back the entire line of positions all the way to the coastal center of Melilla. Within a week or so more than 9,000 Spanish troops were killed or lost as prisoners. Anual became a disaster second only to 1898.

An enormous outcry went up at home. After all the pretensions, demands, and interference of the army in recent years, it seemed that the Spanish military scarcely existed as a fighting force. The temporary Conservative ministry that had been organized following Dato's assassination five months earlier resigned and was replaced by a new "government of concentration" under Maura, who in his old age was serving as "fireman of the monarchy." A broad investigation was undertaken by a special army board, the Picasso commission, and the nuclei of the Junta movement in the peninsular garrisons were officially, though not in fact, dissolved. The Maura government planned to follow a policy of vengeance (*desquite*) for the humiliation of Anual, but decided against any program of conquering and occupying the entire Protectorate. Instead, it proposed a limited offensive to secure the coastline and establish a kind of military hegemony over most of the Spanish zone. Before this could be done, however, the government broke up in March 1922 over social and juridical policy, the Liberal ministers resigning in protest over the continuation of martial law in Catalonia.

The political situation was thus seriously complicated, and again the Spanish government was caught between two fires. Without an effective policy in Morocco the future of the Protectorate, to say nothing of the Spanish Army's self-conceived national mission and its very loyalty to the government, was in doubt. Such a policy could not be prosecuted against a background of domestic turmoil. Yet though social peace under constitutional guarantees had been difficult to achieve, the Liberals insisted that all special means of repression be dropped. Spanish government needed reorganized, functioning political groups to resume the roles of Liberal and Conservative parties. Since 1919 there had slowly been taking form a loosely allied neo-Liberal bloc composed of Alba's Liberal Left, García Prieto's Liberal Democrats, the Romanones Liberals, and the Reformists of Melquiades Alvarez. Should it assume power, there was a real danger that in the prevailing disorder and national dissatisfaction a Liberal government would push the balance too far left to retain stability. Conservative opinion was restive over the social issue and opinion in important branches of the army highly agitated over national "betrayal" by the politicians. The crown felt that a reorganized, reformist Conservative bloc stood a better chance of preserving unity and stability while trying to resolve the Moroccan mess. Such a bloc could also face social and economic reforms along the lines of the earlier programs of Dato and Cambó. Don Alfonso offered power to Maura and Cambó to govern temporarily without parliament and hold new elections; Cambó was willing to cooperate, but Maura said that such an opportunity came too late for him. He was sixty-seven and his hour had passed.

Maura's successor, José Sánchez Guerra, the new leader of the main group of Conservatives, was courageous and forthright but a political mediocrity. His ministry, which lasted from March to December 1922, was the seventh Conservative government in less than four years and lacked a clear parliamentary majority. In July, when the Picasso commission returned its report on the responsibilities for Anual, Sánchez Guerra made the grievous error of throwing the whole issue into the Cortes for further parliamentary investigation, turning the issue into a political football. The ensuing discord and vituperation soon brought his government down, and no one was more to blame than himself. The only alternative remaining was to call to power a Liberal coalition ministry under García Prieto, at the close of 1922.

This was a government of notables from all Liberal factions. It proposed a general program of reform involving total equality of religious practice; reform of the Senate and reduction of its privileges; reform of electoral procedures, establishing proportionate representation; obligatory Cortes sessions for four months each year; new public works; expansion of credit; an irrigation program; labor reforms; and the beginning of a land reform. The coalition, however, was not a unified party, and the government was not united internally. Its dominant figure was the new foreign minister, Alba, who had to face the nation's number-one issue, the Moroccan problem. The nominal prime minister, García Prieto, was a weaker figure than several of his key ministers; his government underwent a series of three internal crises and reorganizations within less than nine months.

The García Prieto ministry followed the policy of its predecessor, the Sánchez Guerra government, in restoring complete freedom to syndical groups and their leaders. Police activity in Barcelona and elsewhere had been greatly reduced and brought under tighter control. Yet the ending of repression did not discourage violence; it gave the anarchists full opportunity. The rate of political violence shot upward drastically in 1923, while the Moroccan stalemate, which occupied the main attention of government, persisted.

In this situation, new elections were held in April 1923 in the face of a deepening apathy of the electorate. Disillusionment with politics was now extremely widespread. Among much of the population that genuinely desired change there was either a feeling that the parliamentary system was hopelessly divided and deadlocked or else a feeling of bitter resentment. In nearly three-eighths of the electoral districts the balloting was uncontested; altogether, less than 42 percent of the electorate voted. The Liberal coalition won a workable majority (223 seats) but there was some doubt as to whether it had really received clear-cut national endorsement.

Taking into account the increase in the number of districts in which a single candidate was not challenged but elected by Article 29, the percentage of real participation in elections had steadily declined

Table 27.   Participation in Spanish Elections, 1910-1923

1910	52.9%	1919	51.7%
1914	53.9	1920	50.5
1916	44	1923	42.1
1918	60.1		

Source: Adapted from *Anuario Estadístico de España, 1922-1923*, in Sevilla Andrés, p. 405.

during the past five years (see table 27). Average abstention in elections for municipal councils was running at more than 50 percent, and for elections to the provincial chambers it was higher than 70 percent. On the other hand, official participation figures for districts in which elections were actually contested showed little decline, averaging about 65 percent for the past decade (see table 28).

The economic situation by and large remained comparatively good. Real wages for Spanish workers had increased 29 percent between 1914 and 1920, and though no longer increasing at that rate, were by no means declining. The García Prieto government prepared a series of social and economic reform measures during the spring and summer of 1923, yet few were actually passed into law.

The relative paralysis of government was a result of the Moroccan problem. Alba appointed a civilian high commissioner to administer the Protectorate and hoped to settle the conflict by negotiation. He also tried to obtain support from France in resolving the revolt, but the French government refused to cooperate with the Spanish, whom they deemed inept and lacking in prestige. The Liberal ministry rejected any attempt at outright conquest. Alba was willing to grant internal autonomy to Abd el-Krim and other Moroccan leaders, and planned to reduce the zone of military operations so as to concentrate Spanish resources. This brought continued frustration, since Abd el-Krim now insisted on complete victory and independence. To army leaders, the Liberal policy seemed to be a strictly "no win" policy; on

Table 28.   Electoral Participation in Districts Where
Seats Were Contested, 1907-1923

1907	67.1%	1918	66.6%
1910	73.7	1919	64.3
1914	68.7	1920	60
1916	68.1	1923	65

Source: Juan J. Linz, "The Party System of Spain: Past and Future," in S. Lipset and S. Rokkan, *Party Systems and Voter Alignments* (New York, 1967), p. 213.

that basis the government could neither resolve the conflict nor extricate Spain from Morocco.

At the same time the government continued to use the disaster of 1921 as a political issue. A special extraparliamentary commission was scheduled to report on the question of "responsibilities," both military and political, in September 1923. Urban terrorism meanwhile increased. The small new Spanish Communist party vied with the anarcho-syndicalists, staging a petty insurrection in Bilbao during August and encouraging a minor mutiny among troop replacements bound for Morocco. The concurrence of these events heightened the sense of political exasperation.

The Primo de Rivera Pronunciamiento (1923)

During 1922 and 1923 the apprehension of the most active leaders of the Spanish army mounted. They feared the army was about to be made a political scapegoat, and that all recent sacrifices would be wasted and national honor besmirched by a humiliating "abandonment" of Morocco. Army officers were bitter against the politicians for failing to provide financial and political support needed for victory. At the same time the commanders were fully aware that much of the public had lost confidence in the parliamentary system. The politically alienated in 1923 constituted over half the country—radicalized workers, landless peasants, disillusioned middle-class people, poor peasant renters and sharecroppers in the north, and much of the cultural elite in the cities. For a year or more there had been talk of some sort of temporary dictatorship to straighten out affairs, yet no group had the power or will to take charge. Only two elements were prepared to break into the system, but the revolutionaries, despite their widespread use of violence, were politically impotent, since all other elements of society, including the armed forces and the most influential institutions, would rally against them. The army was in a stronger position.

Throughout the summer of 1923 a group of generals in Madrid plotted the establishment of a temporary military dictatorship to provide forthright leadership and solve the Moroccan problem. When informed of their activities, the king apparently did not discourage them. Their major problem was lack of a leader to serve as temporary dictator, since none of the plotters had attained the reputation required. Such a figure finally presented himself at the beginning of September 1923 in the person of General Miguel Primo de Rivera, captain general of Catalonia. Primo was a bluff, hearty, talkative commander known for his outspokenness and maverick role in politics. He had twice spoken publicly against too impetuous a course in Morocco, at some risk to his career. In Barcelona he had shown sympathy for the Catalans and had become a popular figure among the middle classes as a symbol of both order and reform, however vaguely conceived. Primo had no clearcut political program, but he held a crucial command, the rank of lieutenant general, and showed himself ready for resolute action.

The Primo de Rivera revolt that began in Barcelona on the weekend of September 12-13 was a typical pronunciamiento in the nineteenth-century tradition, the last such exercise in Spanish history. Primo simply "pronounced" publicly his intention to take over the government. The cabinet demonstrated its customary paralysis, demanding Primo's resignation but failing to take more effective action. Only two of the nine captaincies-general of the Spanish home army stood resolutely behind Primo, but only one supported the government; the rest waited to see what would happen. The king refused to exercise any personal initiative—since he was always being criticized for that—and the government resigned. There was then little alternative to receiving Primo de Rivera in Madrid as head of government, with temporary powers to dissolve parliament and rule by decree. The new military government was received with frank enthusiasm by much of the public; even certain liberal intellectuals announced their satisfaction.

The Primo de Rivera Regime

Establishment of the Primo de Rivera dictatorship was to a large extent the consummation of the antiparliamentary trend that had begun with certain of the patriotic regenerationists and Costa's call for an "iron surgeon," stimulated by the resurgence of the army as a political force since 1917. Primo de Rivera was a garrulous, warm-hearted, patriotic, instinctive, and anti-intellectual man of great ambition for himself and his country. He was no fascist; in his first statements he invoked examples of Prim and Costa rather than Mussolini. The new regime was frank; it was known as and referred to publicly as "the Dictatorship" for the next six and one-half years. Yet D. Miguel at first denied that he was a dictator, insisting that he was merely a reformer governing with decree powers.

The dictatorship had no distinct ideology or political theory. Its original notion was that it had received temporary decree powers from the crown to resolve severe national problems, after which the normal political process would be resumed. During its first period (1923-1925), the new government took the form of a straightforward military directory, composed of eight brigadiers and one admiral. It was greeted with loud applause by much if not all the public, including reformist intellectuals such as Ortega y Gasset who believed that only a drastic solution could cut through the problem of political and constitutional change.

Under terms of martial law, peace and security were soon restored to the cities and industrial areas. Once the hand of authority was imposed and the opportunity for political maneuver and legal manipulation was at an end, disorder vanished. The dictatorship had, however, few ideas about the long-desired constitutional reform. For local government, it appointed a series of military delegates to oversee administrative affairs, even though the qualifications of such officials were often dubious. In 1924 a new local government measure was prepared, offering considerable municipal autonomy with locally elected councils. But the regime never put the new system into operation.

The overriding issue that had brought in the dictatorship was the Moroccan morass. Primo had earlier suggested abandoning north Morocco or trading it to Britain in return for Gibraltar. He had never been an ideal chief for the military movement and had been accepted by army conspirators only for want of alternative leaders among the senior command. During 1923-1924 he tried to arrange a compromise with Abd el-Krim, leaving the Berber chief in real control of most of the Protectorate as long as nominal relations were maintained with the Spanish authorities. But by 1924 Krim believed that he could establish absolute independence for the "Emirate of the Riff" and had extended his offensive to the western half of the Protectorate as well. Finding the Spanish positions there difficult to defend, the Spanish dictator took the resolute decision to shorten his lines, withdrawing at heavy cost all Spanish forces in the west to the "Primo de Rivera" line just outside the capital of Tetuán in the northwestern peninsula of the Protectorate. The wisdom of this decision is not entirely clear, since it cost more casualties than the disaster of 1921. Nevertheless, braving a potential revolt among the africanista veterans of the Spanish forces, Primo carried through this consolidation and began a major reorganization of the combat forces. The great paradox of Primo's Moroccan policy during the first year of his dictatorship was that it was essentially the same program pursued by Alba under the constitutional government. Yet Alba had been driven into exile and was being tried in absentia on trumped up charges.

Abd el-Krim's downfall was brought about by expansion of the Moroccan struggle into a two-front war. The French authorities became increasingly apprehensive about the revolt in the Spanish zone and began to fortify their northern frontier area. Abd el-Krim's rebels were partially dependent on supplies from the northern part of the French zone. The Riff leader decided to try to safeguard his rear and expand his movement by launching a major assault against the French border in 1924. The Berber warriors proved their mettle as effectively against the French as against the Spanish. They bowled over the northern French outposts and at one point were only thirty miles from Fez. Large-scale reinforcements had to be hurried in from France, and for the first time the French government was willing to adopt a program of joint action with the Spanish authorities.

A broad pincers movement was planned for 1925. In September, a reorganized Spanish amphibious force landed in the Bay of Alhucemas at the coastal base of the Riff, catching the heartland of the rebel movement from the rear. Facing a French offensive from the south and with his sources of supply almost completely cut off, Abd el-Krim was increasingly hard pressed and began to lose followers. In 1926 he surrendered to the French, and by the end of that year most of the Spanish zone had been pacified, a work finally completed by smaller campaigns in 1927–1928. The victory could be credited to a change in fortune, but also to persistence and to improved combat capabilities of a partially reorganized military. For the first time since the 1870s, the Spanish Army had a combat-proven military elite, the africanista veterans of Morocco, who ten years later played a crucial role in the Civil War.

The dictatorship enjoyed the advantages of the economic prosperity of the 1920s, which encouraged domestic stability and the political acquiescence of most of the population. By 1925, with victory in sight in Morocco, Primo de Rivera was at the height of his achievement, but was no nearer than ever to achieving constitutional reform, for want of explicit and firm ideas. The dictatorship still lived in the twilight of the age of Spanish liberalism and could not consciously affirm or develop a precise theory of authoritarianism or corporatism. The temporary solution was to form a more conventional government in December 1925, with over half the posts held by civilian appointees.

The regime did not abolish the status quo in church-state relations, but it leaned considerably more toward the church. The small Protestant groups suffered greater harassment, and Catholic activities received stronger official backing. Thus the regime acquired a tinge of clericalism.

The dictatorship never developed an official state party, but it did generate an official political front. The Unión Patriótica, first formed by middle class supporters of the regime in Valladolid during 1924, was later extended into a national organization in 1926. It had no specific doctrine and was little more than the name implied. When

Table 29.   Index of Mining and Industrial Production, 1922-1932
(1906-1930 = 100)

1922	84.7	1925	121.1	1928	135.6	1931	146.1
1923	102.5	1926	133.7	1929	141.9	1932	132.8
1924	117.9	1927	132.8	1930	144.0		

Source: Juan Velarde Fuertes, *La política económica de la Dictadura* (Madrid, 1969),
p. 108.

the regime established an appointive consultative assembly in Madrid in 1927, the UP supplied most of the members.

The principal notion behind Primo's second government (1926–1930) was a sort of technocratic regenerationism. A separate budget was prepared to allow for government borrowing and deficit spending on public works. Though in its later years the dictatorship added considerably to the national debt, it was under Primo de Rivera that the nucleus of the modern Spanish highway system was built. A central state hydropower policy was drawn up for the first time, the biggest achievement of which was the Ebro hydropower confederation (part of which was dismantled by the Republic). There was a considerable increase in rural electrification, and new irrigation projects were undertaken. For the first time in decades significant progress was made in reorganizing and reequipping the railroads, and steps were taken toward a national coordination of the rail network. Municipal governments were assisted in raising money for urban development, so that nearly all the larger Spanish cities increased their facilities and improved services. State banks were established to promote housing and industrial expansion. A state oil monopoly (CAMPSA) was established and operated on profitable terms. A modest beginning was made in land reform, particularly with a 1926 law that set feasible terms by which Galician peasants could redeem their foros. The dictatorship even undertook a reforestation campaign.

Assisted to some extent by state encouragement and protection and even more by the generally favorable economic climate of the period, nearly all industries increased their production, as indicated in table 29. The regime never managed to create a genuinely corporative system, but it did eventually set up a series of corporate committees to regulate and supervise major aspects of the economy. The labor minister, Eduardo Aunós, began in 1926 to establish a nationwide network of *comités paritarios* (arbitration committees) to negotiate working agreements and conditions, thus finally fulfilling a project long encouraged by the parliamentary system. The CNT had been suppressed, but the Socialist UGT was favored by the regime for its

Table 30.   Index of Real Wages, 1914-1930

1914	100.0	1925	106.0
1920	129.0	1930	103.8

Source: Velarde Fuertes, p.157. Figures in E. Aunós, *La política social de la Dicta-dura* (Madrid, 1944), largely coincide. Aunós notes that there were significant wage increases for women in general and also for the largely Socialist-represented workers of Vizcaya, and that the worst decline was suffered by farm laborers in Jaén province.

moderation and discipline and participated in elections for labor representatives to the committees, becoming the principal single spokesman for Spanish labor in the process. The result was not however any major new improvements for labor, whose principal gains had been achieved during the "time of troubles" from 1919 to 1923. Under Primo de Rivera, the Spanish economy enjoyed relatively full employment, prices declined just a trifle, working conditions improved slightly, and the work week was reduced a bit, but wages also declined somewhat, as indicated in table 30.

One of the most progressive aspects of the regime's economic policy was its tax program. The tax reform carried out in 1928 by the capable José Calvo Sotelo, finance minister of Primo's second government, improved tax collection and administration, considerably increased overall levies—a reform long overdue—and equally or more important, established the most progressive rates on personal income ever set before or after in Spanish history. The increase in the index of tax pressure is indicated in table 31.

Fall of the Dictatorship

After formation of the 1926 government, the Dictator gave up the notion of returning to the old legality and spoke vaguely of preparing a new constitution. In 1929 a handpicked assembly prepared the draft of a corporate constitution under which part of parliament would be

Table 31.   Index of Tax Pressure, 1922-1930
(1913 = 100)

1922	83.0	1925	94.6	1928	129.5
1923	86.6	1926	95.5	1929	119.6
1924	104.5	1927	108.0	1930	125.0

Source: Velarde Fuertes, p. 153. Cf. J. Buxó y Abaigar, *Ensayo crítico sobre el impuesto de la renta* (Valencia, 1936).

chosen by indirect, organic elections. Yet Primo de Rivera could not find his way toward the inauguration of a new system. His health was declining (by that point he suffered severely from diabetes), and he was weary and uncertain. His own collaborators were sharply divided and there was mounting opposition among politically conscious elements in Spain as a whole.

By 1929 the dictatorship had alienated every important interest group in Spain, save perhaps the neutral middle classes. The upper classes and business interests were not supporters of the regime because of its reformist and interventionist proposals. Aunós, the Primo labor minister, was denounced as a "white Lenin." The Socialists accepted Primo on sufferance only. Upper class Catalanists of the Lliga had at first acclaimed the Dictatorship because it would repress the left, only to see it repress regionalism as well and dissolve the Mancomunitat. The old political classes were all enemies for obvious reasons. Even the church had begun to draw off, after it became clear that the dictatorship was failing to institutionalize itself. Perhaps the strongest opposition of all came from Spanish intellectuals, subject to partial censorship and moderate suppression and infuriated by the regime's clericalism and lack of ideological order. The university students, many of them organized in a leftist student syndicate (FUE), were among the strongest opponents. By 1928 they were beginning mass strikes and organizations, originally in opposition to equal rights to Catholic schools. Finally, much of the army had turned against the regime. The military had never supported Primo fully. There had always been resentment against compromising the army as an instrument of dictatorial political administration. The artillery corps came out in revolt in 1926 after Primo intervened to break its tradition of iron seniority promotion, and the corps was reorganized. There were several attempted revolts between 1926 and 1929, organized by disgruntled officers, a few opposition politicians, and clandestine elements of the CNT. Moreover, economic pressures increased in 1929 with the depreciation of the national currency that was brought on by persistently adverse payment balances and a bad harvest in Spain. The only direct supporters of the regime were to be found in the heterogeneous ranks of the weakly organized UP.

Don Alfonso had become restive after six years of *primorriverismo.* The Dictator had virtually absorbed the prerogatives of the crown, for there was no parliament and no parliamentary government. If Primo should ever succeed in institutionalizing a more authoritarian system, the royal prerogative might be made superfluous; should Primo continue to grow weaker, he would drag the monarchy down in his eventual failure. Some of Primo's closest collaborators urged local elections or a constitutional plebiscite, but the Dictator could not see his way to a clear course of action. A more extensive conspiracy was begun against him in sectors of the army, and in a public gesture he canvassed the attitudes of military leaders at the end of January 1930. When it became clear that army chiefs were reluctant to continue their support, the crown found it fairly easy to "dismiss" the Dictator, whose weak health, dissillusionment, and lack of backing left little alternative.

The Primo de Rivera dictatorship never escaped the shadow of historic Spanish liberalism. It was probably the most gentle and liberal "dictatorship" of twentieth-century Europe, unstained by a single political execution. The Dictator himself lacked a ruthless will to power; his instincts were paternalistic and semiliberal. At first he looked upon his government as a supplement, rather than a drastic alternative, to the liberal system, and many of the ambitions and practices of his fascist contemporaries in other lands were simply alien to his nature. His intentions were of the highest, his regime was able to resolve a national nightmare—Morocco—and it began major projects of economic development and reform. For six and a half years it brought peace, order, and prosperity to Spain. Yet it destroyed the historic system of representative government, and once the national polity left that road, it never found it again.

Collapse of the Monarchy

Don Alfonso hoped to save the monarchy by getting rid of the dictatorship, but the tiger of authoritarian rule, once mounted, was not easily dismounted. Nearly all the old pre-1923 politicians had been alienated by the dictatorship, and the crown lacked able counselors or collaborators. The two remaining leaders of stature, Cambó and Alba, were both indisposed—Cambó by throat cancer, Alba by his general repugnance for politics under Alfonso XIII, after the experience of 1923.

Through a fatal process of elimination the head of the new government of 1930 was an elderly general, Dámaso Berenguer, former high commissioner of Spanish Morocco in 1921, a sometime opponent of Primo de Rivera, a gentleman and a bit of a liberal, and most important of all, one of the very few figures on whom the crown could rely. But Berenguer was not a political leader; he lacked talent, experience, and goals, and his health was almost as poor as that of Primo. What remained of the old party system had disappeared, and Spain was politically more invertebrate than at any time since the 1870s. There was no consensus even among conservative, monarchist elements about what course should be followed, and so Berenguer let precious months slip by in uncertainty. His government eased up on censorship and police activity, winning for itself the nickname of the *dictablanda*. The CNT began to reorganize, strikes increased, and republican conspirators moved freely. Finally, in January 1931, a year after the resignation of Primo de Rivera, the government announced that it would hold regular parliamentary elections. Melquiades Alvarez's "constitutional" group declared their boycott, demanding a constituent assembly, and most other political spokesmen seconded them, leaving the Berenguer government little alternative but to resign. Alba, in Paris, had persistently refused requests from the crown to form a representative Liberal bloc that might take power. The best successor for the Berenguer ministry that D. Alfonso could find was a hodge-podge cabinet of monarchist notables, led by an obscure admiral, Aznar. The latter was a complete political incompetent whose only qualification was his having held the post of minister of navy in the last constitutional government of 1923. The Aznar government was one in name only; it had neither leadership, unity, nor policy, but was a feeble holding action that almost no one respected.

During 1930 republicanism began to gain its greatest vogue in Spanish history. The new republicanism was extremely vague, and its backing was as much negative as positive; it stood for opposition to the monarchist regime more clearly than for any specific program of its own. The middle classes began to rally to it, and even some of the upper classes resigned themselves to republicanism as the lesser evil, the best alternative to a monarchist system that had recently attempted unpleasant reforms and if perpetuated might provoke radical lower class reaction. What was not appreciated, however, was that at the core of the new republicanism was a spirit of sectarian radicalism, generated among part of the intelligentsia and lower middle classes during the late 1920s in opposition to the dictatorship. This new republican radicalism had developed in a political vacuum, in a mood of emotion and hatred; it was doctrinaire and sectarian, rejecting the compromise tactics of historic parliamentarianism, with which it had little or no acquaintance.

Leaders of the principal republican cliques got together in August 1930 to sign the so-called Pact of San Sebastián, which pledged them to establish a constitutional republic and won the support of the left Catalanists by promising to prepare a statute of regional autonomy. Yet the majority of the people were by no means republican, and so the customary relations were cultivated with dissident elements among the military. The minor military revolts that resulted in December 1930 were a fiasco, but two officers who led them were executed by military courts, providing the republican movement with martyrs.

The chairman of the republican committee, Niceto Alcalá Zamora, was a former monarchist politician whose moderation and Catholicism reassured some of the more conservative elements that might otherwise have been frightened by the growth of republicanism. A group of leading intellectuals, including Ortega y Gasset, rallied to republicanism in February 1931, giving it increased prestige, and the trial of arrested republican leaders in March—dominated by republican propaganda and resulting in only token sentences—was a clear moral victory for the conspirators. When the feeble Aznar government finally initiated the return to representative processes by holding direct municipal elections throughout Spain on April 12, 1931, a majority of voters supported monarchist candidates, but the larger, more liberal cities voted overwhelmingly for republican municipal councillors. For forty years there had tended to be tacit agreement that opinion in these cities was the political bellwether of Spain. Even most of the monarchists gave up hope, and the commanders of the army made it clear that they had little stomach to take up arms against their fellow countrymen in defense of the monarchy. On April 14 D. Alfonso concluded that any attempt to retain power would either be futile, or at best, hopelessly divide Spaniards in a difficult struggle. He left the country rather than risk civil war.

The monarchy had lost moral support through the dictadura and the sterile, hesitant perpetuation of the dictablanda. It then failed in and almost failed to contest the propaganda battle of 1930–1931. The monarchy's only representative support had stemmed from the pre-1923 parties, especially the Conservatives. The old Conservative and Liberal factions had depended on the electoral system to mobilize their constituency, and so had atrophied under the dictatorships. Had elections been held promptly in 1930, it would have been much easier to restore some degree of continuity and stability. The remnants of the former Conservatives had themselves lost confidence in D. Alfonso, while the former Liberals were disillusioned, embittered, and not a little confused. Insofar as there was an underlying political consensus in Spanish society, it was a liberal one, even among the moderately conservative. The experience of the 1920s had discredited authoritarianism, and when the sudden republican movement gave token of moderation and reliability, the will to resist a neoliberal transition evaporated. Even so, the quick crystallization of a vague liberal republican sentiment in the municipal elections surprised the republican leaders, who were still more surprised by the precipitous collapse of the monarchy that followed within less than forty-eight hours. Though almost no one opposed it, almost no one was really prepared for the advent of the new regime on April 14, 1931.

Conclusion: The Breakdown of Constitutional Monarchy in Spain

The constitutional monarchist system of 1875-1923 was the most durable representative, parliamentary government in Spanish history. When it was originally overturned in 1923, comparatively few realized how difficult it would be to restore stable, representative institutions. The numerous deficiencies of the restored monarchy have been widely publicized, but with the passage of time its achievements are slowly being better appreciated. It provided a rather precocious system of parliamentary representation, increasingly impartial constitutional justice, general religious and cultural freedom, not unimportant social reforms, and a period of improved living standards, as well as a certain degree of local and regional autonomy.

The breakdown of the system is commonly blamed either on outrageous social and economic conditions or on the nefarious conduct of the king. In fact, social and economic conditions improved *pari passu* with the breakdown of the system, and closer examination reveals that the discretionary powers of the crown were more frequently exercised in a constructive than a destructive manner. The breakdown of the system was above all else, as Raymond Carr has observed, a political failure. In that process a number of key points and factors merit emphasis:

1. The provocations of Catalan nationalism, resulting in the military intervention of 1905 and the passing of the Law of Jurisdictions. On that occasion the crown capitulated to the right, and in so doing permitted an unbalancing of the Spanish constitutional system, with destructive consequences.

2. Formation of the Left Bloc in 1908-1909, the resulting Maura NO! campaign, and the antiparliamentary dismissal of the Maura government. On this occasion the crown capitulated to the left in almost exactly the same way that it had capitulated to the right four years earlier. Don Alfonso's action was fully constitutional but antiparliamentary. It terminated the most productive reform government that twentieth-century Spain had seen; after 1909 only one more really effective parliamentary government was ever constituted under the regime.

3. Failure to achieve significant political and administrative decentralization, in part because of the premature termination of the Maura long government.

4. The traumatic consequences of the murder of Canalejas.

5. Breakup of the Liberal party over the issue of the most limited sort of autonomy for Catalonia in 1913.

6. The essentially antipolitical position of Antonio Maura in the years following the anti-Maura veto, demanding in effect a kind of unconstitutional vengeance against his persecutors, and the resulting split of the Conservative party. In a sense, it might be said that Maura was willing to save Spain but not to give it political leadership.

7. The fractionalization of parliament as a result of the foregoing and other divisions and rivalries. There was no effective parliamentary majority from 1914 on.

8. The failure of fiscal reform, as, for example, underlined by the opposition to the Alba program in 1916.

9. The persistance of military pressures and interference in politics after 1917.

10. Inability of the more liberal forces to achieve effective alliance for constitutional reform, as demonstrated particularly by the failure of 1917.

11. The suicidal *totorresisme* (all-or-nothingism) of the left Catalanists, as demonstrated in 1908 and 1918-1919.

12. The rise of anarchist terrorism after 1917.

13. The intransigence of business interests in labor disputes, especially in Catalonia.

14. The stubbornness of the Conservative factions in resisting a compromise reunification after the murder of Dato in 1921.

15. The Moroccan problem, which virtually paralyzed political life after 1921.

16. The failure of the fifth (and final) Maura government of 1921-1922, brought down by the Liberals over the issue of civil guarantees in Barcelona, and the subsequent frustration of any forceful effort to resolve the Moroccan problem.

17. The tardiness and relative ineffectuality of the Liberal realignment, first proposed in 1918, then finally given its major opportunity in 1922-1923.

18. The final, neosubversive wave of anarchist and Communist violence during the spring and summer of 1923.

19. The political ineffectuality of Primo de Rivera, who could not resolve the dilemma that he had created.

20. The total absence of leadership in 1930-1931, heightened by the tragic illness of Cambó and the refusal of Alba to assume any responsibility.

The frustrations of parliamentary government were reflected in the shortening of the average life of Spanish cabinets, which had been twenty-two months between 1875 and 1902, fell to ten months between 1902 and 1917, and then only six months between 1917 and 1923. It should be kept in mind that the crisis of Spanish parliamentary government occurred not because the system was growing more corrupt and unrepresentative, but on the contrary, as it became less corrupt and more respresentative.

25

The Second Spanish Republic

The Republican committee that took over the government of Spain on April 14, 1931, was a largely self-appointed group of leaders of several small parties that had been formed within the past two or three years. The prime minister of the new regime, Alcalá Zamora, was a former monarchist politician, but he had no organized party support. There were four principal groups of Republicans: the Republican Action party, the Radical Socialists, the left Catalanists (Esquerra) and left Galicianists (ORGA), and the Radical Republicans. Only the latter, led by Alejandro Lerroux, had an "historic" party with broader national roots. Yet even they were largely reorganized on a new basis in 1931, and despite their name, soon proved themselves to be the only genuinely moderate group among the major Republican organizations. The discontinuity between the personnel and party structure of the new regime, when compared with that of the pre-1923 system, was extreme. Unlike those of France, Germany, and Italy after 1945, representative institutions in Spain were rebuilt largely with new and inexperienced elements. Nevertheless, it is quite clear that in the first months the new regime had either the support or at least the benevolent acquiescence of the great majority of the politically conscious. Hence despite the inexperience and lack of political roots of most of the new leaders and groups, they had an

630

excellent opportunity to lay the basis for a widely popular and progressive new regime.

That this did not happen was in large measure due to the doctrinaire policies and political incompetence of the dominant members of the governing coalition—the Republican left* and the Socialists. Their aim was not merely reform or establishment of a new democratic consensus, but rather paying off old scores and building a sectarian leftist regime. The coalition had four goals: a) reform and reduction of the army; b) separation of church and state and sharp restriction of Catholic rights as well as privileges; c) reform of the unitary structure of the Spanish state to permit Catalan regional autonomy; and d) broad social and economic reforms, though the latter remained vague in the planning of all groups save the Socialists. At first the only one of these goals inherently incompatible with the building of a strong consensual democratic regime was the doctrinaire anti-Catholic bent of the left coalition. The tenor of the new government was revealed within less than a month, on May 11, 1931, when mobs led by anarchists (and some Radical Socialists) sacked monarchist headquarters in Madrid and then proceeded to set fire or otherwise wreck more than a dozen churches in the capital. Similar arson and vandalism occurred in a score of other cities in southern and eastern Spain, in most cases with the acquiescence and in several cases with the assistance of the official Republican authorities. The *quema de conventos* (burning of convents) set the tone for relations between the Republican left and Spanish Catholicism. The climax came with the passage of the Republican constitution in the autumn of 1931. The new charter separated church and state, prohibited public religious processions, and outlawed much of the work of Catholic orders, with the intention of destroying Catholic education in Spain.

Elections for a constituent Cortes were held in June 1931 and were swept by the left and liberal groups. The two largest parties were the Socialists and the Radicals, followed by the Radical Socialists. Conservative elements had still not recovered from the collapse of the monarchy and were not well organized to contest the elections.

The reform of the army was carried on by the new defense minister, Manual Azaña, who emerged as the leader of the Republican left. Azaña was by profession a bureaucrat in the judicial registry office and a writer of some note who had produced an eclectic corpus of work, including imaginative literature, translations, and political and

* The Republican Action party was later reconstituted under the label Republican Left, but used generically, the term refers to the sectarian, ultrarepublican groups— Republican Action, the Radical Socialists, and the left regionalists.

social criticism. He was a doctrinaire anticlerical radical of outstanding rhetorical skill and literary style, splenetic in manner, forceful and direct in his political leadership. He was determined to break the autonomy of the Spanish army, and set about accomplishing this by a series of army reforms stretching over a year. The officer corps was cut 50 percent by allowing all who desired to retire at full pay. The size of the army was reduced, some sections reorganized, and several kinds of privileges and special promotions abolished. Moreover, Azaña, whose public manner was frequently biting and sarcastic, rarely wasted an opportunity to impress upon army officers that the military were completely at the disposal of the government and would never again be in a position to protect their institutional prerogatives or exercise political initiative. Azaña's reforms amounted to something less than a total restructuring of the army, but they shook up the Spanish military, and the arbitrary, insulting manner of the defense minister aroused the permanent hostility of many officers. The army reforms, together with Azaña's vigorous prosecution of anticlerical legislation, raised him to the premiership in October 1931. When the writing of the Republican constitution was completed in December, Azaña's predecessor as prime minister, the Catholic moderate Alcalá Zamora, was elected to the presidency of the Republic.

By and large the Republican constitution was a sound document, providing for full civil liberties and representative rights, with the major exception of Catholic rights. Yet the exclusion of the latter left nearly 25 percent of the Spanish people at war with the Republic or at least the political-constitutional structure of it. This split made it impossible to unite a broad democratic majority and left the body politic divided almost from the start of the regime. Since the Republican left regarded constitutional reform to protect Catholic interests as at the very least treason, the Republic as a democratic constitutional regime was doomed from the outset.

The third major project, Catalan autonomy, was somewhat slower to be achieved. Francesc Macià, the aging leader of ultra-Catalanism, had grouped together most of the Catalan lower middle classes in a federation of the Catalanist Esquerra (Left) that demanded full autonomy as well as reform within the region but was willing to cooperate with the new regime in order to achieve it. The opposition in 1931–1932 came not so much from the right, which was unorganized and nearly impotent, as from centrist liberals and the Socialists, who distrusted middle class Catalanism. It was, however, in part to head off the concession of autonomy to Catalonia that a small group of army officers, together with a few monarchist conspirators, staged an abortive revolt in Madrid and Seville on August 10, 1932. This was easily suppressed, and it swung the political pendulum to the left once more. The Catalan Statute was passed in September, providing for broad internal autonomy for a regional government (Generalitat) of Catalonia, with its own regional parliament, president, and prime minster. Macià became the first president of Catalonia, then died the following year, his goal accomplished.

Yet in the 1930s, as before 1923, the Catalanists could not fully dominate Catalonia because of the rivalry of anarcho-syndicalism. The CNT was reorganized in 1930 and sprang back to full life in 1931. Moreover, the most doctrinaire anarchists, alarmed by the attitudes of economic reform and political action among moderates within the CNT, as well as by Communist efforts to penetrate the movement, in 1927 organized the separate Iberian Anarchist Federation (FAI) of elitist revolutionary anarchists, determined to dominate the CNT and keep it on the path of revolutionary anarcho-syndicalism. During the course of 1931 the FAI took over the main part of the CNT (from which several more moderate or politicist elements split off) and launched it on a course of pseudorevolutionary turmoil. Anarchists denounced the Republic as being worse than the monarchy. During 1931–1933 they carried out scores of strikes and terrorist attacks, culminating in the *tres ochos* of January 8, 1932, January 8, 1933, and December 8, 1933—small-scale pseudorevolutionary strikes and petty insurrections in scattered parts of the country, with the principal focus in Catalonia. The leaders of the Esquerra had originally hoped to reach an understanding with the CNT for cooperation in the building of an autonomous, democratic, socially progressive Catalonia, but the hostility and terrorism of the anarchists eventually drew reprisals from the Catalan government. Three years of frenzied activity and playing at revolution exhausted the CNT; by the end of 1933 its momentum was spent, the movement waning and losing membership.

The fourth major goal of the left Republican–Socialist coalition—social reform—achieved significant, though by no means complete, success. Francisco Largo Caballero, the most prominent leader of the UGT, became Republican minister of labor and instituted an efficient labor inspectorate for the enforcement of social legislation. A system of labor arbitration committees, weighted in favor of labor interests, was established nationwide and gained major wage increases, especially for the ill-paid rural laborers.

The major issue of socio-economic reform was agriculture. The severity of the Spanish agrarian problem was recognized by nearly all political groups, including some conservatives, and agrarian reform was accepted by most as a foregone conclusion. The Socialists wanted a very extensive reform that would expropriate the land of all save smallholders, and they proposed establishment of numerous collective farms. Yet the Republican left, who held the balance of power, were themselves uncertain and divided. Most of their leaders had little knowledge of agrarian problems and were less concerned with this than with the question of church-state relations and constitutional issues. Only after the suppression of the *sanjurjada* (the petty revolt of August 1932) was real progress made. Contrary to the Republican constitution, the land of all grandes was confiscated, and a full agrarian reform measure was finally passed. This was an extremely complicated bill that provided for expropriation of several categories of land. Under its terms, the great majority of the approximately 80,000 landowners subject to partial or nearly total expropriation were medium and small-medium holders, not latifundists. Through technicalities, much of the property of some of the larger owners was allowed to escape. Moreover, all expropriations had to be paid for, and the government had almost no money left; expenditures on agrarian reform were limited to 1 percent of the budget. In the meantime a full cadastre had to be completed and initial operations supervised by an agrarian reform institute representing all the major parties, so that little was accomplished during 1933.

The Socialists were greatly disillusioned by the relative frustration of the agrarian reform. Their initial relationship to the Republic had been ambiguous. Only reluctantly had the Socialist leadership allowed the party to be taken into the Republican coalition, and the Socialists themselves, after cooperating with Primo de Rivera's labor tribunals, had done very little to assist the coming of the new regime. Since 1918 Spanish Socialist ideology had become increasingly vague. Many Socialist spokesmen still considered themselves orthodox revolutionary Marxists, though non-Leninist and non-communist, while others ignored the issue altogether. In 1931 the Socialists made it clear that their goal was a socialist republic, not a liberal middle class parliamentary republic, but what this actually meant was far from clear. Nearly all the Socialist leaders accepted full and disciplined collaboration within a parliamentary regime, on the general notion that this would lead to sweeping changes both in social and economic structure and in public attitudes, preparing for the transition to a socialist regime. The elections of 1931, in which the organized Socialists emerged as the largest single party out of a largely disorganized electorate, had seemed a good augury. So did the Republican constitution, which provided for the legal nationalization of property, and the Largo Caballero labor reforms, which resulted in great gains for labor and enabled the UGT to triple its membership, establishing a mass following among rural laborers. Yet by the beginning of 1933 the momentum was not being sustained. The major socio-economic reform was very far from realization, and the political situation was no longer evolving toward the left. A strong reaction was under way in conservative opinion, particularly among Catholics and in northern Spain, while the governing republican coalition was losing its strength and unity. The Radicals went into opposition, and the Radical Socialists split into three sections—left, right, and center.

The Azaña government was shaken by a series of blows during the first eight months of 1933. The first was a police scandal—the Casas Viejas affair in Cádiz province. During the anarchist insurrectionary effort of January 1933, a detachment of Assault Guards (the newly formed Republican urban equivalent of the Civil Guards) shot down nearly a score of anarchist prisoners. This brought condemnation of the government from nearly all quarters. Several months later, municipal elections were held in numerous small towns of northern Spain whose promonarchist local governments had been ousted by the Republican regime in Madrid two years earlier. Two-thirds of the new municipal officials chosen represented parties in opposition to the government. Finally, in August the first (indirect) elections to the new Republican supreme court returned a majority from groups to the right of the government. Some of Azaña's own supporters believed that the government had gone too far too fast, and his majority began to break up. Since no other coalition was feasible, new elections were scheduled for November 1933. The Socialists felt deceived by political collaboration with the Republic, feeling they had been compromised into reformism while failing to gain the major structural and political changes which they sought. They were alarmed by the political events of central Europe—the establishment of the Nazi dictatorship in Germany and of the Dollfuss regime in Austria, in the course of which two of the strongest Socialist parties in Europe were going under. Failure to adopt a radical prerevolutionary position in Spain would, many Socialist leaders feared, only encourage a Spanish reaction leading to the same sort of tyranny central Europe was suffering.

The leading representative of Spanish conservatism was the new Catholic confederation, CEDA, led by a young law professer from Salamanca, José Ma. Gil Robles. The CEDA capitalized on the reaction among Catholics against Republican anticlericalism and reformism to form a broad nationwide organization, with plentiful financial support from wealthy interests. Its goal was to return conservative forces to power and restore Catholic privilege. Its leaders refused to declare themselves either monarchist or republican, declaring that government forms were accidental and that it was political values and achievements that counted.

In the 1933 elections the Socialists no longer associated themselves with the divided factions of the middle class Republican left, hoping to rally a broad following independently. Conversely, in some districts the CEDA joined forces with the moderate liberal Radicals. Though they did not win a majority, the CEDA emerged with the largest single Cortes representation of any party, and the Radicals had the next largest. The Socialists came third (though second in the popular vote), losing one-third of their seats, while the left Republican parties in their isolation were nearly wiped out.

The parliament chosen in 1933 was made up mainly of moderate liberals and moderate conservatives, which ought logically to have led to a moderate conservative coalition government based on the CEDA, the largest party. But the president of the Republic, Alcalá Zamora, was hostile to the CEDA, which refused to commit itself completely to Republican institutions. Moreover, the Socialists had made it clear that they would not accept a government made up even in part of the supposedly "fascist" CEDA, and threatened revolutionary insurrection. In turn, since the Republican left had harped on the theme that the Republic must be anti-Catholic and that Catholic political groups could not be true Republicans, prevailing pressures naturally worked against the CEDA leadership espousing a position of outright Republicanism. Alcalá Zamora sought a temporary way out of the dilemma by encouraging the formation of a minority Radical-led government that excluded the CEDA. Several transitory Radical ministries under Alejandro Lerroux and one of his lieutenants governed for ten months, until October 1934. The CEDA accepted this arrangement temporarily but soon demanded participation in power, which was its constitutional right as the single largest parliamentary group. At the beginning of October 1934, Alcalá Zamora could resist no longer and appointed a coalition government under Lerroux, this time including three CEDA ministers. That became the signal for revolutionary insurrection in Catalonia and Asturias.

The 1934 revolt sprang from two different sources: radical middle class Catalanism and proletarian revolution. In Catalonia, the Esquerra had retained control of the regional government and then won the municipal elections of January 1934. It had passed a considerable amount of regional legislation in 1933-1934 affecting local affairs, education, sanitation, roads, and so forth, but its most important bill was a Law of Cultivation Contracts that would allow long-term renters (for fifteen years or more) to purchase their land at reasonable rates. The law was fought by landowners. Under the Republican constitution, Catalan agrarian affairs were under the jurisdiction of the Generalitat, but the terms of legal contracts in Catalonia were required to conform to the Spanish norm. The case was referred to the Spanish supreme court, which ruled that until national norms governing revision of rental contracts were determined by legislation pending in the Spanish parliament, the Catalan bill was unconstitutional. This created a great uproar among radical Catalanists, already chafing under the limitations of their broad but not complete autonomy. The Catalan Generalitat in effect renounced the Spanish constitutional system, declared that it would not respect the judicial decision, and passed the legislation once more. The radical youth section of the Esquerra federation, Estat Català (Catalan State), came to the fore, its leaders heading a secret resistance committee to prepare for armed revolt. A compromise was eventually negotiated for the Catalan agrarian reform project, but it was completely ignored by the radical Catalanists, who were determined to exploit the latent polarization for their own purposes: an armed revolt to establish absolute Catalan autonomy, amounting to virtual independence, and the federalization of the Spanish state.

Meanwhile, the Socialists had become fully disillusioned about the possibilities of winning power by parliamentary means, and many of their leaders talked of direct action. Largo Caballero was hailed by youthful militants as leader of the revolutionary "bolshevizing" trend. Revolutionaries gained control of the UGT as well as the Socialist Youth. Though they realized the Socialists were too weak to win power in a *coup d'etat,* they obtained the agreement even of the moderates that entrance of the CEDA into the government must be avoided by force. Meanwhile, the small Marxist parties of Catalonia had formed a broad Worker Alliance in 1933. The Socialists joined this in 1934 as a means of broadening the strength of the working class parties for revolution, but save in Asturias, the CNT remained aloof.

The signal for revolt was in a sense given by the leaders of the small middle class left parties, who handed the president of the Republic virtually identical notes when the new cabinet was formed, announcing that they "were breaking off all association with existing institutions." The subsequent rebellion in Barcelona was pure farce. The Catalanists did not cooperate with the Worker Alliance and were themselves uncertain and divided. After a few timid gestures, the Catalan government offices were occupied by a comparatively small force of army troops from the local garrison.

The revolutionary insurrection of October 1934 in Asturias was entirely different. It was a revolt of Socialist workers, supported by the CNT and the Communists, that occupied the entire mining and industrial district making up the central portion of the province of Asturias. Elite troops had to be called in from Spanish Morocco to quell the revolt, which lingered on for two weeks. More than 1,000 were killed, the majority revolutionaries, and there were atrocities on both sides. The revolutionaries shot nearly 100 people in cold blood, most of them policemen and priests, and an almost equal number of rebels—possibly even more—were executed out of hand by the troops that suppressed the revolt.

The result was to leave government in the hands of the moderate conservative coalition for the next fourteen months. In 1934, when Lerroux and the Radicals largely administered the government, a moderately progressive policy had been followed, continuing agrarian reform, expanding education, and only partially altering the extreme prolabor character of the labor tribunals. In 1935 government policy became reactionary, reforming the agrarian reform to reduce it to ineffectiveness, packing the tribunals with antilabor majorities, and in general, fostering the interests of the possessing classes at the expense of the working classes.

In May 1935 the cabinet was reorganized to give the CEDA five seats, including the vital ministry of war for Gil Robles. It was widely rumored that the CEDA was planning either a *coup d'etat* or imminent constitutional reform to turn the Republic into a clerical, corporative state. In fact, Gil Robles's primary goal as minister of war was to revitalize the Spanish army and secure it against leftist influence, in which task he achieved some success. The more important goal of constitutional reform was harder to bring about. A two-thirds majority was required for constitutional changes, and since the CEDA's religious goals were controversial, the party, with less than half the seats in parliament, might have had difficulty in raising the necessary votes. On the other hand, four years after passage of the Republican constitution, that is, after December 1935, constitutional amendments might be effected by a simple majority vote. Hence no serious effort was made to carry out fundamental constitutional reform during 1935.

Altogether, the year was one of frustration. Some aspects of the economic depression grew worse, and in certain sectors unemployment mounted. The governing coalition limited itself to undoing many of the changes of the Azaña administration without offering viable new policies in their place. This was partly thanks to the heterogeneous nature of the alliance, having to placate both liberal Radicals and reactionary elements on the right. The Radicals suffered especially in these compromises, and by the end of 1935 found themselves morally discredited by a series of minor financial scandals which their enemies succeeded in magnifying out of all proportion.

The judicial prosecution of the 1934 revolutionaries was largely ineffective. At least 15,000 militants were held in prison, and many were tried and sentenced to long terms. The president and the Radicals, however, prevented conservatives from imposing major sanctions against the revolutionaries. None of the revolutionary leaders were condemned to death, and only four of the rank and file were executed, three of them common murderers. None of the leftist organizations were outlawed, and they were allowed to continue official work. In the aftermath of the repression, however, there were cases of police brutality and torture in Asturias. Though the main phase of this lasted little more than a month, the theme of atrocious repression gave rise to a virulent leftist propaganda equal to that of the right, which exaggerated the extent of the "red terror" in Asturias. The whole effect of the insurrection, the repression, and the stagnation of government in 1935 was to polarize political opinion ever more sharply toward the extremes of left and right.

The CEDA planned to remain in power, with the Radicals, through 1936, and to enjoy plenty of time to effect institutional reforms. Yet the real moderating power was not held by the CEDA but by Alcalá Zamora. Though the Catholic president favored moderate constitutional reform, he feared the CEDA and resented its able young leader. Alcalá Zamora took the position that since there was no senate in the Spanish Republican system, it was up to the president to serve as a moderating influence and prevent power from swinging too sharply to one extreme or the other. When the existing ministry collapsed over a minor issue in December 1935, he refused to allow the CEDA leaders to form the next government, and they in turn refused to serve further as subordinate members of a broad coalition. Such an impasse made regular government impossible, so Alcalá Zamora appointed a caretaker ministry under a personal crony, Portela Valladares, who closed parliament for a month. Elections were then scheduled for February 1936.

Alcalá Zamora's dissolution of parliament gave the left its great opportunity for a political comeback. Two major divergent forces were at work among the Spanish left in 1935. One was the struggle by the moderate middle class leftist parties and the moderate, nonrevolutionary sector of the Socialists to build a broad and essentially moderate leftist alliance for electoral purposes, one that could regain government power. This was the origin of the subsequent Popular Front. The other was the rise of the hitherto minuscule Spanish Communist party and the "bolshevization" of the bulk of the Socialist movement, a movement directly opposite to the broad cooperative trend of the moderate left. It was the Communists who gained the propaganda advantage from the 1934 insurrection on the left, falsely claiming for themselves the main role in that tragic drama. The Popular Front alliance was not formed until January 1936, after the new elections were announced. The Socialists agreed to join only because of the need to win amnesty for thousands of imprisoned

Table 32.   Voting in the Elections of 1936

Eligible voters	13,553,710	
Ballots cast	9,864,783	73.0%
Popular Front	4,555,401	
Popular Front with Center (Lugo)	98,715	34.3
Basque Nationalists	125,714	
Center	400,901	5.4
Right	1,866,981	
Right with Center	2,636,524	33.2

Source: J. Tusell Gómez, et al., Las elecciones del Frente Popular en España, 2 vols. (Madrid, 1971), 2:13.

militants and to remove the moderate conservative government from power. The Socialists were indispensable for a leftist victory, and it was at their insistence that the Communists were included as well. The goal of the Popular Front program was further extension of all the earlier reforms and the "republicanization" of official institutions, eliminating all conservative influence.

The conservatives responded with a National Front built around the CEDA, but it was not fully unified and never published an official program. The aim of Alcalá Zamora and Portela Valladares was to build a centrist third force, but they lacked organizational cadres, popular support, or a convincing propaganda line. It has been said that the election of 1936 was in a way a plebiscite on the 1934 insurrection. This is partly correct; the main rightist slogan was "Against the revolution and its accomplices." The slender margin of popular support won by the Popular Front, however, was not so much an expression of enthusiasm for revolutionary insurrection as it was a positive response to Popular Front propaganda, which stressed the "atrocities" wreaked by the repression in Asturias and the need for a renewal of Republican reform.

On the eve of the election, most informed opinion expected a victory for the right. The slender Popular Front triumph came as a surprise even to the leading leftists, and the margin was very close, as indicated in table 32, drawn from the only detailed scholarly study of the electoral results.

Under the majority bloc system, what counted was not so much the total popular vote as the way it was concentrated province by province. Thus a slender plurality of votes for the left was transformed into a decisive majority of Cortes deputies. At the same time the center was wiped out. The only previously strong national centrist party, the Radicals, had been discredited by the scandals and frustrations of 1935—a discrediting in which the president had played a major role. To Alcalá Zamora's own discomfiture, this cut the ground from under the possibility of any third force alternative. Hence his gamble was a complete failure.

The first electoral returns were the signal for a new leftist outburst in the streets of many cities, opening jails and bringing minor disorders. The Portela government abruptly resigned three days after the elections, before the results were fully tabulated and certified, and before the second round elections were held. A new all-left Republican cabinet under Azaña was hastily sworn in and then presided over the registration of the electoral results. After this was completed the Popular Front ended up with a clear majority of the seats in the new Cortes, a majority made even stronger by the work of the credentials committee of the new Cortes, which annulled the election of 17 rightist and 3 centrist deputies. This finally resulted in 271 seats for the Popular Front, 137 for the right, and 40 for the center, though the Socialist president of the credentials committee, Indalecio Prieto, resigned in protest over the fraud.

Thus the Popular Front had complete control over Spanish government in 1936, with an even stronger majority than Azaña had held in 1931-1932. The new ministry proposed to carry out the Popular Front program immediately, and an amnesty was promulgated for all leftist prisoners without bothering to observe full constitutional requirements. Measures were taken to prepare for reinstatement of and full compensation for leftist workers fired for political reasons. Catalan autonomy, partially suspended since the insurrection, was reestablished. Measures were taken to extend the agrarian reform and to appoint more left Republicans to government service.

The Azaña ministry was, however, outflanked almost immediately by the revolutionaries. Without waiting for the extension of the agrarian reform, the UGT peasant sections occupied large sections of land, mostly in Badajoz province, amounting to 250,000 hectares. These seizures were then legalized ex post facto by the government. By July 535,000 hectares had been expropriated, much of it not according to regulations. During the spring, a wave of revolutionary strikes began whose object was not to win economic improvements but to break the Spanish economic structure. At one point in June a million workers were out on strike, roughly 25 percent of the labor force. During May and June a number of small and medium-sized businesses were forced into bankruptcy. Capital fled the country, the exchange balance and peseta value declined, and it became increasingly difficult to fund the national debt.

A new wave of terrorism and political street violence began the day after the elections, initiated by the victorious revolutionary groups. Their main targets were members of the Falange, the small (10,000- to 20,000-man) Spanish fascist movement organized in 1933 by José Antonio Primo de Rivera, eldest son of the late dictator. After the Falangists struck back in an abortive attempt on the life of a Socialist professor, the party's leaders were arrested in mid-March and most of its local sections closed.

Pressure against the government was maintained not from the right, which had lost most of its parliamentary leverage and was quite disoriented, but from the revolutionary left. The Socialists and Communists called for the immediate completion of the Popular Front program and then the implementation of radical social and economic changes. Though moderate Socialists retained control of the executive commission of the party, the revolutionaries gained the support of most of the membership, and were the main factor in the Spanish disorders of the spring of 1936. The Communists were growing by leaps and bounds and claimed to have expanded from 30,000 to 100,000 members between February and July. They pressed a hyper-revolutionary line, calling for a transition to a "worker-peasant" government as soon as Azaña completed the Popular Front program, and had organized their own paramilitary militia (MAOC). The "bol-shevizing" trend won the sympathy of most young Socialist leaders, and in April the Socialist and Communist youth movements were unified under Communist control. The CNT was also expanding and engaged in a helter-skelter policy of revolutionary rivalry with the UGT, contributing to further violence and economic disorder.

A major aim of the Popular Front was to completely eliminate conservative influence from Spanish government. The only remaining nonleftist authority in Spain was that of the president, Alcalá Zamora, who was removed from office on the specious and hypocritical charge of having exceeded his authority by dissolving parliament twice. The constitution provided that when a president dissolved the Cortes a second time during one term in office, his action would be reviewed by the new Cortes, and the Popular Front forces, who before January had demanded that the president dissolve parliament immediately, then used this technicality to get rid of him for acting upon their own insistence. He was the last remaining guarantee of moderation within the government, and the elevation of Azaña to the presidency in May 1936 established full leftist control of power.

Yet by that time Azaña had worked himself into a hopeless situation. He was not a revolutionary and wanted to preserve the Republican constitution while eliminating the power of the conservative elements. He more than anyone else was responsible for the organization of the Popular Front alliance, but in the spring of 1936 he found the power of the left being used to bypass the Republic and its constitutional system. The revolutionary parties had control of the streets and insisted on a constantly accelerating program of radical changes. The middle class left parties behind Azaña were too weak to govern by themselves, the center had been eliminated, and all bridges to the conservatives burnt. Azaña found himself the virtual prisoner of the extreme left, and disheartened by the situation, withdrew to the less active role of president. He was replaced as prime minister by a close associate, Casares Quiroga, who completely lacked the balance, tact, and insight for governing a country undergoing a process of civic dissolution.

Much of the Spanish middle class was benumbed by the experiences of the spring of 1936. The conservative groups were impotent, their leaders barely allowed to speak in parliament. The government and the leftist parties made it clear that they did not intend to permit conservative groups to regain a major voice in Spanish affairs. Given the complete leftist control of civic processes, the weakness of the organized right, and the incipient collapse of the political system, a purely political reaction was impossible.

Elements of the Spanish army officer corps had begun to conspire as early as 1933, but a serious military revolt against the government did not start to develop until May 1936. It took root only among a minority of military activists, most of them of junior and middle rank. Their leader was General Emilio Mola, commander of the garrison in Pamplona, who had first won notice in the Moroccan campaigns and then served as the last national police director under the monarchy. It proved very difficult to develop a firmly committed conspiracy, however, for the Azaña government had given nearly all the senior command positions to officers of liberal or moderate principles, and most rank-and-file officers were reluctant to take a stand, being aware of the failure of most military interventions in politics and dubious of the success of a revolt against the leftist government and the mass revolutionary movements.

Last minute support was won, however, by the wave of reaction that followed the climax of political terrorism. On July 12, leftist police officers and Communist militia, enraged by the killing of a leftist officer by Falangists, dragged from his home and murdered a leader of the parliamentary opposition, José Calvo Sotelo, head of a small protofascist movement (Bloque Nacional) and former finance minister under Primo de Rivera. It was a political murder without precedent in the history of west European parliamentary regimes and symbolized the breakdown of the Republican constitutional system. It became the signal for the start of the Spanish Civil War.

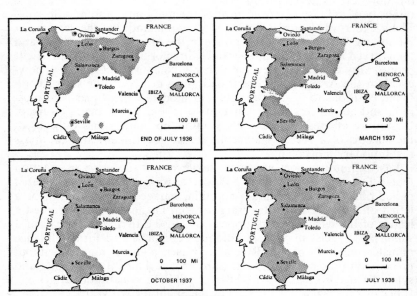

Expansion of the Nationalist Zone, 1936–1939

UWCL

26

The Spanish Civil War
of 1936–1939

The Spanish Civil War began on July 17, 1936, with the revolt of elite
units of the Spanish army in the Moroccan Protectorate against the
left Republican government of Azaña and Casares Quiroga. In accordance with the ill-coordinated conspiracy organized by General
Mola, they were joined within the next seventy-two hours by something more than half the units of the Spanish army, primarily in the
north, west, and extreme south of the peninsula. Subsequent propaganda presented the rising as a move to prevent an imminent Communist seizure of power that was supposed to have begun only a few
weeks later. Some rebel officers did indeed believe that a leftist coup
was about to occur, but their leaders did not assume any such timeta-
ble. Rather, their goal was simply to put an end to extreme political,
social, and economic disorder and quash leftist power in Spain.

Up to the last minute the Azaña-Casares Quiroga government
refused to believe that any sizable portion of the army would rebel.
Azaña knew that nearly all the senior commanders appointed after
the Popular Front victory were reliable. Moreover, he had switched
around scores of less reliable officers during the late winter and spring
of 1936, but had hesitated to make further moves against the military
for fear of antagonizing them still more and of leaving the government completely defenseless vis-à-vis the revolutionary left. Azaña
was essentially correct in his judgment of senior commanders; the

rebellion was not a "generals' revolt" but a rising by the active nationalistic middle strata of the officer corps that in some cases swept reluctant generals along with it or simply deposed them and seized their commands.

Finally, on the night of July 18-19, Azaña did what he had hitherto refused to do since the beginning of the Republic: attempt a compromise with non-liberals. The Casares Quiroga cabinet was hastily replaced by a more moderate ministry led by Diego Martínez Barrio, the most temperate middle class leader within the Popular Front coalition. Martínez Barrio offered major concessions to the rebels, including the ministry of defense for Mola, the leader of the conspiracy. Thirty days earlier some such arrangement might have worked, but by July 19 it was too late. Polarization was almost complete, and Mola refused to go back on the pledges the conspirators had made among themselves not to rest until the present system was overthrown.

From that point the lines were drawn. The Martínez Barrio ministry gave way to an all-left Republican cabinet under José Giral that immediately acceded to leftist demands for the "arming of the people," meaning not of course the "people" but the organized leftist groups. This completed the division of forces; before midday on July 19 fewer than half the units in the army had come out in direct rebellion. By July 20 a slight majority had done so. The insurgents occupied Spanish Morocco and the Canary Islands, all of north-central Spain save the Basque country, Santander and Asturias, all the west, and an edge of the extreme south. In most cases, these were the more conservative areas of the country which had voted for the right in the February elections and which more or less supported the revolt. In the largest cities (save Seville and Zaragoza) and throughout the center, east, and southeast, the revolutionary parties assisted loyal police and military forces in smothering revolts by those army units which tried to resist the Giral government.

The Spanish Revolution

The leftist zone has been variously designated "Republican," "loyalist," and "Popular Front." Of those terms, the adjective "loyalist" is somewhat misleading, for there was no attempt to remain loyal to the constitutional Republican regime. If that had been the scrupulous policy of the left, there would have been no revolt and civil war in the first place. Instead, the long-threatened revolution finally erupted in almost every part of Spain that was not occupied by the rebellious military. The great irony was thus that the revolution was not initiated by the revolutionaries' own planning but in response to and as a result of the opportunity provided by the counterrevolutionary revolt of the military.

The Giral government exercised authority only in the greater Madrid district, and even there it was highly limited. In Catalonia an Anti-Fascist Militia Committee exercised de facto power in a system of revolutionary dualism parallel to the merely nominal authority of the Catalan Generalitat. The committee was made up of representatives of all the leftist parties but was largely dominated by the anarchists of the FAI-CNT, who played a major role in quashing the attempted military revolt in Barcelona. Regional coalition revolutionary committees of the leftist parties and movements also seized de facto, sometimes temporarily de jure, control of the regions of Valencia, Asturias, and Santander. Militia columns of Catalan anarchists soon occupied eastern Aragón and set up their separate regional Council of Aragón in September. The moderate, Catholic Basque Nationalists remained loyal to the nominal Republican government in return for the passage of a Basque autonomy statute, similar to that of Catalonia, at the beginning of October. A regional government of "Euzkadi" (a Basque nationalist neologism referring to the Basque country) was then established over Vizcaya and western Guipuzcoa. Provincial revolutionary committees held de facto power in most other provinces of the leftist zone. Thus after July 1936 what remained of the constitutional Republic gave way to the "revolutionary Republican confederation" of 1936–1937.

The revolutionary committees, the syndicates, and the militia groups began at once to in some cases requisition and in other cases expropriate whatever they considered most important to their needs or their work. Franz Borkenau estimated that something like 70 percent of the industrial establishments in Barcelona were taken over by workers, 50 percent of those in Valencia, and 30 percent of those in Madrid. Certainly the urban socio-economic revolution went farther in Catalonia than in any other part of the leftist zone. For two months the Catalan Generalitat accepted a system of revolutionary dualism in which real power was held by the Anti-Fascist Militia Committee. Yet, though the CNT had become the major power in Catalonia, it found itself unable to carry out the complete revolution of "libertarian communism" that it postulated. The revolution was occurring in conditions of total civil war, and even though CNT syndicates had seized large sectors of Catalan industry, they lacked the resources to operate these alone. For the first time in the movement's history, the CNT agreed to regular collaboration in a formal government, their representatives joining a reorganized Catalan cabinet at the close of September 1936. The new Catalan government then set to work to legitimize the economic revolution. Its counselor of economics, a CNT economist named Juan Fàbregas, prepared a decree in October establishing the compulsory collectivization of all factories with more than one hundred employees, as well as for those with between fifty and one hundred employees if a majority of the employees demanded it. Moreover, provisions were made for "industrial concentrations" that would bring small shops in some sectors under the control of large collectives.

In the main part of the leftist zone, particularly in areas where Socialists rather than anarcho-syndicalists predominated, there was much less interest in de jure collectivization. Most important businesses were requisitioned or in one way or another taken under syndical control, but the process was never systematized and many firms were operated in much the same way as before. In the autonomous Basque country, there was no real economic revolution at all. The Basque government requisitioned the use of war-related and other industries, but there were no basic changes in ownership or structure.

Acceleration of the agrarian reform was sustained in the main part of the leftist zone, thanks in part to Communist concern. The problem was to rally the support of landless peasants against "fascism," while avoiding alienation of smallholders through reckless expropriation. Lands of all overt supporters of the Nationalists were soon seized, as were all larger properties. The expropriations were progressively extended, until by August 1938 the following number of hectares had been expropriated in the main part of the leftist zone:

Confiscated for political reasons	2,162,402
Expropriated for reasons of "social utility"	2,008,470
Occupied directly by peasants under provisional title	1,252,340
	5,423,212

This amounted to nearly 35 percent of the arable land in the leftist zone. A total of 316,777 peasants received land, and 2,213 cooperatives were formed, though under wartime conditions most were not especially successful.

In the anarchist fief of eastern Aragón, the CNT collectivized most of the land, forming several hundred cooperatives. Some of these were later broken up when government control was restored in this area in the summer of 1937. In Catalonia there was much less expropriation than in most other areas, largely because land was better distributed and peasant smallholders often supported the left Catalanists. Only a small number of rural cooperatives were created, but Catalan legislation later provided for comprehensive reforms, reducing all holdings to limited size and even guaranteeing 20 percent shares of small-farm profits for each hired laborer.

The revolution of 1936–1937 had a sweeping effect on economic structure in much of the leftist zone, but the social effects were somewhat less drastic. Save in some of the larger urban areas, there was no abrupt change in mores. In Barcelona and certain key centers there was great emphasis on "proletarian style," and in Catalonia inexpensive abortion facilities were set up, but the personal behavior of very many of the Spanish lower classes remained surprisingly conservative, and there was comparatively little emulation of Russian-style "revolutionary morality."

The Terror

During the first months of the fighting most of the deaths did not come from combat on the battlefield but from political executions in the rear—the "Red" and "White" terrors. In some cases the murder of political opponents began more or less spontaneously, but from the very beginning there was always a certain degree of organization, and nearly all the killings after the first few days were carried out by organized groups. Murder of the political opposition was an almost inevitable result of conditions of revolutionary civil war and the constant incitement to violence, particularly by the left, in the years leading up to it. Fear was also a major ingredient. Both sides knew that they had reached a showdown and were eager to eliminate potential opposition before it was too late.

The Red terror began with the murder of some of the rebels as they attempted to surrender after their revolt had failed in several of the key cities. From there it broadened out to wholesale arrests, and sometimes wholesale executions, of people associated with right-wing groups or the Catholic church. In general, this was not an irrepressible outpouring of hatred by the man in the street for his "oppressors," as it has sometimes been painted, but a semi-organized activity carried out by sections of nearly all the leftist groups. In the entire leftist zone the only organized political party that eschewed involvement in such activity were the Basque Nationalists.

Within a matter of weeks Socialist and anarcho-syndicalist leaders tried to bring such killings under control. "Control patrols" were organized in many areas and a series of revolutionary "people's courts," that in most cases imposed much lighter penalties, were formed to channel the repression of anti-leftists. After about six months, when a reorganized Popular Front government began to reassert authority, most of the random executions were ended, but under more centralized control, political killings continued through-out the leftist zone until the end of the war.

The repression in the Nationalist zone was more centralized and much more effective. Though often carried out by right-wing civilian groups, the White terror was almost from the beginning nominally institutionalized under military courts-martial. It was also more efficient, for, being under more coordinated direction, it was concentrated against the most dangerous opposition elements. By contrast, particularly during the first six months, each Red terror group operated on its own in a frequently irrational fashion, murdering innocent people and letting some of the more dangerous go free. Moreover, one of the main targets of the Red terror was the clergy, most of whom were not engaged in overt opposition.

The toll taken by the respective terrors may never be known exactly. The left slaughtered more in the first months, but the Nationalist repression probably reached its height only after the war had ended, when punishment was exacted and vengeance wreaked on the vanquished left. The White terror may have slain 50,000, perhaps fewer, during the war. The Franco government now gives the names of 61,000 victims of the Red terror, but this is not subject to objective verification. The number of victims of the Nationalist repression, during and after the war, was undoubtedly greater than that.

Grim as the reality was, it was immediately exaggerated by both sides, eager to deepen the guilt of their adversaries and underline the sufferings of their own people. Thus the legend of the *millón de muertos,* which exaggerated both terrorist and battlefield deaths by approximately 200 percent, was widely accepted after the war and gave rise to a contemporary variant of the Black Legend that stressed the supposedly uniquely sanguinary propensities of the Spanish.

In fact, compared with other revolutionary civil wars of twentieth century Europe, the Spanish Civil War was not remarkably lethal, either on the battlefield or behind the lines. In Finland, in 1918, approximately 1 percent of the population was killed during and in the aftermath of a four-month civil war.* It took the Spanish nearly three years to destroy proportionately as many of themselves, but

* The principal study of the killings in the Finnish Civil War is Jaakko Paavolainen, *Poliittiset väkivaltaisundet Suomessa 1918,* 2 vols. (Helsinki, 1967). It concludes that approximately 31,000 deaths resulted, or about 1 percent of the Finnish population of 3,200,000. The bulk of these were direct or indirect victims of the White terror, which killed about 8,400 outright. Another 11,800 (included in the general totals) died afterward in camps. (I am indebted for this source to my colleague Prof. Pekka Hamalainen.)

when this occurred in Spain it was put down by foreign observers to the "innate savagery" of the Spanish.

In addition to the deaths that resulted, the twin terrors in Spain left another, equally fateful, legacy. They left a gulf of enduring hatred between opposing sectors of society that made a final resolution of the conflict much more difficult.

International Reaction to the Civil War

Outbreak of the civil war caught all the great powers by surprise. Spain had not been involved in major international disputes since the partition of Morocco early in the century. The Republic can hardly be said to have had a foreign policy, and refused to take an independent stand on major international issues, save to blandly endorse the League of Nations. Both sides immediately looked for outside military support when the war began. The Republican government turned to France, which was also ruled by a Popular Front coalition—though in the case of France nonrevolutionary—and which held official contracts to supply the Spanish military. The initial French response was positive, and small numbers of planes and supplies were dispatched, but after indication of German and Italian support to the rebels, and mounting opposition among moderate and conservative opinion in France, the French government grew more cautious. It feared conflict with the central European fascist powers and followed the British policy of noninvolvement. During the month of August 1936 agreements were worked out for a nonintervention pact signed by all the great powers, implemented by an official committee sitting in London. This theoretically would deny arms support for both sides. Republican authorities protested that theirs was the legitimate government, and hence entitled under recognized rules of international law to purchase arms in all countries with which Spain had diplomatic relations. The reality of the revolution, however, discouraged other states from taking this claim too seriously.

The rebel military leaders sent representatives to both the German and Italian governments at the end of the first week of fighting. Neither Hitler nor Mussolini could gain a clear picture of the situation in Spain, but both were eventually attracted by the idea of helping establish a right-wing government in Spain favorable to them, while throttling the efforts of the revolutionary left. At the end of July both fascist governments sent small quantities of planes and material, but at first neither would commit itself to a major investment in the Spanish conflict.

This paralleled the attitude of the Soviet Union. The Comintern had encouraged the overthrow of the Spanish Republic from its very inception, and after the Popular Front elections the Communist party called for a rapid transition to a "worker-peasant" dictatorship, but this line changed abruptly as soon as the civil war began. The Communists were more keenly aware than were anarchists and revolutionary Socialists that the support of liberal and moderate middle class people would be needed to win the struggle. Moreover, Stalin was eager to strengthen the Soviet Union's position vis-à-vis Britain and France in opposition to Nazi Germany, and a regime of the extreme left in Spain would alienate moderate and conservative opinion in the western countries. Hence the Communists immediately announced that the goal of the civil war was not to establish a proletarian revolutionary regime but simply to defend a middle class parliamentary republic (though that had already ceased to exist). During the first two months of the civil war the Soviet government sent very little military equipment to the leftist zone, and, like Germany and Italy, signed the nonintervention agreement. However, at the very same time, the first official Soviet ambassador was dispatched to Madrid, a special military advisory commission was sent, and an NKVD section for intelligence activities was installed in the erstwhile Republican capital. All Communist assistance was eagerly received—save by the anarchists—for this seemed to be the only significant source of foreign support for the left.

Franco's Nationalist Government

The military revolt began with only a vague, general political plan. The rebel chiefs realized that a brief civil war could hardly be avoided, but Mola proposed to bring enough forces from northern Spain and from Morocco within two or three weeks to choke off resistance and capture Madrid. He planned to establish an all-military government which would create joint military-civilian local governing bodies staffed by officers and conservative leaders. The strength of the leftist reaction and the failure of the revolt in the navy, which made it impossible at first to move large numbers of troops from Morocco, upset much of this plan. However, a National Defense Junta was set up at Burgos on July 22, 1936, composed of senior army officers and nominally led by a mere figurehead, General Miguel Cabanellas, the senior active general in the army.

The real leaders were Mola, in command of rebel forces in the north, and General Francisco Franco, who led the elite Moroccan units. Franco had been a hero of the earlier Moroccan campaigns and the youngest general in the Spanish army. He had been director of the national military academy from 1928 to 1931, demoted by Azaña and then made chief of the general staff in 1935. He had more prestige than any officer in the army but had never before played an active role in politics. In reputation and authority he stood above all the other leaders, and it was his representatives who negotiated the first arrangements for German and Italian assistance. By September, it was clear that the civil war had become a bitter struggle that was likely to continue for some time and that a strong unified command was needed. Once the principle of the *mando único* was decided upon, it was almost a foregone conclusion that Franco would become commander in chief and head of government. When formation of a Nationalist government under Franco was announced on October 1, 1936, he assumed the title of head of state as well.

The main support for the Nationalist counterrevolutionary movement came from the middle classes, the conservative peasant smallholders of the north, and Catholic opinion in general. The Catholic clergy had little to do with the genesis of the antileftist insurgence, and during the first year of the Civil War the church hierarchy maintained an officially neutral stance for fear of being compromised should the Nationalists collapse. In fact, it was inevitable that nearly all Catholic opinion would rally to Franco after the orgy of church-burning and priest murder that wracked most of the leftist zone during the first six months of the war. The main exceptions were the Catholic Basque Nationalists, but even in the Basque country one-third of the people backed Franco. Finally in mid-1937, the Catholic Church gave its official blessing to the Franco regime; a joint pastoral letter of Spanish bishops denounced the left and proclaimed the Nationalist struggle to be a crusade. Religious fervor was probably the major source of emotional support for the Nationalists in the Civil War.

The Franco government began as a rather simple and uncertain military dictatorship. It had no clear doctrine or program other than national unity and the defeat of the left. Franco was a cautious, thoroughly professional soldier with no training in politics or economics. He had to devote most of his time to military leadership, and the real political architect of the first phase of the Franco regime was his brother-in-law, Ramón Serrano Súñer, former secretary of the CEDA youth movement.

The new political ideas of antileftist dynamism in the European air were those of fascism and the totalitarian state. The catastrophe of the Republic and the disaster of all-out civil war completely discredited the CEDA's conservative tactic of parliamentarianism. Serrano Súñer and certain other government collaborators embraced the idea of a Spanish fascism, though its content was vague. The only real

Spanish fascist movement, the Falange, had achieved no importance whatever before the spring of 1936. All its main leaders were killed by the left in the first months of the civil war. However, it enjoyed an enormous influx of membership from frightened and disillusioned middle class people and by the beginning of 1937 had several hundred thousand affiliates. It was helping to organize scores of thousands of militiamen and auxiliaries and playing a major role in bolstering the Nationalist rear guard. The only other organized political group providing significant support were the Carlists, who volunteered en masse and contributed some of the Nationalists' most effective shock troops. After preparations by Serrano, on April 19, 1937, Franco established an organized political front for the regime by decreeing the fusion of the Falange and the Carlists' "Traditionalist Communion" in a new entity to be called the Falange Española Tradicionalista, henceforth declared the official state party (*partido único*) of the Nationalist regime.

Franco was not, however, turning his government into a Falangist state. Rather, he was simply making the revamped Falange the fascist state party of his eclectic military dictatorship. In his unification speech he emphasized that the new party would constitute a broad national front of people from disparate moderate and conservative (and sometimes leftist) backgrounds, and that its program and ideology would be subject to change and elaboration. The formation of a Spanish fascist state party was naturally pleasing to the German and Italian governments, but Franco did not plan the Falange as an imitation of the Nazi or Fascist parties. The "totalitarian" state that he spoke of would, he said, derive its norms from Spanish tradition, going back to the authoritarian monarchy of Fernando and Isabel. It did provide his government with a vague ideology and a bureaucratic following.

Franco's first regular government was not organized until 1938, and even then half its members were army officers. Plans were drawn up for corporate economic organization, elaborating on Primo de Rivera's system under the rubric of Falangist "national syndicalism." So long as the war lasted, however, the Franco government paid little attention to domestic changes. Having rallied the support of much of the middle classes, it devoted itself to maintaining unity and order and to winning the military struggle.

The Spanish People's Republic

The only leftist group that had a policy for prosecuting the leftist revolution in terms that might make possible both military and political victory was the Communist party. The essence of the Communist program was the reestablishment of central government authority in the leftist zone and the formation of an organized army to win the war. Abroad, the Comintern usually advertised the struggle as one of basic parliamentary democracy against fascism. This line was too conservative to be effective within the leftist zone, where the Communist policy tried to channel the revolution within limits compatible with the political and economic demands of the war. While encouraging government control and a certain degree of nationalization of industry, the Communists discouraged all-out collectivization to avoid frightening the lower middle classes and driving them completely into the arms of Franco.

Communist influence, still only secondary before the fighting started, increased enormously during the first months of the civil war. Only the Communists had a united party with a consistent program. The Socialists were divided and the CNT incapable of concerted, organized action. Communist emphasis on paramilitary activity enabled them to exert influence on military organization in the Madrid district far exceeding their party membership. Moreover, the diplomatic and military support of the Soviet Union gave Spanish Communism a decisive voice that it could never otherwise have achieved. Communist party membership increased more rapidly than did that of any other group in the leftist zone.

The revolutionary Socialists also admitted the need for a more representative and organized government, after the disastrous military defeats of the left in the second month of the civil war. Consequently the first all-Popular Front government was organized under Largo Caballero in September 1936. This cabinet included two officially Communist ministers and one crypto-Communist, as well as one Catalanist and one Basque Nationalist. Four CNT representatives joined in November.

Over a period of six months, from the fall of 1936 to the spring of 1937, there developed an increasingly tense struggle between the forces of centralization and state control, led by the Communists, moderate Socialists, and middle class left on the one hand, and the supporters of continuing revolutionary dualism and local autonomy, led by the CNT and the small independent revolutionary Marxist POUM in Catalonia on the other. One of the main bones of contention was the organization of the new People's Army. Largo Caballero was the head of the Popular Front government that was reestablishing authority, yet his personal attitude was ambiguous. His own military appointees began organization of the People's Army, but he was reluctant to repress the local revolutionary committees completely, as the Communists and others demanded. Indeed, by April

1937 Largo Caballero, the nominal leader of the "bolshevizing" Socialists, had become bitterly anti-Communist. He feared the growing influence of the Communist party and the Soviet Union in the leftist zone. In 1936 the Communists had stolen most of the Socialist youth movement to form their own JSU (United Socialist Youth), and had taken over the Catalan section of the Socialist party to form their own new Catalan Communist party (PSUC). They dominated military organization in the main zone of operations and tried by every means to impose their views on the government. In April 1937 Largo rebelled, attempted to reduce the number of Communist military appointees, and began secret negotiations with representatives of the four leading west European powers to try to reach a compromise that would end the war and force the Soviet presence out of Spain.

The climax of the struggle between the revolutionary extreme left and neo-Republican Popular Front state occurred in Barcelona in May 1937. Communist-led police tried to reoccupy the Barcelona telephone center in the name of the Catalan Generalitat. This led to full-scale resistance by the CNT and POUM, who soon occupied most of Barcelona. The government had to move in reinforcements, and the CNT leaders, already collaborating with the state, were eager to avoid conflict. Republican troops occupied Barcelona and the extreme left acquiesced.

The Communists then forced Largo from office, and he was replaced by Juan Negrín, a pro-Communist Socialist who was willing to cooperate with them fully and pursue a policy of central authority and all-out resistance to the Spanish Nationalists. In October 1937 the seat of government was moved from Valencia (where it had been located in November 1936) to Barcelona; in the meantime government control had been extended over nearly all the local revolutionary committees. In Catalonia this process had been begun months earlier by the Catalan Generalitat, yet under the Negrín regime the Catalanists saw their own sphere of autonomy shrink rapidly. During the first year of the civil war Catalonia had failed to provide its share of assistance to the military effort, and during the second half of the war Catalan autonomy was honored only in the breach. The whole experience was one of disillusion and bitterness for the Catalanists, who at one point walked out of the Negrín government.

In 1937–1938 the Communists exercised general hegemony in the politics, military affairs, and propaganda of the leftist zone, but the wartime Republican government never became a Communist regime. Soviet policy was eager to avoid giving the appearance of a Communist-controlled state in Spain. That would have completed the alienation of the lower middle classes in Spain and of most opinion in Britain and France at a time when support from all these elements was vital to the international situation. The Republican government remained a multiparty regime (exclusively of the left) under general Communist tutelage but not complete Communist control.

The Communists and most other left groups hailed it as a "people's republic," a progressivist leftist regime that had eliminated all conservative influence and major capitalist economic power, as well as that of the church. This gave a new twist to the phrase *República popular,* used before the war by the middle class left to mean a "people's" or "popular" republic standing for constitutional democracy in the interests of the majority of the population. The Communists used "people's republic" to mean a left-wing transition regime that would lead to the worker-peasant dictatorship, the first such regime in modern Europe. After 1945, when hybrid "people's democracies" were instituted in the east-central European countries occupied by the Red Army, they pointed to the Spanish regime of Negrín as their predecessor.

The Military Struggle

Militarily, the Spanish Civil War may be divided into eight phases: 1) the rebellion and taking up of positions, July 17-30, 1936; 2) the Nationalist march from the south, August-October 1936; 3) the battles around Madrid, November 1936-March 1937, which ended in stalemate; 4) the Nationalist conquest of the northern Republican zone, April-October 1937, which tilted the balance of power; 5) the Republican offensives in Aragón, October-December 1937, and the ensuing Nationalist counteroffensive of January-February 1938; 6) the Nationalist offensive in Aragón, March-June 1938, which divided the remaining leftist zone in two; 7) the Battle of the Ebro, July-November 1938; and 8) the Nationalist conquest of Catalonia, December 1938-February 1939, leading to the end of the war at the close of March 1939.

The beginning struggle gave the left control of most of the large cities, the center, the east, and most of the south, as well as the greater part of the northern coast. The rebels gained control of approximately one-third of peninsular Spain, mainly in the north-center and west, with a toehold in the extreme south from Córdoba to Cádiz. At first, nearly half the police and regular army remained with the nominal Republican authorities, and they were put to effective use against the rebels during the first days. Organized forces were all distrusted by the extreme left, however, and after two weeks most organized units had been dissolved in favor of untrained, poorly led, undisciplined militia units from the left groups.

The main strength of the Nationalists lay in the elite 25,000-man Army of Africa, but leftist control of most of the navy and the Moroccan straits, as well as of three-quarters of the air force, at first made it impossible to move these forces across to the peninsula. The first Italian and German aerial assistance, some forty planes, facilitated the beginning of the aerial (and later the naval) convoy of troops to Spain at the close of July. Poor leadership and organization prevented the left from using its naval and air superiority effectively, some of the naval officers having been killed by revolutionary crewmen. Thus a march northward from Seville by the Army of Africa was begun on August 3.

During the next ninety days the Army of Africa, assisted by very small units from other sectors of the rebel army and by right-wing militia, conquered nearly all of southwestern Spain. Militia columns dispatched by the Socialist and Communist organizers of Madrid far outnumbered the forward units of the Nationalists and were in general at least as well equipped, but they were grossly deficient in military leadership, training, and organization. By the first week of November, Franco's small field force of little more than 25,000 combat troops was just outside the capital.

At this crucial moment, when all seemed lost for the left, the defense of Madrid stiffened dramatically. Several factors were responsible: a) the numerical weakness of Franco's units, tired and overextended; b) the greater effectiveness of the Republican militia in fighting from defensive positions, along with the knowledge that there could be no more retreat; c) the arrival of the first sizable shipments of Russian material in October, which gave the left great superiority in armor and continued air control; and d) the appearance of the first two International Brigades of foreign volunteers recruited and organized by the Comintern. After the first attack on Madrid was blunted by mid-November, Franco attempted several flanking attacks to the north in December and January 1937, but these were stopped as well.

During the autumn of 1936 both sides devoted much energy to building up a mass army for what might be a long struggle. On the central front the militia columns began to give way to the first units of a new Republican People's Army, whose organization was extended to nearly all parts of the leftist zone by the close of 1937. However, since the revolutionaries had made it impossible to use most of the thousands of professional army officers within the Republican zone, the People's Army never solved the problem of staffing and leadership, its organizational cohesion remaining distinctly inferior to that of the Nationalist forces.

Meanwhile, increased Russian intervention brought counterescalation from Germany and Italy. Early in November the first units of a new 100-plane German air corps began to arrive, together with more German equipment and military instructors. In December Mussolini began to dispatch regular ground forces to Spain, where 40,000 Italian troops were operating by the spring of 1937. Moreover, the bulk of the equipment of the Nationalist forces was provided by Italy.

The last of the battles in the Madrid region occurred in February and March 1937, when two more Nationalist offensives, one to the south across the Jarama, the other to the northeast in the Guadalajara region, were halted by the Republican defense.

Failure to conquer Madrid directly led Franco to open the fourth phase of the war—Nationalist conquest of the northern Republican zone in the spring and summer of 1937. Since July 1936 the provinces of Asturias, Santander, and Vizcaya (the latter, together with western Guipuzcoa, making up the newly autonomous Euzkadi) had been separated from the main Republican territory. They never formed a unified district but were governed by revolutionary committees in Asturias and Santander and by the Basque regime in Vizcaya. Vizcaya and Asturias contained the bulk of the heavy industry in the Republican zone and were a great prize. In the offensive that began in April 1937, Franco was able to conquer each of the three main regions of the northern Republican zone in isolation, concentrating his forces against them one at a time. Completion of their occupation in October 1937 greatly increased the economic and human resources of the Nationalist zone and shifted the balance of the war.

The major Republican offensives began in July 1937 with a full-scale assault at Brunete, northwest of Madrid, by the best units of the new People's Army. Its object was to relieve pressure on the north, but the Republican forces lacked leadership and cohesion in open offensive maneuvers. The attack was a failure, temporarily exhausted the People's Army, and left it without further means of support for the north.

The next Republican offensive was launched far to the northeast against the thinly held Nationalist lines in Aragón. After initial successes, it, too, ground to a halt. Nonetheless, following the loss of the north, the People's Army command tried to keep the initiative and throw Franco off balance before he could launch another major offensive on the central front. The result was the second Republican Aragonese offensive, this time against Teruel, in December 1937. It scored an initial success, knocked the Nationalists off balance, and seized Teruel, the only provincial capital conquered by the People's Army during the war. But Franco regrouped and opened a counteroffensive of his own in January-February 1938 that rewon all the lost territory and once more exhausted the Republican forces.

That opened the way for the great Nationalist offensive in Aragón in the spring of 1938. It cut the Republican zone in two, driving to the Mediterranean at Alcañiz, moving into western Catalonia, and pushing slowly but steadily southward down the coast toward Valencia. At this point, when the People's Army seemed nearly finished, it staged a major comeback. While Franco's strength was directed southward toward Valencia, the Republican forces regrouped and launched a new offensive southwestward across the Ebro. This caught the Nationalists in the rear, forced them to suspend offensive operations, and brought a four-month battle of attrition along the Ebro. When it was over, the last reserves of the People's Army were exhausted. Franco's conquest of Catalonia that began in December 1938 was a rather slow but simple and steady advance against increasingly weak opposition.

Franco's Victory

Franco's primary achievements in the Civil War were to maintain unity among the Nationalists, build an adequate mass military machine, and guarantee enough support from Germany and Italy to sustain his forces. Hitler never made a major commitment to the Spanish struggle. His concern was to use it as a focal point for rallying anti-Communist sentiment throughout western Europe and to divert attention from Germany's own rearmament and expansion. By 1938 he considered withdrawing German support from Spain altogether and leaving the field to Mussolini, who had involved Italy much more deeply. The Italian government was committed as a matter of prestige, particularly after the military stalemate at Guadalajara in March 1937. The bulk of the material for the Nationalist forces was supplied by Italy. Yet, contrary to leftist propaganda, Franco was able to maintain this flow of support without compromising the independence of his regime. Mining concessions had to be made to Germany in 1938, but beyond that the large volume of material from both fascist powers was made essentially as a loan without binding strings attached.

By comparison, Russian assistance to the Republican side began to wane after about nine months, that is, in mid-1937. Stalin's goal was to brace the Republican war effort, increase Communist influence to the point of general hegemony, and through the struggle in Spain hold at bay Germany and Italy while winning support from France for the new Russian policy of collective security. Communist policy within the leftist zone was generally successful. The aim was not to set up an outright Communist regime, which would have been difficult to achieve and would have alienated the western powers, but to make of

Republican Spain a loyal satellite. This had been largely if not completely achieved under the People's Republic of Negrín, but the larger design of Russian policy had been a failure. France and other western countries had not rallied to the so-called anti-fascist struggle in Spain. Hence after mid-1937 Stalin found it imprudent to maintain a significant commitment under parlous circumstances at the opposite end of the continent. The Russian effort was reduced but not altogether ended, for, as in the case of Hitler, it suited Stalin's calculations to keep the Spanish war going as long as possible. Continued leftist resistance in Spain might prove a useful bargaining point for Stalin should direct negotiations with Hitler ever materialize, and conversely, might be a useful lever should war with Germany ever break out.

During 1938, morale in the Republican zone steadily sagged. Those of moderate opinion no longer supported the struggle (if they ever did), while the anarchist extreme left felt that the achievements of the revolution were being sacrificed to the demands of the war and the policies of the Negrín regime. Concessions were made to the moderate middle classes on one hand while controls increased on the other. Similarly, the CNT officially began to give up its traditional revolutionary apoliticism and took steps during 1938 to convert itself into a Spanish Libertarian Movement (MLE) that would function as a regular political party. All the while, anarchists sought an alternative to the Negrín regime.

Military defeat and lack of supplies ground down the Republican troops. Communist hegemony in politics and propaganda increased the malaise of leftists on the home front, many of whom saw no reason to continue to fight for the Negrín government. After the loss of all Catalonia in the winter of 1939 resistance became hopeless, yet the government and Communist leaders insisted on a struggle to the last, their only real hope being that a broader European war might soon break out and rally foreign powers to their aid.

One of the great ironies of the Spanish Civil War was that it ended almost the same way it began, with a rebellion by a minority of the nominally Republican army against the Republican government on the grounds that it was in the process of becoming a Communist dictatorship. In March 1939, leaders of the non-Communist leftist parties in Madrid formed a National Defense Council (almost the same title used by Mola's first rebel council in July 1936) under the anti-Communist commander of the Republic's Madrid garrison, Col. Segismundo Casado. It declared that Negrín had been deposed and it hoped to start negotiations with Franco. While the prime minister and top Communist leaders fled Spain by air, a bitter battle ensued between Communist and non-Communist Republican units in Madrid. The latter won control of the capital, only to surrender unconditionally to Franco at the close of March 1939.

The Nationalists thus won a complete military victory in the most bitter civil war in Spanish history, a war that reflected the major ideological and spiritual conflicts of the twentieth century. Though both sides had relied on foreign material, it had been a war fought essentially by Spaniards. Approximately 2,000,000 men were mobilized by the rival regimes out of a total Spanish population of 25,000,000. Few more than 200,000 were killed as a result of the fighting (some 70,000 Nationalists, 100,000 or more Republicans), but about 100,000 more were killed in political executions. Altogether there had been at least 300,000 violent deaths in Spain, and a great chasm of fear, hatred, and bitterness, as well as of persecution and oppression, had been opened in the country.

27

Portugal under the Salazar Regime

In Portugal, the parliamentary Republic gave way to a conservative, authoritarian Republic through a simple pronunciamiento followed by seven years of institutional change. There was no apocalyptic civil war as in Spain, and the ultimate leader of the new regime was a university professor, not a generalissimo. The move to the right came ten years earlier in Portugal, and in part because of the absence of such clear and almost total polarization as in Spain, the new authoritarian system developed in a framework of institutional continuity. This was the easier because political mobilization and participation in Portugal had been minimal compared with Spain; Portugal had still not experienced mass movements.

The military coup of May 1926 took advantage of the disgruntlement with the dominant liberal elites felt in highly diverse sectors of society. At the time, it was by no means clear that the pronunciamiento had put an end to the liberal parliamentary system. The revolt was supported by most of the army but lacked ideological consistency or clear planning. It was in general a "popular" coup in that the majority of politically conscious elements not associated with the governing group at first accepted it. Forces ranging from the moderate left to the extreme right hoped to benefit from the shift in power, and newspapers of widely varying tendencies hailed the new government.

On June 2, 1926, two days after the coup succeeded, Bernardino Machado resigned the presidency to Mendes Cabeçadas, the sometime Republican naval officer (and antimonarchist conspirator of 1910) who had initiated the revolt. Within a few weeks, however, Cabeçadas was shouldered out by the military for not being sufficiently "apolitical." He was replaced as president and prime minister by General Gomes da Costa, Portugal's prime war hero, veteran of African campaigns and commander of the Portuguese Expeditionary Corps in the World War. Gomes da Costa was, however, in many ways but a simple soldier, subject to amnesia from the fevers contracted in Africa and uncertain in his leadership. Within twenty days he was replaced by General António Oscar de Fragoso Carmona, a senior administrative officer who had led the revolt in southern Portugal.

The new regime had no grand design but set out to govern "apolitically," promising to restore order and establish efficiency and economy in government. Strikes were outlawed and controls were placed on firearms; parliament was dissolved and censorship imposed. The reaction finally occurred in February 1927, when leftists and former Democrats rebelled in Lisbon and Porto. The struggle lasted several days and cost 160 lives before it was put down. This resulted in further tightening of the military regime. Carmona was elected president of the Republic for a special five-year term in a plebiscite held in March 1927. He was then replaced as prime minister by another officer, Col. José Vicente de Freitas.

Of the two main problems facing the dictatorship, public order and public finance, the former was at least being precariously maintained against a multiplicity of petty conspiracies and several more small, sputtering revolts. Yet the financial problems grew worse because of the lack of technical ability of the military regime and the destructive effects of several new manipulative devices. When they applied for a foreign loan, the regime's leaders were astounded to find that Portugal's government and finances were held in such low esteem that the same terms exacted of defeated countries such as Austria and Hungary—international control of part of state finance—would be demanded of them. After it was formed, the Freitas government saw little alternative to turning over state finance to the leading conservative in the field, a professor of political economy at the University of Coimbra named António de Oliveira Salazar.

Born in 1889, Salazar came from a rural lower-middle-class family in northeastern Portugal. He studied in a seminary during his youth but later turned to law and economics. A lifelong bachelor, austere and ascetic in his personal life, Salazar was a pious Catholic and one of the leaders in the Centro Académico da Democracia Cristã

(CADC), a movement of the Catholic intelligentsia founded in 1910. It followed the doctrines of Leo XIII and was more concerned with defending Catholic interests than with promoting democracy. The CADC was strictly practical on the issue of regimes; from the beginning of his academic career Salazar had made it clear that what was needed was a different spirit in public affairs and a new form of civic tutelage rather than a change of regime per se. Elected as one of the three CADC deputies in the 1921 parliament, he resigned his seat after one session in disgust over the corruption and ineptitude of the assembly. During the next five years Salazar began to make a name for himself in conservative circles as a financial expert, and was made finance minister in the dictatorship's first government of June 1926. At that time he found that little could be done without drastic change, and resigned when the regime refused to give him full veto power over financial measures. His recall in 1928 was a recognition of the ineffectuality of the military regime and the overriding need for strong, competent direction of finance. In 1928 Salazar was granted the full veto power over finance that he had demanded earlier, and within a year he managed to balance the budget, at least on paper, and eliminate the floating debt. Public employees were reduced in number and expenditures in most branches of state administration significantly lowered. Taxes were raised slightly, the efficiency of their collection and administration much improved, and strict controls placed on credit and foreign trade. By the beginning of 1930 Salazar had become the indispensable strong man of the government.

Three and a half years after its inception the Portuguese regime was uncertain and divided over the course it should pursue. Collapse of the Primo de Rivera government in Spain raised new doubts about the future of the Portuguese dictatorship. Its original minimal program had been more or less completed, but what lay beyond that was uncertain. Some of the military favored continuation of a sort of military dictatorship with a corporate social and economic system in the fashion of Italy and Spain; others preferred a more strongly institutionalized presidential republic that could return to normalcy. The CADC had always had a doctrine of Catholic corporatism, and the first leaders of the regime had mentioned a corporate form of organization in their earliest announcements. The monarchist minority was divided between constitutionalists and authoritarians, the main expression of the latter being the radical Integralismo Lusitano, modeled on the Action Française and with considerable support in the universities, particularly Coimbra, and among the intelligentsia. The arbiter of the regime was its president, General Carmona, who showed himself not lacking in political talent as he maneuvered among sectors of the military and their civilian supporters. The government had been reorganized under yet another general, Ivens Ferraz, in mid-1929, but after internal disagreement led to its breakdown at the beginning of 1930 the new prime minister, Gen. Domingos Oliveira, formed a cabinet that represented an almost complete victory for Salazar's policies.

Opposition centered on three aspects of the regime, the political, economic, and religious. All the more liberal elements opposed continuation of authoritarian rule; vocal elements among the lower classes and some business leaders were restive about the financial restrictions that raised the cost of some staples and tended to discourage new production and expansion; anticlericals both within the army and among civilians resented the relaxation of all forms of restriction against Catholicism on which Salazar had insisted. In addition, many officers resented the great influence of a civilian minister on a military regime. However Carmona, a Catholic, had gone along with Salazar on nearly all the key issues, while balancing intradictatorship internal politics between monarchists and republicans, clericals and anticlericals. On the basis of Salazar's ideas and policies and Carmona's political arbitration, the dictatorship finally began to take doctrinal and institutional form, as defined by Salazar in key speeches of May 28 and July 30, 1930. He indicated that the regime would create a corporate republic based on a strong state. Such a system would transcend military dictatorship, and grounded in patriotic unity and the moral doctrines of Catholic corporatism, provide cooperation and stability without indulging in the glorification of authoritarian rule found in Fascist Italy or Bolshevist Russia. An amorphous political organization, the National Union, was then formed along the lines of Primo de Rivera's late Patriotic Union, to provide semiorganized citizen support for the regime.

Antigovernment conspiracies and revolts persisted. A plot by the Democrats and other groups was aborted in mid-1930, but Madeira, the Azores, and Portuguese Guinea were held briefly by military rebels in April 1931. An uprising in Lisbon in August 1931, the twenty-third antigovernment revolt (not counting minor conspiracies and bombings) in twenty-one years, cost eighty lives before it was put down.

One of the great strengths of the dictatorship lay in the fact that most Portuguese opinion was weary of politics and after the vicissitudes of two decades was largely willing to accept a regime that could bring peace and stability. Despite the pressure which his financial policies placed on much of the population, especially the lower classes, Salazar pursued his program with little deterrence, completing the balancing of state finances and the stabilization of Portuguese currency. In July 1932 his tutelage of the government finally became official when he replaced the ailing Domingos Oliveira as prime minister. The way had been cleared for the institutionalization of the Portuguese "New State."

The new Portuguese constitution of 1933 was anounced as the "first corporate constitution in the world," which in a formal sense it was. It provided for a president elected for a seven-year term by an electorate of literate adult males or males paying at least 100 escudos annually in taxes, as well as literate adult women who either paid 200 escudos in taxes or had a secondary education. This meant an electorate of slightly more than 1,200,000 in a country of 7,000,000. The president held authority to appoint the prime minister, as well as the rest of the cabinet on the prime minister's recommendation, and the government was made responsible to the president, not the national assembly. The national assembly was to be composed of 120 deputies chosen for a term of four years. Both the government and the assembly had the right to initiate legislation, but the assembly could not initiate measures that required new expenditure or that reduced state income. Civil governors of the eighteen provincial districts and heads of municipal councils were to be named by the central executive, as they had been under the constitutional monarchy. Finally, the constitution of the New State provided for the selection of a consultative "Corporate Chamber" in lieu of a senate, chosen by cultural and professional associations and economic groups. This constitution represented Salazar's concept of a system of order and stability that would foster the established national interests without adopting overt statism or formal authoritarianism. Some have noted that the new charter bore a strong resemblance to the original corporative doctrine first defined by the Catholic Union of Fribourg in 1884. After a plebiscite in March 1933 it was announced that 60 percent of the eligible voters had cast ballots in favor of the new constitution.

Establishment of the Estado Novo constitution was met by a successful military and civilian revolt in Madeira and the Azores which spread almost immediately to Cape Verde and the west African possessions. Though it was snuffed out in Africa, it was sustained for a month in the Atlantic islands, until finally put down by a special expedition from the mainland. By that time the only formidable rivals of Salazar's leadership were several potentially dissident groups in the military, some of whom felt that the army did not enjoy sufficient influence or reward under the New State. A minor attempt at military revolt in August 1933 led to reorganization of the cabinet; a subsequent petty mutiny at Bragança in October was probably motivated by liberal conspiratorial residues in the military.

By the time that the New State was inaugurated, the old circles of lower-middle-class radicalism had become disheartened and disarticulated. The other remaining opposition lay in the clandestine labor movements: the syndicalist CGT, dominated by the Portuguese anarchist FARP; the socialist FOP (Portuguese Worker Federation); and the small Communist Inter-Syndical Commission. The labor system of the new state was defined by the National Labor Statute of September 1933 that reaffirmed the ban on strikes (and lockouts), formed workers into official syndicates, regulated their activities, and defined their legal and bargaining relationship with the "guilds" of employers that were to be organized. The statute was more directly influenced by the Italian Fascist system than was the constitution and was aimed mainly at workers in the cities, who were more troublesome. The response was an attempt at general strike and insurrection on January 18, 1934, carried out mainly by the anarcho-syndicalists, that enjoyed fleeting success only at Coimbra. Events were precipitated by Communist terrorism, and though the Communists refused to cooperate with the anarcho-syndicalists in the main insurrection, the whole effort was labeled bolshevist and led to renewed, more effective repression.

Formation of the New State and suppression of the left opened the question of the internal politics of the regime; political organizations had not arisen to fill the void left by the elimination of the old groups. A variety of small nationalist societies and youth groups had been formed in recent years, but the National Union had not taken effective shape and the roots of the liberal cliques and local liberal notables survived in sectors of Portuguese society. The most serious of the new nationalist groups was the National Syndicalist movement, founded in 1932 and to become the principal exponent of Portuguese fascism. The National Syndicalists were led by former Integralists who had moved in a radical direction in their stress on social issues and the lower classes. Their head, Rolão Preto, was known to be a friend of Salazar, and the movement burgeoned under the apparent benevolence of the regime. As the most dynamic and "modern" of the nationalist groups its support grew rapidly; by 1934 the National Syndicalist leaders claimed 50,000 members—a number which if valid would have represented a major mobilization in Portugal—and eighteen newspapers, as well as the support of several hundred army officers. Like their Spanish counterparts, the National Syndicalists adopted the blue shirt as their insignia and touted their social fascism as the logical goal of a modern authoritarian nationalist regime. Thus the Blue Shirts threatened the leadership, goals, and equilibrium of the New State within a year of its founding.

Salazar finally took action in June 1934, exiling Preto and purging the Blue Shirt leadership. On the following July 29 Salazar denounced the National Syndicalists as "inspired by certain foreign models" and singled out their "exaltation of youth, and the cult of force through direct action, the principle of the superiority of state political power in social life, [and] the propensity for organizing masses behind a single leader"* as fundamental differences between fascism and the Catholic corporatism of the New State. Soon afterward the remaining National Syndicalists announced their dissolution as a separate party in order to incorporate themselves into the government's National Union. Elections under the new constitution were then held in December 1934 without opposition of any kind, and Carmona was subsequently reelected to a formal seven-year term as president, his moderating functions now having been almost entirely assumed by Salazar. In March 1935, after reports of new conspiracies by Masonic groups, all secret societies were outlawed in Portugal. The final anticlimactic round in the consolidation of the regime occurred in September 1935, when a few hard-core National Syndicalists, a small group of disgruntled army officers, and a handful of anarcho-syndicalists attempted an armed revolt in Lisbon that was easily crushed.

Salazar faced his first major problem in foreign affairs with the outbreak of the Spanish Civil War. Till that time official relations between the Portuguese authoritarian state and the Spanish Republic had been quite correct, though the latter permitted its leftist associates to assist efforts at overthrow of the former and the former permitted Spanish rightists to live and operate on Portuguese territory. The Portuguese government immediately grasped what was at stake in the Spanish contest and had every reason to fear the long-range consequences of a victory for the revolutionary left. Within little more than a week it agreed to cooperate with the Spanish insurgents; Portuguese transportation and communications facilities were vital in the Nationalist war effort. Nonetheless, Salazar adhered to the international nonintervention agreement, having no intention of making Portugal a belligerent and recognizing that nonintervention was a convenient diplomatic device for avoiding further complications. Subsequently, a contingent of Portuguese enlisted in the Nationalist forces. At the end of the war the government announced that there had been 18,000 volunteers and more than 8,000 casualties. Conversely, in September 1936 the crews of two small Portuguese warships mutinied and tried to join the Spanish left.

The Spanish war resulted in a radicalization of the Portuguese regime. Though Salazar declared his opposition to all the "grand heresies" of the contemporary world, including nazism and fascism as well as communism and materialism, new security and mobilization measures were carried out. In September 1936 the regime announced

* Jacques Ploncard d'Assac, *Salazar* (Paris, 1967), p. 107.

creation of a Portuguese Legion, trained by reserve army officers, as a special auxiliary militia system. Soon afterward a general youth organization, the Mocidade, was established on a compulsory basis to train all school children through university years in civic discipline and extracurricular activity, though it was never extended to the entire school population. A loyalty oath was introduced for state employees, and a purge was conducted in the civil service and universities, discharging employees of doubtful reliability. For the first time in the history of the regime an official state culture and propaganda agency was established. The response of the opposition was a bomb that exploded some ten feet from Salazar on July 4, 1937, deafening his chauffeur but leaving its target unharmed.

From the beginning of the Spanish war, the Portuguese government alone of all powers save the Soviet Union made it perfectly clear which side it supported. Though Franco's regime was not officially recognized, on December 1937 Salazar sent a special delegate to the Nationalist government and at the close of the war signed a treaty of friendship with it. At the same time the historic alliance with Britain was retained, and as the danger of war with Germany increased, the British government made clear its acceptance of the "independent" position of the Portuguese state.

Salazar was careful to avoid involvement in the outbreak and development of the Second World War. In 1937 official relations had been broken with Czechoslovakia, but only after the Czech government had for political reasons forced cancellation of an arms contract negotiated by Czech industry. Salazar shared Franco's dismay over the German invasion of Poland; after the fall of France, the two peninsular governments added an additional protocol in July 1940 to their treaty of friendship and nonagression, providing for mutual consultation to preserve their independence and integrity. Unlike Spain, Portugal never felt real pressure to enter the war. The British alliance, from the vantage point of neutrality, gave Portugal a special relationship to the allied powers that was also of help to Spain. In September 1943 Salazar granted Britain and the United States the use of military bases in the Azores, and in 1944 finally curtailed shipment of certain strategic materials, mainly wolfram, to Germany. The two remaining Far Eastern possessions, Macau and Timor, were both occupied by Japan in 1942 but recovered at war's end. After the conclusion of the conflict, the Portuguese regime was made a target of the international Communist "antifascist" campaign, along with Spain, Argentina, Sweden, and Switzerland. However, retention of the form of a republican parliamentary system stood the regime in good stead, and pressure against Portugal never became extreme.

One major internal problem that was finally regulated during the war years was that of religion, settled by an official concordat with the Vatican in 1940. Republican separation of church and state was maintained, but the state restored nearly all privileges enjoyed by the church under the monarchy, including educational and moral jurisdiction and financial support. This completed the process of reaffirmation of Catholicism begun by the government in 1928 and in religious society by the Fátima experience of 1917. It reversed the anticlerical and eventually anti-Catholic trend of Portuguese history from 1760 to 1925.

In October 1945 Salazar announced a drastic liberalization program designed to make Portugal appear in step with the democratic swing of events in the immediate postwar period. These measures included a general political amnesty, restoration of press freedom, curtailment of legal repression, and a promised introduction of the right of habeas corpus. Parliamentary elections were announced, and the opposition formed a broad Movement of Democratic Unity based in Porto with participation that ranged from ultra-Catholics and fringe elements of the extreme right all the way to the Portuguese Communist party. The nominal list of electors, however, was tightly controlled by the government, which announced that some 900,000 people were eligible to vote, a decrease of 25 percent since 1933 in an expanding population. The opposition then withdrew and boycotted the elections, in which the government announced that 56 percent of registered voters cast their ballots for the official ticket. Restrictions that had been temporarily lifted were then increasingly reimposed. The regime easily put down a minor military revolt in October 1946, but the Lisbon dockworkers' strike of April 1947 proved more difficult to handle and was accompanied by unrest in the armed forces. A potentially far-reaching plot uncovered in the military command involved both liberals and monarchists; six general officers were imprisoned, including the aging Mendes Cabeçadas, who had played a major role in the overthrow of the two preceding regimes in 1910 and 1926.

Despite the essentially authoritarian character of the regime, Portugal, unlike Spain, was accepted into both the Marshall Plan (1947-1948) and the North Atlantic Treaty Organization (1949). As a member, it did what it could to secure the admission of Spain to NATO, but to no avail. The first direct shipments of Marshall Plan aid did not reach Portugal until 1950.

During the principal years of the Cold War there was no fundamental change in the nature or structure of the Estado Novo. An opposition candidate, the elderly liberal Gen. Norton de Matos, stood against Carmona for the first time in the presidential election of 1949 but withdrew before the balloting on the grounds of repression and discrimination. Carmona died in 1951 and was succeeded as president by Gen. Craveiro Lopes, a man closely tied to the regime and a former commander of Portuguese volunteers in the Spanish Civil War. Censorship was maintained save for a brief thirty-day period before each election, and all but a tiny handful of opposition candidates invariably withdrew before balloting began. The major exception occurred in the presidential election of 1958. Salazar and other top figures were dissatisfied with Craveiro Lopes's tenure as president, because of his willingness to tolerate pressures for liberalization. He was replaced as government (National Union) candidate by the reliable naval minister, Admiral Américo Tomás. The opposition candidate was an emotional, quixotic former government collaborator, Gen. Humberto Delgado, who refused to withdraw despite efforts at repression, and according to official announcement received one-fourth of the approximately one million votes cast. In 1959, a year after Tomás's election, the choice of the president was switched from direct elections to indirect selection by the two parliamentary bodies and representatives of provincial municipal councils.

The Legion was maintained as an elite militia of the regime. It was given naval and air arms, was placed in charge of civil defense, and later received counterinsurgency training. As a special force recruited on the basis of political qualification, it was considered a more reliable instrument of the regime than the semi-autonomous army. The youth organization, the Mocidade, was limited to children between seven and fourteen (excluding some of the rural areas), but continued to receive special perquisites, including a modicum of political instruction and some paramilitary training for older boys.

The basic goal of the regime was depoliticization, which was the more easily achieved since most of the people had never become politically conscious anyway. Hence the joke about the diversion of Portuguese interest toward the "three *F*s": Fátima, football, and fado. Opposition, such as it was, remained limited to small groups of students and intellectuals and a handful of middle class activists and military men.

Repression was efficiently handled by security forces, the three most important of which were the secret police (PIDE), the urban police (PSP), and the Guarda Nacional Republicana, converted into a rural constabulary along the lines of the Spanish Civil Guard. Between 1948 and 1959 the annual number of prosecutions for illicit political activity oscillated between 700 and 2,000.

Social and Economic Development

The social structure of Portugal has changed more slowly than that of any other west European country save perhaps Ireland, but population increase in the twentieth century has been rapid:

1900	5,423,000
1920	6,032,991
1930	6,825,883
1940	7,722,152
1950	8,441,312 (incl. 584,399 in the islands)
1970	9,800,000 (approx.)

The rate of population growth in the middle decades was greater than that of Spain, explained in part by the peace and continuity in Portuguese society. Though infant mortality in Portugal was cut in half between 1920 and 1960, neither the birth rate nor the death rate has dropped as rapidly as in other west European countries:

	Portuguese birth rate per 1,000	*Death rate per 1,000*
1900	31.0	20.3
1920	32.2	22.8
1940	24.6	16.1
1950	24.8	12.6
1958	23.6	10.2

Figures in both categories are higher in the islands than in mainland Portugal.

The illiteracy rates remained the highest in Europe outside parts of the Balkans. Illiteracy among those above seven years of age declined through the following levels:

1911	70 percent
1920	66
1930	61
1940	49
1950	40

By 1970 it was estimated to be a little more than 15 percent.

Agriculture, the base of the Portuguese economy and society, changed very little during the first generation of the Estado Novo. The strength of the Portuguese rural economy has always been that its poverty is, at least in the northern half of the country, an evenly distributed poverty. Though the proportion of land held in large estates of more than 100 hectares is approximately the same as in Spain—roughly 50 percent—the proportion of Portuguese farmland owned in small properties of 10 hectares and less is one and a quarter times greater in Portugal than in Spain (32.2 percent compared with

Table 33.   Portuguese Farm Properties by Categories of Size, c. 1960

Size in hectares	Percent of all farms	Percent of all farm area
Up to 10	94.9	32.2
Over 10 but less than 200	4.8	28.7
Over 200	.3	39.0

Source: Relatorio Final Preparatorio do II Plano de Fomento, vol. 2, in V. X. Pintado, Structure and Growth of the Portuguese Economy (EFTA, 1964), p. 63.

14.73 percent). This distribution of property, combined with traditional culture and the absence of new ideas, had been the foundation of the stability and quiescence of the apolitical peasantry. Hence the regime has been eager to protect the structure of rural society, showing little inclination to expose it to the effects of rapid change or development.

As of 1952-1954 there were 853,568 agricultural units in Portugal, divided into the following categories of exploitation:

Farmed by owner	525,335
Rented	131,320
Share-cropped	28,134
Mixed	168,779
	853,568

The fractionalization of agrarian cultivation units is impressive, as indicated in table 34. A law of 1926 prohibited subdivision of any property of less than one hectare, but subdivision of only slightly larger properties has continued steadily, and table 34 if anything is incomplete. The actual number of landholders is, however, considerably smaller than the number of cultivation units, as indicated in table 35.

Between 1874 and 1957, land under cultivation increased approximately 50 percent, from 4,598,500 to 6,630,000 hectares. The latter figure represents approximately three-quarters of the 8,906,000 hectares of land in Portugal, but 40 percent (or about 2,500,000 hectares) is partially productive forest land. Only 668,000 hectares are classified as completely unfit for any productive use. As in the nineteenth century, most of the land brought into new use lies in central and southern Portugal, and the extension of cultivation has been most notable in wheat, vineyards, and olives.

In 1950 the distribution between the employment sectors of both the Spanish and Portuguese economies resembled those of France

Table 34. *Size of Portuguese Cultivation Units in Hectares*

Size of unit	No. of properties
to .25	130,038
.25-.5	112,554
.51-1.	157,877
1.1-3.	238,519
3.1-5	68,914
5.1-10	52,921
10.1-20	22,872
20.1-50	10,874
50.1-100	3,047
100.1-200	1,516
200.1-500	1,182
500.1-1000	500
1000.1-2500	276
2500.1-5000	61
5000.1-10,000	8
10,000.1-20,000	3

Source: Albert Pasquier, *L'Economie du Portugal* (Paris, 1962), p. 72.

Table 35. *Dispersion of Portuguese Agricultural Properties, 1952-1954*

No. of holdings in farm	Percent of all landowners
1	24.2
2 noncontiguous	15.3
3-5 noncontiguous	28.2
6-10 noncontiguous	18.7
11-20 noncontiguous	9.6
more than 20 noncontiguous	4.0

Source: INE, *Inquérito às Explorações Agrícolas do Continente,* vol. 3, in Pintado, p. 64.

nearly 80 years earlier. Since 1950, employment in the primary sector has declined rapidly in both countries and at approximately the same rate. According to government statistics, employment of the Portuguese labor force has changed as follows:

Sector	1940	1950	1960	1970
Primary	49.3	48.4	42.8	29.8
Secondary	20.4	24.9	29.5	36.7
Tertiary	30.3	26.7	27.7	33.5

The financial policies of the first decade of the regime bore heavily on the lower classes, temporarily decreasing the standard of living and probably hampering Portuguese production. As indicated earlier, the autonomous trade unions were eventually broken up after 1926 and replaced by official syndicates. State syndical regulations were promulgated in 1933, but syndicates were not organized for all branches of urban labor until the end of the decade. At best they would have affected only a minority of the population, for in 1940 only 25 percent of the Portuguese people lived in cities of 10,000 or more inhabitants. For most of the lower classes—rural laborers and dwarfholders—the regime planned local "Casas do Povo" in each rural district to set up savings accounts and administer insurance benefits. By 1959 there were 319 syndicates with 894,845 members, but only 570 rural Casas do Povo with 480,000 members. Though a total of 45 percent of the active population was enrolled by that time, this included only about 20 percent of the rural population.

By 1959, 501 employers' guilds had been organized: 234 in agriculture, 169 in commerce, and 43 in industry. In most branches of enterprise guilds were not compulsory, and none had been formed in either textiles or metallurgy; the Estado Novo was for a long time a corporative state without full state economic corporations. The first full corporations to coordinate employers' guilds and workers' syndicates were not organized until 1956.

In 1945, neutral Portugal presented a pleasant and in some respects prosperous-looking contrast to most of devastated Europe. Without war damage and with foreign credits earned by shipments to belligerent powers, the country was in the most favorable economic position vis-à-vis western Europe that it had seen in many generations. This did not survive long into the postwar period. By the early 1950s, with the recovery of western Europe under way (including even, to some extent, Spain), it became clear that the real gap between the Portu-

Table 36.   *Expansion of Cultivated Area by Products, Portugal,*
1874–1957 (in hectares)

	1874	1957
Wheat	260,000	814,000
Corn	520,000	483,000
Rice	7,000	37,000
Vineyard	204,000	360,000
Olives	200,000	420,000
Oak groves	370,000	1,000,000
Pine groves	210,000	1,170,000

Source: Virginia Rau, *Estudos de história económica* (Lisbon, 1961), p. 30.

Table 37. General Index of Portuguese Industrial Production, 1933-1962
(1953 = 100)

1933	43	1947	80	1952	101	1957	137	1960	172
1943	60	1948	88	1953	100	1958	147	1961	186
1944	62	1949	84	1954	111	1959	155	1962	192
1945	65	1950	91	1955	119				
1946	75	1951	102	1956	130				

Source: Pintado, p. 164.

Table 38.   Portuguese Economic Growth, 1962-1969
(1963 = 100)

	1962	1964	1965	1966	1967	1968	1969
General Industrial Index	92	112	119	127	134	142	154
Mining	115	96	101	102	112	115	106
Manufacturing	92	112	119	127	135	143	154
Electricity	89	111	108	130	138	143	157
Agriculture	95	—	—	88	99	98	91

Source: *United Nations Statistical Yearbook,* 1970.

guese and west European norm had not been reduced. Industrial production had made up only 31 percent of the Portuguese gross national product in 1938 and rose very slowly to 33.7 in 1953 (at which time the corresponding figure in France was nearly 45 percent).

Consequently in 1953 the Portuguese government adopted its first official plan for national economic development, embracing the six years 1953-1958. It emphasized development of basic facilities (such as electric power) and relied largely on domestic financing, stipulating that 60 percent of new investment would be provided by public capital. The plan stimulated industrial growth to the rate of 8 percent a year but fell short of its goals in agriculture. The second six-year plan, for 1959-1964, stressed industry and recruited 25 percent of its capital from abroad, maintaining the same industrial growth rate on a slightly more sophisticated plane. The third, or interim, plan, covering only the years 1965-1967, emphasized producing for export, while the fourth development plan for 1968-1973 returned to the stress on industrial expansion.

Portuguese industry sustained a commendable growth rate through the 1960s, as indicated in tables 37 and 38. The gross national income and real wages for workers and farm laborers also increased considerably. Between 1961 and 1967 the rise in real wages for industrial workers was approximately 4 percent a year and that for farm laborers even more.

Nevertheless the Portuguese growth rate was considerably below

Table 39. Economic Growth in Portugal Compared with
Other South European Nations

	GNP per capita	Rate of growth of GNP	
	1961	1938-58	1953-57
Portugal	$301	3.0	4.5
Spain	303	3.3	6.0
South Italy	305	—	4.1
Greece	435	1.2	6.9
Turkey	210	3.5	2.6
Yugoslavia	266	4.4	10.5

	Rates of Investment as Percentage of GNP		
	1952-56	1957-61	1952-61
Portugal	14.5	17.7	16.3
Spain	15.6	17.5	16.6
South Italy	24.2	24.6	24.5
Greece	14.6	17.6	16.3
Turkey	13.6	14.6	14.3
Yugoslavia	27.5	28.6	28.2

Source: Pintado, pp. 14, 19, 22.

that of Spain, with its greater resources and broader market. Portuguese per capita income, despite recent increases, has remained about one-quarter lower than the Spanish and is still far and away the poorest in western Europe. As in Spain, economic expansion is not yet sufficient to absorb population increase and the results of social and technological transformation.

As in Spain and most other developing countries, agriculture has been neglected and continues to do poorly. Though there has been a steady increase in mechanization, this is not directly reflected in a proportionate rise in productivity. Agricultural production declined in 1958-1959, and rose at a rate of less than 1 percent a year for the entire period of the first two plans. During the mid-1960s it remained static.

Portuguese industry and finance have become increasingly concentrated, as is true in most developing economies. By 1959, 45 percent of the industrial labor force still worked in shops with 10 or fewer employees, but 44 percent worked in plants with more than 100 employees each. Moreover, the top 1 percent of all enterprises in

Table 40. Rates of Change of Personal Consumption, 1950-1960

| | Annual rate of growth in percentages | | Ratio of column 1 to column 2 |
	Per capita consumption	Per capita GNP	
Czechoslovakia	1.24	4.3	.28
Poland	3.00	3.0	1.00
Hungary	3.10	3.5	.89
France	3.06	3.4	.90
Greece	3.99	5.27	.76
Italy	3.56	5.15	.70
Portugal (1952-60)	3.24	3.02	1.07
West Germany	6.49	6.05	1.07
United States	1.61	1.17	1.38

Source: V. Holesovsky, "Personal Consumption in Czechoslovakia, Hungary and Poland, 1950-1960: A Comparison," *Slavic Review* 24, no. 4 (Dec., 1968): 622-35.

industry and services earned 42 percent of the income in those sectors, while the small firms making up 83 percent of all enterprises earned less than 11 percent. The six largest banks held approximately 60 percent of Portuguese deposits and credit.

As noted in table 40, the ratio of consumption to production was comparatively high in the Portuguese economy during the 1950s and 60s. Though the distribution of consumption has been somewhat less egalitarian than in certain other west European countries, this nonetheless indicates a not inconsiderable diversion of national income to the lower classes. A weak economy presumably cannot do otherwise if it is to maintain the most minimal subsistance level, yet this also results in a slower rate of investment. Another feature of the Portuguese system lightening somewhat the burden of the lower classes is that it has had a nominally more progressive tax structure than the three larger countries of southwestern Europe. By 1960, 35.7 percent of Portuguese state income was derived from direct taxes, compared with only 27.5 percent in France.

During the second half of the Salazar era there was increased investment in education. By the 1960s schools, for the first time in Portuguese history, became available for nearly all children, though a very small minority were still unprovided for. By 1970 illiteracy was estimated at slightly more than 15 percent, and less than 8 percent among adults under forty.

One of the most remarkable things about contemporary Portuguese society is the extent to which, despite population growth and economic development, it has remained basically rural. As recently as 1950 over half the workers in industry and construction lived in very small country towns with fewer than 2,000 inhabitants. Since then the rate of urbanization has increased, but only slowly when compared with other countries. By 1958 only 16.4 percent of all Portuguese lived in genuine cities, of 20,000 or more, whereas 39.8 percent of Spain's population lived in cities.

Portuguese rural society has produced a steady population surplus for the past century, but the bulk of it has emigrated overseas rather than moved to the cities. Since 1945 nearly one million people have left Portugal, and the rate of departure has accelerated since 1961. Only 22 percent of all rural migrants during the decade 1950–1960 moved to Portuguese cities. Most have sought cheap industrial jobs in France and other advanced west European countries; it has been said that by 1970 the greater Paris district had the third, or even the second, largest Portuguese urban population in Europe. After Porto, the largest Portuguese urban concentration under Portuguese domin-ion is found in the Angolan capital of Luanda.

Recent Portuguese history and social structure have shown a greater continuity than those of any other country in Europe. As Herminio Martins has written,

> it is one of the few European nations which within the last forty years has failed to experience civil war or defeat and occupation by another power or both. Neither has it experienced major inflation-ary bursts or major balance of payments crises. Urbanization, in-dustrialization, increases in media density, access to secondary and higher education and the granting of minimal social rights have kept pace in a fairly synchronized and harmonious fashion.[*]

Thus the Salazar regime has managed to implement its leader's insis-tence upon conservation and continuity. Portuguese social structure since 1930 has been altered comparatively less than that of any other European country. Only one new major source of pressure has emerged in recent years, the rebellion in the African territories.

Portuguese Africa

The expansion and tightening of Portuguese control in Africa is not merely a product of the Estado Novo but has its roots in the late Republican period. Though the Republican government had made an effort to decentralize government in the overseas territories, its main

---

[*] H. Martins, "Portugal," in *Contemporary Europe: Class Status and Power,* ed. M. S. Archer and S. Giner (London, 1971), p. 84.

accomplishment was to regularize administration and place each major territory under its own high commissioner, who dominated local affairs much more thoroughly than before. An example was the most important high commissioner of early twentieth century Angola, Gen. José Norton de Matos (Salazar's later adversary for the government leadership), who administered the region from 1921 to 1923. It was during his regime that the local press and political groups were brought under tight government control. It was also under the Republic that the requirement of the *caderneta* (labor notebook) for each native worker was fully developed. Angola in particular was wracked by persistent petty revolts between 1910 and 1922. Pacification of inland Angola and Moçambique was not completed until the mid-1930s, and during that period the nineteenth-century ideal of potential Portuguese citizenship for the African population was given up.

By 1929 a clear line had been drawn between the *indigenato,* or native population, and the tiny minority of *assimilados* literate in Portuguese. The subsequent Colonial Act of 1930 recategorized the overseas as colonies instead of the provinces they had been up to that time, though a later measure of 1951 changed the classification to overseas provinces. The original goal of the Estado Novo was to make Portuguese Africa self-sufficient and eliminate the drain on the central budget. A small amount of foreign capital was attracted, but the pace of development was slow. Output of raw materials and agrarian exports, particularly in Angola, began to increase rapidly only after 1945 with the great expansion of coffee production. In 1950 only 30,000 of the more than 4,000,000 native inhabitants of Angola had become assimilados, and by the end of that decade schools had been provided for no more than 10 percent of the children. Portuguese immigration had increased considerably but was still less than 5 percent of the population in Angola and only about 2 percent in Moçambique. Portuguese Africa seemed at first untouched by the movement toward independence in other colonial regions, but an increase in minor disorders during the late 1950s led to a tightening of security.

The storm finally broke in 1961 when armed revolt erupted in northwestern Angola. There was considerable opinion in the Portuguese government in favor of avoiding further complications by pulling out as Britain, France, and Belgium had done elsewhere. Salazar, however, stood firm, though he had to quell an incipient military revolt to do so. Reinforcements were rushed to Angola, and the insurgency was confined to one tribal group in the northwest. Meanwhile the Indian government seized the opportunity to occupy Goa and the last remaining Portuguese possessions on the Indian coast.

There were native insurrections in Portuguese Guinea in 1962 and in Moçambique in 1964. The communist and third-world blocs mustered all their propaganda resources against the Portuguese regime. In 1965 the Security Council of the United Nations (to which Portugal had been admitted nine years earlier) demanded that Portugal grant independence to its African territories, and the General Assembly urged that diplomatic and commercial relations with Portugal be severed. Subsequently, one of the two remaining Portuguese outposts in east Asia, Macau, was made a virtual protectorate by China in 1967.

Through this tempest the Portutuese government made clear its determination to stand fast in Africa. Officially it was argued that Portugal had never been racist but had always encouraged assimilation and miscegenation, which was partly but not fully true. Beyond Portugal's "mission," leaders of the regime felt that the shock of losing the remainder of the empire would be too severe for the system to survive at home. Major reforms were undertaken in Portuguese Africa in 1961-1962. Equal rights were established nominally for the entire native population, and forced contract labor was abolished. Schools and sanitary facilities were improved and economic development speeded up. It could soon be demonstrated that living standards in Angola were higher than in most surrounding independent African states; meanwhile the growth of Angola's coffee and diamond production and the discovery of oil increased the economic desirability of holding firm.

It is difficult to measure the cost of Portuguese policy. By 1970 few more than 200,000 of 4,800,000 inhabitants of Angola were Portuguese, in Moçambique only 130,000 of 6,600,000, and in Guinea only a handful out of 500,000. In recent years more than 100,000 Portuguese troops have been regularly deployed in counterinsurgency, not counting tens of thousands of native auxiliaries. Portugal has borne a heavier burden of military service than any other west European country. Throughout the history of the regime, the armed forces have taken nearly 40 percent of the budget, but the figure has increased somewhat in recent years and may amount to 7 percent or more of the gross national income of Portugal. Only the firm control of the government in Lisbon, supported by a definite sentiment of nationalist determination among some of the home population, has made the effort possible. Thus the revolts in Angola and Moçambique have been largely contained, though the one in Guinea has been more successful, dominating at least half the countryside in the least important of the three Portuguese African territories.

The Demise of Salazar and the
Continuity of the Regime

In September 1968 a chair collapsed under the seventy-nine-year-old Salazar, who fell heavily, later suffering a stroke that left him in a coma for months. (He did not die until over a year later.) The president, Admiral Tomás, temporarily took over the government, and appointed as the new prime minister Dr. Marcello Caetano, an internationally known jurist and scholar who had held numerous state administrative positions and was considered the leader of the "liberals" within the regime. In 1958 Caetano had been dismissed from the key post of administrative minister of the presidency for being too "advanced," and in 1962 had resigned the rectorship of the University of Lisbon in protest against police intervention. As leader of Portugal in the post-Salazar transition, he proposed to guide the country into a phase of accelerated development and of discreet liberalization. In his first speech to the nation on September 27, 1968, Caetano declared that "fidelity to the doctrine brilliantly taught by Dr. Salazar should not be confused with obstinate attachment to formulas or solutions which he once might have adopted."*

Under Caetano the Portuguese regime has maintained its basic structure and policies. There is, however, greater emphasis on rapid expansion, and Caetano's cabinet, like the contemporary government of Franco in Spain, includes a high proportion of so-called technocrats. Police repression was eased considerably, and the opposition enjoyed greater freedom in the elections of October 1969 than at any time in more than thirty-five years. Approximately 62.4 percent of nearly 1,700,000 registered voters participated, and the two main opposition groups won about 12 percent of the votes cast. Nonetheless, the opposition remained weak, divided, and in no position to contest the strength of the government.

Two main question marks were left for the future: the outcome of the African struggle and the direction of internal development. Despite the domestic growth of the 1960s, the Portuguese government could hardly rest secure while the country continued to register at the bottom in nearly all categories of west European social and economic statistics.

* Hugh Kay, *Salazar and Modern Portugal* (New York, 1970), p. 418.

28

Spain in the Franco Era

Spain presented an ambivalent spectacle in the spring of 1939. On the one hand there was rejoicing among the Nationalists who had won the war and held great expectations for the future. Franco and many other Nationalist leaders genuinely believed that the moment was at hand for a rebirth of Spain. Economic destruction had not been overwhelming, and government leaders hoped for a revitalization of the Spanish economy during the next five years. Beyond that, Franco expected to lead Spain to a position of renewed influence in foreign affairs, and adopted the vague Falangist rhetoric about "the return to empire." The structure of the regime remained eclectic, with most of the top positions given to military men, Catholic conservatives, and monarchists. Though fascism was the new political vogue in Europe, Franco shrewdly avoided committing his government to a completely fascist program and system. The Falange was the official state party and had a nominal membership of 900,000 in a country of 25,000,000, but its leaders held only a minority of important positions. The most important figure in the regime aside from Franco was his brother-in-law Serrano Súñer, minister of the interior and chief dispenser of patronage.

On the other hand were the defeated left, who still commanded the loyalty of a large minority of the population. At the close of the war a quarter million leftist militants were imprisoned and during the next two years most of them were brought to trial. This thorough-going purge was directed at all those who had held positions of leadership, initiative, and responsibility of any kind. Punishment was meted out on the basis of investigation, not blanket proscription. Most sentences involved moderate prison terms, but many were extremely harsh. The regime has subsequently recognized the figure of 40,000 executions during the five years following the Civil War, and the true figure may be higher than that. A total of 528,000 people fled Spain during the final months of the conflict, and only a little more than 100,000 returned during the course of 1939. Several thousand Republican soldiers took to the hills rather than surrender. They formed guerrilla and bandit bands in several of the more desolate parts of the country, but presented only a minor security problem in the immediate aftermath of the war.

Economic difficulties proved more difficult than Nationalist leaders had hoped. If actual destruction was not overwhelming, the dislocation that resulted from the war was severe. Shortages of skilled labor and supplies made it completely impossible to regain prewar production levels, general economic indices in the first postwar years standing at only about 80 percent of earlier figures. Spain's economic distress was then compounded by the outbreak of general war in Europe.

Spanish Neutrality in the Second World War

Signing of the Nazi-Soviet Pact in August 1939 and the resultant German-Russian invasion of Catholic Poland, leading to a general state of war in Europe, filled most Spanish leaders with apprehension. It confirmed the repugnance felt by Catholic conservatives toward Nazism, and though he had signed the German-inspired Anti-Comintern Pact at the close of the Civil War, Franco himself seems at first to have doubted the likelihood of a German victory. This attitude changed after the fall of France in June 1940. Franco, Serrano, and most of Spain's leaders became convinced of the inevitability of a German victory. The problem was then one of accommodating Spain most effectively to the Nazi new order. Spanish forces occupied the international district of Tangier (which they held until 1945), and Franco made known to Hitler his willingness to enter the war on the side of Germany in return for major economic and military assistance, as well as cession of much of French northwest Africa. In October 1940 Serrano Súñer, identified somewhat inaccurately with a strongly pro-Axis line, was made minister of foreign affairs. Germany's attack on the Soviet Union in June 1941 drew an enthusiastic response among Spanish Nationalists. Franco immediately announced preparations to dispatch a Spanish "Blue Division" to fight on the Russian front. Between 1941 and 1943, 40,000 Spanish volunteers served there. More than 6,000 were killed, twenty times the number of Germans who fell assisting the Nationalists in the Civil War.

From the start, however, Franco carefully measured his pro-German orientation. Each change in the international situation increased his wariness, and he knew enough about war and Spain's own weakness to prefer continued neutrality (technically "non-belligerency," after mid-1940). In his famous day-long interview with Hitler at Hendaye in October 1940, Franco held his own with great effectiveness and made it clear that Germany would have to meet Spain's price. Hitler did not think it worth that. Though his interest in a joint German-Spanish attack on Gibraltar momentarily increased in the winter of 1941, the west Mediterranean was not important enough to his plans to bribe or force the Spanish regime into war. Between 1940 and 1942 there was no doubt that Spain was more friendly to the Axis than to the antifascist allies, and Franco himself came to hope for some sort of Nazi victory, if for no other reason than that he did not believe his regime would be permitted to survive by a victorious anti-German coalition. Spain also provided intelligence facilities and submarine supply stations for the German forces, but all the while Franco was careful to underline Spanish independence and maintain correct relations with the allied powers. At one point he indicated to the Germans that should their forces violate Spanish territory in a movement against Gibraltar or other allied positions the Spanish army would resist.

Churchill and Roosevelt largely understood Franco's position. Neither Britain nor the United States wanted to complicate the military situation by adding Spain as an enemy. When the allied counteroffensive began in North Africa in November 1942, Franco was assured by Roosevelt that it was in no way directed against Spanish interests, which would be fully respected. Even before that point, however, Franco was working to dissociate himself further from Germany and Italy. After a minor intraregime political crisis, Serrano was ejected from the government and never again played a role in Franco's state. The treaty of friendship between Spain and Portugal that had been signed in 1939 was expanded into an Iberian Bloc agreement at the close of 1942, with the aim of protecting the interests and independence of the two peninsular states. By 1943, the Spanish regime had developed a three-war theory of the global conflict: in the war between Communists and anti-Communists in eastern Europe, Spain was declared to favor the German anti-Communists, where her own troops had until recently been engaged; in the war between the Axis and Allies in western Europe, Spain was neutral; in the struggle between the western allies and Japan in the Far East, Spain favored the allies. Anti-Nazi refugees were given sanctuary in Spain and transit rights elsewhere, and the regime later extended Spanish citizenship to several thousand Sephardic Jews in the Balkans to try to save them from extermination.

Throughout the war, a delicate diplomatic contest was played between Spain and the two English-speaking allies over commercial relations and economic supplies—particularly food and fuel—for the beleaguered Spanish domestic economy. The years 1940 to 1945 were a time of extreme privation for most Spaniards, in some respects as bad or worse than the Civil War. In moments of allied weakness, economic shipments to Spain were increased to guarantee continued neutrality; once the allied star was in the ascendant, an increasingly tough line was adopted in economic relations.

The Spanish Regime Ostracized, 1945-1949

When the war ended, hostility against the Spanish government was widespread among the victors. Franco for a while enjoyed the dubious distinction in international opinion of being the most hated head of state in Europe, a supposed fascist residue who regrettably had not been eliminated along with Hitler and Mussolini. The Soviet Union orchestrated an international campaign, which also had as lesser targets the supposedly pro-fascist governments of Argentina, Portugal, Sweden, and Switzerland. In March 1946 France closed its frontier with Spain, and at the end of that year a United Nations resolution condemned the Spanish regime. Ambassadors from all member states were withdrawn from Madrid.

Franco responded to the new situation with formal efforts to liberalize and regularize the regime. As early as 1942, Falangist writers had begun to emphasize that the Spanish system was not fascist or totalitarian in the central European sense. In 1943 a new Cortes, its members nominated by government agencies and elected through corporate and indirect suffrage by heads of families, assembled in Madrid. In 1945 offices in municipal government were made elective by heads of families and a new "Spaniards' Charter" (Fuero de los Españoles) was proclaimed soon afterwards. It amounted to a Spanish bill of rights, enumerating civil liberties with the proviso that they might be suspended in case of emergency. The one thing that Franco might have done that would genuinely have mollified foreign antagonism, however—disbanding the Falange—he refused to do. The Falange provided the only organized political following fully committed to the regime, and Franco still found it indispensable.

International ostracism was intended to weaken the regime and make its overthrow by the left possible. It had the opposite effect, however, for the regime had managed to institutionalize itself to a certain degree, held all the levers of power, and by 1945 had as much popular support as the defeated leftist groups. The international campaign against it could be presented as the modern version of the Black Legend. The campaign was labeled a machination by the forces of anti-Spain and was used to rally support for the government. Since 1939 millions of Spaniards had reestablished themselves in life and were not eager for the disruption of a new political upheaval. In 1947 Franco received overwhelming nominal approval in a popular referendum for his Law of Succession. This established his full powers as head of state for as long as he chose, his successor to be selected preferably from the main line of the Spanish Bourbon dynasty, restoring the monarchy within the framework of the Franquist state. The decision rested with Franco, who retained authority to select an alternative candidate as prudence might dictate.

The hopes of the left for mounting pressure against the regime, leading to insurrection, were completely dashed. Several efforts by Communist and anarchist groups to organize guerrilla incursions from France in 1944–1945 came to naught, because they were routed through conservative Pyrenean peasant territory and received little or no support. Urban bank robberies and rural terrorism and banditry continued at a diminishing rate until about 1952. According to the Civil Guard, 2,166 *bandoleros* were killed between 1943 and 1952 and approximately 3,400 captured.

Franco Rehabilitated: The Spanish-American Pact

The period of ostracism was brought to a close by the manifest stability of the regime and even more by the intensification of the Cold War between the Communist world and the West. The French border was reopened in 1948, and foreign ambassadors returned to Madrid. The west European left remained intensely hostile, but military and strategic leadership in the United States became increasingly interested in making use of Spain in the western defense system. There was no doubt about the anti-Communism of Franco, who was, as conservative American politicians said with some slight inaccuracy, "the only commander-in-chief who ever completely defeated a Communist army." Franco received the first American military emissaries in 1949, and negotiations began in 1951. There could be no question of bringing Spain into the North Atlantic Treaty Organization because of the opposition of the west European left. The result was a bilateral Spanish-American Pact in 1953 establishing a ten-year agreement for the construction and use of three American air bases and one naval base in Spain. It provided for American military and economic assistance and was renewed at reduced terms for shorter periods in 1964 and 1970.

The agreement with the United States has never been especially popular in Spain. Traditional and contemporary American attitudes are still resented by diverse elements of society. There has been considerable feeling that the United States was using Spain, involving it in a potential nuclear confrontation with the Soviet Union without making it a full partner or ally. Spain was excluded from the Marshall Plan, and the economic assistance under the bases agreement has amounted to but a fraction of the aid given to much wealthier countries such as Britain and France.

Nevertheless the relationship with the United States did provide needed economic support, and even more, bolstered the prestige and security of the regime. It gave Franco a degree of respectability among the western powers for the first time and helped to stabilize Spain's position in the postwar world.

Social and Economic Development

During the 1940s Spanish economic policy aimed at self-sufficiency, both because of the regime's quasi-Falangist ideology of independent self-development and because of the virtual impossibility of broadening foreign trade and gaining outside assistance under conditions of world war and international ostracism. Most of the economy was organized under a structure of national syndicates, with separate organizations for workers and employers. The state labor system, in a loose sense similar to that of Fascist Italy, precluded any form of independent union activity, and was developed by Falangist leaders as their main institutional function within the pluralistic regime. A rigid series of controls were established over virtually the entire economy, setting prices, wages, allocation of supplies, and import quotas.

A full ten years were required to recover from the effects of the Civil War, production indices finally regaining prewar levels in 1949-1950. During the 1950s industrial output expanded at a satisfactory rate, and after the miseries of the 1940s there was a sense of modest prosperity, at least in the cities. The percentage of national income devoted to wages compared favorably with that of other countries,

Table 41.   Increase in Industrial Production, 1929–1959

Years	Electricity	Iron	Chemical Products	Textiles
1929–31	100	100	100	100
1941–45	171	79	76	98
1946–50	230	84	95	98
1951	319	100	129	81
1952	362	113	183	99
1953	380	112	199	105
1954	395	135	214	96
1955	471	150	217	101
1956	534	152	214	106
1957	551	165	233	113
1958	610	195	258	128
1959	610	216	259	114

Source: *Anuario Estadístico de España 1960.*

taking into account Spain's level of economic development, as table 42 illustrates.

Agriculture, however, did much more poorly and failed to keep pace with the growth of population, which passed the figure of 30,000,000 by 1960. The policy of the Franco regime was typical of that of nearly all developmental programs in underdeveloped countries in that it stressed industry to the detriment of agriculture. The massive revolutionary property transfers in the Republican zone were

Table 42.   Comparison of Percentages of National Incomes
Devoted to Wages, 1958, 1962

Country	1958	1962
Austria	61	61
Belgium	57	58
Brazil	48	47
Denmark	59	—
France	59	61
Germany	61	64
Peru	38	37
Sweden	65	70
United Kingdom	73	75
United States	70	72
Spain	56	67.5

Source: H. París Eguilaz, *Desarrollo económico español: 1906–1964* (Madrid, 1965), in and corroborated by C. W. Anderson, *The Political Economy of Modern Spain* (Madison, 1970), p. 50.

Table 43.   Variations in Spanish Agricultural Production, 1940-1958
(1931-35 = 100)

Year	Index of agrarian production	Population level	Agrarian production per capita
1940	82.8	106	78.1
1945	72.5	110	65.9
1950	86.5	115	75.1
1955	104.9	119	88.2
1958	117.3	122	96.1

Source: Spanish Ministry of Agriculture.

canceled completely by the Nationalist victory, and the property structure was restored to the pre-Civil War state. The conditions of the million or more landless rural laborers in the southern half of the country improved little, if at all, for a long time. Without any provision for land redistribution, the dilemma of the rural proletariat could be solved only by emigration, which was under way in the 1950s and

Table 44.   Distribution of Agrarian Property by Category of Owner

Size of property	Number of owners	% of all owners	Property in hectares	% of all property	Parcels per owner	Average property per owner
Minifundia						
Less than 1 ha.	3,128,953	52.23	1,808,747	4.23	15.56	.57
Small properties						
1 to 5 ha.	1,805,012	30.13	2,707,518	6.33	2.35	1.50
5 to 10 ha.	552,655	9.23	3,592,257	8.40	1.07	6.50
Total	2,357,667	39.36	6,299,775	14.73	—	—
Medium Properties						
10 to 50 ha.	401,922	6.71	8,038,440	18.79	.93	20.
50 to 100 ha.	49,812	.84	3,735,900	8.74	1.34	75.
Total	451,734	7.55	11,774,340	27.53	—	—
Large Properties						
Over 100 ha.	51,283	.86	22,881,100	53.51	.80	446.
Grand Total	5,989,637	100.	42,763,962	100.	—	—

Source: G. García-Badell, "La distribución de la propiedad agrícola de España en las diferentes categorías de fincas," *Revista de Estudios Agro-Sociales,* no. 30 (Jan.-Mar., 1960) in Xavier Flores, *Estructura socioeconómica de la agricultura española* (Barcelona, 1969), p. 103.

speeded up during the following decade. That registered unemployment in Spain declined from 500,000 in 1940 to 95,000 in 1959 was due almost entirely to expanded urban employment and rural emigration.

The Spanish economy depended heavily on imports of supplies and machinery to maintain its expansion (and even its equilibrium). Since export in the economy remained weak—limited to foods and raw materials—a steadily unfavorable trade balance persisted in the postwar period. This was aggravated by the high costs of unrationalized Spanish production artificially protected by a massive tariff. Even worse were the effects of runaway inflation, which began to reach ruinous proportions by the mid-1950s. Inflation was caused by several factors. Among them were deficit state financing, especially to fund the state industrial complex called the National Institute of Industry (INI), which accounted for 15 percent of all Spanish investment. Also important were the demagogic across-the-board wage increases for labor engineered by the Falangist minister of labor, José Antonio Girón (in office, 1946-1957). These did have some small effect in increasing labor's share of real income, but the great bulk of the increase was simply passed along in higher prices.

By 1957 the Spanish state was nearly bankrupt and the economy in jeopardy. Semi-autarchy and statist syndicalization were not working, and Franco, though relatively unsophisticated in economics, realized the need for change. To lead the reorientation, he selected economists and administrators who were members of the new Catholic secular institute, Opus Dei,* several of them occupying the key financial, commercial, and economic posts in the new cabinet. In subsequent years these men, led by Laureano López Rodó, became known as the "Opus Dei technocrats." This is somewhat misleading, since their norms were not those of technocracy but of a form of state-coordinated, neoliberal market economy. This involved drastic reduction of government economic controls, coupled with the Stabilization Plan of 1959 to halt runaway inflation. The latter was an unqualified success and led to greatly increased economic expansion. The new program emphasized Europeanization of the economy, with greater international cooperation and major new opportunities for foreign (especially American) investment in Spain, hitherto greatly restricted. To

---

* Opus Dei, founded in 1928, became the first secular institute in the Catholic Church. Nearly all its members are laymen who have taken special religious vows, and their goal is the restoration of Catholic values and influence in contemporary society. In Spain they became particularly influential in education and economic affairs during the 1950s and 1960s. They are not, however, a monolithic group and do not function as a political unit.

Table 45.   Growth of Industrial and Food Production, 1959-1963

	1959	1960	1961	1962	1963
General industrial production (1958 = 100)	102.8	105.2	123.2	134.5	144.8
Total food production	119	117.5	127.9	133.7	151.1

Source: *Anuario Estadístico de España 1964.*

stimulate and coordinate economic growth, the new economic leadership prepared a system of integrated public-private planning, based on that of France under the Fourth and Fifth Republics. The Spanish plans of the 1960s (1963-1967, 1968-1972) were considerably less precise than their French counterparts because of the inferior statistical data and instruments with which the Spanish worked, but in general terms they were equally successful.

After a temporary slowdown for readjustment, the Spanish economy moved ahead rapidly in the early 1960s, as indicated in table 45. Industrial expansion proceeded even more rapidly than had been planned, and during most of the 1960s, Spain had the highest industrial growth rate in Europe.

Agriculture was still the Achilles heel despite a growth spurt in the first three years of the decade. During the remainder of the 1960s it stagnated. Hydroelectric facilities were being developed at an accelerated pace, with a major program of dam construction, but Spanish agriculture remained technologically backward. Between 1940 and 1964 the number of tractors in Spain increased from 5,300 to 130,000, but this was actually only a medium rate for a developing country. Even so, the decline in the relative demand for farm labor, together with increased mobility, produced a massive flow of emigration to jobs in the more industrialized European countries.

Continued development and the exchange balance depended heav-

Table 46.   Growth of Industrial Production, 1962-1969
(1963 = 100)

	1962	1964	1965	1966	1967	1968	1969
General industrial index	89	111	127	146	154	167	190
Mining	100	98	104	105	104	109	106
Manufacturing	88	112	128	149	157	170	194
Electricity	89	114	122	145	157	176	203
Agriculture	87	—	—	100	99	106	108

Source: *United Nations Statistical Yearbook,* 1970.

ily on continued foreign investment, payments from workers abroad, and especially on the huge tourist business, which developed into one of the four largest in the world and reached a rate of twenty million visitors annually in 1970. Shortages of capital, entrepreneurial skills, and qualified labor were still potentially serious, and the rhythm of Spanish development at the beginning of the 1970s continued to be somewhat precariously dependent on the international economy.

This notwithstanding, the decade of the 1960s opened a relatively prosperous era of mass consumption and greatly increased living standards for most Spaniards. By 1970, the per capita income of the thirty-three million inhabitants of Spain was between $700 and $800, well above the level of $600 used by economists to distinguish between residents of developed and underdeveloped countries. Spain had an almost evenly triangulated occupational structure, the work force divided in approximate thirds between industry, agriculture, and service employment.

The Opposition

The Franco regime was pluralistic from its inception, but a sharp distinction was drawn between pluralism within an authoritarian system and the competition or opposition of groups outside the regime. All opposition was proscribed politically at the start of the Nationalist movement and a rigid repression was maintained for approximately the first decade after the Civil War.

A Republican government-in-exile was established, first in Mexico City and subsequently in Paris. During the 1940s, underground opposition movements were maintained by the CNT, Communist party, Socialists, and regionalist groups. These were also associated in varying degrees with the guerrillero and bandit groups of the period. Their high point came at the close of the Second World War, which was widely expected to portend the overthrow of the regime. These hopes were dashed, and the morale of opposition groups had sagged by the close of the decade.

During the 1950s the regime became more permissive with private as distinguished from public dissidence. Wholesale amnesties in the late 1940s and the 1950s emptied the prisons of the majority of remaining Civil War political prisoners. Small opposition circles might meet fairly freely among themselves so long as they did not engage in open or direct activity against the regime. Such opposition groups increased in number but also in impotence, because of their proliferating fractionalization. Meanwhile, the several hundred thousand political exiles increasingly lost touch with the realities of life in Spain.

Juan Linz has divided opposition and potential opposition into three categories: legal, a-legal, and illegal. The legal opposition is composed mainly of small dissident groups of Carlists and Falangists, dissatisfied with the course of the regime and its failure to adopt their own ideology. They are of little political importance and are tolerated by the regime as long as they do not become too vociferous.

The a-legal opposition is composed of nominally respectable elements who were in one way or another associated with the Nationalists in the Civil War but are more liberal in orientation than the regime. They are mainly Christian Democratic successors of the prewar CEDA, and several groups of monarchists. Though more restricted by the regime than the legal opposition, they as a rule have been rapped on the knuckles rather than vigorously repressed.

The illegal opposition is composed of successors of the defeated leftist and regionalist groups. Though police pressure against them eased in the 1950s, they are still subject to arrest, beatings, and long prison sentences. The leftist groups continue to be divided not only among themselves but even within each group. Regionalist groups are split between moderates and revolutionaries, and the Communists are divided between Muscovite, Maoist, and Castroite groups. Disorders of the late 1960s were primarily the work of university students and, more spectacularly, of the Basque separatist-Marxist group, ETA (Basque Land and Liberty). In general, the opposition has remained fractionalized and impotent.

Twilight of the Franco Regime: Institutional Change and the Succession

At the close of the Civil War, Franco expected to preside over a rebirth of Spanish greatness and influence. The obstacles in his path were more difficult than he supposed, but his regime achieved order and stability and ultimately helped to make major social and economic development possible. During the first half of the regime's history his major accomplishment was to preserve Spain's neutrality and independence in the Second World War. His diplomacy proved skillful in the extreme. Though he had begun by proclaiming the revival of empire, he moved gracefully into decolonization in Spanish Morocco, ceding the independence of the Protectorate (and its incorporation into the new Moroccan state) immediately after the French evacuated their zone in 1956. The coastal enclave of Ifni was yielded in 1969 and Spanish Guinea was granted independence in 1968.

Franco firmly believed that he received an historic mandate to govern Spain for his lifetime, but when he reached the age of seventy-five in 1967 he was fully aware that that life would not likely be extended much longer. Hence several changes were made to institutionalize the regime and prepare for the post-Franco succession. In a referendum of 1967, the nominal Spanish electorate approved an "Organic Law" that slightly reorganized representation in the Cortes, opening 108 of the 565 seats to direct election by heads of families and married women. Secondly, the National Council of the Movement (as the Falange had been known since 1945) was converted into a kind of consultative senate of the Spanish legislature, half its members to be chosen indirectly by local Movement groups.

Franco had first appointed a vice-president of government in 1961, and eight years later, in 1969, he took the much more momentous step of naming a successor: Prince Juan Carlos de Borbón, grandson of Alfonso XIII. This designation, to take effect only upon Franco's death, bypassed the direct heir to the throne, the prince's father, Don Juan, who had been at odds with Franco since the aftermath of the Civil War and was deemed too liberal. Prince Juan Carlos, born in 1938, had been educated in Spain since 1954 and pledged his acceptance of the fundamental laws and structure of the Spanish regime. Thus Franco attempted to guarantee the "installation" (*instauración*) of a corporative-authoritarian monarchy as the continuation of his regime and avoid the "restoration" of a liberal constitutional monarchy by D. Juan on the model of the old Alfonsine system, which would have repudiated the structure and ideology of the dictatorship.

At the end of 1971 Franco entered his eightieth year and was about to become the oldest ruling dictator in modern history. His rule was less vigorous than twenty years earlier, but his regime was still not seriously challenged from within. Strikes had been granted de facto legality since 1964, and all remaining Civil War political prisoners had been granted amnesty in 1966. Prior (but not eventual) censorship of all publications was lifted in 1966, and in 1969-1970 the government budgeted more for education than for military expenses for the first time in Spanish history. The church, whose relations with the regime had finally been regularized in a formal concordat of 1951, had tended to dissociate itself more and more from the government throughout the 1960s, hoping to avoid entanglement in the problem of the political transition.

The mainstay of the regime, as always, was the army. The size of both the army and police forces had been reduced in the 1950s and 1960s, and by 1970 were considerably smaller than under the Republic. Yet Franco had always maintained a special relationship with the senior commanders of the army, and they remained firmly committed to the security and continuity of the regime.

Thirty years after the Civil War Spain had become a more modern country and less at odds with itself. Spanish society was highly depoliticised, though urban workers were restive and the number of strikes had shot upwards since the early 1960s. Workers wanted genuine syndical representation and improved economic conditions. The intelligentsia was as usual discontented with the political and cultural situation, but was the only group in society pressing for actual political change. Continued economic development remained largely at the mercy of favorable international conditions, and the problem of political freedom and representation had not been solved. The viability of a corporative-authoritarian structure in the 1970s after the passing of Franco thus remained an open question, but memories of the Civil War left most Spaniards with no desire to return to the bitter strife of the 1930s.

REFERENCE MATTER

Bibliography

Chapters 16 and 17

The outstanding account of administrative and financial changes in the Succession War is Henry Kamen's *The War of Succession in Spain 1700-1715* (London, 1969). For military developments, see Arthur Parnell's still useful *The War of Succession in Spain during the Reign of Queen Anne, 1702-1711* (London, 1888, 1905).

The most compact and balanced study of eighteenth-century Spanish reformism, also dealing extensively with Spanish reaction to the French Revolution, is Richard Herr, *The Eighteenth-Century Revolution in Spain* (Princeton, 1958). Much detail, not all of it accurate, is given in Desdevises du Dézert, *L'Espagne de l'Ancien Régime*, 3 vols. (Paris, 1897-1904). Luis Sánchez Agesta, *El pensamiento político del Despotismo Ilustrado* (Madrid, 1953), is a useful work on political theory. The principal historian of the realignment of Catalonia is Juan Mercader, who has written *Felip V i Catalunya* (Barcelona, 1968), and *Els capitans generals* (Barcelona, 1957), which provides an excellent brief account of eighteenth-century Catalonia. Pedro Voltes Bou has written three works on Catalonia and Valencia during the Succession War: *El archiduque Carlos de Austria, rey de los catalanes* (Barcelona, 1953); *Barcelona durante el gobierno del archiduque Carlos de Austria (1705-1714)*, 2 vols. (Barcelona, 1963); and *La Guerra de Sucesión en Valencia* (Valencia, 1964). The pressures of the Bourbon regime against Basque fueros are chronicled in two works of Francisco Elías de Tejada, *El*

701

señorío de Vizcaya (hasta 1812) (Madrid, 1963), and *La provincia de Gui-púzcoa* (Madrid, 1965).

The most detailed account of the reign of Carlos III is Antonio Ferrer del Río, *Historia del reinado de Carlos III en España*, 4 vols. (Madrid, 1856). Vicente Rodríguez Casado, *La política y los políticos en el reinado de Carlos III* (Madrid, 1962), is a recent brief treatment of the politics of the reign. Some of the better biographies of leading eighteenth-century government and reform leaders are: Felipe Alvarez Requejo, *El Conde de Campomanes* (Oviedo, 1954); Marcelin Defourneaux, *Pablo de Olavide* (Paris, 1959); C. Alcázar, *El Conde de Floridablanca* (Murcia, 1934); Jesús Casariego, *Jovellanos* (Madrid, 1943); and Patricio Peñalver, *Modernidad tradicional en el pensamiento de Jovellanos* (Seville, 1955). F. Aguilar Pinal's *La Sevilla de Olavide, 1767-1778* (Seville, 1966), gives a broad portrait of Seville in the reformist period.

The broadest treatment of the Spanish enlightenment is Jean Sarrailh, *L'Espagne éclairée de la seconde moitié du XVIIIe siècle* (Paris, 1954). G. Delpy, *L'Espagne et l'esprit européen: L'Oeuvre de Feijóo (1725-1760)* (Paris, 1936), deals with its beginnings. There are several studies of the universities and leading intellectuals and scientists: A. Alvarez de Morales, *La 'Ilustración' y la reforma de la universidad en la España del siglo XVIII* (Madrid, 1971); George M. Addy, *The Enlightenment in the University of Salamanca* (Durham, N.C., 1966); Vicente Peset, *La Universidad de Valencia y la renovación científica española (1687-1727)* (Castellón de la Plana, 1966); *El Padre Feijóo y su siglo*, 3 vols. (Oviedo, 1966); Ignacio Casanovas, *Finestres y la Universidad de Cervera* (Barcelona, 1953); Leandro Silván, *Los estudios científicos en Vergara* (San Sebastián, 1953); Alejandro Sanvisens, *Andrés Piquer* (Barcelona, 1953); E. Moles, *El momento científico español 1772-1825* (Madrid, 1934), which deals especially with physics and chemistry; Hans Juretschke, *Alberto Lista* (Madrid, 1951); Juan Mercader, *Historiadors i erudits a Catalunya i a Valencia en el segle XVIII* (Barcelona, 1966); and André Mounier, *Jerónimo de Uztáriz* (Bordeaux, 1919).

Vicente de la Fuente, *Historia de las universidades, colegios y demás establecimientos de enseñanza en España*, 3 vols. (Madrid, 1884-1889), provides a lot of disorganized data on education, and E. Luzuriaga, *Documentos sobre la historia escolar de España* (Madrid, 1916), is useful on the state of elementary education. On the development of Spanish journalism in this period, see Henry F. Schulte, *The Spanish Press, 1470-1966* (Urbana, 1968), and L. M. Enciso Recio, *Nipho y el periodismo español del siglo XVIII* (Valencia, 1956). On relations with Italy, see V. Cian, *Italia e Spagna nel secolo XVIII* (Turin, 1896).

The religious history of the period is treated in La Fuente's *Historia esclesiástica de España*, vol. 6 (Madrid, 1875). See also M. Miguélez, *Jansenismo y regalismo en España* (Madrid, 1905), and R. Eguía, *Los jesuitas en el Motín de Esquilache* (Madrid, 1947).

The best study of Spanish society in this period is Antonio Domínguez Ortiz, *La sociedad española del siglo XVIII* (Madrid, 1955). Part of the agrarian economy is surveyed by Gonzalo Anes, *Las crisis agrarias en la España moderna* (Madrid, 1970), but the title is grossly extravagant for a book which primarily studies eighteenth-century price fluctuations. Pierre Vilar, *La Catalogne dans L'Espagne moderne*, 3 vols. (Paris, 1963), constitutes a monumental study of the eighteenth-century Catalan economy. Miguel Capella and A. Matilla Tascón, *Los cinco Gremios Mayores de Madrid* (Madrid, 1957), deal with the merchant aristocracy of the capital. The problem of tax reform is treated in Matilla Tascón's *La única contribución y el catastro de Ensenada* (Madrid, 1947). Rudolf Leonhardt, *Agrarpolitik und Agrarreform in Spanien unter Karl III* (Munich, 1909), is still basic on agrarian reform. The state textile mills are studied in J. C. La Force, Jr., *The Development of the Spanish Textile Industry, 1750-1800* (Berkeley, 1965). A. Rumeu de Armas's *Historia de la previsión social en España* (Madrid, 1944) contains useful material on the struggle against the guilds. Rafael Labra, *Las Sociedades Económicas de Amigos del País* (Madrid, 1904), remains the only general study of the economic societies. The backward transportation facilities of central Spain are scrutinized in David Ringrose's *Transportation and Economic Stagnation in Spain, 1750-1850* (Durham, N.C., 1969).

Chapter 18

The classic near-contemporary history of the Portuguese restoration, Conde de Ericeira, *Portugal restaurado*, 2 vols. (Lisbon, 1679-1698), is still of some use. There is no satisfactory biography of João IV; on his queen, see Hipólito Raposo, *Luisa de Gusmão* (Lisbon, 1947). The principal historian of the period of João V is Eduardo Brazão; see especially his *Relações externas: Reinado de João V* (Porto, 1938) and *D. João V* (Barcelos, 1945). There is no definitive treatment of Pombal. Marcus Cheke, *Dictator of Portugal* (London, 1938) gives an introduction in English. The classic account is still S. J. da Luz Soriano, *História do Reinado de El-Rei D. José I e da administração do Marquez de Pombal*, 2 vols. (Lisbon, 1867). On the penultimate ruler of the old regime, see Caetano Beirão, *D. Maria I* (Lisbon, 1944).

The best general survey of the empire in this period, as for the earlier epoch, is C. R. Boxer, *The Portuguese Seaborne Empire* (New York, 1969). For Brazil and its relations with Portugal, see Boxer's *Salvador de Sá and the Struggle for Angola and Brazil* (London, 1952) and his *The Golden Age of Brazil* (Berkeley, 1962); and Visconde de Carnaxide, *D. João V e o Brazil* (Lisbon, 1952). David Lopes treats an important aspect of Portuguese influence overseas in *A expansão da lingua portuguesa no Oriente nos séculos XVI, XVII e XVIII* (Barcelos, 1936).

There are two excellent French studies of aspects of the Portuguese economy in this period: Frédéric Mauro, *Le Portugal et l'Atlantique au XVIIe siècle (1570-1670)* (Paris, 1960), deals with seventeenth-century commerce, and Albert Silbert, *Le Portugal méditerranéen à la fin de l'ancien régime*, 2 vols. (Paris, 1967), provides an exhaustive treatment of agriculture in south-central Portugal. A. D. Francis, *The Methuens and Portugal, 1691-1708* (Cambridge, 1966), and H. E. S. Fisher, *The Portugal Trade* (London, 1971), explain the trade with England. Three other important economic studies are V. Magalhães Godinho, *Prix et monnaies au Portugal 1750-1850* (Paris,

1955), and Jorge B. de Macedo's *A situação económica no tempo de Pombal* (Lisbon, 1951) and *Problemas da história da indústria portuguesa no século XVIII* (Lisbon, 1963). Descriptions of the Lisbon earthquake and daily life are given by Sir T. D. Kendrick, *The Lisbon Earthquake* (Lisbon, 1956), and Suzanne Chantal, *La Vie quotidienne après le tremblement de terre de Lisbonne de 1755* (Paris, 1962).

The Portuguese enlightenment may be approached through four works: Hernani Cidade, *Ensaio sobre a crise mental do século XVIII* (Coimbra, 1929); J. S. da Silva Dias, *Portugal e a cultura europeia* (Coimbra, 1953); L. Cabral de Moncada, *Mística e racionalismo em Portugal no século XVIII* (Lisbon, 1952); and José Tengarrinha, *História da imprensa periódica portuguesa* (Lisbon, 1965).

Chapter 19

The most detailed account of Spanish government from 1785 to 1795 is still Hermann Baumgarten, *Geschichte Spaniens zur Zeit der französischen Revolution* (Berlin, 1861). The last chapters of Richard Herr, *The Eighteenth-Century Revolution in Spain* (Princeton, 1958), deal with the politics of the 1790s. A recent brief account is Carlos Corona, *Revolución y reacción en el reinado de Carlos IV* (Madrid, 1962). Antonio Elorza, *La ideología liberal en la Ilustración española* (Madrid, 1970), gives examples of the passage from Enlightenment reformism to political preliberalism. Salvador de Moxó, *La incorporación de señoríos en la España del Antiguo Régimen* (Madrid, 1959), treats measures to reduce seigneuries.

General study of nineteenth-century Spain should begin with Raymond Carr's *Spain 1808-1939* (Oxford, 1966). Political history is supplemented by Diego Sevilla Andrés, *Historia política de España (1800-1967)* (Madrid, 1968). The best work on the quarter-century of Fernando VII is Miguel Artola, *La España de Fernando VII* (Madrid, 1968). Gabriel Lovett's *Napoleon and the Birth of Modern Spain*, 2 vols. (New York, 1965), provides a descriptive account of Spain during the War of Independence. The classic Spanish narrative is the Conde de Toreno's *Historia del levantamiento, guerra y revolución de España*, 5 vols. (Madrid, 1835-37). Several key aspects of the struggle are studied in the symposium *La Guerra de la Independencia española y los sitios de Zaragoza* (Zaragoza, 1958), and V. Genovés Amorós, *València contra Napoleó* (Valencia, 1967), treats the conflict in the Levant. On the rise of Spanish liberalism during the war, see two works by Miguel Artola, *Los orígenes de la España contemporánea* (Madrid, 1959), and *Los afrancesados* (Madrid, 1953); Hans Juretschke, *Los afrancesados en la Guerra de la Independencia* (Madrid, 1962); Ramón Solís, *El Cádiz de las Cortes* (Madrid, 1958); the special volume devoted to the 1812 constitution by the *Revista de Estudios Políticos*, no. 126 (Nov.-Dec., 1963); and Manuel Ardit's booklet, *Els valencians de les Corts de Cadis* (Barcelona, 1968).

The conflict between traditionalism and liberalism has been reinterpreted by Frederico Suárez Verdaguer in *La crisis política del Antiguo Régimen en*

España (1800-1840) (Madrid, 1950). José Luis Comellas has written two important works in the same vein: *Los primeros pronunciamientos en España, 1814-1820* (Madrid, 1958), and *Los realistas en el primer trienio constitucional, 1820-1823* (Pamplona, 1958). Luis Alonso Tejada, *El ocaso de la Inquisición* (Madrid, 1969), deals with the extreme right in the last decade of Fernando VII. Spanish Masonry can be approached through Vicente de la Fuente, *Historia de las sociedades secretas antiguas y modernas,* 2d ed. (Barcelona, 1933), and Iris M. Zavala, *Masones, comuneros y carbonarios* (Madrid, 1971).

There is no adequate history of Carlism, but see Román Oyarzun, *Historia del Carlismo* (Madrid, 1940), and Melchor Ferrer et al., eds., *Historia del Tradicionalismo español,* 30 vols. (Seville, 1930-1959). Edgar Holt, *The Carlist Wars in Spain* (London, 1967), is a brief descriptive account. Jesús Pabón, *La otra legitimidad* (Madrid, 1965), is a careful study of the claims of dynastic legitimacy. The revolt of 1826 – 1827 is studied by Jaime Torras Elías, *La guerra de los Agraviados* (Barcelona, 1967). R. Rodríguez Garraza, *Navarra de Reino a provincia (1828-1841)* (Pamplona, 1968), treats Navarrese politics in the 1830s.

A thorough study of the initial political structure of the Isabeline monarchy has been made by J. T. Villarroya, *El sistema político del Estatuto Real (1834-1836)* (Madrid, 1968). Eric Christiansen, *The Origins of Military Power in Spain, 1800-1854* (Oxford, 1967), is an excellent study of the Spanish Army and its political activities for those years. The best synthesis on any region of nineteenth-century Spain is Jaime Vicens Vives's *Cataluña en el siglo XIX* (Madrid, 1961). Salvador de Moxó, *La disolución del régimen señorial en España* (Madrid, 1965), is an able study.

E. Allison Peers, *A History of the Romantic Movement in Spain* (Liverpool, 1940), is a classic. See also Leon-François Hoffmann, *Romantique Espagne: L'Image de l'Espagne en France entre 1800 et 1850* (Paris, 1961), and J. F. Montesinos, *Costumbrismo y novela* (Valencia, 1960).

The standard history of Spanish foreign relations in the nineteenth-century is Jerónimo Becker, *Historia de las relaciones exteriores de España durante el siglo XIX,* 3 vols. (Madrid, 1924-1926). On the emancipation of the mainland colonies, see Julio F. Guillén, *Independencia de América,* 3 vols. (Madrid, 1953). Jaime Delgado, *España y México en el siglo XIX,* 3 vols. (Madrid, 1950-1953), deals mainly with the years 1820-1845. See also L. M. Enciso Recio, *La opinión española y la independencia hispanoamericana, 1819-1820* (Valladolid, 1967). Giorgio Spini, *Mito e realtà della Spagna nelle rivoluzioni italiani del 1820-1821* (Rome, 1950), shows the influence of early Spanish liberalism in Italy.

Chapter 20

The main work on Spanish politics from 1844 to 1854 is J. L. Comellas, *Los Moderados en el poder* (Madrid, 1970). Two general works on early liberalism are Luis Sánchez Agesta, *Historia del constitucionalismo español* (Madrid, 1955), and Luis Díez del Corral, *El liberalismo doctrinario* (Madrid,

1956). V. G. Kiernan, *The Revolution of 1854 in Spanish History* (Oxford, 1966), provides a descriptive account.

The principal narrative of Spanish politics from 1868 to the end of the century is Melchor Fernández Almagro, *Historia política de la España contemporánea*, 2 vols. (Madrid, 1956, 1968). Clara Lida and Iris Zavala, eds., *La Revolución de 1868* (New York, 1970), provides a general introduction to the revolutionary sexennium. The best study of the Republican period is C. A. M. Hennessey, *The Federal Republic in Spain* (Oxford, 1962). Antonio Jutglar, *Federalismo y revolución: Las ideas sociales de Pi y Margall* (Barcelona, 1966), and Carmen Llorca, *Emilio Castelar* (Madrid, 1966), explain the ideas of the two key Republican presidents. On the Democrats, see Antonio Eiras Roel, *El Partido Demócrata español (1849-1868)* (Madrid, 1961). Important insights into Carlism may be gained from J. Aróstegui Sánchez, *El Carlismo alavés y la guerra civil de 1870-1876* (Vitoria, 1970). J. M. Cuenca Toribio, *La Iglesia española ante la revolución liberal* (Madrid, 1971), analyzes the relationship between the church hierarchy and politics.

The attention devoted to the history of the working class movement in the years 1868-1875 is entirely disproportionate to its influence. This topic can first be approached through Maximiano García Venero, *Historia del sindicalismo español* (Madrid, 1961), and *Historia de las Internacionales en España*, vol. 1 (Madrid, 1956). The key work on early Spanish anarchism is Max Nettlau's *La Première Internationale en Espagne (1868-1888)*, 2 vols. (Dordrecht, 1969). Other noteworthy books are Fernando Garrido, *Historia de las asociaciones obreras en España*, 2 vols. (Madrid, 1870); Casimiro Martí, *Orígenes del anarquismo en Barcelona* (Barcelona, 1959); José Termes Ardévol, *El movimiento obrero en España: La Primera Internacional (1864-1881)* (Barcelona, 1965); and, on the only social revolution in 1873, R. Coloma, *La revolución internacionalista en Alcoy* (Alicante, 1959).

Two general introductions to modern Spanish economic history are J. Nadal Oller, "La economía española (1829-1931)," in *El Banco de España: Una historia económica* (Madrid, 1970), pp. 315-417, and J. A. Lacomba, *Introducción a la historia económica de la España contemporánea* (Madrid, 1969). Agriculture has been little studied, but on prices and the beginning of industrialization, see Juan Sardá, *La política monetaria y las fluctuaciones de la economía española en el siglo XIX* (Madrid, n.d.); L. Beltrán Flórez, *La industria algodonera española* (Barcelona, 1943); and F. Sánchez Ramos, *La economía siderúrgica española* (Madrid, 1945). The principal railroad history is F. Wais San Martín, *Historia general de los ferrocarriles españoles* (Madrid, 1967). There has been very little study of nineteenth-century Spanish society. On the growth of the bullfight, the basic work is J. M. Cossío, *Los toros*, 3 vols. (Madrid, 1943).

Chapter 21

The best narrative survey of the formal political life of the Restoration period will be found in the two volumes of Melchor Fernández Almagro's *Historia política de la España contemporánea* (Madrid, 1956, 1968). Miguel M. Cuadrado, *Elecciones y partidos políticos de España (1868-1931)*, vol. 1 (Madrid, 1969), is indispensable for this period. There are two multivolume accounts of the regency of María Cristina (1885-1902): Juan Ortega y Rubio, *Historia de la Regencia de Doña María Cristina Habsbourg-Lorena*, 5 vols. (Madrid, 1905-06), and Gabriel Maura y Gamazo's more interpretive *Historia crítica del reinado de Alfonso XIII . . . bajo la Regencia . . . ,* 2 vols. (Barcelona, 1919, 1925). The two principal biographies of Cánovas are by Fernández Almagro (1951) and more recently by J. L. Comellas (1965). The only biography of Sagasta is a sketchy little book by the Conde de Romanones (1934). The most famous critique of Restoration politics is Joaquín Costa's *Oligarquía y caciquismo como la forma actual de gobierno en España* (Madrid, 1902). There are considerable data about protests against caciquismo in R. W. Kern's dissertation, "Caciquismo versus Self-Government: The Crisis of Liberalism and Local Government in Spain 1858-1910" (University of Chicago, 1966).

Organicist philosophy in late-nineteenth-century Spain is treated in J. J. Gil Cremades, *El reformismo español* (Barcelona, 1969). On the great polymath of the period, see Pedro Laín Entralgo's *Menéndez Pelayo* (Madrid, 1944). The main books on Krausism and the Institución Libre are Juan López Morillas, *El krausismo español* (Mexico City, 1956); Vicente Cacho Viu, *La Institución Libre de Enseñanza* (Madrid, 1962); and M. D. Gómez Molleda, *Los reformadores de la España contemporánea* (Madrid, 1966). The basic problems of education can be approached through Yvonne Turin, *La educación y la escuela en España de 1874 a 1902* (Madrid, 1967).

The key works on the development of regionalism are Maximiano García Venero, *Historia del nacionalismo catalán (1793-1936)*, vol. 1 (Madrid, 1966), and *Historia del nacionalismo vasco* (Madrid, 1967); J. L. Varela, *Poesía y restauración cultural de Galicia en el siglo XIX* (Madrid, 1958); and Alfons Cucó, *El valencianisme polític (1868-1936)* (Valencia, 1971). On the phylloxera problem in Catalonia, see Josep Iglesies, *La crisi agrari de 1879-1900* (Barcelona, 1968).

Two items in diplomatic history may be recommended: Julio Salom, *España en la Europa de Bismarck* (Madrid, 1967), and an essay by Jesús Pabón, *El 98, acontecimiento internacional* (Madrid, 1952). H. Wayne Morgan, *America's Road to Empire* (New York, 1965), is a well-reasoned, brief defense of United States policy.

Chapter 22

There have been several efforts to conduct a regional and social analysis of early Portuguese liberalism. The most useful is Fernando Piteira Santos, *Geografia e economia da Revolução de 1820* (Lisbon, 1962), but see also Julião Soares de Azevedo, *Condições económicas da Revolução portuguesa de 1820* (Lisbon, 1944). Victor de Sá's *A crise do liberalismo e as primeiras manifestações das ideias socialistas em Portugal (1820-1852)* (Lisbon, 1969), and his brief *A revolução de setembro de 1836* (Lisbon, 1969) are incisive, if slightly tendentious, works. Still of importance for the study of nineteenth-century Portugal is J. P. de Oliveira Martins' *Portugal contemporáneo*, 5th ed., 2 vols. (Lisbon, 1919). Marcello Caetano, *Constituições portuguesas* (Braga, 1958), gives an outline of Portuguese political parties and constitutions. There are few decent biographies dealing with this period; P. M. Laranjo Coelho, *Mousinho da Silveira* (Lisbon, 1918), can perhaps be recommended. On Portuguese Africa, see R. J. Hammond, *Portugal and Africa 1815-1910, a Study in Uneconomic Imperialism* (Stanford, 1966), and Luis Vieira de Castro, *Dom Carlos I* (Lisbon, 1936).

Social and economic affairs are treated in Armando Castro, *Introdução ao estudo da economia portuguesa* (Lisbon, 1947); Paul Descamps, *Histoire sociale du Portugal* (Paris, 1959); Bento Carquejo, *O Povo portuguez* (Porto, 1916); and the best contemporary work, Charles Vogel, *Le Portugal et ses colonies: Tableau politique et commerciale* (Paris, 1860).

There has been little study of the collapse of the monarchy. The most that can be recommended, and that with qualification, are Jesús Pabón's one-sided *La revolución portuguesa*, vol. 1 (Madrid, 1941), and three personalistic, anecdotal volumes by Rocha Martins: *D. Carlos* (Lisbon, 1926), *João Franco e o seu tempo* (Lisbon, n.d.), and *D. Manuel II* (Lisbon, 1931).

Chapter 23

The Portuguese parliamentary republic has received very little attention from scholars. A.-H. de Oliveira Marques has written a very helpful structural and topical analysis, *A Primeira República portuguesa* (Lisbon, 1971), and a brief introduction to the period, "Revolution and Counterrevolution in Portugal— Problems of Portuguese History, 1900-1930," in *Studien über die Revolution* (Berlin, 1969), pp. 403-18. The lengthiest treatment is Jesús Pabón's overtly biased *La revolución portuguesa*, 2 vols. (Madrid, 1941-1944), which is narrative and anecdotal. V. de Bragança-Cunha's *Revolutionary Portugal (1910-1936)* (London, 1937), is fairer but still superficial. Other accounts are Arthur Ribeiro Lopes, *Histoire de la République portugaise* (Paris, 1939), and the *Suplemento* to Damião Peres, ed., *História de Portugal* (Barcelos, 1954-1958). On the background of Republican ideology and propaganda, see Luis de Montalvor, ed., *História do Regimen republicano em Portugal*, 2 vols. (Lisbon, 1930-1932). Carlos Ferrão, *O Integralismo e a República*, 2 vols. (Lisbon, 1964-1965), deals with the most salient monarchist group.

Three books on economic problems should be mentioned: Ezequiel de Campos, *O enquadramento geo-económico da população portuguesa* (Lisbon, 1943); Anselmo de Andrade, *Portugal económico* (Coimbra, 1918); and Marcello Caetano, *A depreciação da moeda depois da guerra* (Coimbra, 1931). On the working class movements, see Costa Junior, *História breve do movimento operário português* (Braga, 1967).

There are abundant memoirs and polemical literature for these years. Events and personalities of the conservative forces have been sketched by Rocha Martins in three volumes: *Pimenta de Castro, dictador* (Lisbon, n.d.), *Memorias sobre Sidónio Pais* (London, 1921), and *A monarquia do norte* (Lisbon, 1923).

Chapter 24

For this period, as for the entire preceding century, Raymond Carr's *Spain 1808-1939* (Oxford, 1966) provides lucid guidance. Salvador de Madariaga's *Spain: A Modern History* (New York, 1957) is refreshingly objective though very general. Two standard political histories are Melchor Fernández Almagro, *Historia del reinado de D. Alfonso XIII* (Madrid, 1934), and Gabriel Maura y Gamazo, *Bosquejo histórico de la Dictadura* (Madrid, 1930). These two authors collaborated on an important study of party politics, *Por qué cayó Alfonso XIII*, 2d ed. (Madrid, 1948), hostile to the crown. Gerald Brenan's well-known *The Spanish Labyrinth* (London, 1944), is a standard work on the sociopolitical background, through rather ill informed on the constitutional monarchy. Two key works on parties and elections are the second volume of the work by Miguel M. Cuadrado and Juan J. Linz, "The Party System of Spain: Past and Future," in *Party Systems and Voter Alignments*, ed. S. Lipset and S. Rokkan (New York, 1967), pp. 187-282. The role of the army has been studied in my *Politics and the Military in Modern Spain* (Stanford, 1967). Gabriel Solé Villalonga, *La reforma fiscal de Villaverde, 1899-1900* (Madrid, 1967), is an instructive monograph. Joan Connelly Ullman has written an excellent account in *The Tragic Week* (Cambridge, Mass., 1968). Though his interpretations are exaggerated, J. A. Lacomba has provided a useful study in *La crisis española de 1917* (Madrid, 1970). On the slow rise of Basque nationalism, see García Venero's *Historia del nacionalismo vasco* (Madrid, 1968). Juan Velarde Fuertes, *Política económica de la Dictadura* (Madrid, 1968), is brief but important.

The principal biographies for this period are Jesús Pabón, *Cambó*, 3 vols. (Barcelona, 1952-1969); Diego Sevilla Andrés, *Antonio Maura* (Barcelona, 1954), and *Canalejas* (Barcelona, 1956); García Venero's *Melquiades Alvarez* (Madrid, 1954), and *Santiago Alba* (Madrid, 1963); and Vicente Pilapil, *Alfonso XIII* (New York, 1969). Carlos Seco Serrano, *Alfonso XIII y la crisis de la restauración* (Barcelona, 1969), offers an interesting reevaluation.

The main literature on the early history of the working class movement has been given in the bibliography to chapter 21. Albert Balcells has written two important monographs on social struggles in Catalonia, *El sindicalisme a Barcelona, 1916-1923* (Barcelona, 1966), and *El problema agrari a Catalunya, 1890-1936* (Barcelona, 1968). See also Joan Lacomba, *Crisi i revolució al país valencià* (Valencia, 1968).

The best introduction to the Generation of Ninety-Eight is Pedro Laín Entralgo, *La generación del 98* (Madrid, 1946). On Costa see Rafael Pérez de la Dehesa, *El pensamiento de Costa y su influencia en el 98* (Madrid, 1966); C. Martín-Retortillo, *Joaquín Costa* (Barcelona, 1961); and E. Tierno Galván, *Costa y el regeneracionismo* (Barcelona, 1961). On the other main cultural figures, see Julián Marías's books *Miguel de Unamuno* (Madrid, 1943) and *Ortega* (Madrid, 1960); José Ferrater Mora, *Ortega y Gasset* (Barcelona, 1958); and Vicente Marrero, *Maeztu* (Madrid, 1955).

There are several useful books on Spain in Morocco, beginning with the general works by Tomás García Figueras, *La acción africana de España en torno al 98 (1860-1912)*, 2 vols. (Madrid, 1966), and *España y su protecto-*

rado en Marruecos (1912-1956) (Madrid, 1957). On diplomatic preliminaries, see José Ma. Campoamor, *La actitud de España ante la cuestión de Marruecos (1900-1904)* (Madrid, 1951). A. Mousset, *L'Espagne dans la politique mondiale* (Paris, 1925), treats Spanish policy during the era of World War I. A useful account of Hispanist ideologies and intra-Hispanic relations is given by Fredrick B. Pike. *Hispanismo 1898-1936* (Notre Dame, 1971).

Chapter 25

The most extensive and fully documented history of the Second Republic in one volume will be found in Ricardo de la Cierva's *Historia de la Guerra Civil española,* vol. 1, *Antecedentes: Monarquía y República 1898-1936* (Madrid, 1969). Gabriel Jackson's *Spanish Republic and Civil War* (Princeton, 1965) is a concise, well-written account from the viewpoint of the moderate middle class left. Joaquín Arrarás, *Historia de la segunda República española,* 4 vols. (Madrid, 1956-1967), is the most detailed narrative and is quite hostile to the Republican experience. The *Historia de la segunda República española,* 4 vols. (Barcelona, 1940-1941), by José Pla, is more moderate. Though limited to formal politics, it was an impressive achievement in the immediate aftermath of the Civil War. Some new perspectives are offered in a symposium edited by Raymond Carr, *The Republic and Civil War in Spain* (London, 1971).

The best monograph on any aspect of Republican problems is E. E. Malefakis, *Agrarian Reform and Peasant Revolution in Spain* (New Haven, 1970). R. A. H. Robinson, *The Origins of Franco's Spain: The Right, the Republic and Revolution, 1931-1936* (Devon, 1970), provides a lucid account of the conservative and rightist groups. My *Spanish Revolution* (New York, 1970) treats the revolutionary left. Manuel Ramírez Jiménez, *Los grupos de presión en la segunda República española* (Madrid, 1969), analyzes the major groups and problems of Republican affairs. J. Tusell Gómez et al., *Las elecciones del Frente Popular en España,* 2 vols. (Madrid, 1971), provides an exhaustive study of the final elections.

Chapter 26

Until Ricardo de la Cierva completes his two-volume history of the Civil War, the principal account will remain Hugh Thomas, *The Spanish Civil War,* 2d ed. (London, 1966). The second half of Gabriel Jackson's *Spanish Republic and Civil War* (Princeton, 1965) also presents a general history of the conflict. On the outbreak of the war and political developments in the Nationalist zone, see V. Palacio Atard, R. de la Cierva, and R. Salas Larrazábal, *Aproximación histórica a la guerra española (1936-1939)* (Madrid, 1970), and my *Falange* (Stanford, 1961). The two best biographies of Franco are J. W. D. Trythall, *El Caudillo* (New York, 1970) and Brian Crozier, *Franco* (London, 1967). The most accurate military studies are the "Monografías de la Guerra de España" (Madrid, 1968–) by Col. J. M. Martínez Bande, of which seven volumes had been published by 1972.

On internal developments in the Republican zone see, in addition to the two general accounts mentioned above, P. Broué and E. Témime, *La Révolution et la guerre d'Espagne* (Paris, 1961), and my *Spanish Revolution* (New York, 1970). Burnett Bolloten, *The Grand Camouflage* (New York, 1961), provides a detailed and documented narrative of revolutionary politics during the first ten months of the war. J. M. Bricall, *Política econòmica de la Generalitat (1936-1939)* (Barcelona, 1970), is an excellent study of economic policy and developments in Catalonia.

International diplomacy attending the conflict is treated in P. A. M. van der Esch, *Prelude to War* (The Hague, 1951). On the intervention of Germany and the Soviet Union see Manfred Merkes, *Die deutsche Politik gegenüber dem spanischen Bürgerkrieg* (Bonn, 1961), and David T. Cattell, *Soviet Diplomacy and the Spanish Civil War* (Berkeley, 1957).

Chapter 27

The best account of Salazar and his policies is Hugh Kay, *Salazar and Modern Portugal* (New York, 1960). An excellent brief analysis of the structure of the regime will be found in H. Martins, "Portugal," in S. J. Woolf, ed., *European Fascism* (New York, 1969), 302–36. Of recent brief descriptive books the most balanced is Pierre Debray, *Le Portugal entre deux révolutions* (Paris, 1963). The best economic study is Albert Pasquier, *L'Economie du Portugal* (Paris, 1962), but see also V. Xavier Pintado, *Structure and Growth of the Portuguese Economy* (EFTA, 1964). Ralph von Gersdorff, *Portugals finanzen* (Bielefeld, 1961) is a semi-official account. Paul Descamps, *Le Portugal: La Vie sociale actuelle* (Paris, 1935), provides a detailed description of Portuguese society as of the early 1930s. Ludwig Renard, *Salazar, Kirche und Staat in Portugal* (Essen, 1968), presents a juridical account of the legal terms of church-state relations.

During the past decade and more, most of the ink spilt on Portuguese affairs has dealt with Portuguese Africa. The only detailed and reliable book on contemporary Angola is D. Wheeler and R. Pélissier, *Angola* (London, 1971). There is a brief general survey by Ronald H. Chilcote, *Portuguese Africa* (Englewood Cliffs, N.J., 1967). The Portuguese position is given in F. C. C. Egerton's *Angola in Perspective* (London, 1957); Dr. Franco Nogueira, *Portugal and the United Nations* (London, 1964); Hélio Felgas, *Guerra em Angola* (Lisbon, 1961) and *Os movimentos terroristas de Angola, Guiné, Moçambique (Influência externa)* (Lisbon, 1966); and Mugur Valahu, *Angola clé de l'Afrique* (Paris, 1966).

Chapter 28

There is as yet no complete history of Spain in the Franco era. The best one-volume treatments will be found in George Hills, *Spain* (New York, 1970);

Jacques Georgel, *Le Franquisme* (Paris, 1970); and Carlos Seco Serrano, *Epoca contemporánea* (Barcelona, 1968), vol. 6 of *Historia de España*. Considerable data is also given in Max Gallo, *Histoire de l'Espagne franquiste*, 2 vols. (Verviers, 1969). My *Franco's Spain* (New York, 1967) provides a short summary to 1966. Franco's wartime diplomacy is treated at some length in Crozier's biography of Franco, but see also C. B. Burdick, *Germany's Military Strategy and Spain in World War II* (Syracuse, 1968). The second half of Trythall's biography of Franco gives a lucid exposition of the regime's politics. An informative account of the late 1950s and early 1960s will be found in Benjamin Welles's *Spain: The Gentle Anarchy* (New York, 1965). The Equipo Mundo's *Los noventa ministros de Franco* (Barcelona, 1970) offers interesting data on the governmental elite, and R. Fernández-Carvajal, *La Constitución española* (Madrid, 1969), expounds the formal legal structure of the state.

Charles W. Anderson, *The Political Economy of Modern Spain* (Madison, 1970), analyzes economic policy and development in the late 1950s and 1960s. A general description of the economy has been written by Ramón Tamames, *Introducción a la economía española* (Madrid, 1967). Xavier Flores, *Estructura socioeconómica de la agricultura española* (Barcelona, 1969), is perhaps the best treatment of the agrarian system. Juan Muñoz, *El poder de la banca en España* (Madrid, 1969), is an extensive critique of the financial system, while C. Iglesias Selgas, *Los sindicatos en España* (Madrid, 1966), describes the formal structure though not the functioning reality of the syndical system.

Study of contemporary Spanish society should begin with the Fundación FOESSA's *Informe sociológico sobre la situación social de España 1970* (Madrid, 1970). Insights into the structure of religiosity may be obtained from J. M. Vázquez, *Realidades socio-religiosas de España* (Madrid, 1967).

Index to Both Volumes

TEXT DESIGNED
BY IRVING PERKINS
JACKET DESIGNED BY KAREN FOGET
MANUFACTURED BY THE GEORGE BANTA CO., INC., MENASHA, WISCONSIN
TEXT AND DISPLAY LINES ARE SET IN TIMES ROMAN, DISPLAY
FIGURES IN BODONI BOLD

Library of Congress Cataloging in Publication Data
Payne, Stanley G
A history of Spain and Portugal.
Bibliography: p. 701-712.
1.   Spain—History.   2.   Portugal—History.   I.   Title.-
DP66.P382   946   72-7992
ISBN 0-299-06280-5   (v. 2)

The illustrations that follow have been made available through the generosity of the Spanish cultural relations office, the Casa de Portugal (New York), and Professor A.-H. de Oliveira Marques. Maps in this volume were prepared by the University of Wisconsin Cartographic Laboratory, map 1 abridged from a map by Richard Herr, with his kind permission.

Felipe V

Carlos III, by Mengs (El Prado)

The Charge of the Mamluks (Dos de Mayo), Goya (El Prado)

Executions of the Third of May, 1808 (Tres de Mayo), Goya (El Prado)

Fernando VII, by Goya

The Execution of Torrijos, Antonio Gisbert (Museo de Arte Moderno)

A depiction of Zumalacárregui mortally wounded

Don Carlos talking with Liberal prisoners

Carlists engaged in a mountain battle

Narváez

Prim

Cánovas del Castillo

+ Luis Bolín

Alfonso

Alfonso XIII

Antonio Maura

Antonio Maura

José Canalejas

Primo de Rivera

Franco in Morocco at the age of thirty-three

Revolutionary sailors in the Republican fleet, 1936

Republican troops marching in Barcelona

Republican political and military leaders reviewing troops on the central front near Madrid, November 1937. *Left to right:* José Giral, former prime minister; Juan Negrín, prime minister; Manuel Azaña, president; Gen. José Miaja, commander of central front; Col. Cipriano Mera, anarchist commander

Franco as Nationalist generalissimo in the Civil War

Launching of a new vessel built for
Yugoslavia in the shipyards of El Ferrol

João IV the Restorer

Royal convent and palace at Mafra, built by João V

Mousinho da Silveira

Afonso Costa

Sidonio Pais

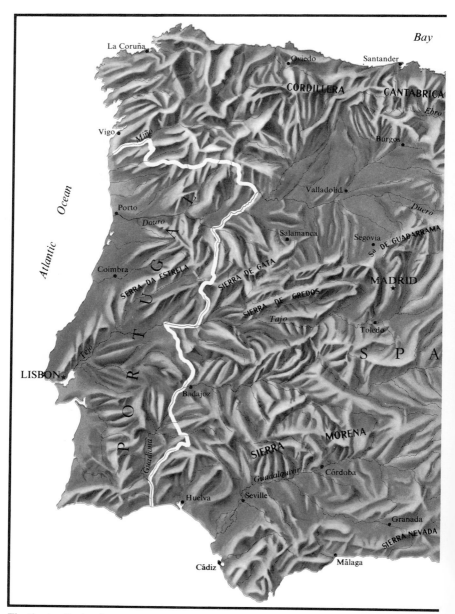

The Iberian Peninsula

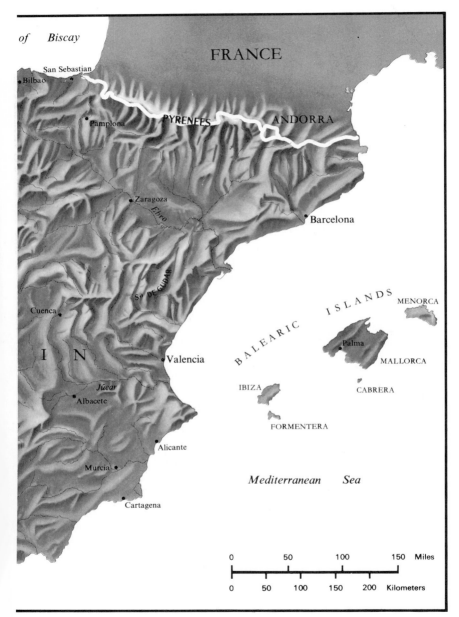

of Biscay

FRANCE

San Sebastian
Bilbao

Pamplona

PYRENEES
ANDORRA

Zaragoza
Ebro

Barcelona

S^a DE GUDAR

Cuenca

I N

Valencia

Júcar
Albacete

BALEARIC

ISLANDS

MENORCA

Palma

MALLORCA

IBIZA

CABRERA

FORMENTERA

Alicante

Murcia

Cartagena

Mediterranean   Sea

0	50	100	150 Miles

0	50	100	150	200	Kilometers

Dr. António de Oliveira Salazar

The new bridge over the Tejo outside Lisbon